Ecuador
& the Galapagos Islands
a travel survival kit

D0778337

Ecuador & the Galapagos Islands – a travel survival kit
First edition

Published by
Lonely Planet Publications
PO Box 88, South Yarra, Victoria 3141, Australia
PO Box 2001A, Berkeley, CA 94702, USA

Printed by
Colorcraft, Hong Kong

Cover photographs by
Rob Rachowiecki – thanks to Randy Nadler for the iguana stand-off on the front cover.

Other photographs by
Rob Rachowiecki, Tony Wheeler

Published
February 1986

National Library of Australia Cataloguing in Publication Data

Rachowiecki, Rob.
  Ecuador and the Galapagos Islands – a travel survival kit.

  Includes index.
  ISBN 0 908086 79 2.

  1. Ecuador – Description and travel – 1981– – Guide-books. 2. Galapagos Islands – Description and travel – Guide-books. I. Title.

918.66'0474

Rob Rachowiecki was born near London and became interested in travel while still a teenager. He has visited countries as diverse as Greenland and Thailand. He spent several years in Latin America, where he now works as a tour leader for Wilderness Travel, an adventure tour company. His first book, with Hilary Bradt, was *Backpacking in Mexico & Central America* (2nd edition, 1982). He spent most of 1982 climbing Ecuador's major mountains; his guidebook *Climbing & Hiking in Ecuador* was published in 1984. This is Rob's first book with Lonely Planet, and at present he is leading treks in the Peruvian Andes and working on a Travel Survival Kit for Peru. He lives with his American wife, Cathy, in California for half the year, and dreams of some day sailing around the world.

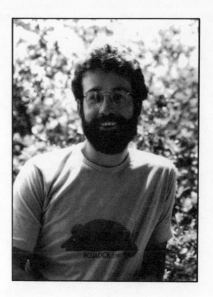

This book is dedicated to Scabby-nose and Strawbear, two very experienced travellers.

Acknowledgements
Many travellers whom I met in Ecuador helped with their information and experiences. Particularly, I'd like to thank Chuck and Maleah, Randy, and Judy who accompanied me on wonderful trips to various parts of the country. David Eskin wrote a useful letter about Amazonian river travel. My most special thanks go to Cathy, who travelled with me in Ecuador and made my Galápagos visit of January 1985 the most memorable ever, and who helped with immeasurable support when the writing had to be done.

This Edition
Apart from Rob Rachowiecki's hard work a number of other people lent their expertise in its production. Elizabeth Kim did the editing at Lonely Planet's California office. Back in Australia the typesetting was done by Ann Logan, mapping by Fiona Boyes, paste-up by Richard Holt, indexing and final proof reading by Sue Tan.

And the Next
Things change, prices go up, new places open, old places close. So if you find things betters, worse, cheaper, more expensive, or even simply different, please write and tell us about them. We love getting letters from 'our travellers' out on the road. And as usual the best letters will be rewarded with a free copy of the next edition or another Lonely Planet guide if you prefer.

Contents

Introduction

Ecuador is the smallest of the Andean countries, and in many ways it is the easiest and most pleasant to travel in. From the beautifully preserved colonial capital of Quito, located in the highlands at 2850 metres (9300 feet) above sea level, you can travel by frequent buses to Andean Indian markets, remote jungle towns and warm Pacific beaches. In fact, starting from Quito, you can get to most points in this tropical country in less than a day by public transport.

The highlands have many colourful Indian markets, some world famous and deservedly so, and others which are rarely visited by foreigners but are no less interesting. Any journey in the highlands is dominated by magnificent volcanoes such as Cotopaxi – at 5897 metres (19,348 feet) one of the highest active volcanoes in the world – and many others.

Jungle travel in Ecuador is easier than in most other countries simply because the distances involved are far less, so you can be in the jungle after just a day of bus travel from Quito. There are many exciting opportunities to hire local guides or strike out on your own from jungle villages such as Misahuallí on the Río Napo, a tributary of the Amazon.

The coast, too, has much to offer. Go to a picturesque fishing village and watch the fishermen expertly return their traditional balsa-wood rafts through the ocean breakers to the sandy shore, or help them pull in their nets in return for some of the catch. Laze on the beach in the equatorial sun, swim in the warm seas, and in the evening listen to salsa music in a local bar.

The Galápagos Islands, 1000 km off the Pacific coast of Ecuador, are high on the list of destinations for travellers interested in wildlife. Here you can swim with penguins and sea lions, or walk along beaches while pelicans flap by and huge land iguanas scurry around your feet. The wildlife is so unafraid of humans that at times it's difficult to avoid stepping on the animals.

Ecuador – a travel survival kit tells you everything you'll need to know about travelling around this enchanting country. The most interesting sights, the best-value hotels and restaurants, details on taking all forms of public transport from cheap air flights to dugout canoes, and a host of background details will make this guide an indispensable part of your trip. And you can do it for as little as US$5 a day – or more if you want some comfort.

Finally, Ecuador is one of the safest and most stable countries in Latin America and the problems of pickpockets and revolutions are much less noticeable than in other countries in the region. You really can't go wrong in Ecuador, even if it's your first time travelling in a foreign country. Enjoy it!

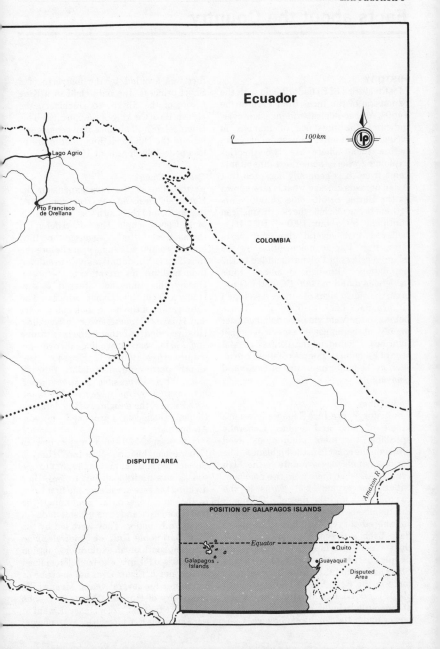

Ecuador

0   100km

Lago Agrio

Pto Francisco
de Orellana

COLOMBIA

DISPUTED AREA

Amazon R.

POSITION OF GALAPAGOS ISLANDS

Equator

Galapagos
Islands

Quito

Guayaquil

Disputed
Area

Facts about the Country

HISTORY

Most histories of Ecuador begin with the expansion of the Incas from Peru in the 1400s. Archaeological evidence, however, indicates the presence of humans in Ecuador for many thousands of years before then. There are two theories explaining where the earliest inhabitants came from. It is generally accepted that Asian nomads crossed what is now known as the Bering Strait some 25,000 years ago and began reaching the South American continent by about 12,000 BC. It is believed that several thousand years later, trans-Pacific colonisation by the island dwellers of Polynesia added to the population. Although stone-age tools have been dated to 9000 BC in the Quito area, the oldest signs of a more developed culture date back to 3200 BC. These belong to the Valdivia period and consist mainly of ceramics – especially small figurines – found in the central coastal area of Ecuador. Examples of these can be seen in the major museums of Quito and Guayaquil.

Early Tribes

The history of pre-Inca Ecuador is lost in a tangle of time and legend. Generally speaking, the main populations lived either on the coast or in the highlands. The earliest details we have date to the 11th century AD when there were two dominant tribes: the expansionist Caras in the coastal areas and the peaceful Quitus in the highlands. The Caras, led by Shyri, conquered the Quitus, but it seems to have been a peaceful expansion rather than bloody warfare. The Cara/Quitu peoples became collectively known as the Shyri nation and they were the dominant force in the Ecuadorean highlands until about 1300 AD, by which time the Puruhá of the southern highlands had also risen to power under the Duchicela lineage. Con-

flict was avoided by the marriage of a Shyri princess, the only child of a King Caran of the Shyris, to Duchicela, the eldest son of the king of the Puruhás. This Duchicela/Shyri alliance proved successful and the Duchicela line ruled more or less peacefully for about 150 years.

The Inca Empire

At the time of the Inca expansion the Duchicela descendants still dominated the north, and the south was in the hands of the Cañari people. The Cañari defended themselves bitterly against the Inca invaders and it was some years before the Inca Tupac-Yupanqui was able to subdue them and turn his attention to the north. During this time he fathered a son, Huayna Capac, by a Cañari princess. The subjugation of the north took many years and Huayna Capac grew up in Ecuador. He succeeded his father to the Inca throne and spent years travelling all over his empire, from Bolivia to Ecuador, constantly putting down uprisings from all sides. Wherever possible, he strengthened his position by marriage and his union with Paccha, the daughter of the defeated Cacha Duchicela, produced a son, Atahualpa.

The year 1526 is a major one in Ecuadorean history. The Inca Huayna Capac died and left his empire, not to one son as was traditional, but to two, thus dividing the Inca empire for the first time. In the same year, on 21 September, the first Spaniards landed near Esmeraldas in northern Ecuador. They were led by the pilot Bartolomé Ruiz de Andrade, who was sent south on an exploratory mission by Francisco Pizarro, who himself remained further north. Pizarro was not to arrive as conqueror for several years. Meanwhile, the rivalry of Huayna Capac's two sons grew. The Inca of Cuzco, Huascar, went to war against the Ecuadorean Inca, Atahualpa.

After several years of fighting, Atahualpa defeated Huascar near Ambato in central Ecuador and was thus the ruler of a weakened and still divided Inca empire when Pizarro arrived in 1532 with plans to conquer the empire.

The Spanish Conquest

Pizarro's advance was rapid and dramatic. His horse-riding, armour-wearing and cannon-firing conquistadors, though few in number, were believed to be godlike and spread terror among the Indians. In late 1532, a summit meeting was arranged between Pizarro and Atahualpa. Although Atahualpa was prepared to negotiate with the Spaniards, Pizarro had other ideas. When the Inca arrived at the pre-arranged meeting place of Cajamarca in Peru on 16 November, he was ambushed by the conquistadors, who massacred most of his badly armed guards and captured Atahualpa. He was held for ransom, and incalculable quantities of gold, silver and other valuables poured in to Cajamarca. When the ransom was paid, the Inca, instead of being released, was put through a sham trial and sentenced to death. His crimes were incest (marrying one's sister was traditional in the Inca heritage), polygamy, worship of false gods, and crimes against the King. He was executed on 29 August 1533, and the Inca empire was effectively at an end.

Despite Atahualpa's death, his general Rumiñahui fought on against the Spaniards in Ecuador for two more years. Pizarro's lieutenant, Sebastián de Benalcázar, finally battled his way to Quito in late 1534, only to find the city razed to the ground by Rumiñahui, who preferred destroying the Inca city to leaving it in the hands of the conquistadors. Quito was refounded on 6 December 1534, and Rumiñahui was captured, tortured and executed in January of 1535. The only important Inca site in Ecuador which remains more or less intact today is at Ingapirca, near Cuenca.

The Colonial Era

From 1535 onwards, the colonial era proceeded with the usual intrigues amongst the Spanish but with no major uprisings by the Ecuadorean Indians. Francisco Pizarro named his brother, Gonzalo, as governor of Quito in 1540. Gonzalo hoped to conquer the Amazon and find more gold, and in 1541 his lieutenant, Francisco de Orellana, left Quito to prospect. He and his force ended up floating all the way to the Atlantic, the first men to descend the Amazon and thus cross the continent. It took them almost a year. This feat is still commemorated in Ecuador and constitutes part of Ecuador's historical claim to a greater part of the Amazon basin than they actually have.

Lima, Peru was the seat of the political administration of Ecuador during the first centuries of colonial rule. Ecuador was first known as a *gobernación* (or province) but in 1563 became the *Audiencia de Quito*, a more important political division. In 1739 the *audiencia* was transferred from the viceroyalty of Peru, of which it was a part, to the viceroyalty of Colombia (then known as Nueva Grenada). Ecuador remained a peaceful colony during these centuries, and agriculture and the arts flourished. Various new agricultural products were introduced from Europe, including cattle and bananas, which still remain important in Ecuador today. There was prolific construction of churches and monasteries which were decorated with unique carvings and paintings resulting from the blend of Spanish and Indian art influences. This so-called 'Quito school of art' has left an indelible stamp on the colonial buildings of the time and is much admired by visitors today.

Life was comfortable for the ruling colonialists, but the Indians, and later *mestizos*, under their rule were treated abysmally. A system of forced labour was not only tolerated, but encouraged, and it was no surprise that by the 18th century there were several uprisings of the Indians against the Spanish ruling classes. Both poor and rich died in violent fighting. One of the best-remembered heroes of the early revolutionary period was Eugenio Espejo, born in Quito in 1747 of an Indian father and a mulatto mother. Espejo was a brilliant man who obtained his doctorate by the age of 20 and became a major literary voice for independence. He wrote political satire, founded a liberal newspaper, and spoke out strongly against colonialism. He was imprisoned several times and died in jail in 1795.

Independence

The first serious attempt to liberate Ecuador was by a partisan group led by Juan Pío Montúfar on 10 August 1809. The group managed to take Quito and install a government, but this lasted only 24 days before royalist troops were able to regain control.

Independence was finally achieved by Simón Bolívar, the Venezuelan liberator who marched southward from Caracas, freed Colombia in 1819, and supported the people of Guayaquil when they claimed independence on 9 October 1820. It took almost two years before Ecuador was entirely liberated from Spanish rule. The decisive battle was fought on 24 May 1822, when Field Marshal Sucre, one of Bolívar's best generals, defeated the royalists at the Battle of Pichincha and took Quito.

Bolívar's idealistic dream was to form a United South America, and he began by amalgamating Venezuela, Colombia and Ecuador into the independent nation of Gran Colombia. This lasted only eight years and Ecuador became fully independent in 1830. In the same year, a treaty was signed with Peru drawing up a boundary between the two nations. This is the boundary that is marked on all Ecuadorean maps. In 1942, after a war between the two countries, the border was redrawn in Rio de Janeiro and it is this border that is found on non-Ecuadorean maps. However, it is not officially acknowledged by the Ecuadorean authorities.

Independent Ecuador's internal history has been a typically Latin American turmoil of political and open warfare between liberals and conservatives. Quito emerged as the main centre for the church-backed conservatives and Guayaquil has traditionally been considered liberal and socialist. This rivalry continues on a social level today; Quiteños have nicknamed Guayaquileños as *monos* (monkeys) and the lively coastal people think of the highland inhabitants as very staid and dull. The rivalry between the groups frequently escalated to extreme violence: conservative President García Moreno was shot to death in 1875 and liberal President Eloy Alfaro was killed and burned by a mob in Quito in 1912. The military began to take control and the 20th century has seen more periods of military rule than of civilian. Ecuador's most recent period of democracy began in 1979 when President Jaime Roldós Aguilera was elected. He was killed in an aeroplane crash in 1981 and his term of office was completed by his vice president, Osvaldo Hurtado Larrea. In 1984 the conservative, León Febres Cordero, was elected and remains in power as this goes to press.

Despite intense and bloody rivalry between liberals, conservatives and the military during the earlier part of this century, Ecuador has remained peaceful in recent years and is, at present, one of the safest countries to visit in South America.

PEOPLE

The (provisional) results of the 1982 census, according to figures available in Quito, give a total population of 8,053,280. The actual figure is probably tens of thousands higher than this. This is approximately 10 times the number of Indians estimated to have been living in the area at the time of the Spanish conquest. The population density of about 30 people per square km is the highest of any South American nation. About 40% of this total are Indians and an equal number are *mestizos* (mixed Spanish/Indian stock). About 10% are white and the remainder black or Asian. Of the Indians, the majority are Quechua-speaking descendants of the inhabitants of the Inca empire and live mainly in the highlands. A few other small groups exist in the lowlands. About 49% of the population live on the coast (and the Galápagos) and over 47% in the highlands. The remainder live in the jungle region of the Oriente, and colonisation of this area is slowly increasing.

ECONOMY

Until recently, Ecuador was the archetypal 'banana republic.' Until the early 1970s, bananas were the most important export and almost all other exports were agricultural. This changed very rapidly with the discovery of oil. Petroleum exports rose to first place in 1973 and by the 1980s accounted for about half of the total export earnings. Bananas still remain important, accounting for about 7% of the nation's exports, as do shrimp and coffee.

The new-found wealth produced by oil export has definitely improved the standards of living. Nevertheless, Ecuador remains a poor country. Distribution of the wealth has been patchy, and much of the rural population continues to live at the same standards it did a decade ago. Education and medical services have improved, however.

GEOGRAPHY

Geographically, Ecuador is one of the world's most varied countries despite its small size (at 283,520 square km it is only a little larger than Great Britain). It straddles the equator on the Pacific coast of South America, and is bordered by only two countries, Colombia to the north and Peru to the south.

The country is divided into three regions. The backbone of Ecuador is the Andean range, rising to 6310 metres with its highest peak Chimborazo. The mountains run from north to south and split the country into the western coastal lowlands and the the eastern jungles of the upper Amazonian basin (known in Ecuador as the Oriente). In only 200 km as the condor flies, you can climb from the coast to snowcaps at over six km above sea level and descend back down to the steaming rain forest on the eastern side.

The central highlands consist of two volcanic mountain ranges, about 400 km long, with a valley nestled between them. This valley was appropriately dubbed 'The Avenue of the Volcanoes' by the German explorer Alexander von Humboldt, who visited Ecuador in 1802. Within the valley are the capital, Quito – at 2850 metres above sea level the second highest capital in the world – and many other towns and tiny villages often of great interest to the traveller for their Indian markets and fiestas.

This book begins with Quito and continues with the northern highlands, proceeds down into the central and southern highlands, swings around into the jungles of the Oriente and then describes the western lowland coastal areas. It concludes with a section on visiting the Galápagos.

RELIGION

In common with that of most Latin

American countries, the religion is predominantly Roman Catholic. Some of the older towns have splendid 16th- and 17th-century Catholic churches. Although churches of other faiths can be found, they form only a small minority. The Indians, while outwardly Roman Catholic, tend to blend Catholicism with their traditional beliefs.

FESTIVALS & HOLIDAYS

Many of the major festivals are oriented to the Roman Catholic liturgical calendar. These are often celebrated with great pageantry, especially in highland Indian villages where a Catholic feast day is often the excuse for a traditional Indian fiesta with much drinking, dancing, rituals and processions. Other holidays are of historical or political interest, for example Columbus Day on 12 October. On the days of the major holidays, banks, offices and other services are closed and transportation tends to be very crowded, so book ahead if possible.

The following list describes the major holidays, but they may well be celebrated for several days around the actual date.

1 January
New Year's Day

6 January
Epiphany

March-April
Carnival Usually held the last few days before Lent, the Carnival is celebrated with water fights. Ambato has its fruit and flowers festival.

April
Easter Palm Sunday, Holy Thursday, Good Friday, Holy Saturday and Easter Sunday are celebrated with religious processions.

1 May
Labour Day Workers' parades.

24 May
Battle of Pichincha National holiday celebrates the decisive battle of independence from the Spanish in 1822.

June
Corpus Christi Religious feast day combined with traditional harvest fiesta in many highland towns. Processions, street dancing.

24 June
St John the Baptist Fiestas in Otavalo area.

29 June
Sts Peter & Paul Fiestas in Otavalo area and other northern highland towns.

24 July
Simón Bolívar's Birthday National holiday to celebrate the liberator's birthday.

25 July
Founding of Guayaquil A major festival for the city of Guayaquil.

10 August
Quito's Independence Day

1-15 September
Fiesta del Yamor Held in Otavalo.

9 October
Guayaquil's Independence Day

12 October
Columbus Day National holiday to celebrate the discovery of America (also known as Americas Day).

1 November
All Saints' Day

2 November
All Souls' Day (Día de Difuntos) Celebrated by flower-laying ceremonies in the cemeteries. Especially colourful in rural areas, where entire Indian families show up at the cemeteries to eat, drink, and leave offerings in memory of their departed relatives. The atmosphere often becomes festive rather than sombre.

3 November
Cuenca's Independence Day

6 December
Founding of Quito Celebrated throughout the first week of December with bullfights, parades and street dances.

24-25 December
Christmas Eve, Christmas Day

28-31 December
End-of-year celebrations Parades and dances culminate in burning of life-size effigies in the streets on New Year's Eve. In addition to these major festivals, there are many smaller ones. Most towns and villages have their own special day.

LANGUAGE

For the traveller, Spanish is the main language. Most Indians are bilingual, with Quechua being their preferred language and Spanish their second tongue. Apart from the Quechua-speaking Indians of the highlands, there are small lowland groups speaking their own languages. These include the Shuar (Jivaro), Auca, Cofan, Secoya, Cayapa and Colorado Indians among others. It is rare to encounter Indians who understand no Spanish at all. Although English is understood in the best hotels, airline offices and tourist agencies, it is of little use elsewhere.

If you don't speak Spanish, take heart. It is an easy language to learn. Courses are available in Quito (see under the Quito section) or you can study books, records and tapes while you are still at home and planning your trip. These study aids are often available for free from many public libraries or you might want to consider taking an evening or college course. Once you have learned the basics, you'll find that you'll be able to travel all over Latin America because – apart from Brazil which is Portuguese-speaking – most of the countries use Spanish.

Spanish is easy to learn for several reasons. First, it uses Roman script. Secondly, with few exceptions, it is spoken as it is written and vice versa. Imagine trying to explain to someone learning English that there are seven different ways of pronouncing 'ough.' This isn't a problem in Spanish. Thirdly, many words are similar enough to English that you can figure them out by guesswork. *Instituto Geográfico Militar* means the military geographical institute, for example.

Even if you don't have time to take a course, at least bring a phrase-book and dictionary. Don't dispense with the dictionary, because the phrase-book limits you to asking where the bus station is, and won't help you translate the local newspaper. My favourite dictionary, incidentally, is the paperback *University of Chicago Spanish-English, English-Spanish Dictionary*. It's small enough to travel with, yet has many more entries than most pocket dictionaries. It also contains words used in Latin America but not in Spain.

Although the Spanish alphabet looks like the English one, it is in fact different. 'Ch' is considered a separate letter, for example, so *champú* (which simply means 'shampoo') will be listed in a dictionary after all the words beginning with just 'c.' Similarly, 'll' is a separate letter, so a *llama* is listed after all the words beginning with a single 'l.' The letter 'ñ' is listed after the ordinary 'n.' Vowels with an accent are accented for stress and are not considered separate letters.

Pronunciation is generally more straightforward than it is in English, and if you say a word the way it looks like it should be said, the chances are that it will be close enough to be understood. You will get better with practise of course. A few notable exceptions are 'll' which is always pronounced 'y' as in 'yacht,' the 'j' which is pronounced 'h' as in 'happy,' and the 'h' which isn't pronounced at all. Thus the phrase *hojas en la calle* (leaves in the street) would be pronounced 'o-has en la ka-yea.' Finally, the letter 'ñ' is pronounced as the 'ny' sound in 'canyon.'

Facts for the Visitor

VISAS & DOCUMENTS

Travellers entering Ecuador as tourists do not require visas. You need your passport (valid for six months or more) and a T-3 tourist card which is obtainable on arrival in Ecuador. There is no charge for this card, but don't lose it as you will need it for stay extensions, passport checks and leaving the country. If you should lose it, you can get another at the immigration office in Quito or Guayaquil, or at the exit point from the country.

On arrival, you are normally asked how long you want to stay. If you're lucky and the duty officer is in a good mood, you can get 60 days. You are given an identical stamp on both your passport and tourist card which indicates how long you can stay. The maximum is 90 days, but usually less is given. There is no set pattern in this; during 1983 there was a two-month period when everyone got 30 days irrespective of whether they wanted to stay for three days or three months. Whatever happens, keep cool. If you argue with the official who gave you only 30 days when you wanted 45, he could hassle you further. It's easy and quick to get a stay extension in Quito at Avenida Amazonas 2639.

The main problem with staying in Ecuador is undoubtedly the 90-day rule. This means that you can't stay in the country for more than 90 days in any 12-month period. Ecuador isn't a large country and 90 days is more than enough for most people. A longer stay with a tourist card is flatly refused and the only official way to stay on is with a business, work, student or residence visa. Obtaining one in Ecuador is often a time-consuming, frustrating and costly process, and it's usually better to apply for a visa at your nearest Ecuadorean consul if you are a bona fide businessperson or whatever.

If you don't fall conveniently into one of the above categories and you want to stay longer than 90 days, simply leaving the country (across to Peru, for example) and returning a few days later doesn't work. The officials check your passport for entry and exit dates and are quick to notice if your 90 days have been used up. Should you go to Peru and get a new passport at your embassy because your previous one was lost, stolen or expired, then returning to Ecuador is another story. With no Ecuadorean stamps in your brand-new passport you have no problem. If you leave Ecuador with, say, only 60 of your 90 days used, you will receive your balance of 30 days upon re-entry with no problem.

In addition to your passport and tourist card, you officially need a ticket out of the country and evidence of sufficient funds for your stay (US$20 per day). This is the law and if you turn up at the border stoned or looking as if you haven't washed or eaten for a week, the law will be enforced. However, in about 10 trips to Ecuador, I was never asked for an onward ticket and was only asked to show sufficient funds once. They didn't count it too carefully – I just waved a bunch of travellers' cheques. I have heard a story of passengers on an Ecuatoriana flight from Miami to Quito being refused entry without an onward ticket – I don't know the details. If you're flying in, it's safest to buy an onward ticket. It can be refunded if you don't use it. Most reputable airlines will refund your ticket as long as it hasn't expired. In Ecuador this can take a couple of weeks but they'll give you the money in dollars. Don't worry about an onward ticket at the land borders; it's very unlikely that the rule will be mentioned if you arrive looking reasonably respectable.

You should always carry your passport (or at least a photocopy of the pages with your photo and passport number and you T-3 card), as there are occasional document checks on public transport – you can be arrested if you don't have identification. Another document you can use for identification is a driver's licence (as long as it is of the type with a photo on it) or any similar official-looking document that has a recent photo of you.

Colombian Visas

Ecuador is bordered only by Colombia to the north and Peru to the south. To enter Colombia, most nationalities need a visa. Nationals of the following countries do not require a visa: Argentina, Austria, Barbados, Belgium, Chile, Costa Rica, Denmark, El Salvador, Finland, Holland, Ireland, Israel, Italy, Japan, Liechtenstein, Luxemburg, Norway, South Korea, Spain, Sweden, Switzerland, Trinidad and Tobago, UK, Uruguay, West Germany. As of 9 November 1983, all other nationalities require a visa, which costs anywhere from US$5 (French) to US$20 for citizens of most other countries. This includes Australians, New Zealanders, Canadians and US citizens, among others. If you don't already have your visa, go to the Colombian Consul which has offices in Guayaquil, Quito and Tulcán. (See the sections on those cities for further information.)

Peruvian Visas

Most European nationalities – the French being a notable exception – do not require a visa to enter Peru. Most Latins, except Chileans and Venezuelans, do not require visas. Canadians and US citizens do not require visas. Travellers from most communist countries and some African and Asian countries (not Japan) do require visas. Australians and New Zealanders, for some perverse reason, also require visas. If you need a Peruvian visa, you can get one at the consul in Quito, Guayaquil, Macará and Machala. (See the sections on those cities for further information.)

Other Paperwork

International vaccination certificates are not required by law, but vaccinations are advisable. See the 'Health' section.

Student cards are of little use, as the number of places that give discounts for students are very limited.

MONEY

The currency in Ecuador is the sucre, usually written as S/. It has nothing to do with sugar; in fact it is named after General Sucre, who defeated the Spanish colonialists at the Battle of Pichincha on 24 May 1824, thus opening the way to independence for Ecuador. There are bills of 1000, 500, 100, 50, 20, 10 and 5 sucres. There is a one-sucre coin which is divided into 100 centavos, but the latter are little used. There are two rates of exchange; the lower one is used in international business transactions and is of no concern to the traveller. The higher rate is available at all exchange houses. The sucre is frequently devalued, so it is impossible to give accurate exchange rates. The following table gives some idea:

1981	30 sucres per US dollar
1982	65 sucres per US dollar
1983	95 sucres per US dollar
1985	120 sucres per US dollar

The easiest currency to exchange is the US dollar. Although hard currencies such as other dollars, pounds sterling, French and Swiss francs and German marks are exchangeable in Quito and Guayaquil, outside of these cities you should try to travel with US dollars. It is best to try to exchange as much money as you need in the major cities, as exchange rates are lower in the smaller towns. In some places, notably the Oriente, it is very difficult to exchange any money at all. If you are stuck in a small town and are out of sucres, try the banks. Even if they don't officially do foreign exchange, the bank manager may be persuaded to change a small amount of US cash dollars from his personal account, or he may know of someone who will do so. Also ask at the best hotels, restaurants and stores in town. Missionaries, Peace Corps volunteers and other travellers may help you exchange dollars.

Where you should exchange your money varies from month to month. On my last visit to Ecuador, there was an embargo on foreign exchange at all banks so I had to change at *casas de cambio* (exchange houses). I understand that banks are once again dealing in foreign currency, but you'll have to check the latest situation upon your arrival. Normally, all exchange rates are within 2% of one another, so it's not worth hassling all day for the best deal unless you're changing a sizable sum. Good places to change money are indicated under each town. There is not very much difference between exchange rates for cash and travellers' cheques. There is no black market and street changers are limited to the borders.

With the lack of a black market, there isn't much advantage in carrying all your money in cash. Travellers' cheques are much safer because they are refunded if they are lost or stolen. I've had no difficulty in exchanging major brands of travellers' cheques in Ecuador. I definitely do not recommend using First National Citibank cheques, however. They took over a year to reimburse me for US$200 in stolen cheques and had the gall to charge me about US$20 for handling. (The theft, I should add, occurred in Peru.) But don't bring all your money in travellers' cheques;

it's always useful to have a supply of cash dollars for the occasions when only cash is accepted.

Credit cards are also useful and most major cards are widely accepted. Some transactions are classified as 'business' and you get the lower exchange rate, so check carefully. The best use for credit cards is buying dollars from a bank.

If you run out of money, it is a simple matter to have more sent to you, assuming, of course, that there's someone at home kind enough to send you money. A bank transfer is most quickly done by telex, although this will take at least three days. All you need to do is pick an Ecuadorean bank which will cooperate with your bank at home (eg Bank of America, Bank of London & South America) and telex your family, friend or bank manager to deposit the money in your name at the bank of your choice. Unlike many Latin American countries, Ecuador allows you to receive the money in the currency of your choice (US dollars!). If you are planning on travelling throughout Latin America, you'll find that Ecuador is one of the best countries to have money sent to.

Banks are open for business from 9 am to 1 pm Monday through Friday. In some cities banks are open on Saturday, mainly if Saturday happens to be market day. In some cities, banks may stay open later. *Casas de cambio* are usually open from 9 am to 6 pm Monday through Friday and until noon on Saturday. There is usually a lunch hour, which varies from place to place.

Should you change more money than necessary, you can buy back dollars at international airports when leaving the country. The loss depends on fluctuations of the dollar; sometimes you get back more than you paid but usually you lose a few percent. Airports are good places to change money on Sundays when *casas de cambio* are closed. If you aren't flying out, you can change money at the major land borders.

COSTS

Costs in Ecuador are among the lowest in Latin America. In four years of travelling in Ecuador, I've noticed that the price of travel basics such as hotels, meals and transportation have almost halved. It seems, if anything, to be getting cheaper and you may find that the already low prices in this book are lower still by the time you read this. All good things come to an end, however, so the reverse may also be true. Because of the inflation rate, I've used US dollars in all my price quotes.

If you're on a very tight budget, you'll find that you can easily manage on the classic bare-bones budget of US$5 per day, including the occasional luxury such as a bottle of beer and a movie. If you're really economical, you could manage on less than US$3 per day if you stay in the cheapest US$1 pensiones and eat the meal of the day in restaurants.

If you can afford to spend a little more, however, you'll probably enjoy yourself more. The luxury of a simple room with a private hot shower and a table and chair on which to write letters home can be had for as little as US$2.50 per person if you know where to go – this book will show you where. Saving time and energy by flying back from a remote destination which took you several days of land travel to reach is also recommended. At present, the most expensive internal flight on the Ecuadorean mainland is about US$16 and many flights are much cheaper. A taxi, particularly when you're in a group, isn't expensive and usually costs less than a dollar for short but convenient rides.

Travelling hard, eating well, staying in rooms with a private bath, writing an average of one letter each day to friends/family, buying a daily newspaper, seeing a movie once in a while, and drinking a couple of beers with dinner most nights sounds expensive – almost decadent – to the 'purist' budget traveller. I did that for several months while researching this book, and averaged less than US$10 a day. Even if you demand the best available, in most parts of Ecuador it will cost much less than wherever home may be.

I sometimes meet travellers who spend most of their time worrying how to make their every penny stretch further. It seems to me that they spend more time looking at their finances than looking at the places they're visiting. Of course, many travellers are on a grand tour of South America and want to make their money last, but you can get so burned out on squalid hotels and bad food that the grand tour becomes an endurance test. I'd rather spend eight months travelling comfortably and enjoyably than a full year of strain and sacrifice.

There is one major stumbling block for budget travellers and that is the Galápagos Archipelago. Getting there is very expensive and staying there isn't particularly cheap. I suggest you read the chapter on the Galápagos before you decide whether you want to go.

WORKING

Officially, you need a work visa to be allowed to work in Ecuador. You can, however, get a job teaching English in language schools, usually in Quito. They often advertise for teachers on the bulletin board at the almost legendary budget travellers' Hotel Gran Casino. They expect you to be a native English speaker, but I know of one fluent Dutchman who got a job. Pay is low but enough to live on if you're broke. It's best to start looking soon after you arrive, because it's not easy to get a work visa and you may have to leave in 90 days. If, in addition to speaking English like a native, you actually have a bona fide teaching credential, so much the better. Schools such as the American School in Quito will often hire teachers of maths, biology and other subjects, and may often help you get a work visa if you want to stay on. They also pay much better than the language schools. I don't know of other jobs which are readily available without a working visa.

Another way of making money, if you're in that unfortunate position of needing it, is selling good-quality camping or camera equipment, etc. Good gear can be sold for a reasonable though not excessive price – again, use the notice board at the Gran Casino.

CLIMATE

Ecuador's climate follows a pattern very different from the one travellers from temperate regions are used to. Instead of the four seasons, there are wet and dry seasons. The weather patterns also vary greatly depending on which geographical region you are in.

The Galápagos and coastal areas are influenced by ocean currents. The warm El Niño current from the north causes a hot and rainy season from January through April. It doesn't rain all the time but you can expect torrential downpours which often disrupt communications. Daytime temperatures average about 31°C (88°F) but are often much higher and this time of year is generally an unpleasant time to be travelling in the coastal regions. From May to December the cool Humboldt current from the south keeps temperatures a few degrees lower and it rarely rains.

If you want to travel in the Oriente, bring your rain gear as it rains during most months. September through December are usually the driest, and June through August are the wettest – with regional variations. It's usually almost as hot as the coast.

The dry season in the highlands is from June through September and a short dry season also occurs during the month around Christmas. It doesn't rain daily in the wet season, however. April, the wettest month, averages one rainy day in two. Daytime temperatures average a high of 20 to 22°C (68 to 72°F) and a low of 7 to 8°C (45 to 48°F) year round, though you should expect more extreme variations on occasion. These figures are based on climatic data from Quito.

Despite all these statistics, you should remember the Ecuadorean adage that they can experience all four seasons in one day. Without a doubt, the most predictable aspect of Ecuador's weather is its unpredictability.

HEALTH

It's true that most people travelling for any length of time in South America are likely to have an occasional mild stomach upset. It's also true that if you take the appropriate precautions before, during and after your trip, it's unlikely that you will become seriously ill. In six years of travelling in Latin America, I'm happy to report that I've picked up no major illnesses.

Before You Go

Vaccinations are the most important of your pre-departure health preparations. Although the Ecuadorean authorities do not, at present, require anyone to have an up-to-date international vaccination card to enter the country, you are strongly advised to read the following list and receive the ones appropriate for your trip. Pregnant women should consult with their doctor before taking these vaccinations.

Yellow fever vaccination is very important if you are planning a trip to the jungles of the Oriente, but not necessary if you intend to avoid the Oriente altogether. This vaccination lasts 10 years.

Typhoid vaccination consists of two injections taken four weeks apart, so you have to think ahead for this one. This vaccine makes some people feel unwell and often gives you a sore arm, so try not to schedule the last shot for the day you're packing. You should get a booster shot every three years, but this doesn't normally feel so bad.

Most people in developed countries get a diphtheria-tetanus injection and oral polio vaccine while they are at school. You should get boosters every 10 years.

A cholera vaccination is only necessary if an epidemic has been declared in Latin America. Protection only lasts six months.

Smallpox was eradicated worldwide in 1978 and protection is no longer necessary.

Hepatitis

The diseases mentioned above are dangerous but relatively uncommon. A depressingly common disease is hepatitis, which is caused by ingesting contaminated food or water. Salads, uncooked or unpeeled fruit, unboiled drinks, and dirty syringes (even in hospitals) are the worst offenders. Infection risks are minimized by using bottled drinks, washing your own salads with purified water, and paying scrupulous attention to your toilet habits. If you get the disease you'll know it. Your skin and especially the whites of your eyes turn yellow, and you literally feel so tired that it takes all your effort to go to the bathroom. There is no cure except bed rest. If you're lucky, you'll be on your feet in a couple of weeks. If you're not, expect to stay in bed for a couple of months. Research is currently underway to find a 100% effective prophylaxis; meanwhile you are strongly advised to get a gamma globulin shot as close to departure as possible. Although it is not 100% effective, your chances of getting hepatitis are minimized. The shot should be repeated every six months, although some authorities recommend more frequent shots.

If you do get hepatitis, it's not the end of the world. You may feel deathly ill but people almost never suffer from permanent ill effects. If you're on a long trip, you don't have to give up and go home. Find a hotel that has a decent restaurant and get a room which isn't two flights of stairs and three hallways away from the nearest bathroom. Arrange with the hotel staff to bring you meals and drinks as you need them, and go to bed. Chances are that you'll be fit enough to travel again within a month.

Malaria

This is another disease to think about before leaving. Malarial mosquitoes don't live above 2500 metres, so if you plan on staying in the highlands you needn't worry about them. If you plan on visiting the lowlands, you should purchase anti-malarial pills in advance because they have to be taken from two weeks before until six weeks after your visit. Dosage and frequency of pill-taking varies from brand to brand, so check this carefully.

Some people who spend a great deal of time in tropical lowlands prefer not to take anti-malarial pills on a semi-permanent basis. The side effects, if any, of long-term anti-malarial drug use have not been fully researched. In this case you should avoid getting bitten by always wearing long-sleeved shirts and long trousers, using frequent applications of an insect repellent, and sleeping under a mosquito net. Sleeping under a fan is also effective; mosquitoes don't like wind. The most effective ingredient in insect repellents is *diethyl-metatoluamide*, also known as 'Deet.' You should buy repellent with 90% or more of this ingredient; many brands, including those available in Ecuador, contain less than 15%, so buy it ahead of time. I find that the rub-on lotions are the most effective, and sprays are good for spraying clothes, especially at the neck, wrist, waist and ankle openings.

Other Predeparture Precautions

Several other things must be thought about before leaving home. If you wear prescription glasses, make sure you have a spare pair and the prescription. The tropical sun is strong, so you may want to have a prescription pair of sunglasses made. Also buy suntan lotion, as the lotions available in Ecuador are not very effective. Ensure that you have an adequate supply of the prescription medicines you use on a regular basis. If you haven't had a dental examination for a long time, you should have one rather than risk a dental problem in Ecuador. Put together a small first-aid kit (see next section).

However fit and healthy you are, *do* take out medical insurance, preferably one with provisions for flying you home in the event of a medical emergency. Even if you don't get sick, you might be involved in an accident.

First-Aid Kit

How large or small your first-aid kit should be depends on your knowledge of first-aid procedures, where and how far off the beaten track you are going, how long you will need the kit for, and how many people will be sharing it. The following is a suggested checklist which you should amend as you require.

Antiseptic cream
Aspirin
Lomotil for diarrhoea
Antibiotics such as ampicillin and tetracycline
Throat lozenges
Ear and eye drops
Antacid tablets
Motion-sickness medication
Alcohol swabs
Water purifier
Lip salve
Foot and groin powder
Thermometer in a case
Surgical tape, assorted sticky plasters (band-aids), gauze, bandages, butterfly closures
Scissors
First-aid booklet

A convenient way of carrying your first-aid kit so that it doesn't get crushed is in a small plastic container with a sealing lid, such as Tupperware.

Water Purification

If you use tap water for drinking or washing fruits and vegetables, you should purify it first. The most effective method is to boil it continuously for 20 minutes, which is obviously inconvenient. Various water-purifying tablets are available but most of them aren't wholly effective – the hepatitis virus often survives. Also, they make the water taste strangely and are not recommended for frequent and long-term use. The most effective method, and one that doesn't make the water taste as bad, is to use iodine. You can use a few drops of prepared iodine solution but the problem is that it's difficult to know exactly how strong the solution is in the first place and how many drops you should use. The following method is one that I learnt at the South American Explorer's Club in Lima. I find it eliminates these problems and works very well.

Get hold of a small, one-oz glass bottle and put about two to three mm of iodine crystals in it. Don't use a plastic bottle as the iodine will make it brittle and cause it to crack. Both iodine crystals and suitable glass bottles can be obtained from pharmacies. When you need a purifying solution, fill the glass bottle with water and shake it well for about a minute, and then let the crystals settle to the bottom. Only a minute amount of the crystals actually dissolve in the ounce of water and you now have one oz of saturated (not concentrated) iodine solution which is always the same (saturated) strength. Carefully pour the ounce of saturated iodine solution into a quart (or litre) of water and leave it for 15 minutes to produce clean drinking water. The advantage of this method is that only the iodine solution is used to purify your drinking water and the crystals are left at the bottom of the bottle; they can be used and reused hundreds of times. This is a safe and recommended method except for people who have been treated for thyroid problems and for pregnant women. Also you should be extremely careful not to transfer any of the actual crystals to the drinking water. The saturated solution is quite safe but accidentally swallowing a whole iodine crystal would not do you any good at all.

Diarrhoea

The drastic change in diet experienced by travellers means that they are often susceptible to minor stomach ailments, such as diarrhoea. After you've been travelling in South America for a while, you seem to build up some sort of immunity, which just goes to show that most of the stomach problems you get when you first arrive aren't serious.

The major problem when you have diarrhoea is fluid loss leading to severe dehydration – you can actually dry out to the point of death if you go for several days without replacing the fluids you're losing. So drink plenty of liquids. Caffeine is a stomach irritant, so the best drinks are weak tea, mineral water and caffeine-free soft drinks. Avoid milk. If you can, fast. By giving your body plenty of fluids and no food, you can often get rid of diarrhoea naturally in about 24 to 36 hours. Rest as much as you can.

If it's important (eg just before a flight or journey that has to be done), you can stop the symptoms of diarrhoea by taking Lomotil or Imodium. These pills will not cure you, however, and it is likely that your diarrhoea will recur after the drug wears off. Rest, fast, and drink plenty of fluids.

Dysentery
If your diarrhoea continues for several days and is accompanied by nausea, severe abdominal pain and fever, and you find blood in your stool, it's likely that you have contracted dysentery. Although many travellers suffer from an occasional bout of diarrhoea, dysentery is fortunately not very common. There are two types: amoebic and bacillary. It is not always obvious which kind you have. Although bacillary responds well to antibiotics, amoebic – which is rarer – involves more complex treatment. If you contract dysentery, you should seek medical advice.

Altitude Sickness
This occurs when you ascend to high altitude quickly, for example if you fly into Quito (2850 metres) from sea level. The best way to prevent altitude sickness is to spend a day or two travelling slowly to high altitudes, thus allowing your body time to adjust. Even if you don't do this, it is unlikely that you will suffer greatly in Quito because it is still relatively low. A very few people do become seriously ill, but most travellers experience no more than some shortness of breath and headache. If, however, you travel higher than Quito, you may well experience much severer symptoms, including vomiting, fatigue, insomnia, loss of appetite, a rapid pulse and irregular (Cheyne-Stokes) breathing during sleep.

The best thing you can do upon arriving at high altitude is to take it easy for the first day, and to avoid smoking and alcohol. This will go a long way to helping you acclimatize. If you feel sick, the best treatment is rest, deep breathing, an adequate fluid intake and a mild pain killer (aspirin isn't recommended; try Tylenol or something similar) to alleviate headaches. If symptoms are very severe, the only effective cure is oxygen. The best way to obtain this is to descend to a lower elevation.

Heat & Sun
The heat and humidity of the tropics make you sweat profusely and can also make you feel apathetic. It is important to maintain a high fluid intake and to ensure that your food is well salted. If fluids and salts lost through perspiration are not replaced, heat exhaustion and cramps frequently result. The feeling of apathy that some people experience usually fades after a week or two.

If you're arriving in the tropics with a great desire to improve your tan, you've certainly come to the right place. The tropical sun will not only improve your tan, it will also burn you to a crisp. I know several travellers who have enjoyed themselves in the sun for an afternoon, and then spent the next couple of days with severe sunburn. An effective way of immobilizing yourself is to cover yourself with suntan lotion, walk down to the beach, remove your shoes and badly burn your feet (which you forgot to put lotion on and which are especially white). The power of the tropical sun cannot be overemphasized. Don't spoil your trip by trying to tan too quickly; use strong suntan lotion frequently and put it on all exposed skin. Ecuador doesn't sell strong suntan lotion – bring it from home. Wearing a wide-brimmed sun hat is also a good idea.

Insect Problems

Insect repellents go a long way in preventing bites (see Malaria section). When you do get bitten, avoid scratching; unfortunately this is easier said than done. To alleviate itching, try Hydrocortisone cream, Calamine lotion, or soaking in baking soda. Scratching will quickly open bites and cause them to become infected. Skin infections are slow to heal in the heat of the tropics and all infected bites as well as cuts and grazes should be kept scrupulously clean, treated with antiseptic creams, and covered with dressings on a daily basis.

Another insect problem is infestation by lice or crabs and scabies. Lice or crabs crawl around in your body hair and itch. To get rid of them, wash with a shampoo which contains benzene hexachloride, or shave the affected area. To avoid being re-infected, wash all your clothes and bedding in hot water and the shampoo. It's probably best to just throw away your underwear if you had body lice or crabs. Lice thrive on body warmth; clothing which isn't worn will cause the beasties lurking within to die in about 72 hours.

Scabies are mites which burrow into your skin and cause it to become red and itchy. To kill scabies, wash yourself with a benzene benzoate solution, and wash your clothes too. Both benzene hexachloride and benzoate are obtainable from pharmacies in Ecuador.

Scorpions and spiders can give severely painful – but rarely fatal – stings or bites. A common way to get bitten is to put on your clothes and shoes in the morning without checking them first. Develop the habit of shaking out your clothing before putting it on, especially in the lowlands. Check your bedding before going to sleep. Don't walk barefoot, and look where you place your hands when reaching to a shelf or branch. It's extremely unlikely that you will get stung, so don't worry about it.

Snakebite

This is also extremely unlikely. Should you be bitten, the snake may be a non-venomous one. In any event, follow this procedure: First, try and kill the offending creature for identification. Second, don't try the slash-and-suck routine. One of the world's deadliest snakes is the fer-de-lance, and it has an anti-coagulating agent in its venom. If you're bitten by a fer-de-lance, your blood coagulates twice as slowly as the average hemophiliac's and so slashing at the wound with a razor is a good way to help you bleed to death. The slash-and-suck routine does work in some cases, but this should be done only by someone who knows what they are doing. Third, get the victim to a doctor as soon as possible. Fourth, keep calm and reassure the victim. Even the deadly fer-de-lance only succeeds in killing a small percentage of its victims. Fifth, while reassuring and evacuating the victim, apply a tourniquet just above the bite if it is on a limb. Release pressure for 90 seconds every 10 minutes, and make sure that the tourniquet is never so tight that you can't slide a finger underneath it. If circulation is cut off completely, worse damage will result.

In Australia, which has a fair amount of snake bite experience, a new method of treatment is now recommended. This is to simply immobilise the limb where the bite took place and bandage it tightly (but not like a tourniquet) and completely. Then with the minimum of disturbance, particularly of the bound limb, get the victim to medical attention.

Rabies

Rabid dogs are more common in Latin

America than in more developed nations. If you are bitten by a dog, try and have it captured for tests. If you are unable to test the dog, you must assume that you have rabies, which is invariably fatal, so you cannot take the risk of hoping that the dog was not infected. Treatment consists of a long series of injections which used to be painful but modern techniques are quicker and less painful. Rabies doesn't develop for several weeks, so if you are bitten, don't panic. You've got plenty of time to get treated.

Rabies is also carried by vampire bats, who prefer to bite the toes of their sleeping human victims. So don't stick your toes out from your mosquito net or blanket if you're sleeping in an area where there are bats.

Medical Attention in Ecuador

If you've taken the precautions mentioned in the previous sections you can look forward to a generally healthy trip. Should something go wrong, however, you can get good medical advice and treatment in the major cities. In Quito, the Hospital Vozandes is at Vallalengua 263, next to the radio station of the same name. The No 1 Iñaquito bus passes it. They have some English-speaking staff and both outpatient and emergency rooms. A small fee is charged. In Guayaquil, the best English-speaking hospital is the Clínica Kennedy.

Many prescription drugs are available in Ecuador, some of which are sold over the counter. If you need to buy any, make sure that they haven't expired and that they have been kept in a cool or refrigerated storage area.

BOOKS & BOOKSHOPS

There are only two good bookshops in Ecuador which sell books in English (French and German, too). One is in Guayaquil and one is in Quito. In Guayaquil go to the Librería Científica on Luque 223. In Quito there is Libri Mundi, the best-known bookshop in Ecuador. They

are at Juan León Mera 851 and have a branch on the ground floor of the Hotel Colón. Both shops also have a good selection of Spanish books.

Guidebooks

Apart from months of legwork, I used a great many books in compiling the information in this guidebook. I hope you like it, because I couldn't find any other comprehensive guidebooks on Ecuador. There are, however, some good books on South America in general which have a chapter on Ecuador. They are mainly recommended for the traveller who wants one book for his 'grand tour' of Latin America.

For the budget traveller, *South America on a Shoestring* by Geoff Crowther, 3rd edition 1986, published by Lonely Planet, is recommended for its many maps and money-saving information, as well as its interesting synopses of the historical/political situation in Latin countries.

A broader approach is available in *The South American Handbook*, edited by John Brooks and published annually by Trade & Travel Publications, Bath, UK. It has been referred to as the 'South American Bible' by some travellers and it weighs about as much as one and is quite pricey. Its main drawbacks are sometimes overdue updates and paucity of good city maps. It is suitable for everyone from penurious budget travellers to expense-accounted businesspeople, so there is a lot of extraneous information for most readers. Nevertheless, it is the best general guide to the continent.

Another book which I enjoyed is Lynn Meisch's *A Traveler's Guide to El Dorado & the Inca Empire* published by Penguin Books. It's full of interesting details on the crafts, cultures, markets, fiestas and archaeology of Colombia, Ecuador, Peru and Bolivia, and has good background information for the traveller. However, it doesn't set out to help with specific information on hotels, restaurants or transport.

Various other guidebooks are available in Ecuador. One is Arthur Weilbauer's booklet *A Guide for Excursions by Car in Ecuador*. This is available in Spanish, German and English although the English translation is entertainingly garbled – 'There are hotels of all denominations, but luckily no high-rise damage the aspect.' Only the Spanish version has maps. Most of the other books available are of the coffee-table variety – fun to look through in the store and suitable as a souvenir or present rather than as a travel guide.

There are also 'mainstream' guides by Frommer, Waldo, Birnbaum, Fodor and others, which seem to cater to the 'today's Tuesday, so it must be Rio' crowd, and are fine if that's what you're looking for.

The Outdoors

My first two years in Ecuador were spent trying to climb as many of its mountains as I could. At that time, there was only one climbers' guide available: *The Fool's Climbing Guide to Ecuador & Peru* by Michael Koerner, Buzzard Mountaineering, USA – now, as far as I know, out of print. It was a whimsical little booklet from which I derived a great deal of pleasure, and although its mountain descriptions were not very detailed it remains a great favourite of mine.

More favourite still, though I must admit to a certain prejudice because I wrote it, is *Climbing & Hiking in Ecuador* which is published by Bradt Enterprises, UK and USA (see below). It is a detailed guide to climbing Ecuador's mountains and also describes many beautiful hikes, some of which are simple day hikes suitable for the beginner.

My favourite of all is Edward Whymper's *Travels Amongst the Great Andes of the Equator*, first published in Britain in 1891 and now quite rare, though a good public library might be able to get it for you. This exceptional book describes an 1880 mountaineering expedition which made eight first ascents of Ecuadorean peaks,

including the highest, Chimborazo. There are also fascinating descriptions of travel in Ecuador a century ago and the woodcut engravings are pure delight.

Backpacking in Venezuela, Colombia & Ecuador by George and Hilary Bradt describes more Ecuadorean hikes. It is published by Bradt Enterprises, 41 Nortoft Road, Chalfont St Peter, Bucks SL9 0LA, UK; or 95 Harvey St, Cambridge, Massachusetts 02140, USA. This company publishes an excellent and varied collection of outdoor guides to various regions of the world, including seven books on Latin America.

Books on Ecuador's wildlife are sadly few. *The Birds of Ecuador & the Galápagos Archipelago* by Thomas Butler is merely a check list. A proper field guide by Ridgely and Greenfield will be available in the late 1980s; meanwhile ornithologists have to avail themselves of either guides to the whole continent, or to nearby countries, eg de Schauensee and Phelps' *A Guide to the Birds of Venezuela* which covers approximately half of Ecuador's species. Books on plants and animals are also lacking. The only one I know of is *Fauna del Ecuador*, Quito, 1978, by Erwin Patzelt, in Spanish, and now out of print (though there is frequent talk of a new edition). There are however, several excellent books on South American natural history generally, which contain some information on Ecuador. My favourite is Michael Andrews' *Flight of the Condor*. Tony Morrison's *Land Above the Clouds* and *The Andes* are also very good.

Galápagos

The handiest small guide to the history, geology and both plant and animal wildlife of these islands is the *Galápagos Guide* by Epler and White, available at the Libri Mundi bookstore in Quito. It costs only about US$2.50. Other useful guides are *A Field Guide to the Birds of the Galápagos* by Michael Harris, published by Collins, London. This excellent handbook illustrates and fully describes every Galápagos bird species. Amateur botanists will want Eileen Schofield's booklet *Plants of the Galápagos Islands*, Universe Books, New York. This describes 87 common plants and is much more convenient than the classic, but encyclopaedic, *Flora of the Galápagos Islands* by Wiggins and Porter, Stanford University Press, USA.

In addition to these guides, there are several good books of a general nature about the Galápagos. The following are particularly recommended: *Islands Lost in Time* by Tui de Roi Moore; *Galápagos – Islands of Birds* by Bryan Nelson; and *Darwin's Islands: A Natural History of the Galápagos* by Ian Thornton. There are many others.

The most famous of the visitors to the Galápagos was Charles Darwin in 1835 and you can read his *On the Origin of Species by Means of Natural Selection* or his accounts of *The Voyage of the Beagle*. These 19th century books are rather dated and make heavy reading today. You may prefer modern biographies of Darwin such as Irving Stone's excellent *The Origin* or Alan Moorehead's illustrated *Darwin & the Beagle*.

Miscellaneous

One of my favourite books about travel in Ecuador is Henri Michaux' prose/poetry account of his 1928 visit. Michaux was a Belgian poet and mystic and his *Ecuador – A Travel Journal* is an intriguing look at his impressions of the country more than half a century ago. It was republished by Peter Owen in 1970 and is available in Libri Mundi bookstore.

Various good books are available about the Indian populations of Ecuador. *The Awakening Valley* by Collier and Buitron, University of Chicago Press, 1949, is a photographic anthropological study of the people of the Otavalo region. The Shuar are studied by Michael Harner using their old name, *The Jivaro: People of the Sacred Waterfall* from Doubleday/Anchor, 1973. A well-illustrated multilingual book available in Quito is *The Lost World of the Aucas* by K D Gertelmann. Other books about Ecuador's and South America's Indian peoples are available at Libri Mundi.

Books about the history or politics of Ecuador are hard to find. Going back to the arrival of the Spanish conquistadors, the best book is undoubtedly John Hemming's excellent *The Conquest of the Incas*. Although this mainly deals with Peru (the heart of the Inca Empire) there are several sections on Ecuador. I have yet to find a readable book about the more recent history or politics of the country.

Maps

The bookstores have a limited selection of Ecuadorean maps. The best selection is to be had from the IGM (*Instituto Geográfico Militar*), which is on top of a hill on Avenida T Paz y Miño, off Avenida Colombia in Quito. The building can be recognized from some directions by a map of Ecuador painted on one of its outside walls. There are no buses; walk or take a taxi (about a dollar). A permit to enter the building is given to you at the main gate in exchange for your passport. Opening hours are from 8 am to 3 pm Monday through Friday. Few city maps are published, and except for perhaps a detailed map of the whole of Quito, you'll find the city maps in this book are generally the best available. The IGM does have some excellent large-scale maps of the whole country, ranging from a 1:1,000,000 one-sheet Ecuador map to 1:50,000 topographical maps. Most maps are freely available for reference. Some areas, especially the Oriente and parts of the western lowlands, are inadequately mapped.

NEWSPAPERS & MEDIA

Although Ecuador is a small country, there are literally dozens of newspapers available. Most towns of any size publish a local newspaper which is useful for finding out what's playing in the town cinemas and reading the local gossip, but has little national news and even less international news. The best newspapers are available in Quito and Guayaquil, although many of these are sensationalist rags which luridly portray traffic-accident victims on the front page while relegating world affairs to a few columns behind the sports section.

There are good newspapers; one of the best is *El Comercio* published in Quito. *Hoy* is also good. In Guayaquil *El Telégrafo* and *El Universo* are recommended. These papers normally cost about 15c each in the city of publication. The further away from the city you are, the more you pay. For example, a day-old *El Comercio* in a small jungle town will be 20-25c.

Foreign newspapers and magazines are available at Libri Mundi bookstore, the Hotel Colón shopping mall, and sometimes at the airport. The Hotel Oro Verde in Guayaquil and the airport of that town also have foreign periodicals.

Ecuador has five television channels, but the programming leaves much to be desired. I remember one evening when Ecuador was playing Peru in a soccer match; every channel was carrying coverage of the match. If you're not much interested in sports, you can watch very bad Latin American soap operas or re-runs of old and equally bad North American sit-coms. The news broadcasts every evening are quite good, especially for local news. Occasionally, a National Geographic special makes its way to the screen. These kinds of programmes are advertised days ahead in the better newspapers.

If you carry a portable radio when you travel, you'll find plenty of stations to choose from. There is more variety on the radio than the TV, and you can listen to programmes in Quechua as well as Spanish.

FILM & PHOTOGRAPHY

Definitely bring everything you'll need. Camera gear is very expensive in Ecuador and film choice is limited. Some good films are unavailable, eg Kodachrome slide film. Others are kept in hot storage cabinets and are sometimes sold outdated, so if you do buy any film in Ecuador, check its expiry date.

Don't have film developed in Ecuador if you can help it. Processing is shoddy. On the other hand, carrying around exposed film for months is asking for washed-out results. It is best to send it home as soon after it's exposed as possible. The Ecuadorean mail service isn't very reliable so what I normally do is send it home with a friend. You'll often meet people heading back to whichever continent you're from and they can usually be persuaded to do you this favour, particularly if you offer to take them out to dinner. I always buy either process-paid film or prepaid film mailers so I can place the exposed film in the mailer and not worry about the costs. The last thing you want to do on your return from a trip is worry about how you're going to find the money to develop a few dozen rolls of film.

Equatorial shadows are very strong and come out almost black on photographs. Often a bright but hazy day gives better photographs than a very sunny one. Photography in open shade or using fill-in flash will help. The best time for shooting is when the sun is low – the first and last two hours of the day. If you are heading into the Oriente you will need high-speed film, flash, a tripod, or a combination of these if you want to take photographs within the jungle. The amount of light penetrating the layers of vegetation is surprisingly very low.

The Ecuadorean people are both picturesque and varied. From an Indian child to the handsomely uniformed presidential guard – the possibilities of 'people pictures' are endless. However, most people resent having a camera thrust in their faces and people in markets will often proudly turn their backs on pushy photographers. Ask for permission with a smile or a joke and if this is refused don't become offended. Some people believe that bad luck can be brought upon them by the eye of the camera. Others, more sophisticated, are just fed up with seeing their pictures used in books, magazines and postcards. Somebody is making money at their expense. Sometimes a 'tip' is asked. Be aware and sensitive of people's feelings – it is not worth upsetting someone to get your photograph.

POST

The Ecuadorean postal service is depressingly bad. The majority (though by no means all) of the letters which I've sent from Ecuador have arrived at their destinations, sometimes in as little as a week to the US or Europe. Incoming mail is another matter. Some letters have taken as long as two months to arrive. I would estimate that 10 to 20% of my mail never arrived. It has reached the point where I ask that important letters are photocopied and sent twice to lessen the risk of my never receiving them. I buy aerograms at the post office and use those. Because they contain no enclosure, they're more likely to arrive safely. For a few cents extra, you can send them *certificado*, and although I haven't experienced a loss mailing them this way, there doesn't seem to be much you can do if it doesn't arrive. You'll get some peace of mind, if nothing else.

The post office in each town is marked on the town maps. In some smaller towns it is often just part of a house or a corner of a municipal office. In Quito and Guayaquil there are several post offices dotted around town, but you are advised to go to the central office for greatest efficiency. The hours are usually 9 am to 5 pm Monday through Friday. In the bigger cities they're open a half day on Saturday. For reasons I don't understand, letters to the same destinations but mailed from different towns are often charged different postage. It appears that some post offices aren't sure what the correct postage is! As a general rule, however, postage costs about two-thirds of what you'd expect to pay in Europe or North America.

There are several places where you can receive mail but most travellers use either the post office or American Express. Sometimes embassies will hold mail for you, but some embassies refuse to do so and will return it to the sender. Ask before using your embassy. You can also have mail sent c/o your hotel, but it's liable to get lost. If you have mail sent to the post office, you should know that the mail is filed alphabetically; so if it's addressed to John Gillis Payson, Esq it could well be filed under 'G' or 'E' instead of the correct 'P.' it should be addressed to John *PAYSON*, Lista de Correos, Correos Central, Quito (or town and province of your choice), Ecuador. Ask your loved ones to clearly print your last name and avoid witticisms such as 'World Traveller Extraordinaire' appended to your name. American Express will also hold mail for their clients at J *PAYSON*, c/o American Express, Aptdo 2605, Quito, Ecuador. Their street address is Avenida Amazonas 339 and they are open from 9.30 am to 12.30 pm and 2.30 to 6 pm Monday through Friday and 9 am to noon on Saturdays. (My sincere thanks to my father-in-law for letting me use his name.)

TELECOMMUNICATIONS

IETEL is the place to go for long-distance national and international telephone, telex and telegram services. The IETEL offices are required by law to be open from 6 am to 10 pm on a daily basis, except in the case of offices in small and remote towns where they can keep shorter hours if they have a dispensation from the government. I checked on the IETEL office in every town I visited and found that in places of any size, they were indeed open during the specified hours. You will find the IETEL office locations marked on all the street plans in this book. The bigger towns have telex and telegram services; the smaller towns have only the phone.

Even the most remote villages can often communicate with Quito and connect you into an international call. These cost about US$6 for three minutes to the US, and about US$8 to Europe. Waiting time can sometimes be as short as 10 minutes, though it can also take an hour or more to get through. Rates are cheaper on Sundays. The best hotels can connect international calls to your room at almost any time. Collect or reverse-charge phone calls are possible to a few countries which have reciprocal agreements with Ecuador – these seem to vary from year to year so you should ask at the nearest IETEL office.

ELECTRICITY

Ecuador uses 110 volts, 60 cycles, AC.

TIME

The Ecuadorean mainland is five hours behind Greenwich Mean Time and the Galápagos are six hours behind. Because of Ecuador's location on the equator, days and nights are of equal length year round and there is no 'daylight savings time.'

It is appropriate to mention here that punctuality is not one of the things that Latin America is famous for.

MEASUREMENTS & CONVERSIONS

Ecuador uses the metric system, and I have done so throughout this book. For those travellers who still use miles, ounces, bushels, leagues, rods, magnums, stones and other quaint and arcane expressions, the following table may be of use:

To Convert:

Multiply By:

Inches to centimetres	2.54
Centimetres to inches	0.3937
Feet to metres	0.3048
Metres to feet	3.281
Yards to metres	0.9144
Metres to yards	1.094
Miles to kilometres	1.609
Kilometres to miles	0.6214
Acres to hectares	0.4047
Hectares to acres	2.471
Imperial gallons to litres	4.546
Litres to imperial gallons	0.22
US gallons to litres	3.785
Litres to US gallons	0.264
Ounces to grams	28.35
Grams to ounces	0.03527
Pounds to grams	453.6
Grams to pounds	0.002205
Pounds to kilograms	0.4536
Kilograms to pounds	2.205
British tons to kilograms	1016.0
Kilograms to British tons	0.0009842
US tons to kilograms	907.0
Kilograms to US tons	0.000907

Five imperial gallons are equal to six US gallons.
One British ton is equal to 2240 pounds.
One US ton is equal to 2000 pounds.

To convert °Centigrade to °Fahrenheit, multiply by 1.8 and then add 32.

To convert °Fahrenheit to °Centigrade, subtract 32 and then multiply by 0.55555r (five ninths).

INFORMATION

The government tourist information agency is called DITURIS and they have offices in the major cities; the location of each of these is listed under the appropriate towns. DITURIS seem mostly geared to affluent tourists wishing to see the standard tourist sights and I rarely found them of much help when it came to information about budget hotels, buses to remote villages, or inexpensive nightclubs where the locals go. English was spoken sometimes, but not always. Usually they were friendly and tried to help as much as their limited resources allowed, but at other times I found them bored and disinterested.

It's still worth trying them if you have a problem, because at times they really do go out of their way to be of assistance. I remember complaining to a man at the Esmeraldas tourist office that I couldn't find a bank that would change money for me. He took me to a bank and personally introduced me to a sub-manager he knew, told him I was a personal friend of his, and made sure that I got some dollars changed. I've never been elevated from the status of complete stranger to personal friend so quickly!

A useful source of information is the telephone directory. You can borrow one from your hotel or the IETEL office. They have a section, usually of green pages, full of useful information and telephone numbers of travel and transport companies, tourist offices, police, airports and other services.

ACCOMMODATION

There is much variety and no shortage of places to stay in Ecuador. It is almost unheard of to arrive in a town and not be able to find somewhere to sleep, but during major fiestas or the night before market day, accommodation can be rather tight. For this reason, I have marked as many hotels as possible on the town maps in this book. Most of the time, many of these hotels will be superfluous, but once in a while you'll be glad to know of as many hotels as possible. The fact that a hotel is marked on a city map does not necessarily imply that I recommend it – read the 'Places to Stay' sections for descriptions of the hotels. If you are going to a town

specifically for a market or fiesta, try and arrive a day early if possible, or at least arrive by early afternoon of the day before the market.

Sometimes it's a little difficult to find single rooms, and you may get a room with two or even three beds. In most cases, though, you are only charged for one bed and don't have to share, unless the hotel is full. You should ensure in advance that you won't be asked to pay for all the beds or share with a stranger if you don't want to. This is no problem 90% of the time. If you are travelling as a couple, or in a group, you can't automatically assume that a room with two or three beds will be cheaper per person than a room with one bed. Sometimes it is and sometimes it isn't. If I give a price per person, per night, or each, then usually a double or triple room will cost two or three times a single. If more than one price is given, this indicates that double and triples are cheaper per person than singles. Couples sharing one bed (*cama matrimonial*) are usually, though not always, charged the same as a double room with people in separate beds. To avoid making my figures instantly obsolete because of inflation, I have used US dollars for costs.

Look around the hotel if possible. The same prices are often charged for rooms of widely differing qualities. Even in the dollar-a-night cheapies, it's worth looking around. If you get shown into a horrible airless box with just a bed and a bare light bulb, you can ask to see a better room without giving offence simply by asking if they have a room with a window, or explaining that you have to write some letters home and is there a room with a table and chair. You'll often be amazed at the results. *Never* rent a room without looking at it first. In most hotels, even the cheapest, they'll be happy to let you see the room. If they aren't, then it usually means that the room is filthy anyway. Also ask to see the bathroom and make sure that the toilet flushes and the water runs if you want a wash. If the shower looks and smells as if someone threw up in it, the staff obviously don't do a very good job of looking after the place. There's probably a better hotel at the same price a few blocks away.

Bathroom facilities are rarely what you may be used to at home. The cheapest hotels don't always have hot water. Even if they do, it might not work or be turned on only at certain hours of the day. Ask about this if you're planning on a hot shower before going out to dinner – often there's only hot water in the morning. Another intriguing device you should know about is the electric shower. This consists of a single cold-water shower head hooked up to an electric heating element which is switched on when you want a hot (more likely tepid) shower. Don't touch anything metal while you're in the shower or you may discover what an electric shock feels like. The power is never high enough to actually throw you across the room, but it's unpleasant nevertheless. I managed to shock myself by simply picking up the soap which I had balanced on a horizontal water pipe (there wasn't a soap dish). Some hotels charge extra for hot showers and some simply don't have any showers at all. You can always use the public hot baths – there's one in every town.

As you have probably gathered by now, Ecuadorean plumbing leaves something to be desired. Flushing a toilet creates another hazard – overflow. Putting toilet paper into the bowl seems to clog up the system, so a waste receptacle is often provided for the paper. This may not seem particularly sanitary, but it is much better than clogged bowls and water on the floor. A well-run hotel, even if it is cheap, will ensure that the receptacle is emptied and the toilet cleaned every day.

Most hotels will give you a key to lock your room, and theft from your hotel room is not as frequent as it is in some other countries. Nevertheless, carrying your own padlock is a good idea if you plan on staying in the cheaper hotels. Once in a

while you'll find that a room doesn't look very secure – perhaps there's a window that doesn't close or the wall doesn't come to the ceiling and can be climbed over. It's worth finding another room. This is another reason why it's good to look at a room before you rent it. You should never leave valuables lying around the room. It's just too tempting for a maid who makes US$2 a day for her work. Money and passport should be in a secure body pouch; other valuables can usually be kept in the hotel strongbox. (Some cheaper hotels might not want to take this responsibility.) Don't get paranoid though. I haven't had anything stolen from my room in years of travelling in Ecuador, and rarely hear of people who have.

In smaller towns, I usually lump the accommodation together in one section. In larger towns, however, I separate them into groups. 'Bottom-end' hotels are the cheapest, but not necessarily the worst. Although they are usually quite basic, with just a bed and four walls, they can nevertheless be well looked after, very clean, and amazing value for money. They are often good places to meet other travellers, both Ecuadorean and foreign. Prices in this section range from just under US$1 to about US$3 per person. Every town has hotels in this price range and in smaller towns there aren't any hotels more expensive. Although you'll usually have to use communal bathrooms in the cheapest hotels, you can sometimes find rooms with a private bathroom for as little as US$2 each.

Hotels in the 'middle' category usually cost from about US$3-8 per person, but are not always better than the best hotels in the bottom end price range. On the whole, however, you can find some very good bargains here. My wife and I stayed in some really pleasant places in this range. For example, a huge carpeted room with a beautiful countryside view, large and comfortable bed, plenty of furniture, and a clean private bathroom (with twin sinks!) cost a princely US$9 for the two of

Top: Giant tropical snail, western lowlands (RR)
Left: Scarlet Macaw (RR)
Right: Land Iguana, Plaza Island, Galapagos (TW)

Top: 'Cuy' or roast guinea-pig, a traditional Inca delicacy (RR)
Bottom: The Extraterrestrial Chicken Restaurant, Quito (RR)

us. Even if you're travelling on a budget, there are always special occasions (your birthday?) when you can indulge in comparative luxury for a day or two.

'Top-end' hotels are still very cheap by western standards. There is some overlap in prices with the top of the middle-range hotels because often the best place in town costs less than US$8 each. Again, there are some good bargains to be found here if you demand some comfort. Luxury hotels are to be found only in the major cities.

Youth hostels as we know them in other parts of the world aren't found in Ecuador. The cheaper hotels make up for this lack anyway. There are climbers' refuges on some of the major mountains and you can camp in the countryside. If you're carrying a tent or want to hike up to a mountaineering refuge, I suggest you get a copy of my *Climbing & Hiking in Ecuador*. There are rarely campsites in the towns; again, the constant availability of cheap hotels makes town campsites redundant.

If you're really travelling far off the beaten track, you may end up in a village that doesn't have even a basic pensión. You can usually find somewhere to sleep by asking around, but it might be just a roof over your head rather than a bed, so carry a sleeping bag or at least a blanket. The place to ask at first would probably be a village store – the store owner usually knows everyone in the village and would know who is in the habit of renting rooms or floor space. If that fails, you can ask for the mayor (*alcalde*) or at the *policía*. You may end up sleeping on the floor of the schoolhouse, the jail or the village community centre, but you'll probably find somewhere if you persevere. People in remote areas are generally hospitable.

LAUNDRY

There are no self-service laundry machines in Ecuador. This means that you have to find someone to wash your clothes for you or wash them yourself. Many hotels will have someone to do your laundry; this can cost very little in the cheaper hotels (under a dollar for a full change of clothes). The major problem is that you might not see your clothes again for two or three days, particularly if it is raining and they can't be dried. There are laundromats (*lavanderías*) in Quito and Guayaquil but you still have to leave the clothes for at least 24 hours. Most of these lavanderías only do dry cleaning anyway. If you wash the clothes yourself, ask the hotel staff where to do this. Most hotels will show you a huge cement sink and scrubbing board which is much easier to use than a bathroom washbasin. Often there is a well-like section next to the scrubbing board and it is full of clean water. Don't dunk your clothes in this water to soak or rinse them as it is often used as an emergency water supply in the case of water failure. Use a bowl or bucket to scoop water out instead, or run water from a tap.

FOOD

If you're on a tight budget, food is the most important part of your trip expenses. You can stay in rock-bottom hotels, travel 2nd class, and never consider buying a souvenir, but you've got to eat well. This doesn't mean expensively, but it does mean that you want to avoid spending half your trip sitting on the toilet.

The worst culprits for getting you sick are salads and unpeeled fruit. With the fruit, stick to bananas, oranges, pineapples and other fruit that you can peel. With unpeeled fruit or salads, wash them yourself in water which you can trust (see Health section). It actually can be a lot of fun getting a group of you together and heading out to the market to buy salad veggies and preparing a huge salad. You can often persuade someone in the hotel to lend you a suitable bowl, or you could buy a large plastic bowl quite inexpensively and sell or give it away afterwards.

As long as you take heed of the salad warning, you'll find plenty of good things to eat at reasonable prices. You certainly don't have to eat at a fancy restaurant; their kitchen facilities may not be as clean as their white tablecloths. A good sign for any restaurant is if the locals eat there – restaurants aren't empty if the food is delicious and healthy.

If you're on a tight budget you can eat from street and market stalls if the food looks freshly cooked, though watch to see if your plate is going to be 'washed' in a bowl of cold, greasy water and wiped with a filthy rag – it's worth carrying your own bowl and spoon. Alternately, try food that can be wrapped in paper, such as pancakes.

Good local dishes to try at markets and street stands (and restaurants too, of course) are the following:

Caldo Soups and stews are very popular and are often served in markets for breakfasts. Soups are known as *caldos, sopas,* or *locro.* Chicken soup, or *caldo de gallina,* is the most popular. *Caldo de patas* is soup made by boiling cattle hooves and, to my taste, is as bad as it sounds.

Cuy Whole roasted guinea pig. This is a traditional food dating back to Inca times. The sight of the little paws and teeth sticking out and eyes tightly closed is a little unnerving, but cuy is supposed to be a delicacy and some people love it.

Lechón Suckling pig. Pigs are often roasted whole and are a common sight at Ecuadorean food markets. Pork is also called *chancho.*

Llapingachos Mashed-potato-and-cheese pancakes that are fried, these are my favourite. They are often served with *fritada* – scraps of fried or roast pork.

Seco Stew. The word literally means 'dry' (as opposed to a 'wet' soup). The stew is usually meat served with rice and can be *seco de gallina* (chicken stew), *de res* (beef), *de chivo* (goat), or *de cordero* (lamb).

Tostadas de maíz Tasty fried corn pancakes.

Yaguarlocro Potato soup with chunks of barely congealed blood sausage floating in it. I happen to like blood sausage and find this soup very tasty; many people prefer just straight *locro* which usually has potatoes, corn, and an avocado or cheese topping.

This is just a selection of the more typical local foods frequently found at markets. In a restaurant, there'll be other dishes to choose from. For breakfast, the usual eggs and bread rolls or toast are available. *Huevos fritos* are fried eggs, *revueltos* are scrambled, and *pasados* or *a la copa* are boiled or poached. These last two are usually semi-raw, so ask for *bien cocidos* (well cooked) or *duros* (hard) if you don't like your eggs too runny. *Tostadas* are toast and *panes* are bread rolls which you can have with butter and jam *mantequilla y mermelada.* A good local change from eggs are sweet corn tamales called *humitas,* often served for breakfast with coffee.

Lunch is the biggest meal of the day for many Ecuadoreans. If you walk into a cheap restaurant and ask for the lunch of the day (*almuerzo*), you'll get a decent meal for well under a dollar – highly recommended for the economy minded. An *almuerzo* always consists of a *sopa* and a *segundo* or 'second dish,' which is usually a *seco* (stew) with plenty of rice. Sometimes the *segundo* is fish (*pescado*), or a kind of lentil or pea stew (*lenteja, arveja*), but there's always rice. Many, but not all, restaurants will give you a salad (often cooked), juice and dessert (*postre*) as well as the two main courses.

The supper of the day is usually similar to lunch. Ask for the *merienda.* If you don't want the *almuerzo* or *merienda,* you can choose from the menu, but this is always more expensive. However, the set meals do tend to get a little repetitious after a while and most people try out other dishes – which can still cost little over a dollar. A *churrasco* is a hearty plate with a slice of fried beef, one or two fried eggs, vegetables (usually boiled beet slices, carrots and beans), fried potatoes, a slice of avocado and tomato, and the inevitable rice. If you get *arroz con pollo* then you'll be served a mountain of rice with little bits of chicken mixed in. If you're fed up with rice, go to a *Pollo a la Brasa* restaurant where you can get fried chicken, often with fried potatoes on the side. *Gallina* is usually boiled chicken as in soups, and *pollo* is more often spit-roasted or fried. *Pollo* tends to be underdone but you can always send it back to get it cooked longer.

Parrilladas are steak houses or grills. These are recommended places to eat if you like meat and a complete loss if you don't. Steaks, pork chops, chicken breasts, blood sausages, liver and tripe are all served on a grill which is placed on the table. Every time I order a parrillada for two people, I find there's enough for three but they'll give you a plastic bag for the leftovers. If you don't want the whole thing you can choose just a chop or a steak. Although parrilladas aren't particularly cheap, they are reasonably priced and very good value.

Seafood is very good, even in the highlands, as it is brought in fresh from the coast and iced. The most common types of fish are a white sea bass called *corvina* and trout (*trucha*). *Ceviche* is popular throughout Ecuador. This is seafood marinated in lemon and served with popcorn and sliced onions. It's delicious. Ceviche can be *de pescado* (fish), *de camarones* (shrimp) or *de concha* (shellfish such as clams or mussels). You can go the whole hog (if you pardon the expression) and get a *ceviche mixto*. A lobster dinner (*langosta*) costs about US$5 – a bargain by western standards.

Most Ecuadorean meals come with rice (*arroz*), and some travellers get fed up with it. Surprisingly, one of the best places to go for a change from rice is a Chinese restaurants. These are known as *chifas* and are generally inexpensive and good value. Apart from rice, they serve *tallarines*, which are noodles mixed with your choice of pork, chicken, beef or vegetables (*legumbres, verduras*). Portions tend to be filling. Vegetarians will find that *chifas*

offer the best choice for non-meat dishes, or you can go to a *cevichería* if you don't consider seafood to be meat. Vegetarian restaurants are rare in Ecuador. If you have any kind of strict diet, you would be advised to bring a camping stove with you and cook your own. Most hotels don't mind this, especially the cheapest ones. Just don't burn the place down.

If you want inexpensive luxury, go for breakfast at the fanciest hotel in town (assuming they have a restaurant or cafeteria). You can relax with coffee and rolls and the morning paper, or get a window seat and watch the world go by. Despite the elegant surroundings and the bow-tied waiter, you are only charged an extra 10c for your coffee. Makes a nice change and the coffee is often very good.

Cities big enough to have first-class hotels also have good but expensive (by Ecuadorean standards) international restaurants. These are often right in the hotels themselves.

DRINK

I don't recommend drinking tap water anywhere in Latin America. *Agua potable* means that the water comes from the tap but it's not necessarily healthy. Even if it comes from a chlorination or filtration plant, the plumbing is often old, cracked and full of crud. Salads washed in this water aren't necessarily clean. One possibility is to carry a water bottle and purify your own water. (For more about this see the Health section.) If you don't want to go through the hassle of constantly purifying water, you can buy bottled mineral water very cheaply. Don't ask for mineral water, ask for *Güitig* (pronounced Weetig) which is the best known brand. Another brand is *Manantial* but everyone still asks for *Güitig*. A large two-thirds of a litre bottle costs about 25c in most restaurants and less in a store.

The advantage of buying a bottled drink in a store is that it is very cheap; the disadvantage is that you have to drink it at the store because the bottle is usually worth more than the drink inside. (Canned drinks cost up to three times more than bottles.) You can pay a deposit, but you have to return the bottle to the store you bought it from; a different store won't give you any money for it. What many travellers do is pay a deposit on (effectively buy) a bottle of pop, beer or mineral water and then trade it in every time they want to buy a drink in a different place.

All the usual soft drinks are available, as are some local ones with such endearing names as Bimbo or Lulu. Soft drinks are collectively known as *colas* and the local brands are very sweet. Seven-up is simply called *seven*, so don't try calling it 'siete arriba' or no one will have any idea what you're talking about. You can also buy Coca Cola, Pepsi Cola, Orange Fanta or Crush (called *croosh*) and Sprite – the latter pronounced *essprite*! Ask for your drink *helada* if you want it out of the refrigerator, *al clima* if you don't. Remember to say *sin hielo* (without ice) unless you really trust the water supply. Diet soft drinks aren't available – the concept of Third World countries paying for a drink with no calories is a little absurd.

Juices (*jugos*) are available everywhere and are usually better than colas to my taste, but they cost more. Make sure you get *jugo puro* and not *con agua*. The most common kinds are *mora* (blackberry), *naranja* (orange), *toronja* (grapefruit), *piña* (pineapple), *maracuya* (passion fruit), *sandía* (watermelon), *naranjilla* (a local fruit tasting like bitter orange), or *papaya*.

Coffee is available almost everywhere but is often disappointing. A favourite Ecuadorean way of making coffee is to boil it for hours until only a thick syrup remains. This is then poured into cruets and diluted down with milk or water. It doesn't taste that great and it looks very much like soy sauce, so always check before pouring it into your milk (or over your rice)! Instant coffee is also served. Espresso is available only in the better

restaurants. *Café con leche* is milk with coffee, and *café con agua* or *café negro* is black coffee. Tea (*té*) is served black with lemon and sugar. If you ask for tea with milk, British style, you'll get a cup of hot milk with a tea bag to dunk in it. Hot chocolate is also popular.

Finally we come to those beverages which can loosely be labelled 'libations.' The selection of beers is limited, but they are quite palatable and inexpensive. Pilsener usually comes in large, –2/3-litre bottles and is my drink of choice. Club is slightly more expensive, has a slightly higher alcohol content (3.9% as opposed to 3.5% if you're interested), and comes in small –1/3-litre bottles. Malta is a sweet, dark beer and is sometimes mixed in a blender with eggs and sugar to make a breakfast drink at the markets. I have never been able to bring myself to try it. Lowenbrau is made in Ecuador and tastes like Club with a different label. All other beers are imported and available only in the most expensive of restaurants or at speciality liquor stores.

Local wines are truly terrible and should not be experimented with. Imported wines from Chile, Argentina or Peru are good but cost much more than they do in their country of origin – I suggest you wait till you visit them. Californian and European wines are available but are more expensive still, and Australian wines haven't made it to Ecuador.

Spirits are expensive if imported and not very good if made locally, with some notable exceptions. Rum is cheap and good. The local firewater, *aguardiente* or sugar cane alcohol, is an acquired taste but is also good. It's very cheap; you can get a half bottle of Cristal aguardiente for about 75c. If you're desperate for gin, vodka or whisky, try Larios brand – probably the best of a bad bunch.

THINGS TO BUY

Souvenirs are good, varied and cheap. Although going to villages and markets is fun, you won't necessarily save a great deal of money. Similar items for sale in the main cities are often not much more expensive, so if you're limited on time you can shop in Quito or Guayaquil. If you only have the time or inclination to go on one big shopping expedition, I definitely recommend the Saturday market at Otavalo as being both full of variety and convenient. In markets and smaller stores, bargaining is acceptable, indeed expected, though don't expect to reduce the price by more than about 20%. In 'tourist stores' in Quito, prices are usually fixed. Some of the best stores are quite expensive; on the other hand, the quality of their products is often superior.

Clothing

Woollen goods are popular and are often made of a pleasantly coarse homespun wool. Otavalo is good for these and you can find sweaters, scarves, hats, gloves and vests. A thick sweater will cost US$5-10 depending on size and quality, so if you're planning trips high into the mountains you can get some good warm clothes in Ecuador. Wool is also spun into a much finer and tighter textile which is used for making ponchos. Otavaleño Indian ponchos are amongst the best anywhere.

Clothing made from orlon is also to be found. It's cheaper than wool but looks garish and unattractive. It's easy to tell the difference just by looking at it, but if you're not sure, you can try the match trick. Take a tiny piece of lint from the material and set light to it. If it melts, it's orlon; if it burns, it's wool. Many people think that only woolen items are traditional, earthy, cool, ethnic, etc. While that may be true, if you see an orlon sweater that you like, there's nothing to stop you buying it and it'll be one of the cheapest sweaters you've ever bought.

Hand-embroidered clothes are also attractive but it's worth getting them from a reputable shop; otherwise they may shrink or run. Cotton blouses, shirts, skirts, dresses and shawls are available.

Ecuadorean T-shirts are among the best I've seen anywhere. If you're a T-shirt collector you'll find all sizes and colours to choose from. The most popular designs are of Galápagos animals, but many others are available. The best designs are by Peter Mussfeldt and the shirts cost about US$3 each.

Panama hats are worth buying. A good panama is so finely made that it can be rolled up and passed through a man's ring, though it's unlikely that you'll find many of that quality. They are made from a palmlike bush which grows abundantly in the coastal province of Manabi. Montecristi and Jipijapa are major centres. Their name dates back to the 1849 Californian gold rush, when prospectors travelling through the Panama Canal bought the hats, but they are originally Ecuadorean.

Weavings

A large variety of mainly woolen weavings are to be found all over the country, with Otavalo as usual having a good selection. They range from foot-square weavings which can be sewn together to make throw cushions or shoulder bags, to weavings large enough to be used as floor rugs. Designs range from traditional to modern; M C Escher styles are popular.

Bags

Apart from bags made from two small tapestries woven together, you can buy *shigras*, shoulder bags made from agave fibre that are strong, colourful and eminently practical. They come in a variety of sizes and are expandable. Agave fibre is also used to make net bags (macramé).

Leather

A famous centre for leatherwork is Cotacachi, north of Otavalo. Prices are cheap in comparison to those in more developed countries, but quality is very variable, so examine possible purchases carefully. Although the best leatherwork in Ecuador is supposedly done in the

Ambato area, it's difficult to find any for sale. Leatherwork items range from full suits to coin purses, and wide-brimmed hats to luggage bags.

Woodwork

The major woodworking centre of Ecuador is San Antonio de Ibarra, and any items bought elsewhere are likely to have been carved there. Items range from the utilitarian (bowls, salad utensils, chess sets, candlesticks) to the decorative (crucifixes, statues, wall plaques). Again, prices are very low, but quality varies.

Balsa wood models are also popular. They are made in the jungles of the Oriente and sold in many of Quito's gift stores. Brightly painted birds are the most frequently seen items, but other animals and boxes are also sold.

Tagua nut carvings are typical of Ecuador. The tagua nut is actually the seed of a coastal palm. The egg-sized seed is carved into a variety of novelty items such as napkin rings, egg cups and chess pieces. Riobamba is a well-known tagua nut centre.

Jewellery

Ecuador isn't famous for its gemstones but it does have good silver and gold work. Chordeleg near Cuenca is a major jewellery centre. Beautifully filigreed work can be obtained here.

Other

Baskets made of straw, reeds, or agave fibres are common everywhere. Painted and varnished ornaments made of bread dough are unique to Ecuador and are best obtained in Calderón, a village just north of Quito. Onyx (a pale, translucent quartz with parallel layers of different colours) is carved into chess sets and other objects.

WHAT TO BRING

As an inveterate traveller and guidebook writer, I've naturally read many guidebooks. I always find the What to Bring section depressing, as I'm always told to bring as little as possible; I look around at my huge backpack, my two beat-up duffel bags bursting at the seams, and I wonder sadly where I went wrong. I enjoy camping and climbing, so I carry tent, ice axe, heavy boots etc. I'm an avid birdwatcher, and I'd feel naked without my binoculars and field guides. And of course I want to photograph these mountains and birds, which adds a camera, and lenses, and a tripod, and other paraphernalia. In addition, I enjoy relaxing just as much as leaping around mountains taking photographs of birds, so I always have at least two books to read as well as all my indispensable guides and maps. Luckily, I'm not a music addict, so I'm able to live without a guitar, a portable tape player or a shortwave radio.

It appears that I'm not the only one afflicted with the kitchen-sink disease. In Latin America alone, I've met an Australian surfer who travelled the length of the Pacific coast with his board, looking for the world's longest left-handed wave; a couple of Canadian skiers complete with those skinny boards; a black man from Chicago who travelled with a pair of three-foot-high bongo drums; an Italian with a saxophone (a memorable night when those two got together); a Danish journalist with a portable typewriter; a French freak with a ghetto blaster and (by my count) 32 tapes; and an American woman with several hundred weavings which she was planning on selling. All of these were budget travellers staying for at least 1½ months and using public transport.

After confessing to the amount of stuff I travel with, I can't very well give the time-honoured advice of 'travel as lightly as possible.' I suggest you bring anything that is important to you; if you're interested in photography, you'll only curse every time you see a good shot (if only you'd brought your telephoto lens), and if you're a musician you won't enjoy the trip if you constantly worry about how out of practice your fingers are getting.

A good idea once you're in Quito is to

divide your gear into two piles. One is what you need for the next section of your trip. The rest you can stash in the storage room at your hotel (most hotels have one). Ecuador is a small country so you can use Quito as a base and divide your travelling into, say, coastal, highland and jungle portions, easily returning to Quito between sections and picking up necessary gear.

There's no denying, however, that travelling light is much less of a hassle, so don't bring things you can do without. Travelling on buses and trains is bound to make you slightly grubby, so bring one change of dark clothes that don't show the dirt, rather than seven changes of nice clothes for a six-week trip. Many people go overboard with changes of clothes, but one change to wash and the other to wear is the best idea. Bring clothes that wash and dry easily. (Jeans take forever to dry.) The highlands are often cold, so bring a wind-proof jacket and a warm layer to wear beneath, or plan on buying a thick sweater in Otavalo. A hat is indispensable; it'll keep you warm when it's cold, shade your eyes when it's sunny, and keep your head dry when it rains. A great deal! A collapsible umbrella is great protection against sun and rain as well.

You can buy clothes of almost any size if you need them, but shoes are limited to size 43 Ecuadorean, which is about 10½ North American. Suffice it to say that I have US size 12 feet (don't laugh, they're not that big!) and I can't buy any footgear at all in Ecuador. This is also true of most Latin countries, so bring a spare pair of shoes if you're planning a long trip.

The following is a checklist of small items you will find useful and probably need:

Pocket torch (flashlight) with spare bulb and batteries
Travel alarm clock
Swiss Army-style penknife
Sewing and repairs kit (dental floss makes excellent, strong and colourless emergency thread)

A few metres of cord (also useful for clothesline and spare shoelaces)
Sunglasses
Plastic bags
Soap and dish, shampoo, tooth brush and paste, shaving gear, towel
Toilet paper (rarely found in cheaper hotels and restaurants)
Ear plugs for sleeping in noisy hotels or buses
Insect repellent
Suntan lotion (strong blocking lotions are not available in Ecuador)
Address book
Notebook
Pens and pencils
Paperback book (easily exchanged with other travellers when you've finished)
Spanish-English dictionary
Small padlock
Large folding nylon bag to leave things in storage
Water bottle
First-aid kit (see Health section)

Tampons are available in Ecuador, but only in the major cities and in regular sizes, so make sure you stock up with an adequate supply before visiting smaller towns, the jungle or the Galápagos. If you use contraceptives, then you'll also find them available in the major cities. Choice of oral contraceptives is limited, however, so if you use a preferred brand, you should bring it from home; they don't weigh much anyway.

A sleeping bag is useful if you plan on travelling on a budget (or camping), because some of the cheaper hotels don't supply enough blankets and it can get cold at night. Most hotels will give you another blanket if you ask, however, so a sleeping bag is useful but not indispensable if you're planning on staying mainly in the major tourist areas.

You need something to carry everything around in. A backpack is recommended because carrying your baggage on your back is less exhausting than carrying it in your hands, which are left free. On the other hand, it's often more difficult to get at things inside a pack, so some travellers prefer a duffel bag with a full-length zipper. Whichever you choose, ensure that it is a good, strongly made piece of luggage, or you'll find that you spend much of your trip replacing zippers, straps and buckles. Hard travelling is notoriously hard wearing on luggage, and if you bring a backpack, I suggest one with an internal frame. External frames snag on bus doors, luggage racks and airline baggage belts, and are liable to be twisted, cracked or broken.

SAFETY & SECURITY

Although rip-offs are a fact of life in Latin America, you'll find Ecuador is safe compared with the worst offenders, Peru and Colombia. You should, nevertheless, take some simple precautions to avoid being robbed.

Armed robbery is still very rare in Ecuador, although parts of Guayaquil and some coastal areas do have a reputation for being dangerous. Sneak theft is more common, and you should remember that crowded places are the haunts of pickpockets. This means ill-lit bus stations or bustling markets.

Thieves look for easy targets. Tourists who carry a wallet or passport in a hip pocket are asking for trouble. Leave your wallet at home; it's an easy mark for a pickpocket. Carrying a roll of bills loosely wadded under a handkerchief in your front pocket is as safe a way as any of carrying your daily spending money. The rest should be hidden. Always use at least an inside pocket or preferably a body pouch, money belt or leg pouch to protect your money and passport.

Don't accept food from strangers. I know of one person who ate some cookies given him by some smooth-talking 'friends' on a bus – he woke up two days later in an alley with just his shirt and trousers. I've heard of several reports of this; Ecuadorean authorities claim that it's Colombians who do it. Unopened packages of cookies and other foods are injected with horse tranquilizers using hypodermic syringes. I know it sounds weird, but it's true.

Every year or so, you hear of a couple of night bus robberies in the Guayaquil area. Night buses are simply held up at a road block and robbed by armed men. These are always long-distance buses, so you should avoid taking night buses that go through Guayas province unless you have to. It happens to less than one bus in several thousand so don't get paranoid if your schedule demands a night bus through the area.

You should carry the greater proportion of your money in the form of travellers' cheques. These can be refunded if lost or stolen. Some airlines will also reissue your ticket if it is lost. You have to give them details such as where and when you got it, the ticket number and which flight was involved. Usually a reissuing fee – about US$20 – is charged, but that's much better than buying a new ticket.

It is a good idea to carry an emergency packet somewhere separate from all your other valuables. This emergency packet could be sewn into a jacket (don't lose the jacket!) or even carried in your shoe. It should contain a photocopy of the important pages of your passport in case it is lost or stolen. On the back of the photocopy you should list important numbers such as all your travellers' cheques serial numbers, airline ticket numbers, credit card or bank account numbers, telephone numbers. Also keep one high-denomination bill in with this emergency stash. You will probably never have to use it, but it's a good idea not to put all your eggs into one basket.

Take out travellers' insurance if you're carrying really valuable gear such as a good camera. But don't get paranoid; Ecuador really is a safe country and in almost two years of travelling there I didn't get robbed at all.

Getting There

There are three ways of getting to Ecuador: air, land and sea. However, very few people even consider the ocean route these days, as it is more expensive and less convenient than flying.

AIR

If you fly to Ecuador, bear in mind that the main hub for flights to and from western South America is Lima, Peru. You can often fly more cheaply to Lima and finish your journey to Ecuador by land. Bus travel from Lima to the Ecuadorean border takes about 30 hours and costs about US$20. If you prefer to travel direct to Ecuador, frequent international flights arrive and depart from either Quito or Guayaquil.

The ordinary tourist or economy-class fare is not the most economical way to go. It is convenient, however, because it enables you to fly on the next plane out and your ticket is valid for 12 months. If you want to economize further, there are several options. Students and those under 26 can get discounts with most airlines. Whatever age you are, if you can purchase your ticket well in advance and stay a minimum length of time, you can buy an advance purchase excursion (APEX) ticket which is usually about 30 or 40% cheaper than the full economy fare. Normally the following restrictions apply. You must purchase your ticket at least 21 days (sometimes more) in advance and you must stay away a minimum period (about 14 days on average) and return within 180 days (sometimes less). Individual airlines have different requirements and these change from time to time. APEX tickets do not allow stopovers and there are extra charges if you change your dates of travel or destinations. Stand-by fares are another possibility. Some airlines will let you travel at the last minute if they have available seats just before the flight.

These stand-by tickets cost less than an economy fare but are not usually as cheap as APEX.

The cheapest way to go is via the so-called 'bucket shops,' which are legally allowed to sell discounted tickets to help airlines fill their flights. These tickets are usually the cheapest of all, particularly in the low seasons, but they often sell out fast and you may be limited to only a few available dates. While APEX, economy and student flights are available direct from the airlines or from a travel agent (there is no extra charge for any of these flights if you buy them from an agent rather than direct from the airline), discount bucket shop tickets are available only from the bucket shops themselves. Most of them are good and reputable companies, but once in a while a fly-by-night operator comes along and takes your money for a super-cheap flight and gives you an invalid or unusable ticket, so check what you are buying carefully before handing over your money.

Bucket shops often advertise in newspapers and magazines; there is much competition and a variety of fares and schedules are available. Fares to South America have traditionally been relatively expensive, but bucket shops have recently been able to offer increasingly economical fares to that continent.

From the USA

In the United States, the best way to get cheap flights is by reading the major newspapers (*The Los Angeles Times* on the west coast and *The New York Times* on the east coast). These will have cheaper fares advertised in their travel classified advertisements. Generally speaking, however, the United States does not have such a strong bucket shop tradition as Europe and Asia, so it's a little harder getting cheap flights from the US to South

America. Ticket availability tends to be limited and there are often many restrictions. Prices are sometimes not much lower than the APEX fares with one of the several airlines serving Ecuador.

In 1985 the best deal to South America from the US was, surprisingly, via Canada. Canadian Pacific Air have excellent non-stop flights from Vancouver and Toronto to Lima in Peru. Travel agents could offer this flight for around US$600 return including the connecting CP Air flight from San Francisco or Los Angeles to Vancouver. This is a really good deal and probably better than any straightforward fare direct to Ecuador.

From Europe

From Europe, it is relatively simple to find fares which are cheaper than the APEX prices. In London, bucket shops advertise in *The Times* and *Time Out* classifieds. *Trailfinder* magazine is available free from Trailfinders, 42-48 Earl's Court Rd, London W8 6EJ. Trailfinders are a reputable company who advertised roundtrip fares to Quito for as little as £418 in 1985. Typical one way fares to Quito from London are around £225 to 250. Trailfinders will also help with other travel details; many bucket shops provide only a ticketing service. Another agency which specializes in cheap fares and tours to Latin America is Journey Latin America at 16 Devonshire Rd, Chiswick, London W2 2HD.

There are also bucket shops in various European countries. Try the following for cheap fares: Le Point, 2 Place Wagram and Uniclam-Voyages, 63 Rue Monsieur le Prince, both in Paris. In Zurich there's Sindbad at 3 Schoffelgasse. German travellers often find that an Aeroflot flight to Lima (sometimes via Moscow or Cuba) is the cheapest way to go.

From Australia

There is no real choice of routes between Australia and South America and there are certainly no bargain fares available. The only direct route is to fly from Australia to Tahiti and connect from there with the weekly Lan Chile flight to Santiago in Chile. One way this costs A$1124, return costs vary with the season – A$1824 in the low season, A$2067 in the high season. From Chile you could then fly or travel overland through Peru to Ecuador.

The other alternative is to fly to the US west coast and from there either fly to South America or make your way overland through Mexico and Central America. One-way fare from Australia to Los Angeles or San Francisco is A$1013, the return fare again varies with season – from A$1446 in the low season, A$1786 in the shoulder, A$1966 in the high. You won't find any special deals offered on the Lan Chile flight but by shopping around you should be able to knock the fares to USA down by a reasonable amount. Check the ads in the travel pages of papers like the Melbourne *Age* or the *Sydney Morning Herald*.

From Asia

There is also very little choice of direct flights between Asia and South America apart from Japan and there certainly won't be any bargains there. The cheapest way will be to fly to the US west coast and connect from there.

Departing Ecuador

There is a US$5 departure tax on international flights from Ecuador.

LAND

If you live in the Americas, it is possible to travel overland. However, if you start from North or Central America, the Pan American highway stops in Panama and begins again in Colombia, leaving a 200-km roadless section of jungle known as the Darien Gap. This takes about a week to cross on foot and by canoe in the dry season (January to mid-April) but is much heavier going in the wet season. Most travellers going by land fly around the Darien Gap. From South America it is straightforward to travel by public transport from Peru or Colombia into Ecuador.

SEA

It may occasionally be possible to find a ship going to Guayaquil, the main port for Ecuador.

Getting Around

Ecuador has a more efficient transport system than most Andean countries. Also, it is a small country, which means you can usually get anywhere and everywhere quickly and easily. The bus is the most frequently used method of transportation; you can take buses from the Colombian border to the Peruvian border in 18 hours if you want to. Airplanes and boats (especially in the Oriente) are also frequently used, but trains less so.

Whichever form of transport you use, remember to have your passport with you and not left in the hotel safe or packed in your luggage. To board most planes and boats, you need to show your passport. Buses have to go through a transit police check upon entering any town; although passports are infrequently asked for, it's as well to have it handy for the one time in 20 that you are asked to show it. If your passport is in order, these procedures are no more than cursory. If you're travelling anywhere near the borders or in the Oriente, you can expect more frequent passport controls.

AIR

Even the budget traveller should consider the occasional internal flight. With the exception of flying to the Galápagos, internal flights are comparatively cheap, and even the most expensive flight is currently only US$16. Almost all flights originate or terminate in Quito or Guayaquil, so the most useful way for the traveller to utilize these services is by taking a long overland journey from one of these cities and then returning quickly by air.

Ecuador's most important domestic airline is TAME, which flies to almost all the destinations in the country. Their closest competitor are SAN-Saeta (formerly two airlines) who have a good schedule of flights between Quito, Guayaquil and Cuenca. Prices from both companies are the same, so if travelling between these major cities, use the one whose schedule most closely matches yours. A third airline is TAO, which flies small aircraft between Puyo and Macas in the Oriente. There are other small local airlines. The military have been known to provide flights, as have the missions and the oil companies. You hear about this less and less, however. These days, with improving air services, it's usually easier to pay a few dollars for a scheduled flight than to spend several days lining up a flight with someone else.

TAME flies from Quito to Guayaquil, Cuenca, Macas, Coca, Tarapoa, Lago Agrio, Tulcán, Esmeraldas, Manta, Port-oviejo and the Galápagos. A service to Loja via Cuenca is planned for 1985 or '86. TAME also flies from Guayaquil to Quito, Cuenca, Loja, Macará, Machala, Manta and the Galápagos. Except for the major cities, flights usually operate several times a week but not on a daily basis. For more details, see the Air sections under the appropriate cities.

Flights are frequently late, but not very much so. Flights first thing in the morning are more likely to be on time but by the afternoon things tend to have slid a half hour behind schedule. You should show up about an hour early for domestic flights, as baggage handling and check-in procedures tend to be rather chaotic. There are about eight flights a day between Quito and Guayaquil (and return). If you show up early for your flight, you can often get on the earlier flight if there is room. If you paid for your ticket with cash (not credit card) then TAME will accept your SAN-Saeta ticket and vice versa.

There are no seating assignments on domestic flights so you choose your seat aboard on a first-come, first-served basis. There are no separate sections for smokers and non-smokers. Many of the flights give extraordinarily good views of the snow-capped Andes and it is worth getting a window seat even if the weather is bad because the plane often rises above the clouds, giving spectacular views of volcanoes riding on a sea of cloud.

Once in a while you may get treated to a special mountain fly-by. This happened to me once on the flight from Macas to Quito. We flew by Cotopaxi and the pilot decided to give us a closer look so he banked sharply and did a complete circuit of the volcano. For over a minute we were able to have wonderful views of the top of the mountain with a rare look directly down into the crater. TAME scored a lot of points that day! So try to get on the plane early and study a topographical map to see which side of the plane will be best for you. Flying from Quito to Guayaquil, you will get the most spectacular mountain views on the left-hand side; flying to Macas the view is on the right-hand side. Many of the other flights have mountains on either side. You should decide which specific peaks you would prefer to have a good look at and also consider the time of day so that you won't be looking into the sun. Good views are to be had about half the time so make an effort to plan your trip and get good seats.

Flights on the mainland cost the same no matter whether you are Ecuadorean or foreign. Flights to the Galápagos are a different matter, however. Although Ecuadoreans pay only about US$40 for the round trip from Guayaquil, all foreigners have to pay about US$310 for the same flight, and they are not treated to better in-flight service. There is nothing you can do about this except be thankful that the rest of the internal flights cost the same for all nationalities.

Wherever you want to fly, don't despair if you can't get a ticket. It's always worth going to the airport in the hopes of someone not turning up for the flight. Make sure that you're there early and get yourself on a waiting list if there is one. If you do have a reservation, make sure you confirm it. And reconfirm it. And reconfirm it again. As a general rule, I would confirm flights both 72 and 24 hours in advance, as well as when you arrive in Ecuador. Ecuadoreans are notorious for bumping you off your flight if you don't reconfirm. If it's impossible for you to reconfirm because you're in the middle of nowhere, tell them so that they know. Try to have it on the computer if possible. And try to find someone to reconfirm for you.

A final point about air travel from Ecuador. You can't buy international charter or other economy flights in Ecuador. You have to pay full first-class or full tourist-class fare. In addition to the fare you must pay a 10% tax, so it is best to buy your international ticket ahead of time in your home country. There is a US$5 international departure tax but no taxes for domestic flights.

BOAT

Boat transportation is commonly used in Ecuador and can be divided into four different types.

The most commonly used is the motorized dugout canoe, which acts as a water taxi or bus on the major rivers of the Oriente and parts of the coast. In the Galápagos, you find medium-sized motor cruisers or motor sailboats which are used by small groups to visit the different islands of the archipelago, either on day trips or for trips of several days' duration. Thirdly, there are large vessels used either for carrying cargo and a few passengers or as cruise ships for many passengers. Finally, many rivers are crossed by ferries, which can vary from a paddled dugout taking one passenger at a time to a car ferry capable of taking half a dozen vehicles across the river. These are sometimes makeshift transportation to replace a bridge which has been washed out, is being repaired, or is still in the planning stages.

Dugout Canoes

Dugout canoes often carry as many as two dozen passengers and are the only way to get around many roadless areas. Wherever they are found, you can hire one yourself to take you anywhere, but this is very expensive. If you take a regularly scheduled one with other passengers, however, it is quite affordable, though not as cheap as a bus for a similar distance. This is simply because an outboard engine uses more fuel per km than a bus engine, and because a dugout travels more slowly than a bus.

The most likely places that you will travel any distance in dugouts are Misahuallí to Coca in the jungles of the Oriente and San Lorenzo to La Tola on the north-west coast.

Most of the boats used are literally dugouts, with maybe a splashboard added to the gunwales. They are long in shape and short on comfort. Seating is normally on hard, low, uncomfortable wooden benches accommodating two people each. Luggage is stashed forward under a tarpaulin, so carry hand baggage containing essentials for the journey. You will be miserable for six hours if you don't take the following advice, which is worth the cost of this book! *Bring seat padding*. A folded sweater or towel will make a world of difference on the trip. Pelting rain or glaring sun are major hazards and an umbrella is excellent defence against both. Bring suntan cream and wear long sleeves, long pants and a sun hat – I have seen people literally unable to walk because of second-degree burns on their legs from a six-hour exposure to the tropical sun. The breeze as the boat motors along tends to keep insects away, and it also tends to cool you so you don't notice the burning effect of the sun. If the sun should disappear or the rain begin, you can get quite chilled, so bring a light jacket. Insect repellent is useful during stops along the river. A water bottle and food will complete your hand baggage. Remember to stash your spare clothes in plastic bags or they'll get soaked by rain or spray.

A final word about dugout canoes: they feel very unstable! Until you get used to the motion of them, you might worry about the whole thing just rolling over and tipping everybody into the shark, piranha, or boa constrictor-infested waters. Clenching the side of the canoe and wondering what madness possessed you to board the flimsy contraption in the first place doesn't seem to help. I've ridden many dugouts and never had a problem, even in rapids and ocean waves. Nor have I met anyone who was actually dunked in. Dugouts feel much more unstable than they really are, so don't worry about a disaster; it almost never happens.

Other Boats

In the Galápagos, you have the choice of travelling in anything from a small sailboat taking four passengers to a large cruise ship complete with 48 air-conditioned double cabins with private bath. The choice is yours. More information on Galápagos boats is given in the chapter on the Galápagos.

In addition to the dugout canoes of the Oriente, there is one cruise ship which makes relatively luxurious passages down the Río Napo. This is the *Flotel*, based in Coca. More information about it is given under the Coca section in the Northern Oriente chapter.

There are a few ratty steamers plying coastal routes. These are mainly cargo boats and are rarely used by travellers. A few boats go out to the Galápagos from Guayaquil, but it's better to fly there and sail around the islands themselves. Otherwise you could get stuck in Guayaquil for weeks. Again, there is more information under the appropriate coastal towns.

Your Own Boat The idea of sailing your own yacht to the Galápagos sounds romantic. Unfortunately, to sail in the Galápagos you need a licence, and these are all limited to Galápagos boats. If you arrive in the islands in your own boat, you will have to moor the boat in Puerto Ayora and hire one of the local boats to take you around. The Ecuadorean authorities give transit permits of only 72 hours for sailors on their own boats.

RAIL

Ecuador's train system was severely damaged by landslides and flooding during the extremely heavy rains of the 1982/83 El Niño wet season. Many km of track were totally destroyed. Roads and bridges were also badly damaged, so available repair money has been channelled into the more important road network; the railway system has to wait until funds become available.

Since the 1982/83 disaster (when thousands of families had their homes and fields flooded) Ecuador has noticed a decline in the amount of tourist revenue entering the country. This has been attributed to the loss of the Quito-Guayaquil railway line, which is one of the most spectacular train rides in the world and was one of the main reasons some tourists visited Guayaquil. The section from Riobamba in the mountains to Guayaquil on the coast is a dramatic descent which has been made famous in a British TV series on the world's greatest train journeys. Although it is hoped that the railway system will be in action again by late 1986, don't be surprised if it's not.

There are two railway networks in Ecuador. Before 1982 the northern lines ran from Quito to Ibarra and from there to San Lorenzo on the coast. The southern lines ran from Quito to Guayaquil with a branch to Cuenca. Neither of these lines are working in their entirety at this time. The northern train runs only between Otavalo and Ibarra and from Ibarra to San Lorenzo. The southern runs from Quito only as far as Riobamba.

Ordinary trains are not normally used except for the short section between Otavalo and Ibarra. Instead, an *autoferro*, which is like a bus mounted on a railway chassis, is used. Space is limited, so you are advised to buy tickets ahead of time if you wish to travel by autoferro. It is not as comfortable as a normal train. Departure times and other details are given under the appropriate town headings.

BUS

Long Distance

Especially in the highlands, and increasingly in the lowlands, Ecuador is developing a system of central bus terminals in each city, which means that if you have to change buses you don't have to go looking for different terminals. All buses arrive and depart from the same place. Once you have located the central bus terminal, often referred to as the Terminal Terrestre, it is a simple matter to find a bus to take you where you want to go. Some towns still haven't completed their main bus terminals so they have several smaller ones.

Throughout this book, I have indicated where the bus terminals are located on the city maps. The accompanying text will tell you the most important destinations served by the terminal, the approximate cost of the journey, about how long it will take to get there, and how frequently buses leave. I have refrained from giving exact schedules, as that is a sure way of making this book obsolete before it is published. Timetables change frequently and are not necessarily adhered to. If a bus is full, it might leave early. Conversely, an almost-empty bus will usually spend half an hour giving *vueltas* or just driving from the terminal to the main plaza and back again with the driver's assistant yelling out of the door in the hopes of attracting more passengers.

Getting around Ecuador by bus is easy, but here are some tips to make your travels more enjoyable. If you go to the terminal the day before your bus trip, you

can usually buy tickets in advance. This means you can choose your approximate time of departure, and often you can choose your seat number too. I'm over six feet tall, and one of my pet hates is being squished in a tiny back seat of a bus. I think it's worth buying tickets in advance so that I can get a front-row seat, which generally means more leg room, much better views and a more exciting trip. Some people prefer second-row seats, to avoid being jostled by passengers getting on and off. Try to avoid those rows where the wheels comes up – usually the third row from the front and the third from the back in the *busetas*, and the fourth or fifth rows from the front and back in larger buses. Ask when buying your ticket about the position of the wheels. Also remember that the suspension at the back of a bus is usually far worse than anywhere else, so try and avoid the back rows.

Some bus companies don't sell tickets in advance. This is usually when they have frequent departures (about twice an hour or even more often). You just arrive and get on the next bus that's going your way.

If travelling during long holiday weekends or special fiestas, you may find that buses are booked up for several days in advance, so book early if you can.

Various types of buses are used; they

Top: Basketware, Saquisilí market (RR)
Left: Pottery Market (RR)
Right: Inspecting weavings in Otavalo market (RR)

Top: River Cuchipamba raft ferry near Gualaquiza (RR)
Left: Bus and buggy, Saquisilí (RR)
Right: Coastal road (RR)

can be roughly grouped into two types. Small buses (*busetas*) usually hold 22 passengers and are fast and efficient. Although standing passengers are not normally allowed, the seats can be rather cramped. Larger coaches have more space, but they often allow standing passengers and so can get rather crowded. They are generally slower than the busetas and at times can take almost twice as long to reach their destinations because they drop off and pick up so many standing passengers. Although they're slow, the big old coaches are sometimes more fun because there's more activity going on with passengers getting on and off all the time, perhaps accompanied by chickens or a couple of hundredweight of potatoes. If you're in any hurry, make sure that you get a buseta. The approximate times given for most of the journeys in this book tend to lean towards the faster times.

If you're travelling very light, it's best to keep your luggage inside the bus with you. If I'm off on a trip for a few days, I often leave much of my luggage in a hotel storage room and travel with a bag small enough to fit under the seat. Local people get away with taking fairly large pieces of luggage aboard so you don't have to put it on the luggage rack, even if the driver tells you to. If your luggage is too big to fit under the seat, it will have to go on top or in a luggage compartment. Sometimes the top is covered with a tarpaulin, but not always, so pack your gear in large plastic bags (trash bags are good) to avoid getting everything wet if it rains. The luggage compartment is sometimes filthy, and your luggage can get covered with grease or mud. Placing your luggage in a large protective sack is a good idea. Most of the Indians use grain sacks as luggage; you can buy them for a few cents in general stores or markets.

Every time a bus stops on the main routes, vendors selling fruit, rolls, ice cream or drinks suddenly appear. So you won't starve. Long-distance buses usually stop for a 20-minute meal break at the appropriate times. The food in the terminal restaurants may be somewhat basic. If you're a picky eater, you should bring food with you on longer trips.

Fares for tickets bought in bus terminals are a set price. The larger terminals often have traveller information booths which can advise you about this, but normally I find that you get charged the correct fare. The booths can give you information on all the routes available from the larger terminals. If you're only going part of the way, or you get on a bus in a small town as it comes by between larger towns, the bus driver will charge you appropriately. About 90% of the time you are charged honestly; once in a while they try and overcharge you. Once I was charged 50c for a ride that I paid 20c for going the other way. I pointed this out to the driver who was adamant that the fare was 50c. The Latin American machismo – he didn't want to admit that he was wrong. Although there's little point in getting uptight about a few cents, this particular example was too blatant for me to just ignore. I told him he could have 20c or we could go talk to the transit police – and he didn't want to talk to the transit police. This sort of thing doesn't happen very often; the only way to guard against it is to know roughly the correct fare beforehand.

If you want to travel somewhere immediately, just go to the terminal and you'll usually find the driver's assistant running around trying to hustle up some passengers for his bus. Often you'll be on a bus going your way within a few minutes of arriving at the terminal. Before boarding a bus, make sure it's going where you want to go. Occasionally drivers will say that they are going where you want to go and then take you only part of the way and expect you to change buses. If you want a direct bus, make sure you ask for it. Also make sure that it is leaving soon, and not in two hours. Finally, if it looks too slow, or too fast, or too old, or too cramped, or you just don't like the bus for some reason, you can usually find another bus leaving soon if you're going to a major destination. Most places are served by several bus companies and you can make the choice that's best for you.

One last word about Ecuadorean buses: toilets. There aren't any. Long-distance buses have rest stops every three or four hours – try not to get onto a bus with a full bladder or you may join the famous traveller who had to pee in his boot.

Local

These are usually slow and crowded, but very cheap. You can get around most towns for about 5c. Local buses often go out to a nearby village and this is a good way to see an area. Just stay on the bus to the end of the line, pay another 5c, and head back again, usually sitting in the best seat on the bus. If you make friends with the driver, you may end up with an entertaining tour as he points out the local sights in between collecting other passengers' fares.

When you want to get off a local bus, yell *Baja!*, which means 'Down!' Telling the driver to stop will make him think you're trying to be a back-seat driver, and you will be ignored. He's only interested if you're getting off, or down from the bus. Another way of getting him to stop is to yell *Esquina!*, which means 'Corner!' He'll stop at the next one.

Trucks

In remote areas, trucks often double as buses. Sometimes they are flatbed trucks with a tin roof, open sides and uncomfortable wooden plank seats. These curious-looking buses are called *rancheros* and are especially common on the coast.

In the highlands, ordinary trucks are used to carry passengers; you just climb in the back. If the weather is OK, you get fabulous views and can feel the wind blow refreshingly by (dress warmly!). If the weather is bad you hunker down underneath a dark tarpaulin with the other passengers. It certainly isn't the height of luxury, but it

may be the only way of getting to some areas, and if you're open minded about the minor discomforts, you may find that these rides are among the best you have in Ecuador.

Payment for these rides is usually determined by the driver and is a standard fare depending on the distance. You can ask other passengers how much they are paying; usually you'll find that the trucks double as buses and charge almost as much.

TAXI

Ecuador is a petroleum-producing country and it keeps down the price of petrol for domestic consumption. It's a low 40-50c a gallon (for some reason petrol is not dispensed in litres). This price combined with low wages means that taxis in Ecuador are very cheap.

The main rule for taking taxis is to ask the fare beforehand, or you'll be over-charged more often than not. A long ride in a large city (Quito or Guayaquil) shouldn't go over US$3 and short hops can cost as little as 50c. In smaller towns fares vary from 30c to about a dollar. Meters are rarely seen, though in 1984 the powers that be were trying fairly successfully to make Quito drivers install meters by law. Even if there is a meter, the driver may not want to use it. This can be to your advantage, because with the meter off the driver can avoid interminable downtown traffic jams by taking a longer route. This saves both you and him time and the extra cost in petrol is negligible. At weekends and at night fares are always about 25-50% higher.

You can hire a taxi for several hours. A half day might cost about US$10 if you bargain. You can also hire pickup trucks which act as taxis to take you to remote areas (eg a climbers' refuge). If you hire a taxi to take you to another town, a rough rule of thumb is about US$1 for every 10 km. Remember to count the driver's return trip, even if you're not returning. A longer trip may average a little less. If you split the cost between four passengers, you'll each be paying between two and three times the bus fare for a round trip.

CAR RENTAL

This is as expensive as a full-price car rental in Europe or the US. Cheap car rentals aren't found. If the price seems reasonable, check to see for what extras you have to pay. Often there is a per km charge and you have to buy insurance. Some cars are not in very good condition (perhaps that's being overly euphemistic). It is difficult to find any kind of car rental outside of Guayaquil and Quito. I checked several places in Quito and was told that I had to have a credit card to be able to rent, as they wouldn't accept a cash deposit. Expect to pay at least US$30 per day.

HITCHING

As mentioned earlier, trucks are used as public transport in remote areas, so trying to hitch a free ride on one is the same as trying to hitch a free ride on a bus. Private cars are not as common in Ecuador as in more developed nations, so hitch-hiking generally is not as easy or successful. It can be done, however.

I have hitched several times on secondary roads in Ecuador and generally I offer to pay the driver. If the driver is stopping to drop off and pick up other passengers, then you can assume that he will expect payment. Talk to other passengers to find out what the going rate is. If you are the only passenger, the driver may have picked you up just to talk to a foreigner, and he may wave aside your offer of payment. This is probably the case in almost half my rides. I have never hitched on roads with good bus services, however, because buses are so cheap. Hitch-hiking isn't normally done and if you want to try, make sure in advance of your ride that you and the driver agree on the subject of payment.

Quito

Quito is my favourite Latin American capital. Situated at about 2850 metres above sea level, it has a wonderfully spring-like climate despite the fact that it is only 22 km south of the equator. It is in a valley flanked by mountains and, on a clear day, several snow-capped volcanoes are visible from the capital. As well as being in a beautiful location, it is rich in history and much of the old colonial town is well preserved.

The site of the capital dates from pre-Columbian times. Early inhabitants of the area were the peaceful Quitu people, who give their name to the capital. The Quitus integrated with the expansionist coastal Caras to give rise to the Indian group known as the Shyris. About 1300 AD the Shyris joined with the Puruhás through marriage, and their descendants fought against the Incas in the late 1400s. By the time of the Spanish arrival, Quito was a major Inca city but it was totally destroyed by Atahualpa's general Rumiñahui shortly before the arrival of the Spanish conquerors in Quito. There are no Inca remains. The present capital was founded on top of the ruins of the Inca city by Sebastián de Benalcázar on 6 December 1534, and many old colonial buildings survive in the old town.

In 1978 UNESCO declared Quito one of the world's cultural heritage sites, and in Quito's old town, development and other changes are strictly controlled. This does not mean that progress has stopped. On the contrary, the old centre is extremely bustling and full of traffic. The buildings haven't changed, however, and a walk down colonial Quito's streets late at night, after the rush hour traffic has finished, is a step into a past era. There are no modern buildings discordantly built next to centuries-old architecture and no flashing neon signs to disrupt the ambience of the past.

Quito has a population of about 860,000 and is thus the second largest city in Ecuador. (Guayaquil is the largest.) It is located along the central valley in a roughly north-south direction and is approximately 17 km long and four km wide. It can conveniently be divided into three segments. The centre (*el centro*) is the site of the old town with its white-washed and red-tiled houses and colonial churches; this is the area of greatest interest to the traveller. The north is modern Quito, with its major businesses, airline offices, embassies, shopping centres and banks. It also contains the airport and middle- and upper-class residential areas. This area is of importance to the traveller who needs to get some business done. Finally, the south consists mainly of working-class housing areas and is of little interest to the traveller except when you want to leave town – the main bus terminal lies at Quito's south end.

Information

DITURIS runs three tourist information offices. The main one is in the new town at Calle Reina Victoria 514 and Roca (tel 239044). They have a branch in the old town, in the Municipal Palace on the south-east side of the Plaza Independencia. Finally, there is a branch at the airport but it keeps irregular hours. They can provide you with brochures, maps and tourist information, and there is often someone available who speaks English.

Warning The elevation of about 2850 metres will make you feel somewhat breathless when you first arrive from sea level. This is a mild symptom of altitude sickness and will disappear after a day or two. It is best to take things easy on arrival. Don't over-exert yourself, eat lightly and cut back on cigarettes and alcohol to minimize altitude problems.

Although Quito is a safe city, you should be aware that pickpockets work crowded areas such as public buses, markets and church plazas. Keep money and other valuables in inside pockets and cameras firmly strapped across your body, and you won't have any problems.

Immigration There are two offices. One is for tourist card extensions and the other is for visas. Most travellers will only need the tourist card extension but if you want to stay longer than 90 days you will need a student, business, work or residence visa. Visas are usually expensive and complicated while the tourist card extension is free and straightforward as long as you haven't used up your 90 days. For tourist card extensions go to Avenida Amazonas 2639 (also numbered 3149 for some strange reason) and República from 8 am to noon and 2.30 to 6 pm Monday through Friday. It takes anywhere from 10 minutes to two hours depending on how busy they are on the day you go. Although onward tickets out of Ecuador and 'sufficient funds' are legally required, they are in fact very rarely asked for. It's still worth bringing any airline tickets or travellers' cheques you may have, just in case. For visas go to the Extranjería at Calle Reina Victoria and Colón. They are open mornings only, Monday through Thursday.

Embassies Most nationalities require visas to enter Colombia and some to enter Peru (see Visas section in Facts for the Visitor). The Colombian consulate is at Avenida Amazonas 353 and Robles and is open 8.30 am to 12.30 pm and 2.30 to 4 pm Monday through Friday. The Peruvian consulate is in the Edificio España at Avenida Amazonas 1429 and Colón.

Money Banks are open from 9 am to 1.30 pm but do not normally change money unless you have an account with them. They will handle money wired from your home bank and pay in US dollars. Most bank offices are on Avenida Amazonas.

Exchange houses, or *casas de cambio*, are the best places to exchange money. Rates vary, but usually not by very much. Rodrigo Paz is the best-known place. They have several branches. Their old town office is at Calle Venezuela 659 and Sucre. In the new town they have an office at Avenida Amazonas 370 and Robles. Their offices are normally open from 9.30 am to 12.30 pm and 3 to 6 pm Monday through Friday, mornings only on Saturday. Other companies have offices near these locations. If you want to change money on Sunday, you will find the Rodrigo Paz airport office open. Also, the office at the Hotel Colón is open on Sunday and they are often open until 7 pm on weekdays.

If you change more money than you need, it is easy to buy back dollars at a rate about 2% below what you sold them for.

Post & Phone There are several post offices but the best one for receiving and sending letters is the central office on Calle Benalcázar behind the Plaza Independencia. They are open from 9 am to 5 pm on weekdays but booths selling stamps are usually open from about 8 am to 6 pm.

The central IETEL office is open from 6 am to 10 pm daily and is on Calle Chile around the corner from the central post office. If you want to mail a package of over a kilogram you have to use the office at Calle Ulloa 943 and Ramirez Dávalos. There are both IETEL and post offices at the airport.

If you are an American Express client you can receive mail sent to you c/o Amex, Aptdo 2605, Quito, Ecuador. Their street address is Avenida Amazonas 339 at the Ecuadorean Tours office, which is open from 9.30 am to 12.30 pm and 2.30 to 6 pm Monday through Friday and mornings only on Saturday.

Bookshops Libri Mundi is the best, with a good selection of books in English, German, French and Spanish. They have books about Ecuador as well as books of a

SAN ROQUE

PANECILLO

SAN JUAN

GONZALEZ
SUAREZ

Cinco de Junio

To Terminal
Terrestre (5 km)
& railway (1 km)

MANOSALVAS

Luis Vargas

SAN SEBASTIÁN

Parque La
Alamed

EUGENIO ESPEJO

1	Gran Casino Hotel	
2	Hotel Monasterio &	
	Transportes Occidental	
3	Transportes Esmeraldas	
4	Pensión Astoria	
5	Caspicara Hotel	
6	Hotel Felix	
7	Hotel Roma	
8	Plaza Santo Domingo	
9	Hotel Juania del Arco	
10	Hotel Interamericano &	
	Supertaxis Cuenca	
11	Hotel Capitalino & Zulia	
12	Banco Central	
13	Hotel Guayaquil & Pacifico	
14	Hotel Restaurant Ingatur	
15	Hotel Indoamericano &	
	Residencial Los Andes	
16	Hotel Colonial	
17	Transportes Ecuador &	
	Hotel Los Andes	
18	Hotel Huasi Continental	
19	Residencial Bolívar & Quitumbe	
20	Hotel Viena	
21	Hotel Viena Internacional	
	& San Agustin	
22	Hotel Los Canarios	
23	Plaza & Teatro Sucre	
24	Rodrigo Paz Casa de Cambio	
	& Auca Hotel	
25	Chifa Hong Kong	
26	Taberna Quiteña	
27	Plaza de la Independencia	
28	House of Sucre	
29	Hotel Sucre	
30	Ecuahotel (Opp. La Merced Church)	
31	Plaza San Francisco	
32	Residencial Marsella	

33	House of Benalcázar
34	Hotel Colón
35	Cine Universitario
36	Casa de Cultura Museums
37	Cine Colón
38	Cathedral
39	Church of La Compañia
40	Church of El Belén
41	Church of El Sagrario
42	Church of La Basilica
43	Monastery of San Agustin
44	Monastery of San Francisco
45	Church of Santo Domingo
46	Instituto Geográfico Militar
47	Buses to Otavalo, Ibarra
	& Tulcán
48	Residencial Italia
49	American Express & Airlines
50	Rodrigo Paz
51	Manolós Pavement Restaurant
52	Taberna Quiteña
53	Hotel Embassy
54	Residencial Cumbes Baqueadano
55	Restaurant La Choza
56	Restaurant Excalibur
57	Libri Mundi Bookstore
58	Colombus Steak House
59	Hotel Embajador
60	Hotel Nueve de Octubre
61	Parcel Post
62	Hotel Residencial Florida
63	Residencial Carrión
64	Central Post Office
65	Hotel Versalles
66	Hotel Majestic
67	Residencial Santa Clara
68	Government Palace
69	Tourist Information (DITURIS)
70	Teatro Prometeo

0   300   60

Major streets only

Quito

more general nature. Their main shop is at Calle Juan León Mera 851 near Veintimilla and is open from 9 am to 7 pm Monday through Friday, and 9 am to 1 pm on Saturday. A smaller branch is open until 8 pm in the Hotel Colón shopping mall (same prices). The other bookshops in Quito sell mainly books in Spanish.

Maps The best maps are available from the Instituto Geográfico Militar (IGM), which is on top of a hill at the end of Calle T Paz y Miño. This small street is found off Avenida Colombia a few blocks southeast of Parque El Ejido in the new town. There are no buses, so walk or take a taxi. The IGM is open from 8 am to 3 pm Monday through Friday. You need to leave your passport at the gate to be allowed in. They have a good selection of country and topographical maps to look at or buy, but their selection of city maps is very limited and you'll be better off with the city maps in this book. Country maps are also available from street vendors and the Libri Mundi bookstore, but they are more expensive than at the IGM.

Spanish Courses There are two places which will teach you Spanish. Classes are available at various levels. The Quito Spanish School is at Avenida Colombia 1140 and Yaguachi (tel 515845). Their mailing address is PO Box 39-C, Quito, Ecuador. They offer four– and six-week courses and provide accommodation with a local family so that you can practise your Spanish out of the classroom. Each student has a private tutor at the school for seven hours a day. Cost for a four-week course including tuition, family accommodation and all meals is about US$340; for six weeks it is about US$480.

If you prefer group classes and providing your own accommodation, then try the Catholic University at Avenida 12 de Octubre and Robles. They have six-week classes for about US$50. They will also provide you with a student card. Although there are few price reductions for students

in Ecuador, the card is very useful in Peru. The university also has classes in Quechua.

Signing up for these classes may be a way of helping you get a student visa.

Things to See

The DITURIS information office told me that churches are open from 9 to 11 am and 3 to 5 pm daily except Sunday, and that museums are open from 9 am to 5 pm daily except Monday. This is not true. Hours are haphazard to say the least. Museums can change hours for reasons varying from a national holiday to staff sickness, so the opening hours in the following sections are meant only as guidelines. Generally speaking, however, Monday is the worst day to visit museums, as many of them are closed. Churches are open every day but are crowded with worshippers on Sunday. Early morning seems to be a good time to visit churches. They are usually closed for a long lunch hour and in the afternoons sometimes remain open until after 6 pm. It's unpredictable. Good luck!

Museums

Casa de Cultura Ecuatoriana If you want to kill several birds with one stone, you should head for the Casa de Cultura Ecuatoriana, the large circular glass building at the corner of Avenidas Patria and 12 de Octubre, to the east of the Parque El Ejido. They have an art museum, open from 9 am to 12.30 pm and 3 to 6.30 pm Tuesday through Friday, and 9.30 am to 4 pm on Saturday. The museum contains more than just an excellent art collection. There is a fascinating display of traditional musical instruments, many several centuries old. The instruments are mainly Ecuadorean, but there are also Asian, African and European oddities. Also on display are examples of traditional Ecuadorean regional dress. The art collection contains both contemporary Ecuadorean work and 19th-century pieces. The contemporary work includes canvases by Ecuador's most famous artists, Guayasamín and Kingman among others. Also in the Casa de Cultura is a small natural history museum open from 9 am to 12.30 pm and 3 to 6.15 pm Monday through Friday, and 10 am to 1 pm on Saturday. Here you can see condor and giant tortoise skeletons and a variety of other exhibits. All the museums in the Casa de Cultura are free.

Catholic University Across the traffic circle from the Casa de Cultura and northeast along Avenida 12 de Octubre is the Catholic University, which has an interesting private archaeology museum on the third floor of the library.

Museo Jijón y Caamaño The entrance to the Museo Jijón y Caamaño is near the intersection with Calle J Carrión. Hours are from 9 am to noon and 3 to 9 pm Monday through Friday. Admission is 30c and you can get a guided tour (sometimes available in English) of the well-displayed archaeological collection. There is also a collection of colonial art.

Museo de Banco Central Another good archaeology museum is that of the Banco Central, on the 5th floor. It houses well-displayed pottery, gold ornaments (including the gold mask that is the symbol of the Museo del Banco Central), skulls showing deformation and early surgical methods, a mummy and many other objects of interest. On the floor above is a display of colonial furniture and religious art and carving. The bank is at the beginning of Avenida 10 de Agosto in front of the apex of the Parque La Alameda. Outside of working hours, the entrance is through the gate to the right of the bank and then through a side door. There is an elevator. Hours are from 9 am to 8 pm Tuesday through Friday, and 10 am to 5 pm on Saturday and Sunday. Entrance is about 30c but is free on Sunday and in the evening from 6 to 8 pm — though it can be crowded then.

Museo de Arte y Historia This museum is in an old building in the centre. It used to be a Jesuit house until 1767, when it became an army barracks. The present museum contains a wealth of early colonial art dating from the 16th and 17th centuries. The building is at Espejo 1147, just off the Plaza Independencia. It is open from 8.30 am to 6.30 pm Tuesday through Friday and 10 am to 3 pm on Saturday and Sunday. Admission is 5c.

Casa de Sucre Several other historical buildings in the centre are now museums. A good one to visit is Casa de Sucre, which is well restored and contains period (1820s) furniture and a small museum. It is on Calle Venezuela 573 and Sucre. Hours are from 9 am to noon and 3 to 6 pm daily, and it's free. An older house is the Casa de Benalcázar, dating from 1534. It was restored by Spain in 1967 and is also free. It's on Calle Olmedo 962 and Benalcázar. There are sometimes classical piano recitals here and it is a delightful site for such entertainment. Check the newspapers or enquire at the house.

Museum of Colonial Art This museum is on the corner of Calle Cuenca and Mejía gets good reviews in old guidebooks but is now closed for restoration. Check to see if it is open yet.

Museo Guayasamín Modern art can be seen at the Museo Guayasamín, the home of Oswaldo Guayasamín, an Ecuadorean Indian painter born in 1919 and now famous throughout the world. The museum is at Calle José Bosmediano 543 in the residencial district of Bellavista to the north-east of Quito. It's an uphill walk and the No 3 Colmena-Batan bus goes near the museum. Make sure the bus has a Bellavista placard, or ask the driver. It is open from 9 am to 12.30 pm and 3 to 6 pm Monday through Saturday, and it's free. You can buy original artwork here.

Museo Camilo Egas Another Ecuadorean painter who has a museum in his name is Camilo Egas (1889-1962). Some 40 of his works are displayed in the Museo Camilo Egas, now under the auspices of the Banco Central. The collection has been recently restored. The museum is open 9 am to 1 pm and 3 to 6 pm Tuesday through Friday, and 9 am to 4 pm on Saturday. Admission is 20c. The address is Calle Venezuela 1302 and Esmeraldas.

Churches

There is a wealth of churches, chapels, convents, monasteries, cathedrals and basilicas in Quito. The old town especially has so many of them that you can hardly walk two blocks without passing a church. Photography is not normally permitted because the intensity of the flash has a detrimental effect on the pigment in the many valuable religious paintings. Slides and postcards can be bought at the post office.

Monastery of San Francisco The oldest church is the Monastery of San Francisco, located on the plaza of the same name. Construction began only a few days after the founding of Quito in 1534 but it was not finished until 70 years later. The founder is commemorated by a statue at the far right of the raised terrace in front of the church. He is the Franciscan mission-ary Joedco Ricke, who is also credited with being the first man to sow wheat in Ecuador.

Although much of the church has been rebuilt because of earthquake damage, some of it is still original. Go to the chapel of Señor Jesus de Gran Poder to the right of the main altar to see original tilework. The main altar itself is a spectacular example of baroque carving, and the roof and walls are also wonderfully carved and richly covered in gold leaf. The church contains excellent examples of early religious art and sculpture; unfortunately it is often too dark to see them properly. Tour guides turn lights on periodically so

keep your eyes open for this. The bells are rung every hour, and often on the quarter hour. You can see the bell-ringer at work in his cubbyhole just to the right of the main door.

To the right of the main entrance is the Franciscan Museum, which contains some of the monastery's finest artwork. Here you can see paintings, sculpture and furniture dating back to the 16th century. One of the oldest signed paintings is a Mateo Mejía canvas dated 1615. Some of the woodcarvings are even older and are covered with gold leaf, paint, period clothing or a fine porcelain flesh finish. Some of the furniture is fantastically wrought and inlaid with literally thousands of pieces of mother-of-pearl. The museum costs 50c to visit, and Spanish-speaking guides are available. It is open from 3 to 6 pm Monday through Saturday. Morning hours are erratic: 9 to 11 am on most weekdays except Tuesday and Friday, when they are open from 9 to 10 am.

La Compañia Looking out across the plain, cobblestoned plaza of San Francisco, you see the ornate green and gold domes of the church of La Compañía de Jesus, just two blocks away. The construction of this Jesuit church began in 1605, the year that San Francisco was completed, and it took 163 years to build. The church is famous as the most ornate in Ecuador; it has been claimed that seven tons of gold were used to gild the walls, ceilings and altars. Note the Arab (Moorish) influence in the intricate designs carved on the magnificent red-and-gold columns and ceilings. There is a beautiful cupola over the main altar. The remains of the Quiteño saint, Mariana de Jesus, who died in 1645, are found here.

The Cathedral One block away from the ornate Jesuit church is the Plaza de la Independencia with the stark cathedral. Although not as rich in decoration as some of the other churches, the cathedral has several points of historical interest. Plaques on the outside walls commemorate Quito's founders. General Sucre, the leading figure of Quito's independence, is buried in the cathedral. To the left of the main altar is a statue of Juan José Flores, Ecuador's first president. Behind the main altar is the smaller altar of Nuestra Señora de los Dolores; the plaque there shows where President Gabriel García Moreno died on 6 August 1875. He was shot outside the Presidential Palace (just across the plaza) and was carried, dying, to the cathedral.

El Sagrario The main chapel of the cathedral was begun in 1657 and was finished 49 years later, but it is now a separate church, El Sagrario. This church is being renovated by Poland's University of Warsaw and is interesting to visit if you want to see how restoration work is done. El Sagrario is on García Moreno, next to the cathedral.

San Augustín Two blocks away from the Plaza de la Independencia is the church where many of the heroes of the battles for Ecuador's independence are buried. This is the church of San Agustín, site of the signing of Ecuador's declaration of independence on 10 August 1809. The church is another fine example of 17th-century architecture. The historical museum where you can see various Independence mementoes as well as colonial art is in the convent to the right of the church. It is open from 9 am to noon and 3 to 6 pm Monday through Saturday and costs 10c to get in.

Santo Domingo The church of Santo Domingo is especially attractive in the evening, when its domes are floodlit. It too dates back to early Quito. Construction began in 1581 and continued until 1650. An exquisite gift from King Charles V of Spain is one of the church's main showpieces. It is a statue of the Virgen del Rosario, found in its own side chapel, which is ornately carved in baroque style.

In the busy Plaza Santo Domingo in front of the church is a statue of General Sucre pointing in the direction of Pichincha, where he won the decisive battle for independence on 24 May 1822.

La Merced One of colonial Quito's most recent churches is that of La Merced, which was begun in 1700 and completed in 1742. Its tower has the distinction of being the highest (47 metres) in colonial Quito and it contains the largest bell of Quito's churches. Inside is a wealth of fascinating art. Paintings show volcanoes glowing and erupting over the church roofs of colonial Quito, the capital covered with ashes, General Sucre going into battle, and many other scenes. The stained-glass windows also show various scenes of colonial life such as early priests and conquistadors among the Indians of the Oriente. It is a surprising and intriguing collection.

Other Churches Moving out of the old town, you can still find several interesting churches. High on a hill on Calle Venezuela is the new basilica, which is still unfinished though work on it began in 1926. Obviously, the tradition of taking decades to construct a church is still alive. At the north end of the Parque La Alameda is the small church of El Belén, which was built on the site of the first Catholic mass to be held in Quito.

Finally, in a precipitous valley on the east side of town, is the Sanctuary of Guápulo, built between 1644 and 1688. The best views of this delightful-looking colonial church are from behind the Hotel Quito at the end of Avenida 12 de Octubre. There is a steep footpath that leads down to the Guápulo and it's a pleasant walk, though somewhat strenuous coming back.

This is just a selection of Quito's most interesting and frequently visited churches. There are dozens more, some of which are closed to the public.

Other Sights

Virgin of Quito The small, rounded hill which dominates the old town is called El Panecillo or the 'the little bread loaf' and is a major Quito landmark. It is topped by a huge statue of the Virgin of Quito. There are marvellous views of the whole city stretching out below, as well as views of the surrounding volcanoes. You can get there from the old town by climbing the stairs at the end of Calle García Moreno – it takes about half an hour. A taxi from the old town costs about US$2 and they will wait and bring you back or you can ride up and make the easier downhill stroll.

Markets At the bottom of the Panecillo is Avenida 24 de Mayo. This used to be a major open-air Indian market. An indoor market was opened in 1981 at the upper end of 24 de Mayo. Some outdoor selling still takes place, however, especially on Calle Cuenca and the streets to the north-west of it.

La Ronda At Avenida 24 de Mayo between Calles García Moreno and Venezuela is the historic alley now called Calle Juan de Dios Morales but known to most people by its traditional name of La Ronda. This street is perhaps the best preserved in colonial Quito and is narrow enough so cars rarely drive along it, which adds to its charm. It is full of old, balconied houses and you can enter several of them. Just walk along the street and you'll see which ones are open to visitors; they usually have handicrafts for sale.

Plaza de la Independencia While wandering around the churches of colonial Quito you'll probably pass through the Plaza de la Independencia several times. Apart from the cathedral you can visit the Palacio de Gobierno, also known as the Palacio Presidencial. It is the low white building on the north-west side of the plaza and has the national flag flying atop of it. The entrance is flanked by a pair of handsomely uniformed presidential guards. Inside you can see a mural depicting Francisco Orellana's descent of the Amazon. The president does indeed carry out business in this building, so sightseeing is limited to the mural and lower courtyard.

Plaza del Teatro At the junction of Calles Guayaquil and Flores is the tiny Plaza del Teatro, where you'll find Teatro Sucre. This is Quito's most sophisticated theatre with frequent concerts and plays.

Parque La Alameda Leaving the old town, you'll see the long, triangular Parque La Alameda with an impressive monument of Simón Bolívar at the apex. There are several other interesting monuments in the park. To the right is a relief map of Ecuador and further in there are statues of the members of the 1736-1744 French Académie des Sciences expedition which surveyed Ecuador and made the equatorial measurements which gave rise to the metric system of weights and measures. In the centre of the park is the Quito observatory, which was opened by President García Moreno in 1864 and is the oldest in the continent. It is used both for meteorology and astronomy and can be visited on Saturday mornings. At the base of the park are a pair of ornamental lakes where rowboats can be hired for a few sucres. It is filled with picnicking families on weekends.

Parque El Ejido A few blocks beyond Parque La Alameda is the biggest park in downtown Quito, the pleasant, tree-filled Parque El Ejido. This is a popular venue for ball games and you can usually see impromptu games of soccer and volleyball, as well as a strange, giant marbles game typical of Ecuador. It is played with golf-ball-sized steel balls.

Avenida Amazonas From the centre of the north end of the park runs modern Quito's showpiece street, Avenida Amazonas. Here are modern hotels and airline offices, banks and restaurants. It is a wide avenue with plenty of room for pedestrians. Buses and trucks are prohibited (except for blue double-decker London buses). There are several outdoor pavement restaurants where you can have a coffee or a snack and watch modern Quito go by.

Quito Zoo Continuing down Avenida Amazonas, you cross Avenida Francisco de Orellana about 1½ km from Parque El Ejido. Here there is a military college which, for some reason, runs the Quito Zoo. The entrance is around the back on Calle La Pradera. It costs 20c to get in and you can see various Ecuadorean species such as giant Galápagos tortoises, Andean condors and monkeys. Some of the cages are quite good, but a few leave much to be desired and are far too small for the comfort of the animals.

Places to Stay

As befits a capital city, Quito has well over a hundred hotels and it would be pointless to list every one. The following selection will give you plenty of choice. As a general guideline, hotels in the old town tend to be less comfortable, older and much cheaper than those in the new town. That is not to say that there are no cheap hotels in the new town.

Places to Stay – bottom end

When I first arrived in Quito in 1981 with a backpack full of climbing gear, no ticket home and about US$150 in my pocket, I went straight to the legendary *Hotel Gran Casino* at Calle García Moreno 330 and Ambato. There is no hotel quite like it in any Latin American capital. If you travel to meet the locals and get away from other travellers, this is not the place to stay. It is always full of budget travellers and is a great place to pick up on the latest travel news. If you've been travelling in Ecuador (or Latin America) for any length of time you often meet someone you know staying here. Its popularity is such that it's been nicknamed the 'Gran Gringo.' They have a cheap restaurant that serves reasonable meals and is usually crowded. There is a notice board, laundry facilities (they'll do it for you in about two days or wash it yourself), left-luggage facilities (25c per week and you are given a claim check), and an excellent view from the roof (don't miss it). The notice board often lists teaching jobs, 'wanted to buy' and 'for sale,' as well as notes from travellers looking for partners to travel with. The rooms are very basic, usually just a bed and a chair, but they vary in quality. If you don't like the first one you see, ask to see another one. Some rooms have excellent views and others have only a door onto the hallway. Singles cost about US$1.40 and tend to go fast. Rooms with two to six beds are about US$1 per person. If you arrive alone, you can share a room if you want to economize. Shared rooms are usually available until fairly late in the evening. There are a few rooms with a private shower for US$2 per person. If you use the communal showers, hot water is available only from 7 am to 3 pm – so if you arrive in the evening you're out of luck. The showers are on the ground floor and there are only three of them so expect to wait in line at about 7.30 am. A bench is provided for waiting. Next door to the hotel are some Turkish baths and sauna where you can soak away your travel grime and tensions for about US$1. It's open from about 9 am to 9 pm and you can spend as long as you want in there.

As you can gather, I've spent a lot of nights here and have developed quite a soft spot for this hotel. There are many other budget hotels to choose from, some of which may well be better, but somehow I always end up staying here.

If the *Gran Casino* is full, the nearest hotels are the *Monasterio* on Avenida 24 de Mayo and García Moreno, and the *Pensión Astoria* at Loja 630 and Venezuela. Neither of them is particularly good but they are cheap at US$1.20 each.

A good place to go looking for cheap hotels is the Plaza Santo Domingo area, and Avenida Maldonado and Calle Flores leaving from it. Here you'll find a score or more of cheap hotels within a few blocks of one another but some of them are not very good. On the Plaza Santo Domingo is the *Hotel Roma* at Rocafuerte 1331 and at the corner of the plaza is the *Caspicara Hotel* at Rocafuerte 1415. Both charge about US$1.60 per person, are basic but clean, and have hot water. The attractive *Hotel Juana del Arco* has hot water and pleasant but noisy rooms (good views) for US$2.50 per person or more with private bath. Just off the plaza at Guayaquil 431 is the *Hotel Felix*, which has pretty flowers in the balconies though the rooms are still basic. It has hot water and it's secure – ring the bell to get in. They charge about US$1 each – good value.

As you head down Avenida Maldonado you'll encounter many hotels. In the first block on the right are the hotels *Interamericano*, *Capitalino* and *Zulia*. The *Interamericano* charges US$1.70-3 each depending on whether or not you have a private bathroom. The *Capitalino* is US$1.60 each and looks basic but clean.

They have hot water all day long. The *Zulia* is a very basic cold-water hotel charging US$1 each. On the left side of the first block of Maldonado are the hotels *Pacifico*, *Guayaquil* and *Ingatur*. The *Pacifico* and *Ingatur* both have hot water and are clean. They charge US$1.50 each. There is a simple restaurant with cheap *almuerzos* and *meriendas* available. The *Guayaquil* charges US$1.40-2.80 per person depending on whether you have a single or double and whether you have a private bathroom or not. There is hot water and the rooms vary; some are good and spacious, others less so.

There are several more cheap hotels further down Maldonado. One of the best is the *Hotel Colonial*, which is down an alley from Maldonado 3035, is quiet and has hot water. Basic but clean rooms are US$1.20 per person; or if you want a private bath the rooms are US$2.75 single and US$5 double. On the other side of Maldonado are several more hotels which cost about US$1.20 but look grimy and have only cold water. These include the hotels *Caribe* and *Los Andes*, and *Residencial Los Andes*. A little better is the *Hotel Indoamericano*, which charges US$1.50 and has hot water in the mornings.

Going in the opposite direction from Plaza Santo Domingo along Calle Flores, you'll find some more hotels to choose from. *Huasi Continental* at Flores 330 and Sucre is recommended. It has spartan but clean rooms with private bathrooms and hot water for US$3 per person. *Residencial Bolívar* at Espejo 832 and Flores has clean, basic rooms for US$1.30 per person but their hot water supply is erratic. *Quitumbe* opposite at Espejo 815 is very clean and secure and has hot water but no private bathrooms. They charge US$3 each. *Hotel Viena* at Flores and Chile charges US$2 and has hot water; the *Viena Internacional* on the other corner is in the middle price category below. Further down is the *Hotel San Agustín* and *Los Canarios*, which charge US$2-4 per person depending on the rooms. Both hotels have hot water and are clean and good.

Two more budget hotels in the old town deserve mention. *Hotel Sucre* on the corner of Plaza San Francisco looks very good from the outside, and the basic rooms have some good views. They will provide you with hot water if you ask, charging only 80c per person. The rather charming *Ecuahotel* at Chile 1427 near Cuenca has a few rooms with good views and charges US$5 for a double room with a private bath.

There are a couple of good budget hotels away from the old town. *Residencial Marsella* at Los Rios and Castro just east of the Parque La Alameda, and *Residencial Italia* at 9 de Octubre 237 and 18 de Septiembre near Avenida Amazonas, both charge about US$2 per person and are clean, have hot water, are family run, and are recommended.

Places to Stay – middle

There are a few mid-range hotels in the old town, of which the *Viena Internacional* at the corner of Flores and Chile is one of the best. They charge about US$6 per person in very pleasant rooms with private bath, hot water, telephone and carpeting. Also good is the *Hotel Juana del Arco*, which has rooms with private showers for US$5 single and US$8 double. The *Auca Hotel* looks spartan and grim but has clean, small rooms with private bathrooms for US$9 single and US$12 double. The *Gran Casino* (see bottom-end hotels) is expanding into the *Gran Casino 2*, which is being built on 24 de Mayo and Bahía de Caráquez. They plan on providing clean, comfortable rooms with private baths for about US$7 each. A restaurant and discotheque is planned.

The best choice of mid-range hotels is in the new town. Most of these will provide full board if you ask them to. There are several good ones in the area between Avenida 10 de Agosto and the university. The cheapest is the *Hotel Versalles* at

Versalles 1442 and Marchena. They charge US$3.50 per person in rooms with a private bathroom. It's OK but nothing fancy. Better is the *Residencial Santa Clara* at Darquea Teran 1578 and 10 de Agosto. The *Residencial* is a pleasant-looking house and it's clean, comfortable and friendly. Rooms are available both with (US$5 per person) and without (US$4 per person) private bathrooms. Meals are available. The *Residencial Florida* at Versalles 1083 and Carrión is excellent value at US$6.50 single and US$10 double in rooms with private bath. Rooms with shared bath are also available cheaper. They are spotlessly clean and have good food in their cafeteria. Around the corner is the slightly more expensive but highly recommended *Residencial Carrión*, which is geared to long-staying guests. *Hotel Majestic* at Mercadillo 366 and Versalles has pleasant, clean rooms with private baths for US$8 single, US$13 double and US$17 triple. They have friendly staff but their hot water supply is sometimes erratic. (Isn't it everywhere?) Most of the hotels in this section are excellent value and highly popular. They are often full so try early in the day.

Two good hotels close to one another and large enough that they usually have rooms available are *Hotel Nueve de Octubre* at 1047 and the *Embajador* at 1046 Calle 9 de Octubre and Colón. They are both friendly and recommended. Rooms are about US$5 single and US$9 double with private showers. The *Nueve de Octubre* has some slightly more expensive rooms with carpets and telephones.

Finally, *Hotel Embassy*, in the heart of a quiet residential district at Presidente Wilson 441 and 6 de Diciembre, is highly recommended as being very good value – it could almost be called a top-end hotel. It is motel-like and rather lacks character, but the comfortable rooms are spotless and complete with carpeting, telephone and private bathroom. Their restaurant is recommended and they charge US$7.50 single and US$12 double.

Places to Stay – top end

The fanciest places in town are *Hotel Quito* on Avenida Amazonas at Patria, complete with shopping mall, casino, swimming pool, three restaurants, two bars, sauna, discotheque, etc, etc; *Hotel Quito*, similar but quieter and smaller on the end of Avenida 12 de Octubre with pleasant gardens; and the *Alameda Real*, which is on Amazonas at Roca and has rooms with private kitchens which can be rented by the week. These hotels charge about US$50 for a double room.

There are several 1st-class hotels which are much more economical. They are often booked up well ahead. One of the best is *Residencia Los Alpes*, in a beautiful old house at Tamayo 223 and Jorge Washington. Comfortable carpeted rooms with spotless bathrooms and a telephone run about US$14 single and US$21 double. Also good and recommended is *Residencial Cumbes Baqueadano* at Baqueadano 164 near 6 de Diciembre. It has clean rooms with private bathrooms for US$10 single and US$16 double. Breakfast is included.

Places to Eat

If you are economizing, it is best to stick to the standard *almuerzos* or *meriendas*. If you're staying at the *Hotel Gran Casino* then you'll find the prices there as cheap as anywhere. There are several cheap restaurants on the 1400 block of Roca-fuerte near the Plaza Santa Domingo. The good *Chifa Hong Kong* is at Guayaquil 1384 near the Plaza Sucre. They serve large and inexpensive portions. There are many other simple and inexpensive rest-aurants in the old town but most of them are unremarkable. The best restaurants are generally in the new town and cost a little more.

Quito is famous for its *cebiches* made of marinated seafood. One of the best *cebicherías* is *Las Redes* at Amazonas 845 and Veintimilla. Have the *cebiche mixta*; it's huge and delicious and costs about US$3. There are cheaper dishes. Other.

excellent seafood restaurants are *El Cebiche* at Juan León Mera 1232 and Calama, and *La Jaiba Mariscos* at Avenida Colón and Reina Victoria. Expect to pay about US$3 for a meal.

Avenida Amazonas is a good place to come and watch the world go by. *Manolo's* pavement café is one of the most popular places and it isn't exorbitant. They serve a decent cup of coffee and don't hassle you if you sit there for hours. It's an extremely popular meeting place. Manolo's is at Amazonas 420 and Robles and there are several similar places nearby. The cafe-terias on the 500 block of Amazonas are inexpensive. Manolo's is also worth bearing in mind as one of the few places in Quito which is open 24 hours. So is the *Colón Cafeteria*, which is not very expensive considering that it is in one of the capital's most luxurious hotels.

Good, typical Ecuadorean food in elegant surroundings can be eaten at *La Choza* at 12 de Octubre and Cordero. You can eat well here for about US$3. Of course, it's much cheaper at a market, but if you have a delicate stomach you can eat here and not get sick. Another place to try 'safe' Ecuadorean food is the *Taberna Quiteña*. There are two locations and they have entertainment at weekends (see Entertainment section.)

For dining with a view of the city you can go to the *Panecillo* restaurant. It's quite elegant and medium priced rather than expensive. The food is OK but the service slow. Better service and a superb view is had at the *La Terraza del Tartaro* on the top floor of the Edificio Amazonas building at Avenida Amazonas and Veint-imilla. An elevator at the back of the lobby will take you up (press button 2 and you automatically get taken to the top floor). This is a classy place and you can expect to pay about US$6-7 each for a meal with a view.

If you like steak, the *Casa de Mi Abuela* at Luis Cordero 1922 and 10 de Agosto is excellent. Steaks are about US$4. Cheaper, and locally popular, is the *Columbus Steak*

Top: Monastery of San Francisco, Quito (RR)
Left: Presidential Palace guard, Quito (RR)
Right: Independence Plaza, Quito (RR)

Top: Author researching Quito nightlife in Taberna Quiteña (RR)
Left: Old Quito and Mt Cayambe (RR)
Right: Virgin of Quito, Panecillo (RR)

House on Avenida Colón at Amazonas. It's good, but don't expect anything but meat. Their *parrilladas* are recommended.

Even the most expensive restaurants in Quito are inexpensive by European standards. You can get a lobster dinner for US$6 in the best restaurants. The most expensive part of any meal will be wine. Ecuadorean wine is not good and imported wine is expensive. While a full meal including hors d'oeuvres and dessert will cost US$10-12 in even the most expensive restaurant, a single bottle of mediocre wine will be more expensive than the meal. If you want to treat yourself to a good meal in elegant surroundings I recommend the *Excalibur* at Calama 380 and Juan León Mera.

Entertainment

Quito is not the world's most exciting capital for nightlife. Read the newspapers for exact details of what is going on. *El Comercio* has the most thorough coverage.

Entertainment reaches its height during the various fiestas. The founding of Quito is celebrated throughout the first week in December and there are bullfights at the Plaza de Toros, just beyond the intersection of Avenida América and 10 de Agosto. There is also street-dancing on the night of 6 December. New Year's Eve is celebrated by erecting life-sized puppets in the streets and burning them at midnight. These puppets are often very elaborate and usually represent politicians. Carnival, which is a movable Catholic feast, is celebrated by intense water fights – no one is spared. Colourful religious processions are held during Easter week.

On a day-to-day basis, films provide cheap and good entertainment. There are some 20 cinemas and at least some of them show good English-language films with Spanish subtitles. The cinemas which consistently show the best films seem to be the *Cine Colón* at the intersection of Avenida Colón and 10 de Agosto, and the *Universitario* at the Indoamerican Plaza on Avenida América

at Perez Guerrero. Other cinemas also show good films once in a while. For their addresses look in the white pages of the telephone directory under 'Cine' or 'Teatro.' Entrance is only about 60c.

If your Spanish is up to it, you can see a play at the *Teatro Sucre* on Guayaquil in the old town, or the *Teatro Prometeo* on Avenida 6 de Diciembre behind the Casa de Cultura in the new town. The Prometeo is the cheapest and sometimes has mime performances which anyone can understand.

Nightlife is usually expensive. Often there is a cover charge or a minimum consumption and you may be expected to wear a jacket or skirt. To listen to local music inexpensively you can go to the *Taberna Quiteña*, which has music on weekends and has no cover. They serve typical Ecuadorean food and aren't cheap but you don't have to order much. They have two locations. In the old town they are at Calle Manabí and Luis Vargas and in the new town at Avenida Amazonas 1259 and Colón. Both have a 'cellar bar' atmosphere. The one in the old town usually has a greater variety of musicians. They often wander from table to table and ask you if you want to hear a request in Spanish. On Avenida Universitaria in front of the university is the *Nuca Canchi Peña*, also good for local music. Other places advertise in the newspaper and are more expensive.

A bar you might want to try for contemporary music is the *Reina Victoria* on the street of the same name near Calle Roca. It's American-run and a place to meet some of the local English-speaking community. They have music evenings about once a week – usually on a weekday – a dart board and an English pub atmosphere. It's not cheap. Another English pub is *El Pub*, next to the British Embassy on Avenida F G Suarez at the end of Avenida 12 de Octubre – again not cheap.

The best hotels have expensive nightclubs and discotheques.

Shopping

The main shopping street in the old town is Calle Guayaquil. Here you can buy most kinds of Ecuadorean handicrafts. There are also handicraft shops around the main plazas and along La Ronda. Bargaining is acceptable and expected.

There are many good stores for souvenir hunters in the new town along and near Avenida Amazonas. If buying on the streets (there are street stalls and ambulatory vendors) you should bargain. In the fancier stores, prices are sometimes fixed, though it does no harm to try bargaining. The better stores are usually more expensive but not necessarily exorbitant, and the items for sale are often top quality. The best, and definitely the most expensive, is the store of designer Olga Fisch, at Avenida Colón 260. At Calle Urbina 111 and Cordero (near the intersection of Avenidas Colón and 6 de Diciembre) is the much cheaper – and highly recommended – Productos Andinos Indian cooperative. Looking in these two shops will give you a good idea of prices and quality. The best place to buy the colourful T-shirts popularly called 'Galápagos T-shirts' – but in fact decorated with various Ecuadorean motifs – is Cosas at Calle Juan León Mera 838.

Getting There

Air There is an international airport departure tax of US$5 payable in either US dollars or sucres. If you are flying internationally, confirm 72 hours in advance, reconfirm 24 hours in advance, and arrive at the airport two hours before your flight. You will probably take off several hours late, but at least you'll be on the flight. The local representatives of international airlines are notorious for bumping you off their frequently overbooked flights – 'Sorry, señor, you're not on the computer.'

There is no departure tax for internal flights, most of which are run by TAME. The exception are flights to Guayaquil and Cuenca, which are also operated by SAN-Saeta. The two airlines will accept one another's tickets if their flights aren't full and if you paid for the ticket with cash. Internal flights (except for the Galápagos) are cheap. Flights to Guayaquil (US$16) leave four to 10 times a day, most frequently on weekdays. Flights to Cuenca (US$16) go one to three times daily.

Only TAME operates services to the following cities: Tulcán (US$8) Monday to Friday mornings; Esmeraldas (US$10) Monday to Saturday mornings; Portoviejo (US$13) Monday and Friday afternoons; Manta (US$13) Monday to Saturday mornings and Sunday afternoons; Macas (US$12) Monday and Friday about midday; Coca (US$11) Monday, Wednesday and Friday mornings; Lago Agrio (US$10) Monday to Saturday mornings; Tarapoa Tuesday and Thursday mornings. To get to Loja you have to connect at Guayaquil but TAME recently announced that they were planning a thrice-weekly service direct from Quito so ask them about this if you're planning on a trip there. Other cities which can be reached from Quito with connections at Guayaquil are Machala and Macará.

The Galápagos are reached from Quito by TAME flights every morning except Sunday. There is usually a change at Guayaquil but your luggage is transferred. The return cost is about US$350 for non-Ecuadorean residents.

The TAME ticket office nearest the old town is at Avenida 10 de Agosto 239. In the new town there is also an office at the corner of Avenida Colón and Reina Victoria. SAN-Saeta has an office at Avenida Colón 535 and 6 de Diciembre, at Avenida Colombia 610, and at Guayaquil 1228 and Olmedo in the old town. In addition, you can buy domestic air tickets from most reputable travel agents at the same cost as direct from the airlines.

Several international airlines have offices in Quito. Almost all of them are on Avenida Amazonas, and many – including Ecuatoriana, Aeroperu, KLM, Eastern and Avianca – are at Amazonas and Jorge Washington.

Rail The famous Quito-Guayaquil train has been suspended since the 1982/83 El Niño floods which destroyed about 80 km of track. It is not known when, if ever, services will resume. Meanwhile there is a daily *autoferro* to Riobamba. It leaves Quito at 2 pm and goes via Latacunga (30c, two hours), Ambato (50c, 3½ hours), to Riobamba (70c, five hours). The train is crowded and you should buy tickets in advance. The ticket booth often doesn't open until an hour before departure and there is a mad scramble. Tickets for the next day's train are sold only reluctantly and with persuasion. The train station is on Avenida P Vicente Maldonado near Llanganates, about two km south of the old town. Most buses to the Terminal Terrestre go there. There is a railway booking office in the old town on Calle Bolívar 443 and Benalcázar, but it remains closed while the line to Guayaquil is down.

Metropolitan Touring (Avenida Amazonas 239) operates a very expensive tourist train trip which includes an overnight at a first-class Riobamba hotel.

Bus At this time the main bus terminal is about five km south of the old town. Most buses to the south, east and west leave from here. It is called the Terminal Terrestre del Sur and is reached by taxi (US$1-2 depending on how far north you are) or by city buses marked 'Terminal Terrestre.' The No 10 from the university along 10 de Agosto, Guayaquil, through Plaza Santo Domingo, goes to the terminal. Also, the No 2 from Avenida Colón to 10 de Agosto continues on a similar route to within three blocks of the terminal.

There are about two dozen bus companies with offices at the terminal. There is also an information window which will tell you which company goes where, although it's fairly obvious. Walk around the small terminal and compare departures. Usually there are several companies serving the same destination at different times. For the most popular destinations you'll find

driver's assistants outside the terminal building hustling passengers for their bus. Only buses departing within a few minutes are allowed to park outside the terminal so you can often be on your way within minutes of arriving. If you do find you have to wait, there is a snack bar. Usually it is easy enough to get onto the bus you want, but if you plan on travelling during holiday periods and just before the weekend it's best to go to the terminal and book in advance.

With literally hundreds of buses departing during the day, it is impossible to give accurate timetables. There are several buses a day to most destinations, and some places – such as Ambato – have two or three departures an hour. Here is a list of the major destinations served and the approximate cost and length of a journey.

The bus ride to Cuenca is over poor roads, and service is erratic.

to	cost	hours
Ambato	US$1	3
Bahía de Caráquez	US$3.50	8
Baños	US$1.30	3½
Coca	US$3	13
Cuenca	US$3-4	9-14
Guaranda	US$1.50	5
Guayaquil	US$2.60	8
Lago Agrio	US$2.60	10
Latacunga	US$0.80	2
Loja	US$4.50	18
Machala	US$3.40	11
Manta	US$3.50	8
Portoviejo	US$3.50	8
Puyo	US$1.80	8
Riobamba	US$1.40	4
Santo Domingo	US$1	2½
Tena	US$2.60	9

For other destinations, you may have to go to the nearest major city and change. Enquire at the bus offices.

Northbound buses do not leave from the Terminal Terrestre. There are several terminals for the north; the majority of them are clustered together in three or four blocks of the streets to the north-west of the Parque El Ejido. Calles 18 de Septiembre and Manuel Larrea are the places to go to find frequent buses for Otavalo (75c, 2½ hours), Ibarra (90c, three hours) and Tulcán (US$1.50, 5½ hours). Buses often leave as soon as they are full and few companies will sell tickets in advance. Buses from here also go to Santo Domingo and Esmeraldas (US$2.20, six hours). Transportes Esmeraldas also has frequent departures from the old town at Avenida 24 de Mayo and García Moreno.

A few other companies have offices in the old town, which could save you a trip to the Terminal Terrestre. Just down from Plaza Santo Domingo at Avenida P Vicente Maldonado 3263 are Supertaxis Cuenca, which have 14-seater minibuses costing US$3.50 for a fast nine-hour trip to Cuenca at 1.45 pm and 9 pm. They also have minibuses to Guayaquil at 8.30 am and 2 pm. Further down the street at Maldonado 3075 is a ticket office for Panamericana, which has buses for Machala. You buy the ticket in advance here and the bus leaves from the Terminal Terrestre. Two blocks further, at Maldonado 2822, is Cooperativa Transportes Ecuador, which has 20 buses a day to Guayaquil.

Near here is the site of the Cumandá Terminal de Buses. This terminal is brand new and was due to open in 1985 but is still under construction. It is expected that buses for most destinations will leave from there – maybe it'll be operational by the time you read this.

There is one other bus office to be aware of. Transportes Occidentales on Avenida 24 de Mayo and García Moreno has two buses to Machala every evening.

There are companies (for example TEPSA) which will sell international bus tickets to Peru or Colombia. Avoid these. The tickets are very expensive and you still have to change buses at the border. Once across the border you often find that only one company will accept your ticket and you can wait for hours until they depart. It's much cheaper and far more convenient to buy tickets as you go.

Getting Around

Airport Quito International Airport terminal is on Avenida de la Prensa about 10 km north of the old town centre. The easiest way to get there by public transport is aboard the blue double-decker London buses which begin from the Casa de Cultura and run along Avenida Amazonas to the airport. The journey in either direction costs only 5c but the bus does not run after dark. Other buses which go to the airport tend to be more crowded. They are usually marked by an 'Aeropuerto' placard. The No 1 Villa Flora-Iñaquito bus runs from Plaza Santo Domingo in the old town to the airport. A taxi costs about US$2.50.

Services at the airport terminal include tourist information, money exchange, cafeteria/bar, post office, IETEL international telephone office and gift shops. The telephone number for airport information is 241580.

Bus The crowded local buses have a flat fare of 5c which you pay as you board. Generally speaking, buses run north-south and have a fixed route. The drivers are usually helpful and will tell you which bus to take if they are not going to your destination. Traffic in the old town is very heavy and you may often find it faster to walk than to take a bus, especially during the rush hours. Buses have both a name and a number, and although they usually have a fixed route, this may vary because of heavy traffic, road repair or the whim of the driver. The narrow streets of downtown are usually one-way. Calles Guayaquil and Venezuela are one-way into the old town towards the Panecillo, and Calles García Moreno and Flores are one-way out of the old town and away from the Panecillo. There are about 40 different routes. A selection of the ones you might use follows:

Iñaquito-Villa Flora Airport – 10 de Agosto – Guayaquil – Santo Domingo – Maldonado – Villa Flora

Colón-Camal Coruña – Colón – 10 de Agosto –
Guayaquil – Santo Domingo – Maldonado –
Camal (three blocks from Terminal Terrestre)
Colmena-Batan La Colmena – 24 de Mayo –
García Moreno – Vargas Torres – Manuel
Larrea – Patria – Juan León Mera – Colón – 6 de
Diciembre – El Batan
Marin-Cotocollao Plaza Marin – 10 de Agosto –
Airport – Cotocollao
Ermita-Las Casas Ermita – 24 de Mayo –
García Moreno – América – University – La
Gasca – Las Casas
San Bartolo-Miraflores San Bartolo – Terminal
Terrestre – Maldonado – Santo Domingo – 10
de Agosto – 18 de Septiembre – Miraflores
El Tejar-El Inca El Tejar – Mejía – La Alameda
– 6 de Diciembre – El Inca (end of 6 de
Diciembre)
Marin-Quito Norte Plaza Marin – 10 de Agosto
– Airport – North Quito
Blue Airport Bus Airport – Avenida Amazonas –
Patria

Some minibuses cost a few cents extra.

Taxi Although a law was passed in 1984
requiring Quito cabs to have meters, many
still don't have them and you have to
arrange the price beforehand. Sometimes
this is to your advantage, as it enables the
driver to take a roundabout route to avoid
traffic thus saving both of you time. Taxi
cabs are all yellow. They can be hired for
several hours or for a day. If you bargain
hard, you could hire a cab for a day for
about US$25 if you don't plan on going
very far. Short journeys downtown cost

from about 60c. To the airport is about
US$2-4 depending on how far south you
are.

Car Rental Car rental in Quito, as elsewhere
in Ecuador, is expensive. There are car-
rental offices at the airport. Expect to pay
at least US$30 per day and make sure that
mileage and adequate insurance are
included.

AROUND QUITO

The most famous excursion is to the
equator at Mitad del Mundo about 22 km
north of Quito. Here there is a large stone
monument and a museum which was
recently closed for restoration but should
be open soon. En route to the equator, the
road passes an intriguing highway art
gallery. Famous Latin American artists
have painted roadside billboards with
weatherproof paint; the works, some two
dozen of them, are stretched out along the
highway. To get there, take a Mitad del
Mundo bus, which leaves about every half
hour from Calle Cuenca at Chile, and
continue north out of town along Avenida
América. The journey takes about an hour
and costs about 15c. A taxi, including
waiting time at the monument, will cost
less than US$10.

The Indian market nearest the capital is
the Sangolquí Sunday morning market.
Frequent local buses go there from Plaza
Marin at Calle Chile and M de Solanda.

North of Quito

The Andean highlands north of Quito are one of the most popular destinations in Ecuador. Few travellers spend any time in the country without visiting the famous Indian market at the small town of Otavalo, where you can buy a wide variety of weavings, clothing and handicrafts. Though many travellers limit their visit to just Otavalo, there is much more to see in the region. The dramatic mountain scenery is dotted with shining white churches set in tiny villages, and includes views of Cayambe, the third highest peak in the country, as well as a beautiful lake district. Several small towns are noted for speciality handicrafts such as woodcarving or leatherwork. Ibarra is a small, charmingly somnolent colonial city worth visiting, both in its own right and as the beginning of the Ibarra-San Lorenzo railway linking the northern highlands with the coast. If you are travelling overland to or from Colombia, it's almost impossible to avoid this region.

CALDERÓN

About 10 km north of Quito on the Pan American highway is the village of Calderón, famous as the best centre of a unique Ecuadorean folk art. Here they make decorations of bread dough ranging from small statuettes to colourful Christmas tree ornaments (such as stars, parrots, angels and tortoises). The ornaments make practical gifts as they are small, unusual and cheap (about 10c each). Some figurines are used for All Soul's Day ceremonies in Calderón and many other Andean villages – it is thought that the figurines represented animal or human sacrifices in pre-conquest times. These are decorative figures and are inedible; preservatives are added to them and they'll last some years. Calderón is a small village so you won't have any difficulty finding many stores on the one main

street. There is nowhere to stay and no proper restaurants.

NORTH TO CAYAMBE

Beyond Calderón the road descends in a series of magnificent sweeps towards the village of Guayllabamba, located in a fertile river valley of the same name and famous for its produce. Roadside stalls offer huge avocados and that strangely reptilian-looking Andean fruit, the *chirimoya*. It's a member of the custard apple family, and perhaps the nearest translation is the sweetsop – I prefer the Spanish name. Its nobbly green skin is discarded and you eat the white pulp inside. The chirimoya definitely tastes better than it looks or sounds.

Some three km beyond Guayllabamba, the road forks and you can take either fork as they both end at Cayambe. About 10 km along the right-hand road you pass a turnoff to the right which leads back to Quito via a roundabout route. (This takes you through Quinche, famous for the Virgin and paintings inside the church, and on through pretty countryside and tiny hamlets to Pifo. Here you turn right and return to Quito via Tumbaco.) A few km further you cross the equator, marked by a monument consisting of a large concrete globe which is much less visited than the ever popular 'Mitad del Mundo' monument north of Quito. Soon you cross the railway tracks of the now defunct Quito-Ibarra train, and 60 km from Quito you reach Cayambe.

The left-hand route, although a little shorter, is somewhat more twisting and slower than the right-hand route; therefore some drivers avoid it. It also crosses the equator but at time of writing there was no marker. It is generally less inhabited and has more barren countryside than the other road. I prefer it for the exciting drive and wild scenery. The only village of any size on this road is Tabacundo. A few km before Tabacundo is a turnoff to the left which leads to Tocachi and the ruins of Cochasquí. These were built by the Cara Indians before the Inca conquest and had been largely forgotten until recently. The area was declared a national archaeological site in 1977 and is currently being excavated and investigated. There are thought to be 15 pyramids, some of which are almost 100 metres long, but there is little to see for the casual visitor and there are no facilities or public transport.

CAYAMBE

Cayambe (population 14,000) is the most important town on the way to Otavalo. It is famous for its dairy industry and there are many stores and restaurants selling a variety of local cheeses and cheese products. Although this is the nearest town of any size to the equator, few people stay here, preferring instead to buy some cheese and continue to Otavalo. Accommodation is limited to the brand new *Hostería Mitad del Mundo* on the south end of town – it looks a bit pricey and there really isn't much reason to stay in Cayambe anyway.

It is a further 50 km to Otavalo. The snow-capped mountain to the right of the road is the extinct volcano of Cayambe, which at 5790 metres is Ecuador's third highest peak. For trivia buffs it is the highest point in the world through which the equator directly passes – at about 4600 metres on the south side. The road climbs and crosses the provincial line from Pichincha to Imbabura, a province known for its lake district. Soon you see the largest of these lakes, Lago San Pablo, stretching away to your right with the high peak of Imbabura (4609 metres) behind it. The area is dotted with many simple villages inhabited by the Otavaleño Indians.

OTAVALO

This small town of some 17,500 inhabitants is justly famous for its friendly people and their Saturday market. The market dates back to pre-Inca times when jungle products were brought up from the eastern lowlands and traded for highland goods. Today's market has two different functions: the local market for buying and bartering animals, food and other essentials; and the crafts market for the tourists.

The story of the phenomenal success of the Otavalen'o weavers is an intriguing one. Their ability as weavers was harshly exploited by the colonialists and later the Ecuadorean landowners who forced them to labour in *obrajes* or sweatshops, often for 14 or more hours a day. Miserable though this was, it did have the effect of instilling a great knowledge of weaving into the Otavaleño people. In 1917 a local weaver had the idea of copying the Scottish tweeds that were then in vogue and this was so successful that it led to recognition of the ability of the Otavaleño weavers. This ability, combined with a shrewd business sense, has made the Otavaleños the most prosperous Indian group in Ecuador and perhaps on the continent. It is difficult to find a town of any size which does not have an Otavaleño store. They also make frequent business trips to neighbouring countries and even to North America and Europe.

The goods they sell are undeniably oriented towards the tourist market and this has led to recent complaints from 'real travellers' that the market is too 'touristified.' This seems to me a kind of reverse snobbism that reveals a lack of concern for the well-being of the weavers. Their prosperity in a changing and difficult world is only to be applauded, but a truer measure of their success is perhaps not only their prosperity but their continuing sense of tribal identity and tradition.

One of the most evident features of the Otavaleños' cultural integrity is the traditional way of dress. This is not just put on specially for the tourists at the Saturday market, but is worn on normal workdays in their houses, villages and fields. The men are immediately noticeable because of

Otavalo

their long single pigtails, calf-length white pants, rope sandals, reversible grey or blue ponchos and dark felt hats. The women are very striking with beautifully embroidered blouses, long black skirts and shawls, and interesting head cloths whose colour and style of folding denotes marital status. The women also enjoy wearing bright jewellery; the most obvious are the many strings of gold-coloured blown glass beads around their necks, and bracelets consisting of long strands of red beads.

Of the 17,500 inhabitants of Otavalo, the majority are whites or mestizos. There are about 35,000 Indians, most of whom live in the many nearby villages and come into Otavalo for market day. Quite a few Indians own stores in Otavalo however, and you can buy most items here if you are unable to visit on market day.

Money

You are strongly advised to bring as much as you think you'll need from Quito. If you must change money, try the Banco del Pichincha on the main plaza. They usually accept cash dollars and travellers' cheques at about 5% below the Quito rate, but it's difficult to negotiate many other currencies (though Colombian pesos are accepted). Some of the better hotels will exchange dollars at an unfavourable rate but normally you have to stay there. It's worth trying to buy souvenirs with cash dollars – often the Indians like to have a little stash of hard currency.

Post & Phone

The post office and IETEL office for local and international calls and telex service are all found together on the García Moreno side of the main plaza.

Bookshops

There are several bookstores which sporadically sell Otavalo maps or guides, though none were available when I was

1 Hotel Yamor Continental	23 Bar Huasipungo
2 Fire Station	24 Pensión Residencial Los Andes
3 Peña de los Chaskis	25 Residencia Otavalo
4 Ali Micui Restaurant	26 Camba Huasy Chicken Restaurant
5 Residencial Centenario	27 Stationary & Restaurant
6 Bahai Institute	Copacabana
7 Parenthese Restaurant	28 Banco Del Pichincha
8 Residencia Samar-Huasy	29 Royal Restaurant Cafeteria & Camba
9 Public toilet	Huasy Fuente de Soda (ice-cream)
10 Hat shop	30 Mama Rosita Restaurant
11 Residencial El Indio	31 Café El Triunfo
12 Pensión Vaca 2	32 Police Station
13 Residencial La Herradura	33 Drug Store
14 Pollo Koko Rico Chicken	34 IETEL & Post Office
Restaurant	35 Chifa Tien An Men
15 El Mesón de Arragon Re	36 Casa de Korea Restaurant
16 Residencias Santa Ana	37 Hotel Otavalo &
17 Residencial Colón	Golden Eagle Restaurant
18 Local villages bus departures	38 Riviera-Sucre Hotel
19 Cockfight Stadium	39 Apollo Theatre
20 Restaurant Centro Latino (chicken)	40 Chifa Restaurant Pekin
21 Cine Bolívar	41 Industria Papelera Stationer
22 Transportes Otavalo	

last there in early 1985. The largest in town is the *Papelería Universal* on Bolívar at Piedranita. There is also a bookstore on Bolívar at the corner of the main plaza, and there are other stationers.

The Market

The main market day is Saturday. There are three main plazas, with the overflow spilling out onto the streets linking them. The Poncho Plaza is where the goods of most appeal to tourists are sold. Here you can buy woolen goods such as ponchos, blankets, scarves, sweaters, tapestries and gloves as well as a variety of embroidered blouses and shirts, shawls, string bags, rope sandals. Bargaining for every purchase is expected. If you buy several items from the same person, you can easily expect a discount of 20% or even more if you are good at bargaining. Some people aren't good at it and feel uncomfortable trying to knock a few sucres off an already cheaply priced item. Just remember that it is expected and make an offer a little below the first asking price (assuming you want to buy the thing). This market gets underway soon after dawn and continues until about noon. It can get rather crowded in mid-morning when the big tour groups arrive. If you come in the early morning there's a greater selection.

The food market sells produce and household goods for the locals, and there is an animal market beginning in the pre-dawn hours (4 to 8 am) on the outskirts of town. These are not designed for tourists but you are welcome to visit them; many people find the sight of poncho-clad Indians quietly bartering for a string of screaming piglets much more interesting than the Poncho Plaza. The animal market is over by early morning, however, so you should plan on an early arrival. It lies over a km out of town – cross the bridge at the end of Morales and follow the crowds to get there.

Fiestas

24 June is St John the Baptist Day, and 29 June is the Day of Sts Peter and Paul. These and the intervening days are an important fiesta for Otavalo and the surrounding villages. There is a bullfight in town and a boating regatta on Lago San Pablo, as well as celebrations in nearby Ilumán. A few km south of Otavalo, on the southern shores of Lago San Pablo, is the village of San Rafael, which has a fiesta on 19 August. Otavalo's best-known fiesta is held in the first two weeks of September. The *Fiesta del Yamor*, as it is known, consists of plenty of music, processions and dancing as well as firework displays, cockfights and election of the Queen of the Fiesta. Precise dates of these can vary from year to year but they are usually well publicised and you can find out what's going on from posters. In addition, there are the usual feast days celebrated throughout the land.

Places to Stay – bottom end

Because Otavalo is such a popular destination, there are many more places to stay than in other, bigger, but less interesting towns. Despite this, it can get rather crowded on Friday nights so arrive early for the best choice. Most places are quite cheap, and new hotels open frequently. If you arrive midweek and plan to stay a few days, a cheaper price can often be negotiated – but late Friday night isn't a good time to expect any favours.

One of the most popular cheapies is the friendly *Residencias Santa Ana*, which is small and tends to fill up quickly. Beds are about US$1 each in quads, and a few cents more in the singles and doubles – but these go really fast. Most of the rooms are large, there's a pretty courtyard, and there are hot (or tepid) showers. A rather larger and also friendly place is the *Pensión Otavalo*. Actually, it's not that much bigger but the rooms are smaller so there's more of them. There's hot water at times and prices are from US$1.20 to 1.50 per person.

The *Residencia Samar-Huasy* is conveniently located half a block from the Poncho Plaza and seems to be gaining popularity recently. The management is friendly and there are many clean rooms. The water is cold and maybe that's why it's only US$1 each. The *Pensión Vaca No 2* has been recommended as good, cheap, clean and with hot water, but I've never visited it. Both *Hotel Riviera-Sucre* and *Residencial La Herradura* are pretty good, with clean rooms, friendly staff, hot showers, and a restaurant in the latter. About US$1.50 each.

The *Residencial El Indio* is a brand-new hotel which has recently opened just off the Poncho Plaza. Because it's new, it's bound to be clean. There's a restaurant and they plan to add rooms with private baths. Rooms with shared baths (hot water) are about US$2 each. If there's no room at any of the above you can try the *Pensión Los Andes* or *Residencial Colón,* which are cheap and basic – I haven't heard any rave reviews about them.

Places to Stay – middle

There's only one better hotel in the town centre, *Hotel Otavalo* (as opposed to the cheap *Pensión Otavalo*). It's clean – in fact last time I was in there it smelt overpoweringly of wax polish – and has rooms with private baths for about US$12 a double. There's a good restaurant. They recommend reservations for the weekend and you can call them at Otavalo 416.

I prefer the *Hotel Yamor Continental* (tel Otavalo 451), which has clean and spacious rooms in a hacienda-like building set in charming flower-filled gardens at the north-east end of town. Supposedly there is a pool – but it's more like an ornamental pond. There's a good restaurant and bar. Rooms with private bath are about US$10 (same price for one or two people). Hot water only runs in the evening and early mornings and you have to make sure that they turn it on; it can take half an hour to warm up. Taxis from the bus station are about 75c or you can

walk in less than half an hour. They are only 10 minutes from the Poncho Plaza.

Places to Stay – top end

Although there aren't any top-notch hotels in Otavalo, there are three good hotels in nearby San Pablo, either by the lake or near the village. On the southern outskirts of the village is the very popular *Hostería Cusín,* which is in a beautiful converted 17th-century hacienda with all the old trimmings. They are only open at weekends and usually booked well ahead. About US$25 for a double with bath, superb home-cooked set meals in the restaurant, a charming bar, beautiful gardens and horses for riding. Call the San Pablo operator and ask to be connected to the Cusín or write to Señora Crichton at the hotel, San Pablo, Imbabura, for reservations. English is spoken at the hotel. In addition, there are the slightly more expensive *Hostal Chicapan* and *Cabañas del Lago,* whose main attraction is their location by the lake. They are modern and comfortable.

Places to Eat

Ali Micui's, on the corner of the Poncho Plaza, is undoubtedly the favourite gringo hangout. They serve both vegetarian and non-vegetarian food. The selection is excellent, the prices reasonable, and the service usually very slow. The restaurant serves dishes made with *quinua,* an Andean grain with a very high protein content and an important traditional food of the Incas. It's rarely found these days. Their banana bread is excellent. Micui's is also a good place to meet people.

If you're on a really tight budget, *Mama Rosita's* is basic and cheap and has been recommended for pancakes. Another cheapie you might try is the *Copacabana* on the main plaza. During the day the stalls at the market are probably the cheapest of all. If you just want a snack, there's the *Royal Cafetería* and *Camba Huasy Fuente de Soda* for ice cream. They are next door to one another on the main plaza.

The *chifas* are, as usual, excellent value and there are several in town. The best is the excellent *Casa de Korea*. *Tien An Men* is also good. For a change you might try the new *Chifa Pekin* – let me know if it's any good. If you're after fried chicken, you'll find a few chicken restaurants marked on the map. None of them seem especially noteworthy.

The most expensive and fanciest restaurant is *El Mesón del Arrayon*, but it's not always open mid-week. Out on the road to the animal market is a new 'French' restaurant, *Parenthese*. It was closed when I last went there for lunch, but you could try it for supper. The restaurants at the better hotels are also worth bearing in mind.

Entertainment

Otavalo is a quiet place during the week but gets livelier on the weekend. There are two movie theatres (see map) with some English-language films. Many people like to hang out at *Ali Micui's* restaurant where you can meet other travellers and read the bulletin board to see what's going on. On Friday and Saturday nights there's a *peña* at *Los Chaskis* which doesn't get under way until after 10 pm and costs about US$1. The music and ambience can vary from abysmal to quite good but there's not much else to do anyway. Finally, there's the weekly cockfight which costs a few cents and is held in the ring at the end of 31 de Octubre every Saturday afternoon about 3 pm.

Getting There & Around

Rail There is a railway station, though trains no longer run to Quito. They do run to Ibarra. At this time there are daily departures at 8 am, 1 pm and 5 pm. The fare is about 10c – half the bus fare – and the trip supposedly takes about an hour. The train is uncomfortable, slow and utilized by the very poorest people – but it might well be a lot of fun. Watch your possessions.

Bus From Quito to Otavalo is totally straightforward. There are several companies and they leave frequently. Go to the area underneath the flyover at Avenida Perez Guerrero and Avenida 10 de Agosto, at the corner of Parque El Ejido in the new town. There are four or five companies located within two blocks. They all charge about 75c for the two– or three-hour ride. If you don't like the departure schedule of one company, go around the corner to the next. They won't sell you tickets in advance. Just turn up when you want to travel and you'll be on your way within an hour.

Reaching the villages of Calderón, Guayllabamba and Cayambe mentioned earlier in this section is not straightforward. The bus companies running between Quito and Otavalo normally don't sell tickets to intermediate points. You can buy a full-price ticket to or from Otavalo and get off where you want, assuming that you know where to get off or speak enough Spanish to explain to the driver. You'll be dropped off at the turnoff from the main road and will have to walk several hundred metres to the village. Some buses run to these villages direct from Quito but they don't leave from the main bus terminals. It's best to catch one of these by standing on the side of the road. A good place to stand is on Avenida 10 de Agosto where it intersects with Avenida Juan de Ascaray near the bull ring in Quito. Flag down any bus that has a sign indicating it's going where you want to go or that looks like it could use some passengers. Start early enough in the day so that you won't get stuck somewhere at nightfall and you'll probably have plenty of adventures.

From the northern towns of Ibarra or Tulcán you'll find buses leaving for Otavalo every hour or so from the respective Terminal Terrestres.

In Otavalo, the main bus terminal is at the strangely named Plaza Copacabana, where you'll probably arrive from Quito. There is a taxi rank if you need it; 50c will take you to most hotels. This is where you catch return buses to Quito and also old local buses to some of the villages south of Otavalo such as San Pablo del Lago. A couple of blocks away, on Avenida Calderón, you'll find Transportes Otavalo, which has frequent buses to Ibarra (about 20c) where you change for buses further north. There are no buses direct to Tulcán at this time. Transportes Otavalo also has Quito-bound buses.

Further down Avenida Calderón, at the intersection with Avenida 31 de Octubre, you'll find a bunch of rather decrepit buses with people waiting hopefully in them. This is a good place to find out about bus services to Cotacachi, Apuela and many of the remoter towns and villages. There is no strict schedule and prices are low. Adventurous travellers might just want to get aboard and see what happens – but leave yourself enough time to get back to a hotel, as most of these villages have absolutely no accommodation.

Taxi You can always hire a taxi from Quito for a few hours and have them take you exactly where you want to go. A taxi for all day can easily be had for US$50 or less if you have any bargaining ability – not too bad if you split it three or four ways.

AROUND OTOVALO
Most of the Indians live and work in the nearby villages of Peguche, Quinchuquí and Ilumán, which are loosely strung together on the north-east side of the Pan American highway a few km away from Otavalo.

Peguche
A popular walk is out of Otavalo to the north and then east off the main highway – you'll be in Peguche in about an hour. Some people go in the hopes of being invited into the Indians' houses and buying the best weavings direct from the loom at bargain prices. That's wishful thinking. Prices aren't much (if at all)

lower than Otavalo's, and people have better things to do than invite curious gringos into their houses. On the other hand, the locals are friendly and you might be lucky – especially if you speak Spanish.

Agato
Another possible village to visit is Agato on the east side of Lago San Pablo, where you can find Co-operativa Tahuantisuyo. They make traditional weavings on back-strap looms and use only natural dyes and products. These weavings are much more expensive than the market weavings, however, and are mainly for those seriously interested in textiles.

San Pablod del Lago
If you wish to continue around the lake, you'll find beautiful views of both the lake and Mt Imbabura behind it. You pass through the village of San Pablo del Lago where there are several good hotels and end up on the Pan American highway. Although people are generally friendly, you should bear in mind that on Saturday afternoons after the market and on Sundays some of the Indians get blind drunk (as happens throughout the Andes) and you may find this an inopportune time for visiting.

COTACACHI
This small village is famous for its leatherwork and is located some 15 km north of Otavalo. Stores are strung out all along the main street and you can find almost anything you might want in the way of leather goods. Market day is Saturday. Most tourists just pay a quick visit to the stores and return to Ibarra or Otavalo but if you wander around to the right of the main street you'll find an attractive main plaza.

Places to Stay & Eat
There's only one hotel, *El Mesón de las Flores*, and it costs about US$15 for a double with private bath. It's at the corners of García Moreno and Sucre, tel

Cotacachi 101. The building is over two centuries old and there is a bar/restaurant. There's also a cheaper restaurant at the corner of the small plaza on the main road.

Getting There
From Otavalo there are buses about every hour.

LAGUNA CUICOCHA
Driving east some 18 km from Cotacachi, you come to an ancient, eroded volcano famous for the deep lake found in the crater. Cheap boat rides (30c) are available to take you on a half-hour trip around the islands on the lake. On sunny weekends it is often popular with some of the poorer locals who seem to think this is a great way to spend their leisure time. Just watching everyone hanging around waiting for a boat can be more interesting than the ride itself. The view of the lake and the extinct volcano Cotacachi (at 4939 metres Ecuador's 11th highest peak) behind it is quite impressive.

Places to Stay & Eat
There is a *Hotel Cuicocha* on the lakeshore, about US$12 a double room, and with a fairly expensive restaurant.

Getting There
A group can hire a taxi or pickup from Cotacachi for about US$10. Buses from Otavalo to Apuela pass by Laguna Cuicocha, or you can hitch-hike.

APUELA
Soon after Laguna Cuicocha the road reaches its highest point and begins to drop down the western slopes of the Andes. The scenery is rugged and this is an opportunity to see some of the remoter and less-visited parts of the highlands. Some 40 km beyond Cuicocha by dirt road, you reach the village of Apuela where there are thermal springs, a very cheap and basic pensión and a simple restaurant.

Getting There
There are five buses a day from Otavalo and more on Saturday. Beyond Apuela there are more remote villages – ask in Apuela about transportation.

IBARRA
Just 22 km north of Otavalo and 135 km north of Quito is the attractive colonial town of Ibarra (population 53,000), which is the provincial capital of Imbabura. One of the main reasons for being here is to take the train from Ibarra to San Lorenzo on the coast. There's not much to do in Ibarra but I enjoy it because it's so old-fashioned. Horse-drawn carts clatter along cobbled streets flanked by colonial buildings, dark-suited old gentlemen sit in the shady parks discussing the day's events, and most good folks are in bed by 10. It's a relaxing sort of place.

Ibarra can be roughly divided into two areas. The south-east around the railway station is the busiest and has the bulk of the cheap hotels, while to the west are the main plazas and the older buildings in a generally quieter and more pleasant area.

Information
The DITURIS information office is on Parque Pedro Moncayo, as is the post office. The IETEL office is half a block from the park. There are no exchange houses and the banks were unwilling to change money when I was last there. Bring enough with you.

Streets in Ibarra are both numbered and named. Roughly north-south streets are numbered *calles*. West-east streets are numbered *carreteras*. Both names and numbers are used on the street signs but the names seem more widely accepted. I use names throughout this section.

Things to See
Plazas Parque La Merced (also known as Peñaherra) has a small museum and a church with a famous image of the Virgin of La Merced. The larger, tree-filled

Parque Pedro Moncayo is dominated by the cathedral. Pedro Moncayo, 1807-1888, was an Ibarra-born journalist and diplomat.

Out at the end of Bolívar is the quaint little Plazoleta Boyaca with a monument to Simón Bolívar to commemorate his victory at the Battle of Ibarra on 17 July 1823. The monument has the rather unlikely scene of an Andean condor attacking an African lion.

Behind the plazoleta is the modern concrete block church of Santo Domingo topped by a huge statue of St Dominic with a giant rosary swinging in the wind. Some people enjoy viewing the paintings in the rather garish interior. A few seem rather tongue-in-cheek: an old-fashioned representation of the Lord throwing the moneylenders out of the temple depicts one of the throng clutching a bag marked '$1000 Petroleo.'

Other Sights Apart from visiting these plazas, there's not much to do. The small, private archaeological museum costs 20c and is closed on Sundays and Mondays. There are two movie theatres. Ibarra is a good base from which to visit some of the surrounding villages and to wait for the train to the coast.

Places to Stay – bottom end

The highest concentration of hotels is near the railway station. Many cost only a dollar or so but are not particularly attractive – basic, noisy with train traffic, and usually with only cold water. These include the residenciales *Guayas, Atahualpa, Tahuando* and pensiones *Olmedo 1 & 2* and *Varsovia.* For a little more money you can find better places nearby. The *Residencial Colón* charges US$2 each, is clean, friendly, and has hot water. Rooms with a private bath are US$3 each and they'll do your laundry for you. *Residencial Familiar* is basic but quite clean and has hot water for US$1.30 each; it's been recommended by several travellers.

As you head away from the train station

you'll find quieter hotels. *Hotel Hong Kong* is US$1.20 each, and they have tepid showers and clean and spacious rooms. It's worth staying here if you get a front room, some with little balconies and views of Parque La Merced. Also on the park is *Residencial La Merced*, which has hot water and the added attraction of being located in the same building as the archaeological museum. About US$1.50 each.

A popular place with travellers is *Hotel Imbabura*, which is run by a friendly old lady and has a delightful little courtyard with flowers, a fish pond and birds. The best rooms are on the quiet street, at US$1.50 each. The rather dark inside rooms are US$1.20 per person. There's hot water. Don't confuse this with the *Residencial Imbabura*, which is US$1 each and quite clean but has only cold water. Similar is the *Residencial Yaguarcocha.* Next door to the *Hotel Imbabura* is the rather dark and uninviting-looking *Residencial Los Ceibos*, which also charges US$1 each and has only cold water.

The cheapest cold-water place in town is the *Pensión Descanso*, which is clean and only 80c each. At the other end of the cheapies price range is the *Residencial Vaca*, which looks pretty good – they charge US$2 each without and US$3 each with private bath. Hot water provided. Other hotels in the US$1-2 range include the residenciales *El Principe, Imperial* and *Los Alpes.* If you stay in a place with cold water and you want a hot shower you can always go to the public baths.

Places to Stay – middle

There's several reasonably priced hotels which provide you with a little luxury if you're getting fed up with always slumming it. For example, the *Residencial Imperio* (not to be confused with the *Imperial*) charges only US$3 each for rooms with a private bath and sometimes a TV! The *Hostal Nueva Colonia* has just opened so it hasn't yet had a chance to become too run down; they also charge US$3 per person

with private bath, as does the *Residencial Majestic*.

For some reason there are two residencials *Madrid*. The one on Olmedo charges US$3.50 single and US$6 double for rooms with private bath; many of the rooms are carpeted and have TV. Around the corner on P Moncayo, the other *Madrid* offers phones in the rooms, which cost about US$1 more per room. The most elegant of the mid-range hotels is the new *Hostal El Ejecutivo*, which is good value at US$5.50/8.50 single/double with private bath.

Places to Stay – top end

There is one fancy hotel in town and it is conveniently located three blocks from the railway station. This is the *Hotel Ibarra* (tel 950091), which has modern, comfortable rooms with private bath for US$8/11 single/double. More expensive still are three hotels on the road south out

of town. The first-class *Hotel Ajaví* (tel 951221) is found halfway between town and the bus terminal. It boasts a good restaurant and bar, swimming pool and relatively luxurious rooms for about US$25 double. A km beyond the bus terminal heading south is the slightly cheaper but still good *Hostería San Agustín* (tel 951888).

A further km south is the best hotel in the Ibarra area, the *Hostería Chorlaví* (tel 950777). This has old-world charm; it is in a converted hacienda and has pretty gardens, a swimming pool and an excellent restaurant/bar. They have a famous buffet-style lunch with folk music on weekends, which is very popular with well-off Ecuadoreans and tour groups after the Otavalo market – perhaps a bit too touristy for many travellers' tastes.

The good hotels often are booked well in advance, particularly at weekends. You may want to call them.

1	Plazoleta Boyaca & Church of Sto. Domingo	24	Residencial Los Alpes
2	Residencial Yahuarcocha	25	Hostal El Ejecutivo
3	IETEL	26	Residencial Vaca
4	Cine Gran Colombia	27	Residencial Imperio
5	Luchino Pizza	28	Residencial Madrid
6	Dituris	29	Residencial Familiar
7	Marisqueria Los Redes	30	Residencial Madrid
8	Bar Restaurant El Dorado	31	Residencial Guayas
9	Hot baths	32	Hotel Imbabura
10	Buses 28 de Septiembre	33	Residencial Los Celbos
11	Buses San Migual de Ibarra	34	Comedor Río Guayas
12	Buses 28 de Septiembre & Buses San Miguel de Ibarra (All buses to Terminal Terrestre & San Antonio)	35	Residencial El Principe
		36	Residencial Majestic & Cafe Pushkin
		37	Chifa Gran Muralla
13	Hotel Ibarra	38	Hotel Hong Kong
14	Buses to La Esperanza	39	Residencial Imbabura
15	Residencial Tahuando	40	Taxis Lagos
16	Pensión Olmedo 2	41	Residencial La Merced, museum & Restaurant La Estancia
17	Railway station	42	Pensión Descanso
18	Obelisk	43	Hostal Nuèva Colonia
19	Cine Popular	44	Post Office
20	Residencial Colón	45	Residencial Imperial
21	Pensión Varsovia	46	To Hotel Agavi (300 m), Terminal Terrestre (750 m), Otavalo (21 km)
22	Residencial Atahualpa		
23	Pensión Olmedo 1		

Places to Eat

A good place to start the day off is *Café Pushkin*, which has decent breakfasts and fresh home-made bread. Cheap lunches and dinners are recommended at *Comedor Río Guayas*. *Chifas* are good and cheap; there are several near the Parque La Merced, of which *Chifa Gran Muralla* is particularly good value. It serves big beers which many other *chifas* don't.

I haven't eaten at the recently opened *Luchino Pizza* on the Parque Pedro Moncayo – you could investigate if you have a sudden craving for Italian food. For fish dishes, the recommended *Marisquería Las Redes* is clean and moderately priced. Across the street the newly opened *Bar Restaurant El Dorado* is trying to be the best place in town, judging by the white tablecloths and shining silverware. Traditionally, the best in town is the pricey *Restaurant La Estancia*. You could also try the better hotels.

Getting There

Rail It used to be that you could get from Quito to Ibarra by train, but this service has been discontinued for some years now. There is a thrice-daily train to and from Otavalo but most people find it more convenient to travel by bus. It's only 22 km anyway. The train service of most interest is the Ibarra-San Lorenzo railway which links the highlands with the coast. At time of writing this is the only coastal train running.

The train is actually a converted school bus mounted onto a railway chassis. There is usually only one departure a day (6.30 am, 90c), so seats are limited. It is best to make a reservation on the previous day, although sometimes you are told that you must buy tickets on the day of departure. This is notoriously difficult – huge crowds of people push and shove to try and get their money into the tiny opening in the ticket grille and you have to be pretty obnoxious to obtain a ticket. It's much better to persuade the official that you really would prefer to buy a ticket in advance. Plead, insist, or tell them you'll pay a 'reservation fee' (about 25c should do it) but whatever you do, keep smiling and don't lose your cool or you won't get anywhere.

The journey is scheduled to take about seven hours but in reality often takes twice as long. Delays caused by landslides, breakdowns and cows on the track are the norm. Every few weeks, a landslide will close the track for a few days and getting tickets for the next available train isn't easy. In short, it can be an exciting trip.

The scenery en route is quite spectacular. You drop from Ibarra at 2225 metres to San Lorenzo at sea level 293 km away. Thus you see a good cross-section of Ecuador. Most of the drop occurs during the first half of the trip as you descend along the Río Mira valley with good whitewater views on the right of the train. At several stops fruit and other food can be purchased but a water bottle and some emergency food is advised. Once in San Lorenzo you can return the way you came or continue by boat – there are no roads.

Bus Buses from Quito leave from several terminals located near the flyover at Avenida Perez Guerrero and Avenida 10 de Agosto at the corner of Parque El Ejido in the new town. Buses leave all day long, once or twice an hour. The trip can take from 2½ to four hours, depending on the company. The fastest is Transportes Andinos at Avenida 18 de Septiembre 801 and Avenida Perez Guerrero, but the buses are small and uncomfortable and you feel like the driver has suicidal tendencies. Other companies within two blocks will take you more slowly and safely. They all cost about 90c. There are also frequent buses from Otavalo and Tulcán.

In Ibarra, the main Terminal Terrestre for buses is about 1-1/2 km south of the town centre. Buses from Quito and Otavalo will drop you here. If you are arriving from Tulcán you could get off before the terminal to save backtracking.

There's little in the way of accommodation near the terminal. A taxi to the centre will cost well under a dollar. There are local buses for about 5c which leave from outside the terminal. They all go within a couple of blocks of the railway station where there are plenty of hotels. From the terminal there are frequent departures for Quito, Tulcán (80c, 2½ hours) and Otavalo (20c, 30 minutes). Two or three times a day there are buses direct to several other major towns which usually involve a stop in Quito but save you having to look for another bus terminal in the capital. There are four daily buses to Esmeraldas, for example, if you can't get on the train.

Taxi If you are in a real hurry to get back to Quito you could use Taxis Lagos on the Parque La Merced. They charge about US$2.50 and cram six passengers into a large taxi. The taxis leave five or six times a day for the 2¼-hour ride.

Getting Around
Bus Local buses leave for the main terminal three or four times an hour near the railway station. They run along Calle Guerrero and are usually marked – if in doubt ask the driver. Two companies run this route: 28 de Septiembre and San Miguel de Ibarra. Some of their buses continue to San Antonio de Ibarra. Different buses leave from the same street for several other local destinations. An exception is the bus to La Esperanza, which leaves about once an hour near the east end of Avenida Sánchez y Cifuentes.

SAN ANTONIO DE IBARRA
This village, which is almost a suburb of Ibarra, is famous for its woodcarving. It has a pleasant main square around which are found a number of stores, poorly disguised as 'workshops.' The most famous is the Galería Luís Potosí, which has some of the best carvings. Señor Potosí is famous throughout Ecuador and sells his work all over the world. Some of his pieces are really beautiful and sell for

hundreds of dollars – the best carvings are to be seen in the upstairs section of his gallery. The atmosphere is totally relaxed; there's no high-pressure salesperson breathing down your neck while you inspect his work. A warning though – should you decide to purchase a large carving and have it shipped home, it's best to arrange for the shipping yourself. Some friends of mine bought a carving, left a deposit for it to be shipped back, and found out many months later that their carving had been sold to someone else a few days later. They received their deposit back but were very disappointed – their once-in-a-lifetime art investment had been sold to someone who paid cash and carried it out. That's Latin America!

There's little wood found in the Ibarra area and most of it comes from the Ecuadorean jungles. A type of cedar and walnut are among the more popular woods used. Various subjects are depicted but the favourites seem to be beggars, religious statues and nude women – again, that's Latin America!

Not all the pieces are expensive and you can buy small, mass-produced carvings for a couple of dollars if you like that sort of thing. It's been recommended by some people that the best deals and selections are to be found on the streets away from the main square. Frankly, I couldn't see any difference.

Places to Stay & Eat
The *Hostería Los Nogales* opened right at the end of '84, rooms were US$2.50 per person and they told me that you could get meals in the bar. There was only cold water – and signs of construction. Maybe it'll be fully functional by the time you read this. There's nowhere else to stay; staying in Ibarra is best. Nor are there any proper restaurants in San Antonio de Ibarra – there's one place a block off the main plaza which serves horribly greasy hamburgers and hot dogs.

Getting There

Transportation from Ibarra is frequent during daylight hours. Buses drop you off at the main plaza. The 15-minute ride costs just a few cents. Or you could walk the five km or so south on the Pan American from Ibarra.

LA ESPERANZA

This is a pretty little village some 10 km south of Ibarra and has recently become a popular place to stay for budget travellers looking for peace and quiet. There's nothing to do except talk to the locals and take walks in the surrounding country-side. It's supposed to be a good place to look for the San Pedro cactus.

Places to Stay & Eat

There is only one very basic but friendly hotel which costs US$1 per person – the *Casa Aida*. You can get good, simple and cheap meals here. There is also the small *Restaurant María* which can rent you a basic room.

Getting There

Buses serve the village frequently along a cobbled country road from Ibarra (see city map) and irregularly continue further south through Olmedo to Cayambe.

SAN GABRIEL

This is the next town of any size north of Ibarra on the Pan American highway. It's almost 90 km away from Ibarra but only 38 km from the border town of Tulcán. It's not a particularly interesting place but I mention it here because Tulcán hotels can occasionally be full and this is the nearest place to stay. It's also a good place to go if you want to be the only gringo in town.

As you drive north from Ibarra you soon pass the highly touted tourist site of Lake Yaguarcocha – Quechua for 'lake of blood.' It was so called after a battle between the Incas and the Caras, when the latter's bodies were supposedly thrown into the lake and turned it red. There's not much to see except for a race track around the lake. The Pan American drops quite steeply to the Chota River valley at about 1600 metres before beginning the long climb to San Gabriel at almost 2900 metres. En route it crosses the provincial line from Imbabura into Carchi and passes the little village of La Paz. Near La Paz are thermal springs and waterfalls; there are buses to the springs from Tulcán. The road north of Ibarra is steep, winding and rather slow, and the scenery is wild.

At San Gabriel there is a bus stop on the Pan American highway; many buses don't enter the town. Walk up the hill on Calle Montalvo for two blocks, then turn right onto Calle Bolívar, which is the main street. Walk three blocks, passing the church, until you reach the Plaza Central, where there is a startling nude statue of Bolívar, the liberator. (Imagine a nude George Washington in a small US town!)

Places to Stay & Eat

On the plaza is the *Residencial Montufar*, which is US$1.25 and doesn't have water. Better is the *Residencial Ideal*, which is only US$1 and has hot water in the mornings. It's on Calle Montufar 8-26, half a block from the plaza. Also on the plaza are two or three simple restaurants, the IETEL office and a movie theatre

Getting There

The Ciudad de San Gabriel bus company is also on the plaza and has buses to Quito every 45 minutes from 3 am to 6.30 pm. The five-hour ride is about US$1.30. For buses to Tulcán it's best to wait on the Pan American highway.

TULCÁN

This small city of 32,000 inhabitants is the provincial capital of Carchi. As you drive through this, the northernmost province of the Ecuadorean highlands, you see frequent farms and ranches, particularly as you get close to Tulcán. It is therefore an important market town, but for most travellers its importance is mainly as the

Tulcán

1 Hotel La Frontera
2 Restaurant Los Redes
3 Minibus to Airport or border
4 Baños Calientes Santa Teresita
5 Post Office
6 Co-operativa Transportes Norte
7 Residence of Colombian Consulate
8 TAME
9 Banco de los Andes
10 IETEL
11 Colombian Consulate
12 Rodrigo Paz Casa de Cambio
13 Restaurant El Bulevar
14 Residencial Oasis
15 Cinema Teatro Lemarie
16 Pensión Minerva
17 Hotel Granada
18 Hotel Carchi
19 Hotel El Paso &
   Chifa Pack Choy
20 Restaurant Danubio
21 Broaster Chicken Restaurant
22 Pensión Avenida & Salon
23 Residencial Española
24 Asadero Pollo Ako

0   200 m

gateway city into Ecuador from Colombia, some seven km away. With the present favourable rate of exchange of the Colombian peso against the Ecuadorean sucre, it has become very popular for Colombian weekend bargain hunters. There is a Sunday street market (no tourist items) and the hotels are often full of Colombian shoppers on Saturday nights. Tulcán lies about 3000 metres above sea level and hence has a rather cold climate. It is the highest provincial capital or town of its size in the country.

Money

Money exchange is best in Tulcán rather than at the border. The bus running between Tulcán and the border will accept both Colombian and Ecuadorean currency. Banco de los Andes is reputedly the only bank doing foreign exchange, but they were not functioning in late 1984 despite a sign in their window which said that they did. There are several exchange houses which pay about 4% less than you can get in Quito. The best known is Casa de Cambio Rodrigo Paz, which will exchange both pesos and dollars (including travellers' cheques at a 1% discount). There are several others nearby; most give rates within 1% of one another. There are also street changers with their little black attaché cases full of money. Because there is no real black market, you won't get much better rates from them than from the exchange houses. If leaving Ecuador, it is best to try and change sucres to dollars and then dollars to pesos when you get to Colombia. If arriving, cash dollars are your strongest currency.

Things to See

The big tourist attraction in town is the topiary garden in the cemetery. Behind the cemetery the locals play paddle-ball at weekends. It's a strange game played with a small soft ball and large spiked paddles that look like mediaeval torture implements. I couldn't figure it out. Parque Isidro Ayora has a rather striking white statue of Abdón Calderón riding a horse. There's one movie theatre. If that's not enough to keep you enthralled, you can call home from the IETEL office or send your first/last postcards from Ecuador through the post office. Both are on the map.

Places to Stay

There aren't any fancy hotels in Tulcán. The best is the *Residencial Oasis*, which costs US$3.50, US$6 and US$8.50 for single, double and triple rooms with shared bathrooms. If you want a room with a private bathroom you'll pay about US$1 extra per room. The next best is the *Hotel El Paso*, which has good clean rooms for US$2.50 each (shared baths) or US$3 (private baths). They have hot water and fill up very fast, especially at weekends. Also recommended is the *Hotel Fronteras*, which is conveniently located near the border bus stop and has hot water. Rooms are US$2.50 per person.

The downtown *Pensión Minerva* is basic, unfriendly, has only cold water and costs US$1.80 per person. Similarly priced, and cold and dingy, is the *Hotel Granada*. *Hotel Carchi* is US$1.60 each and also has only cold water. *Hotel Quito* has been recommended, but was closed last time I was in town. Rumours are that it'll reopen.

There are two hotels out by the main bus terminal. The *Pensión Avenida* is the cheapest place in town at US$1.20 each. Although it has only cold water, the staff is friendly. The *Residencial Española* (no sign, ask at the Kathy Restaurant below) has quite nice rooms but a very erratic water supply. It costs US$1.80 and US$3 per person for rooms without and with private baths. There's supposed to be hot water but I once stayed there and they didn't even have cold, so check the bathrooms before accepting the room.

As usual in highland towns, there are public hot showers (*Baños Calientes Santa Terisita* if you can't face a cold one and the hot water hotels are full.

Saturday evening is a rotten time to arrive in Tulcán, as many hotels are completely full. The next town is San Gabriel, some 40 minutes away. There are two basic hotels here.

Border There is only one place to stay at the border and it is pricey but good. The *Complejo Turistico Rumicacha* is –1/2 km away from the border and offers a swimming pool (50c for non-residents), restaurant, bar, discotheque and supposedly a casino if you can find someone to open it. Prices are US$10/US$14 single/double with private bath.

Places to Eat

Tulcán is not one of the world's great culinary centres. In the town centre there are the usual *chifas*, of which the *Pack Choy* beneath the Hotel El Paso isn't bad at all. A block away is the *Broaster Chicken Restaurant*, which is new and clean and serves, well, chicken. For more Ecuadorean-style food, the *Restaurant Danubio* is clean, quiet and pleasant but has a limited menu. Close to the border bus stop there is the simple but acceptable *Restaurant Las Redes*. There's a restaurant at the main bus terminal which is nothing to write home about, but at least it's cheap. Kitty-corner from it is a basic chicken restaurant, the *Asadero Pollo Piko*.

Out by the border there are a bunch of stalls selling snacks but no restaurants. Many restaurants only open for lunch and supper and close in mid-afternoon.

Crossing the Colombian Border

You don't need an exit or entry stamp in Tulcán. All formalities are taken care of at the Ecuador-Colombia border, 6-1/2 km away at Rumicacha. Fourteen-seater minibuses to the border leave all day long from Parque Isidro Ayora as soon as they are full. They cost about 20c (Ecuadorean or Colombian currency). Return buses from the border will charge the same to the town centre but you can usually persuade the driver to charge double and

take you to the Tulcán bus terminal some 3½ km away if you are in a hurry to head south. Taxis between Tulcán and the border are about US$1.80.

The border is open daily from 8 am to 5.45 pm. They are closed for lunch from noon to 1 pm. There is a lot of traffic from Colombia, and entrance formalities (into Ecuador) are usually no problem. Almost nobody needs a visa, and tourist cards (which you must keep until you leave) are issued at the border. An exit ticket or sufficient funds are rarely asked for unless you look like a bum. They often won't give you the full 90 days that you are allowed, but don't hassle over it – extensions in Quito are normally fast and straightforward.

If leaving Ecuador, you have to get an exit stamp in your passport and hand in your tourist card. If you've lost it they should give you another one free if your passport is in order but it's best not to lose it. Keep it tucked in your passport. If your documents aren't in order, several things could happen. If you've merely overstayed the time allowed by a few days you can pay a fine which is usually about US$10 – this really is a fine, not a bribe. If you've overstayed by several months you may well have to pay a hefty fine or get sent back to Quito. And if you don't have an entry stamp you also get sent back.

Visas Australians, New Zealanders, US citizens and citizens of some 'socialist' Latin American countries need a visa for Colombia. Most western Europeans don't. Whichever category you fall into, you should check in case regulations change. There is a Colombian Consul in office 204/5, in the Delegación de Tulcán building by the Parque La Independencia. They are open from 8.30 am to 12.30 pm and 2.30 to 4 pm Monday through Friday. Supposedly the secretary of the Colombian Consul lives at Junín 441 and he may be able to help you out of business hours if you approach him the 'right way.' To get a Colombian visa you officially need an exit ticket out of Colombia, two photos and sufficient funds (US$10 per day for students, double for others) but this is not always asked for. If you don't need a visa you can get the necessary tourist card at the border.

Getting There & Around

Air San-Saeta used to operate flights but no longer do. TAME has flights to Quito which save you five or six hours on the bus. It operates Monday through Friday but it's best to check at the TAME office at Junín 315 for the latest schedules. The flight takes 30 minutes and costs US$8. That's not a misprint – internal air is inexpensive in Ecuador.

To get to the airport you can take the border-crossing bus, which will leave you there for the same price as going to the border. A taxi will cost about 75c. Or it's a two-km walk. If flying into Tulcán, you have to take a taxi or walk because there are no airport buses.

Bus Buses to and from Ibarra (two to three hours, 90c), and Quito (five to six hours, US$1.50) leave and arrive from the main Terminal Terrestre. There are frequent departures but there is a better selection of times in the mornings. There are also a few daily departures direct for Santo Domingo or Guayaquil if you enjoy the slow form of torture provided by cramped Ecuadorean buses during journeys taking 10 hours or longer.

The main bus terminal is inconveniently located 3½ km uphill from the town centre. City buses (5c) run along Avenida Bolívar and will deposit you at the terminal. If arriving at Tulcán, you have to cross the street in front of the terminal and take the bus from the other side to get to the town centre.

If you wish to travel west of Tulcán along the border to Tufino and Maldonado, you have to take the Co-operativa Transportes Norte buses which leave from the corner of Junín and Arellano. There is a bus to Tufino about every hour until mid-

afternoon (one hour, 25c). There is also one daily bus which leaves about 11 am and continues on to Maldonado, some four hours and US$1 away.

There are also weekend excursion buses leaving from a bus stop in front of the cathedral for day trips to nearby thermal springs. The La Paz hot springs, seven km from the village of that name, are visited on a Saturday excursion leaving at 8 am for US$1 round trip. The Aguas Hediondas thermal baths, beyond Tufino, are visited on the 8 am Sunday-morning trip costing 50c.

TUFINO & MALDONADO

These small villages are right on the border to the west of Tulcán and are rarely visited by gringos. A road is planned, which will continue from Maldonado on to the coast at San Lorenzo, but this won't be completed for many years yet. Meanwhile, Maldonado is the end of the road and adventurous travellers may be intrigued to see what's there – it's a remote area.

At Tufino there are several thermal springs, most of them on the Colombian side of the border. It is easy enough to cross over to Colombia on a day pass to soak in the pools, but you are sent back to Tulcán if you want to enter Colombia properly. However, regulations may have changed. There is a basic restaurant in the village but no hotels. If you ask around, you could probably find someone to rent you a bed or floor space, but it's probably easiest to visit Tufino in the morning and return to Tulcán on an afternoon bus.

The drive beyond Tufino takes you over the Páramos de El Angel, famous for their strange highland vegetation, especially the giant *frailejones*. The dirt road climbs to over 4000 metres before beginning the long descent down the western slopes of the Andes. Maldonado is located in the San Juan River valley at just over 2000 metres. The climate is reportedly pleasant and swimming in the river invigorating, although I've never been there. There are a couple of small pensiones.

South of Quito

A glance at a relief map of Ecuador shows the Pan American highway heading almost due south of Quito along a long valley flanked by two parallel ranges of high mountains. These two ranges consist for the most part of volcanoes, and several of them are still active. It was this feature that prompted the famous German explorer Alexander von Humboldt, who visited the country in 1802, to name Ecuador's central valley 'The Avenue of the Volcanoes.' This name is still used today.

The central valley is only a tiny fraction of Ecuador's land surface, yet it contains almost half of its population. Traditionally, Ecuador's Andean Indians farmed the relatively rich intermontane volcanic soils found here, and after the conquest the Spanish found that the central valley made a good communication route between north and south. Today the same route is used for the Pan American highway, and a string of towns stretches south from the capital to Ecuador's third largest city, Cuenca, some 300 km away. In between lies some of Ecuador's wildest scenery, with nine of the country's 10 highest peaks and scores of tiny villages of Andean Indians leading lives little changed in centuries. Many of these are so remote that access is only on foot; some are easier to get to and provide a fascinating glimpse of Andean life. The larger towns are well connected with one another by road, and travel is generally easy with superb views.

MACHACHI

This small town of 7000 inhabitants is 35 km away from Quito and the first place you arrive at on the way south from the capital. Its main attraction is the Güitig mineral-water bottling plant which you can visit. There's not much else to do.

There is one basic hotel in the centre. Some travellers told me it was a quiet place in which to get away from Quito for a while without having to travel far.

LATACUNGA

It's worth coming here just for the drive from Quito, which is magnificent. Cotopaxi is the ice-cream-cone-shaped mountain looming to the left of the Pan American highway. At 5897 metres, it is the second highest peak in Ecuador and the highest active volcano in the world. The two Ilinizas, also snow capped, are on your right, and several other peaks are seen during the 90-km drive. About 50 km south of Quito the highway crosses a pass at over 3500 metres, and soon after there is an entrance road to Cotopaxi National Park. The road drops and crosses the railway at the small village of Lasso and then continues to Latacunga at about 2800 metres above sea level.

Latacunga (population 29,000) is the capital of Cotopaxi province. Although not a particularly exciting town, it has an interesting history and is a good base for several excellent excursions. It was an important centre for the Puruhá Indians who lived here before the Incas. The town's name originates from the Indian language 'Llacta cunani' which translates rather charmingly into 'land of my choice.' It became an important colonial centre immediately after the conquest but today there is little evidence of this long and varied history. The reason is Cotopaxi, which dominates the town on a clear day. A major eruption in 1742 destroyed the town and it had to be rebuilt. Another eruption 26 years later wiped it out again but the indomitable (or foolhardy) survivors rebuilt it a second time. An immense eruption in 1877 destroyed it a third time – and yet again it was rebuilt on the same site. At present the volcano's activity is minor and it is extremely

To Quito

Rio Yanayacu

F Alfaro
●5

J Andrade
●4

Gas
Station

Railway
Station

Cemetery

C Piño

A Clavijo

6●
●7

F Valencia

26●

25●

Market

●8

13
Plaza
Chile

A Echeverría

2●
●3
●1

5 de Junio

14●

●12

Guayaquil

●20

18●
●15

●19

●21

22●

Parque
Bolívar

P Salcedo

Parque
Vicente
Leon

●9

●16

G Maldonado

17●

●23

●24

Pasaje
Catedral

Tarqui

P Pacha
●10

P Toa

Amazonas

Hnas Paez
●11

M de Maenza

Rio Cutuchi

Pan-American Highway

2 de Mayo

B Quevedo

Quito

S de Urellana

Quijano Y Ordóñez

Ruminahui

To Ambato

Latacunga

0   100   200 m

unlikely that an eruption will occur within the next several years.

Information

The post office and IETEL office are marked on the map. There are no foreign exchange facilities at present. The town closes down early – most restaurants stop serving by 9 pm.

Things to See

Latacunga is a good centre for several excursions, which will be described at the end of this section. In the town itself, there's little to do. A small ethnography museum, the Molinos de Monserrat run by the Casa de Cultura Ecuatoriana, is open from 10 am to 5 pm Tuesday through Saturday. There are several plazas, of which Parque Vicente León is the most attractive with a well-tended garden. At the corner of this plaza is the town hall topped by a pair of stone condors, and the cathedral. Behind the cathedral is a little arcade which includes an art gallery. Many of the buildings are light grey and have been built from the local volcanic rock. There is one tiny theatre which shows bad movies.

Fiestas

Latacunga's major annual fiesta is La Virgen de las Mercedes, held 23-24 September. This is more popularly known as the Fiesta de la Mama Negra, and there are processions, costumes, street dancing, Andean music and fireworks. This is one of those festivals which, although outwardly Christian, has much pagan Indian influence and is worth seeing.

There is also a weekly market on Saturday and a smaller one on Tuesdays. Colourful, but of no special interest.

Places to Stay

There are six hotels open in Latacunga at this time. The newest and most expensive is the *Residencial Los Andes* on the Pan American highway. For US$4 per person you get a clean room with private bathroom and hot water. In the town centre is the rather older *Hotel Cotopaxi* which has rooms with private baths and hot water at US$3.50 each. Some of the rooms have pretty views of Parque Vicente León and are good value.

A good and economical hotel which has clean rooms and hot water in the communal showers is the *Hotel Estambul*, also in the town centre, at US$1.80 per person. There are three basic hotels at US$1.10 each. The *Hong Kong Internacional* and the *Costa Azul* are both over restaurants of the same name close to where you get off the bus on the Pan American highway. (The nearby *Hotel Turismo* is closed.) All

1	Hotels & Restaurants Turismo, Hong Kong & Costa Azul Buses to Ambato, Baños, Riobamba	13	Buses to Joseguango & Mulaló
2	Buses to Pujilí, Zumbahua, Quevedo	14	Restaurant El Calamar Fiestero
3	Buses to Quito	15	Hotel Estambul
4	Salons Panamericana & Cotopaxi Restaurants	16	IETEL & Post Office
5	Residencial Los Andes	17	Restaurant Candilejas
6	Hostal Residencial Jackeline	18	Restaurant La Carreta
7	Buses to Siggchos	19	Pingaino Ice-cream
8	Buses to Saquisití	20	Chifa Tokio
9	Casa de Cultura Ecuatoriana	21	Restaurant Los Alpes
10	Cine Santiago	22	Hotel Cotopaxi
11	General Hospital	23	Cathedral
12	Chifa Restaurant Gran Pekin	24	Town Hall
		25	La Merced Market
		26	Restaurant El Mashca

three are none too clean and the cold showers work only irregularly. The *Hostal Residencial Jackeline* just across the river is cleaner and friendlier, but the last time I was there the showers didn't work – though the manager will show you a place across the street for a wash.

Some 20 km north of Latacunga is the excellent *Hostería La Cienega*, which is in a 400-year-old hacienda belonging to the Lasso family, whose land once spread from Quito to Ambato. The grounds are beautiful and horse riding is available. Their main agents in Quito are Metropolitan Touring, who will book you rooms for about US$20 a double, or you can try just arriving, although they are often full. The hotel is a km west of the Pan American highway a little south of Lasso; there is a sign.

Places to Eat

There are no particularly fine or expensive restaurants in Latacunga. The best are restaurants *Candilejas* and *La Carreta* in the town centre. There are several *chifas*, of which the *Tokio* is recommended. *Pinguino* is good for ice cream and *Restaurant Los Alpes* is open for breakfasts (and all day). *El Mashca* is a chicken restaurant, and for fish try *EL Calamar Fiestero*. There is also a cluster of cheap and simple restaurants which are open all day at the corner of the Pan American highway and Avenida 5 de Junio. Most restaurants close about 9 pm.

The Latacunga area is famous for its *allullas*, sold by local women at every bus stop or checkpoint. Their high-pitched cries of 'aziuuuzias' become quite familiar. Allullas are rather dry biscuits made of flour, pork fat and a local unpasteurized cheese, and I'm afraid they taste no better than they sound.

Getting There

Air There is a Latacunga airport but it is not used for regularly scheduled flights. On rare occasions a plane may be diverted here if it cannot land at Quito. You hear occasional discussion about expanding the airport into an international one for Quito traffic – I can't see it happening this century.

Rail The railway station is located on the west side of the Pan American highway and a km from the town centre. At this time there is no Quito-Guayaquil train; the service goes only as far as Riobamba. The *autoferro* train leaves at 7.30 am for Quito (30c, two hours) and at 4.30 pm for Riobamba (50c, three hours). The train is very crowded and it's best to book in advance.

Bus There is no main bus terminal. Buses from Quito's Terminal Terrestre will usually drop you on the Pan American highway at the corner with Avenida 5 de Junio before continuing to Ambato. This corner is a good place to stand if wanting to catch any north or southbound bus – they pass every few minutes. This may be difficult on holiday weekends, as many buses are full and tend to do the Quito-Ambato-Riobamba run without picking up passengers at Latacunga. Be patient or try to avoid leaving Latacunga on holiday weekends. Occasionally a bus will leave from Quito's terminal direct for Latacunga. Approximate fares and times: Quito, 80c, two hours; Ambato, 40c, one hour; Riobamba, US$1, 2-1/4 hours; and Baños, 75c, 1¾ hours.

Just half a block from the Pan American highway on Avenida 5 de Junio is the bus stop for westbound buses. For Pujilí there are buses several times an hour costing 10c. Beyond Pujilí the road deteriorates but continues down through the western slopes of the Andes to Quevedo in the lowlands. This is the roughest, least-travelled, and perhaps most spectacular bus route joining the highlands with the western lowlands. If you're not pressed for time and don't mind the discomfort, riding a beat-up crowded old bus on this dirt road may be the most interesting way of leaving the highlands. The bus climbs to Zumbagua at 3500 metres (60c, two hours) and then drops to Quevedo at only 150 metres above sea level. Transportes Cotopaxi run this route in six hours at an average speed of less than 30 km an hour and charge about US$1.60. They have departures every two hours all day long.

Buses departing for various nearby villages leave from the Plaza Chile (also known as El Salto) near the market. Refer to the city map for locations of each stop. The bus most frequently used by travellers is the Saquisilí bus, which costs 15c for the half-hour ride. Departures are every few minutes on market-day mornings, and every hour or so at other times. Other destinations served by buses from this plaza are Sigchos, Chugchilán and Mulaló – ask around for other villages.

Plaza Chile is also the place to go to hire pickup trucks for visits to Cotopaxi National Park.

SAQUISILÍ

For many people, the Thursday morning market of Saquisilí is the main reason for coming to Latacunga. It is definitely not a tourist-oriented market, though there are the usual few Otavalo Indians selling their sweaters and weavings. This market is for the inhabitants of remote Indian villages who flood into town to buy (or sell) everything from bananas to homemade shotguns, and from herbal remedies to strings of piglets. The majority of the Indians from the area are recognized by their little felt 'pork pie' hats and red ponchos. There are eight different plazas, each of which sells specific goods. One of my favourites is the animal market, a cacophonous affair with screaming pigs playing a major role. Cattle, sheep and a few llamas are also seen. Ecuadorean economists consider this to be the most important Indian village market in the country and many travellers rate it as the best they've seen in Ecuador.

The bus from Latacunga drops you off near the Plaza La Concordia, which is recognized by its many trees surrounded by an iron railing. On Thursdays this becomes the plaza selling clothes, hats, hardware and homemade shotguns.

Places to Stay

On the Plaza La Concordia at Bolívar 4-88 and Sucre is the *Pensión La Chabela* (also known as La Chabelita), which provides basic accommodation. There is no sign. A bed can also be found at *Salón Pichincha* a couple of blocks away at Bolívar 2-06 and Pichincha. They are likely to be full the night before the market and most travellers find it best to stay in Latacunga – the bus service begins at dawn and you don't miss anything.

Places to Eat

There are no restaurants but plenty of places to eat. I enjoyed breakfast in an unnamed place under a *Viveres* sign at Sucre 7-66 and Bolívar. Inside there's a large smoky kitchen full of Indians and an Elvis Presley poster on the wall. A huge woman supervises the cooking of breakfast over a charcoal brazier and it's a good opportunity to try dishes such as *llaping-achos, fritada, caldo de gallina, tortillas de maíz* and *moté* cooked in traditional style. Makes a change from bacon and eggs! There are similar places nearby and also plenty of street stands. One plaza seems to be nothing but food stalls – if you stick to cooked food and don't have a delicate stomach you'll enjoy it.

Getting There

There are buses returning to Latacunga several times an hour after the market; there are also trucks and buses going to many of the remote villages in the interior such as Sigchos and Chugchilán.

OTHER VILLAGES

Pujilí has a basic unmarked pensión and a couple of simple restaurants on the main plaza. Market day is Sunday. This is a good town for the All Souls Day festivities of 2 November. Further west is **Zumbagua**, a very small village which has an unspoilt

Ambato

and interesting market on Saturdays. Food is available but accommodation is extremely basic (one pensión, no water) and it is best to stay in Latacunga.

North of Zumbagua is the famous volcanic lake of Quilotoa but transportation is both infrequent and irregular. You could hire a vehicle or walk there in three or four hours but carry water – the lake is alkaline. North of the lake on a deteriorating road you can reach **Chugchilán**. This is five more hours on foot. The daily bus from Latacunga arrives via a different, more northern road. At Chugchilán you can sleep in one of the houses on the square. North of Chugchilán is the bigger village of **Sigchos** on a better road and with two or three buses a day to Latacunga. These are all in a very remote area of the Ecuadorean highlands; still more remote communities can be found on foot. The scenery is quite splendid and the Andean Indian inhabitants somewhat withdrawn and not used to seeing strangers. Travellers wishing to spend any time here should be self-sufficient and have some experience in rough travel in strange areas.

COTOPAXI NATIONAL PARK

Pickup trucks can be hired in Latacunga to take you into this national park for about US$20. There is a small museum, a climbers' refuge and camping areas. Apart from Cotopaxi (5897 metres) there are several other peaks within the park of which Rumiñahui (4712 metres) is the most important. The park gives you a good look at the *páramo*, as the typical high-altitude plateaus of Ecuador are called, and there are excellent hiking possibilities. (See my *Climbing & Hiking in Ecuador*.)

SAN MIGUEL DE SALCEDO

This small town is normally called Salcedo and is the next town beyond Latacunga on the Pan American highway. It has a Sunday market. In mid-March they have an important Agricultural and Industrial Fair. Otherwise it's of little interest.

AMBATO

Forty km south of Latacunga is the important town of Ambato, the capital of Tungurahua province. It was badly dam-

1	Hotel Ambato – Casino	20	'Ingahurco' Bus
2	IETEL		to Bus Terminal
3	Teatro Roxi	21	Hotel Tungurahua
4	Post Office	22	Hotel Nacional
5	Cathedral	23	Residencial Lallnios
6	Cambiato (Money Changer)	24	Hotel Asia
7	Pasteleria Quito	25	Cine Bolívar
8	Chifa Nueva Hong Kong	26	Peña Tungurahua Bar
9	Teatro Lalama	27	Mama Miche Restaurant
10	Ecuatoriana	28	Residencial Guayas
11	Residencial Europe 2	29	Residencial San José
12	Museum	30	Residencials Loja & Napo
13	Cine Sucre	31	Residencials Laurita,
14	Restaurant El Alamo –		9 de Octubre & Hotel Guayaquil
	Soda Bar & Café	32	Residencial Ambato
15	Government Office DITURIS	33	Residencials America & Europa
16	Chifa Jao Fua	34	Panaderiia Zurimar
17	EL Alama JR. Self-Service	35	To Residencial Pichincha (600 m)
	Restaurant		Hotel Cumanda & Chifa Hong Kong (700 m)
18	Restaurant El Gran Alamo		Parilladas El Copihue Rojo (800 m)
19	Hotel Vivero		Bus Terminal & Train Station (1200 m)

aged in a 1949 earthquake but a modern city was soon rebuilt. It is prosperous and growing; a population of about 101,000 makes it Ecuador's sixth largest city.

Ambato is famous for its flower festival (Fiesta de Frutas y Flores) which is supposed to coincide with Carnaval, but usually is held during the last two weeks in February. Hotels tend to be full at this time so plan ahead. Otherwise, most travellers just pass through Ambato on their way to Baños, which is one of the more popular destinations in the country. However, it is worth staying here for a night to see the museum, which is little known but interesting.

Information

The DITURIS office may have more tourist information – they are in the process of moving and are temporarily located in the Government Office at Sucre and Castillo. The IETEL and post office are located on or near Parque Juan Montalvo. Banks won't change foreign currency but Cambiato will change both US$ travellers' cheques and cash at rates a little below Quito's.

Things to See

The museum in the Colegio Bolívar on the Parque Cevallos is well worth a visit. Entrance is 25c from 7.30 am to 12.30 pm and 2 to 5 pm, Monday through Friday. It has a variety of exhibits. Primarily there are hundreds of stuffed birds, mammals and reptiles, some of which are quite well done and others rather ratty. In the absence of comprehensive field guides to Ecuadorean wildlife, this is a good museum to visit if you wish to identify species you may have seen in the wild. (There's also a rather gruesome display of freaks such as two-headed calves and six-legged lambs.) I particularly enjoyed the fine display of photographs taken around 1910 by the famous Ecuadorean mountaineer Nicolás Martínez. There are period street and countryside scenes, as well as photographs of early mountaineering expeditions and

Cotopaxi in eruption. The museum curator, Señor Héctor Vásquez, is also a mountaineer with ascents of the highest peaks of Argentina, Peru and Ecuador to his credit. He is knowledgeable and helpful with the exhibits. There are also numismatic, geological, archaeological and other displays.

Because of the recent reconstruction, most of the buildings are new and of no great interest. The main plaza is attractively laid out and dedicated to the famous Ambateño writer Juan Montalvo (1833-1889), of whom there is a statue. On this plaza is the modern and rather bleak cathedral with some good stained-glass windows. The walk to the pleasant modern suburb of Miraflores has been recommended.

The market is held in and around the main market on Mondays, with smaller markets on Wednesdays and Fridays. It is a huge, bustling affair and was once recommended as one of the best in the country. It's still large but modernized and not as interesting as it used to be.

Places to Stay – bottom end

Hotels tend to be full for the flower festival and during Carnaval.

The place for cheap hotels in the city centre is in the Parque 12 de Noviembre area. For about a dollar you can stay in the basic *Residencial América*, which has one of those showers that provides tepid water and electric shocks if you touch any of the pipes, but is probably the best of the super cheapies. Similarly priced are the *Residencials Europa*, which claim to have hot water but don't. *Hotel Nacional* at US$1.25 has hot water in the mornings – sometimes. None of these places are particularly clean or highly recommended except for the penurious.

For US$1.60 you can stay at the *Hotel Guayaquil* which is reasonably clean and friendly and has hot water, as does the similarly priced *Residencial La Unión*. *Hotel Asia* has hot water only in the mornings and the *Residencial 9 de Octubre*

Top: Ibarra-San Lorenzo Autoferro (RR)
Left: Church door in Otavalo (RR)
Right: Topiary at Tulcán Cemetery (RR)

Top: Town of Baños (TW)
Left: Aerial view of Cotopaxi crater (RR)
Right: Private chapel at 400-year old Hacienda La Cienega, Central Highlands (RR)

only has cold water although they also charge about US$1.60. Several other very basic and rather grungy-looking hotels are shown on the map. They include the residencials *Guayas, San José, Loja, Napo, Laurita* and *Ambato*.

If you'd rather stay near the bus terminal, there is the *Hotel Carrillo* right above the terminal for US$2 each. They have hot showers but it's noisy. Walking right along Avenida de las Américas to the traffic circle and left on Avenida 12 de Noviembre brings you to the friendly *Residencial Pichincha* on the right-hand side (five minutes from the terminal). They have clean rooms for US$1.60 single and US$2.80 double but only cold water.

Places to Stay – middle & top end

Just before Residencial Pichincha is the *Hotel Cumandá*, US$4.50 per person in rooms with private baths and hot water. It's the only hotel in this price range near the bus terminal.

If you want some comfort downtown, the most economical is the clean, pleasant and recommended *Hotel Vivero* at US$4 per person without, and US$6.50 with private bath. Also in the city centre is the fancier *Hotel Tungurahua* for US$9.50 single and US$13.50 double. The newest and fanciest hotel in town is the *Hotel Ambato*, which has casino, restaurant and bar, and charges US$13 and US$18 for singles and doubles.

Out on Avenida Miraflores in the suburb of the same name are three quiet and pleasant hotels. All have restaurants and rooms with private baths and are recommended. The closest and cheapest is the *Hotel Florida* with rooms for about US$7 and US$10 single and double. Further along is the *Hotel Villa Hilda*, which is set in large and beautiful gardens and costs US$12 and US$16 single and double. Finally we come to the clean and modern *Hotel Miraflores* with double rooms for US$13.

Places to Eat

The best value is the *Chifa Jao Fua*, where a good meal is to be had for under US$2. Cheaper and almost as good is the *Chifa Nueva Hong Kong*. For breakfast the best bet is one of the cake shops for coffee, juice, and rolls or sandwiches. Try the *Panadería Zurimar* or the *Pastelería Quito*. Also very good are the Swiss-run *El Alamo* restaurants, of which there are three. *Restaurant El Gran Alamo* is quite fancy and expensive. *Restaurant El Alamo* is lower priced and good, and *El Alamo Junior* is a self-service-style cafeteria. *Mama Miche Restaurant* is quite good value considering it's open so late (supposedly 24 hours). Super-cheap meals are to be had around the market.

If you're staying near the bus station there's a basic restaurant in the terminal and food stalls outside. Also there's the *Chifa Hong Kong* opposite the Hotel Cumandá. For steaks you can try *Parrilladas El Copihue Rojo* on the traffic circle at Avenida de las Américas and 12 de Noviembre.

All the best hotels have good restaurants.

Entertainment

There is some nightlife. The *Peña Tungurahua Bar* has *música folklorica* evenings on Fridays and Saturdays but it doesn't get underway until about 11 pm. No cover is charged. There is a casino at the new *Hotel Ambato*. Ambato has six movie theatres, of which one may well be showing a decent film. Consult the map for locations and the local newspaper *El Heraldo* for what's playing.

Getting There

Air There is a small airstrip nearby for emergency and military use only.

Rail The train station is located near the main bus terminal, two km away from the town centre. *Autoferros* leave for Quito at 6.30 am (50c, 3½ hours) and at 5.30 pm for Riobamba (30c, 1½ hours). As usual, it's crowded and advance ticket purchase is recommended.

Bus The Terminal Terrestre is two km away from the town centre and buses to all destinations leave from here. The most frequent departures are for Quito (US$1, three hours), Baños (35c, 45 minutes), Riobamba (50c, one hour), and Guayaquil (US$2.25, six hours). There are also several buses a day to Guaranda (80c, 2-1/2 hours), some of which continue to Babahoyo and a couple to Chillanes. Several companies run a bus to Tena in the Oriente (US$2, six hours depending on road conditions). For northern destinations it's usually best to take a bus to Quito and change. Cuenca buses are erratic; the road is very bad beyond Riobamba and at this time it's best to travel via Guayaquil and change buses. This is also true for most destinations south of Riobamba. There is frequent talk of resurfacing the highland road to Cuenca and by the time you read this there may be better bus services to the south. Check at the terminal for the most up-to-date information; there is an information office.

Getting Around

Bus The most important local bus service for the traveller is the route from the town centre to the terminal. Ingahurco buses marked 'Terminal' leave from the Calle Martínez side of Parque Cevallos – many buses leave from this park so if in doubt, ask. From the terminal, climb the exit ramp to the Avenida de las Américas, which crosses the railway line on a bridge. On this bridge is a bus stop where a westbound (to your right) San Antonio bus will take you to the Parque Cevallos for 5c. A block away from this park is Calle Bolívar, with buses to Miraflores running along it.

Taxi Taxis to the centre will cost about 50c and to Miraflores about US$1.

SALASACA

As you head south-east from Ambato on the Baños road, the first place of interest is Salasaca some 14 km away. The village and its environs are inhabited by some 2000 Salasaca Indians who are famous for their tapestries. They are less well known for their history, which is particularly interesting. Originally they came from Bolivia but were conquered by the Incas in the 1400s. One of the ways in which the Incas controlled the peoples they had conquered was to move them en masse to an area which the Incas had long dominated and where there was less chance of an uprising. This is what happened to the Salasacas. After the Spanish conquest, they remained where they were but retained an unusually high degree of independence and were almost unknown by outsiders until about 40 years ago.

The villagers are recognized by their typical dress, especially the men who are normally seen wearing broad-brimmed white hats, black ponchos, and white shirts and trousers. Traditionally they are farmers and raise their own sheep to obtain wool for their weavings which are a secondary source of income. Their tapestries are all made by hand and are different from work done by other Indian groups (though telling the difference is difficult unless you know something about weaving).

There is no market in Salasaca; the villagers use the nearby Pelileo Saturday market or go to Ambato. You can buy their tapestries in craft stores in Quito and Cuenca and they have their own village store located by the church on the Ambato-Baños road. They make and sell tapestries almost exclusively. There are no restaurants or hotels – stay in Ambato or Baños.

There are many Indian fiestas in the Salasaca area which are worth looking out for. May and June are good months for fiestas all over the highlands. On the Sunday after Easter there is a street dance between Salasaca and Pelileo. On

15 June the Salasacas dress up in animal costumes for Santo Vintio. Corpus Cristi (moveable date in June) is celebrated in Salasaca and Pelileo. Saint Anthony is celebrated at the end of November. All the usual dates (Christmas, Easter, etc) also offer interesting fiesta possibilities.

PELILEO

Some six km beyond Salasaca on the Baños road is the rather bigger village of Pelileo. Despite its 400-year history, today's Pelileo is a very modern village. It was founded by the colonialist Antonio Clavijo in 1570 but destroyed by earthquakes in 1698, 1797, 1840 and 1949. The present site is about two km away from the ruins of the old town. It is the market town for nearby villages including Salasaca. Saturday is market day.

Baños is only 24 km away but the road drops some 850 metres from Pelileo. The descent along the Pastaza River gorge is spectacular and some of the best views of the snow-capped volcano Tungurahua are to be seen on this drive. At 5016 metres, it is Ecuador's 10th highest peak and gives its name to the province.

BAÑOS

The most recent census places the population of this small town at only some 11,000 people, yet there are almost 50 hotels in Baños and its outskirts. It is one of the most important tourist spots in the country, popular with Ecuadoreans and foreigners alike. Surprisingly, it is very pleasant and unspoilt and its popularity remains undiminished despite the many thousands of visitors annually.

Unless you've only just arrived in Latin America, you'll know that Baños means 'baths' and that is precisely what the town is famous for. Some of them are fed by thermal springs upwelling from the base of the active volcano Tungurahua, which means 'little hell' in Quechua. Other baths have melt water running into them from Tungurahua's icy flanks. Locals swear that the baths are great for your health.

While that is a debatable point, it is true that the casual atmosphere of this pretty resort town makes it an excellent place to unwind after some hard travelling, and few travellers can resist the opportunity to relax here for a few days.

The baths are not the only attraction. Baños' elevation of 1800 metres gives it an extremely agreeable climate and the surroundings are green and attractive. There are good opportunities for both short walks and ambitious climbs of Tungurahua and El Altar, an even higher extinct volcano some 25 km south of Tungurahua. Baños is also the gateway town into the jungle via Puyo and Misahuallí. East of Baños the road drops spectacularly and there are exceptional views of the upper Amazonian basin stretching away before you. In the town itself there are more attractions; an interesting Basilica, a small museum, a zoo, and restaurants selling typical local food. Baños became the seat of its *cantón* on 16 December 1936, and an annual fiesta is celebrated on this and the preceding day. There are the usual processions, fireworks, music and a great deal of street dancing. The 1986 celebrations should be especially colourful – it's the town's 50th anniversary. Few people are disappointed by a visit to Baños.

Information

Both IETEL and the post office are on the central plaza. The *Banco Pacifico* (see map) changes both US$ cash and travellers' cheques at rates only a little lower than Quito's. The streets have numbers as well as names.

Things to See

In the town itself the Santuario de Nuestra Señora de Agua Santa is worth seeing. This Dominican church is dedicated to the Virgin of the Holy Water, who is credited with the performance of several miracles in the Baños area. There is an annual celebration in her honour during October

Baños

with much street music and many Indian bands playing, but generally she is the object of devout admiration, as exemplified by the many offerings to her and the paintings depicting her miracles. These are simple but charming, with explanations in Spanish along the lines of 'On January 30th, 1904, Sr X fell off his horse as he was crossing the Río Pastaza bridge. As he fell 70 metres to the torrents below he yelled 'Holy Mother of the Holy Water' and was miraculously saved!' Other paintings show people being miraculously saved from exploding volcanoes, burning hotels, transit accidents and other misfortunes. Reading the explanations is amusing and a great way to practice your Spanish. Please remember that this is a place of worship and act accordingly.

Just above the church is a museum with an eclectic display of stuffed animals, religious paintings, church vestments and local handicrafts. It's open daily from 7.30 am to 4 pm and costs 10c. There is also a small gift shop.

Activities

First of all, relax. This is a laid-back town and most people take it slowly. You're on vacation in Baños.

Baths There are four baths, three in Baños and a fourth out of town. All the baths have a modest entrance fee for which they provide changing rooms and a safe storage system for your clothes. Towels and bathing costumes can be rented and soap is for sale. (Nude bathing is prohibited.) The best-known bath is the Piscina de La Virgen, with hot showers and several pools of different temperatures. They charge 15c. You can't miss them – they're right under the big waterfall at the southeast end of town. You can see it from most parts of Baños. Next door are the as yet unnamed new pools which have bigger

1	La Burbuja Disco	25	Mercedes Restaurant
2	New Swimming Pool & Baths	26	Residencial La Delicia 2
3	Piscina de la Virgen (Hot Baths)	27	Residencial Viena
4	Hotel Sangay	28	Residencial La Delicia 1
5	Hotel Palace		& Bus stop for El Salado
6	Restaurant El Marqués	29	Pensión Turismo
7	Restaurant El Paisano	30	Pensións Jota, Oriente
8	Hostal El Castillo		& Residencial Dumay
9	Sta. Clara Swimming Pool	31	Hotel Humboldt & Paraiso
10	Residencial Villa Sta. Clara	32	Chifa Oriental
11	Hotel Americano & Restaurant	33	Pensión Patty
12	Residencial Sta. Teresita	34	Residencial Ecuador, Hostal
13	Museum		Cordillera, Residencial Puerto
14	Hotel Guayaquil, Hostal Agoyan,		del Dorado
	Residencial Acapulco & Restaurant	35	Residenciales Irmita & Guayas
15	Banco Pacifico		Pensión Quito, Residenciales
16	Residenciales Anita & Panama		Bolívar, Santa Fé & Baños
17	Residenciales Mercedes & Lucy	36	Bus stop to Zoo & Agoyan
18	Villa Gertrudis	37	Residencial Cecilita
19	Hotel Danubio	38	Restaurant Monica
20	Town Hall & Clock Tower	39	Pensión Villa Sta. Clara
21	IETEL	40	Sugar cane stalls
22	Post Office	41	Residencial El Refugio
23	Residenciales Olguita	42	Residencial Julia
	& Los Pinos	43	Residencial El Rey
24	Hospital		

swimming pools (one cold and one hot) but no hot showers. There is a pleasant garden and they charge 25 c. There is also a cold swimming pool at Santa Clara. Most of the better hotels have pools.

If you walk up the hill past the cemetery on Carretera Martínez, you'll end up on a track which crosses a stream (Quebrada de Naguasco) on a small wooden footbridge. The track continues on the other side to a road in front of Cabañas Bascun, where you turn left to reach the Piscina El Salado. Here there are hot and cold showers, several pools of varying temperatures and an ice-cold waterfall to stand under if you're the masochistic sort. A real deal for 20 c. Because these are two or three km of out of town, they're not quite so crowded. There are buses too.

Walks Once you've visited all the pools, there are many walks to take. Here are some suggestions:

The walk down to the Río Pastaza is easy and popular. Just behind the sugar cane stalls by the bus station is a short trail which leads you to the Puente San Francisco. You can continue up the other side as far as you want.

Going south on Calle Maldonado takes you to a footpath which climbs to a building with a white cross high over Baños, and then continues to the tiny settlement of Runtun some two hours away. Great views!

You can walk out of town east on the main road to get to the zoo a couple of km away. There is a bus as well. The zoo, although small, houses an interesting collection of Ecuadorean species, including tapir and the rare harpy eagle.

Continue a further six or seven km beyond the zoo to the famous Agoyan Falls, now being turned into a major hydroelectric project. Buses go here.

Or continue down to the river just beyond the zoo, cross it on the suspension bridge and follow the trail back round to Baños, crossing the Puente San Francisco. It takes an hour or two.

At the police checkpoint at the west end of town, turn right and visit the Cascada Ines María a km away.

At the same check point, find a trail climbing to your left and follow it to the village of Pondoa (two hours), the climbers' refuge (six more hours), and the summit of Tungurahua (for experienced climbers only). For more information on these and other hikes and climbs read my *Climbing & Hiking in Ecuador*.

Horseback Riding Another possible activity is riding horses. Several hotels have information about renting by the hour or day.

Places to Stay – bottom end
There are literally dozens of hotels to choose from and obviously I couldn't spend a night in each! Therefore many of these descriptions are necessarily brief.

For rock-bottom costs there are the extremely basic pensiones *Turismo, Jota, Oriente* and *Residencial Dumay*, all one block from the central plaza on Haiflans; they have little to recommend them. Better cheap hotels are the clean *Hotel Americano* (80c each) with spacious rooms and a restaurant, and the *La Delicia 1*, same price, smaller rooms but clean and friendly. La Delicia has only one hot shower for 22 rooms. Its front rooms (Nos 1 and 2, 18 and 19) face the plaza with great views. At 90c is the *Residencial Santa Teresita*, which is clean and has hot showers sometimes.

There are several hotels for US$1 per person. For many years *Pensión Patty* has been very popular with gringos, with basic but clean rooms, friendly management and information on trekking, climbing, and horse riding in the area. The pensión has one hot and several cold showers, and a communal kitchen if you want to cook your own food. (You sometimes meet a great group of people – everyone chips in with something to eat or drink, conversations flow, a rum bottle gets opened or a guitar appears.) Also good is the *Resid-*

encial *Villa Santa Clara* (by the baths – not to be confused with the pensión by the bus terminal) which offers facilities similar to those at the *Patty* and is set in a garden. On the central plaza the *Residencial Olguita* is also recommended, especially the front rooms with good views. They have hot showers. The new *Residencial La Delicia 2* (not run by the same people as No 1) is also good for a dollar.

A little more expensive at US$1.50 per person are the following: the *Hostal Agoyan* with only cold water but clean rooms; the *Hostal Residencial Lucy*, also clean but with hot water; the old *Hotel Danubio* with hot showers, large rooms and a cheap restaurant; and the *Residencial Anita*, with cold water but spotless rooms and comfortable beds. Perhaps the best in this price range is the *Hostal El Castillo*, clean and quiet with a good restaurant. For US$1.80 the *Hotel Guayaquil* has a restaurant and hot showers. For US$2 each you can get clean rooms with private bathrooms and hot water at the *Hotel Humboldt/Paraiso* (depending on which sign you read). The mattresses in some rooms look rather lumpy though, so go look first.

There are many other hotels for US$2 or under per person. No less than nine are found in one block of Ambato east of the market (see map) and there are three right by the bus station. There seem to be no hotels in Baños for US$2-8 a single. All hotels marked on the map are less than US$2 each with the exception of the following top-end hotels.

Places to Stay – top end

The *Hotel Palace* is clean and pleasant with a good restaurant attached. Rooms with private baths are US$8.50 single, US$11 double and US$14.50 triple – suitable for families. The *Hotel Sangay*, run by Brian Warmington who is an expert on the area (but he's not always there), has a pool, squash courts, restaurant and bar, and runs about the same as the *Palace* in the main building, or a few dollars more in the bungalows. The most expensive in town is the good *Villa Gertrudis*, which charges US$18 per person including meals.

Houses for Rent

Ask at the *El Paisano* restaurant for simple houses to rent by the week or month.

Places to Stay – El Salado Baths

About two km from town by footpath or four km by road is the *Piscina El Salado*, with three nearby hotels. There are two basic US$1 residencials right by the baths – *El Salado* and the *Puerto del Salado* with good views of Tungurahua. About 10 minutes before getting to the baths are the *Cabañas Bascun* for US$7 per person in bungalows with private baths, restaurant, pool and sauna (US$2 extra).

Places to Eat

If you're staying at the more expensive hotels you may as well eat there, as there are no better restaurants in Baños. The 'best' in town is the new *El Marqués* which looks nice but I haven't eaten there.

One of my favourite places in Baños is the *Mercedes* restaurant up the hill towards the cemetery and worth the climb. It has a good book exchange, friendly service, table-tennis and chess, a view of the town, and the food is quite good. There is a self-service honour system on the refrigerator which means that when you arrive hot from the climb up the (little) hill, you can immediately help yourself to a cold beer. The Mercedes also offers 'special' evenings – one New Year's Eve I had a great all-you-can-eat roast lamb dinner which was cooked on a spit outside. It's a good place to meet travellers but it's not used by locals.

Another good restaurant is the simpler *El Paisano*, which has some vegetarian dishes. It's really friendly and run by the children of the woman who runs the *El Paisano* in Misahuallí. Also with vegetarian meals is the restaurant underneath the *Residencial Acapulco* on the church plaza.

The *Chifa Oriental* by the corner of the market is also good. There are many other cheap restaurants on Ambato and around the market. The *Pan de Casa* bakery next to the market is the first place to have fresh bread in the mornings.

On some days you can buy *cuy* at some of the market restaurants. *Cuy* is guinea pig and is a traditional food dating to pre-conquest times. They are normally roasted whole and some people find the sight of their little roasted feet sticking up and their tiny teeth poking out a bit disconcerting. Don't say I didn't warn you! Surprisingly, they taste quite good, a little like a cross between a chicken and a rabbit. In fact the local nickname for them in some areas is *conejo*, which means rabbit.

I am no longer able to recommend *Restaurant Monica*, for many years a favourite gringo hangout with menus in 12 languages hanging on the wall. It's still multilingual but the items on the menu are rarely available. A sign on the wall says 'All items home cooked – Please be patient.' This seems to act as an excuse for incredibly poor service – slow and inefficient. Recently the restaurant seems to be used by local workers who come in for a set meal; meeting them may be the best reason to go there.

Entertainment

Nightlife in Baños consists mainly of chatting with new friends in the restaurants after a strenuous day of soaking in the pools. Generally the town closes down early – most restaurants close by 9 pm. The cinema on the central plaza is closed. *La Burbuja* disco is open nights from Tuesday to Saturday but there's rarely much happening except perhaps weekends after 10 pm. (Bring all your friends and make it happen!) There's no cover but they get you for a minimum consumption of about US$1.50.

Getting There

Buses from Ambato's Terminal Terrestre leave about every half hour for Baños. The fare is 35c and the ride is 45 minutes. From Quito and many other towns it's sometimes quicker to catch a bus to Ambato and change rather than wait for the less frequent direct buses.

The Baños Terminal Terrestre is within walking distance of most hotels – it's a small town. Buses for Quito (US$1.30, 3½ hours) leave almost every hour or you can take more frequent buses to Ambato and change for other destinations. There are frequent departures for Riobamba (40c, one hour) but most of these buses go to Riobamba's Oriente bus terminal which is several km away from the main bus terminal (if you need to make a connection.)

Buses for the Oriente (Puyo or Tena) don't leave direct from Baños. Buses from Ambato or Quito heading for the Oriente pass by the Baños terminal and pick up passengers but sometimes they are full. Ticket offices in Baños will sell you tickets for these buses but usually won't guarantee you a seat nor give you a refund if the bus is full. You can, however, buy a ticket from the driver, so it's best to wait for a bus to pass by and then board if there's room. Alternatively, you can return to Ambato and then backtrack if you're determined to get a seat. (It's possible that the situation will change and that there will soon be eastbound buses leaving from Baños – enquire at the terminal.)

The road between Baños and Puyo is being rebuilt. At one time you had to take a bus to the construction area, drag your luggage across a km or more of churned-up mud, then catch another bus beyond the construction area. Recently buses have been getting straight through, but don't be too surprised if the *trasbordo* (as the mud-slogging system is euphemistically called) goes into effect again. Assuming no problems with road construction, the ride to Puyo costs 80c and takes two hours. To Tena costs US$1.80 and takes five hours.

Getting Around

Buses run along the main street named Ambato. Eastbound buses for the zoo and Agoyan Falls are marked 'Agoyan' and leave every few minutes during daylight hours from the corner of Ambato and Alfaro. Westbound buses leave from the central plaza outside Residencial La Delicia 1. They are marked 'Al Salado' and go to the baths of that name. Fares are about 5c. A taxi to these baths costs about 40c.

GUARANDA

Guaranda is a small town (population 14,000) but nevertheless is the capital of the agricultural province of Bolívar. Its name derives from that of the Indian chief Guarango. Guaranda is a quiet, provincial town which has been described as 'dismal.' I found it dignified rather than dismal, and it is pleasantly located with pretty hills all around. It certainly can't be described as exciting and the main reason you'd want to be here is probably for the bus rides, which are spectacular.

The road from Ambato is newly paved (it was officially inaugurated in November 1980) and comfortable. The 85-km drive climbs from Ambato at 2550 metres to bleak *páramo* at over 4000 metres before dropping to Guaranda at 2650 metres, making this the highest paved road in the country. It passes within 10 km of Chimborazo (6310 metres) and Carihuairazo (5020 metres), the highest and ninth highest peaks in Ecuador. For the best views of these giants you should get seats on the left of the bus (if going to Guaranda). In addition to the mountains, you get a good look at the harsh and inhospitable Andean moorlands known as the *páramo*. The bus ride can get cold so remember to carry some warm clothes onto the bus with you.

When you leave Guaranda there are other equally exciting rides. You can continue on down the western slopes of the Andes to Babahoyo and the coast – a route which was once the most important connection between Quito and Guayaquil but which is now infrequently used. Or you can head due east to Riobamba on a dizzying dirt road which skirts the southern flanks of Chimborazo and gives fantastic views that are not for the faint-hearted (sit on the left of the bus).

Information

Guaranda has an IETEL and post office but no money-changing facilities.

Things to See

There is one movie theatre, which doesn't have shows every day. Main market day is Saturday, with a smaller one on Wednesday. The best place for the market is Plaza 15 de Mayo – even on ordinary days it's worth visiting for its pleasantly quiet, forgotten colonial air (if you ignore the college on one side). The market at Mercado 10 de Noviembre is held in a modern but ugly concrete building. If you've got nothing to do, go down to the Parque Montufar and see if one of the statues there still has a wasps' nest under its right armpit! Walk the streets for a few hours; you'll end up in the last century.

Getting There

Bus Most buses now leave from the new bus terminal a km out of town. Just head east on García Moreno – you can't miss it. A few buses still leave from the bus plaza in town and there are several bus company offices there. As a general rule, the old country buses are likely to leave from the plaza, and the main buses for Riobamba, Ambato and Babahoyo will probably leave from the new terminal. Bus departures are from 4 am to 5 pm and no later. Afternoon buses can get booked up in advance so plan ahead.

The most frequent departures are for Ambato (80c, 2½ hours) and Quito (US$1.50, five hours), with buses for these destinations leaving about once an hour with various companies. Almost as frequently there are buses for Babahoyo (US$1.20, four hours) and Guayaquil

Guaranda

1 Teatro Nilo
2 Flota Bolívar Bus Office
3 Transportes San Pedrito
4 Restaurant El Rosal
5 Public toilet
6 Transportes Caluma
7 Pensión Marivel
8 Hotel Cochabamba &
   Restaurant
9 Pensión Ecuador
10 Post Office
11 Restaurant Santa Fé
12 Residencial Acapulco &
   Restaurant
13 Hotel Bolívar
14 Pensión Tequendama
15 IETEL Office
16 Pensión San José
17 Pensión Rosita Elvira
18 Rooms to Let (sign)
19 Residencial Montufar

(US$1.50, five hours). There are about six daily buses to Riobamba (80c, 2½ hours).

There are also several buses a day to Chillanes, a small town at the end of the road some three hours south of Guaranda. I've never been there nor met anyone who has, but I'm told there's a basic pensión. It certainly would be getting off the beaten track if that's what you want. Chillanes is a coffee and *aguardiente* (sugar cane alcohol) producing area. En route to both Babahoyo and Chillanes, you pass through the old town of San Miguel, which still has wooden colonial buildings with carved balconies.

Places to Stay

You can probably afford to stay in the best place in town, which is the clean and new *Hotel Cochabamba*. It's good value for US$4 each with private bath or US$3 with clean communal showers and hot water. It has a good restaurant downstairs. A bit more run down but still reasonable is the *Hotel Bolívar*, which charges US$3 with and US$2 without private bath per person. It has hot water.

The rest of the hotels in town are cold-water cheapies. *Pensión Tequendama* is US$1.50 per person and has a garage in case you happened to bring your own car. For a dollar each you can stay at the *Pensión Ecuador* which is run by a friendly old woman, or at the *Residencial Acapulco* which has a restaurant attached. Other similarly priced places are shown on the map.

Outside of town is the *Hotel Matiavi* at the bus terminal. It advertises rooms with private baths and hot water but was temporarily closed last time I was in Guaranda. A 15-minute walk out of town on the Quito road is a 'tourist complex' called *Hotel La Colina* which is often empty. Located on a hill, it has some rooms with good views, a restaurant, bar and small swimming pool. They charge US$8 and US$12 single and double with private bath and hot water.

Places to Eat

There are few restaurants and they close early, many by 7.30 pm. The best in town is the reasonably priced *Restaurant Cochabamba* under the hotel of that name, but they don't always have everything on the rather impressive-looking menu. Cheaper are *Restaurant Acapulco* (under the Residencial) and *Restaurant Santa Fé* next door to it. *Restaurant El Rosal* in the bus plaza is OK, and there's a basic place to eat at the main bus terminal.

RIOBAMBA

'All roads lead to Riobamba' proclaims a road sign as you enter this city, and it is indeed true that Riobamba is located at the heart of an extensive and scenic road network. Whichever way you arrive or leave, you should try and plan your journey for daylight hours so as not to miss the great views. The usual way to arrive is on the Pan American highway from Ambato, which is 65 km to the north. The road climbs over a 3600-metre-high pass which gives good views of Ecuador's highest peak, Chimborazo (6310 metres) and Carihuairazo (5020 metres) before dropping to Riobamba at 2750 metres. Another equally spectacular route is the dirt road arriving from Guaranda. There is also a lower road from Baños which follows the Chambo River valley and passes through numerous small villages. One of these, Penipe, is the entrance to the dirt road climbing towards the rugged peak of El Altar, at 5319 metres Ecuador's fifth highest peak. Looking back along this road will also give you views of Tungurahua.

The city itself is fairly important, and with a population of some 73,000 is the capital of Chimborazo province. The area was inhabited long before the Spanish conquest. It was a Puruhá Indian centre before becoming part of the Inca Empire during the late 15th century. The first Spanish colonialists built a city near present-day Cajabamba. This was

Riobamba

destroyed in a 1797 earthquake and the survivors moved to the present site on a large plain surrounded by several snow-capped peaks. The flat terrain of Riobamba enabled it to be built in a regular chessboard pattern with wide avenues and imposing stone buildings. It has rather a sedate air and Ecuadoreans call it the 'Sultan of the Andes.'

Information

There are both IETEL and post offices. The latter can be difficult to find as the sign is tiny and the office is located on the third floor of an office building (see map). Also marked on the map is the Banco Internacional, which is the only place that will change cash dollars and travellers' cheques. Rates are almost as good as in Quito. Normal banking hours are from 9 am to 1 pm, Monday to Friday, but recently they have also been open until noon on Saturdays to cater to market-goers. There is a DITURIS tourist information office on the corner of Parque Maldonado but, regrettably, I am only able to recommend them for friendliness and not efficiency.

Things to See

Market Market day is Saturday and there's much activity in the streets, especially around 5 de Junio and Argentinos. It seems rather incongruous to see a barefooted Indian woman leading a squealing piglet on a string through the streets of a major town. The market certainly is a colourful affair, with thousands of people from many surrounding villages flocking to market. Unfortunately, new market buildings have been constructed which tend to detract from the *ambiente*, and the modern market sells mainly food items and plastic consumer goods. If you look hard you'll still see some crafts but certainly not as many as there used to be.

The most typically Riobambeño handicrafts are the *tagua* nut carvings. These nuts are actually seeds from a type of jungle palm. They are fairly soft until they are carved, but when exposed to the sun and air they become very hard. The seeds are the size of large chicken eggs and are carved into a variety of novelties such as busts, miniature cups and rings. Although the palm grows in many areas, for some reason only Riobamba has become a carving centre for the tagua nut. Another interesting handicraft from the Riobamba area is the *shigra*, a tough woven bag made from agave or century plant fibres. Their durability and practicality make them

1	Hotel Humboldt	17	Hotel Imperio
2	Hotel Whympet	18	Hostal Los Shyris
3	Restaurant La Biblia	19	Restaurant Candilegas
4	Restaurant Monaco	20	Restaurants El Pailón & Monarca
5	Hotel Metro	21	Apart – Hotel Liribamba
6	Residencial Villa Ester & Guayas	22	Restaurant Kikirimiau
7	Hotel Guayaquil & Restaurant Chimborazo	23	Post Offices (3rd floor of office bldg)
8	Restaurant Oriente	24	Chifka Chung Wah
9	Hotel Ecuador	25	Banco Internacional
10	Hotel Americano	26	Restaurant La Cabaña Montekcarb
11	Cine Imperial	27	Teatro T Leon
12	Cine Fenix	28	Museum of Religious Art
13	Residencial Venecia	29	Hotel Segovia
14	Residencial Colonial	30	Chifa Internacional
15	Hotel Atahualpoi	31	Tourist Office
16	Residencial Camba Huasi	32	IETEL

very popular souvenirs for many travellers, who often use them as day bags. Baskets and mats made by the Colta Indians are also to be found. They are woven from the reeds lining the shores of Lake Colta, a few km south of Riobamba. There are many clothing items such as woven belts, fine ponchos and embroidered shawls.

It should be mentioned that the Otavalo market is the most tourist-oriented and convenient place to shop for souvenirs. At the Riobamba market you'll have to do a lot of searching past stalls of potatoes, plastic buckets and polyester pants – less convenient but perhaps more fun!

Museo de Arte Religioso in the old church of La Concepción is famous and worth a visit. The building has been beautifully restored and there are many rooms with a good variety of paintings, sculptures and religious artifacts. Their major piece is a huge, gem-encrusted gold monstrance said to be priceless. Entrance is 60c from 9 am to 12.30 pm and 3 to 6.30 pm Tuesdays through Saturdays. On Sundays and holidays it's open mornings only; closed Mondays.

Parque 21 de Abril has an observation platform from which the city and surrounding countryside can be appreciated. There is also a tilework representation of the history of Ecuador. The view of snow-capped Tungurahua rising behind the church of San Antonio is especially impressive.

Parque La Libertad is another quiet plaza. Its Basilica is famous as the only round church in Ecuador. Begun in 1883, it took over 30 years to complete and was designed, built and decorated mainly by locals – a source of civic pride. It's often closed; try Sundays.

There are several other plazas with impressive buildings and churches. A walk along Primera Constituente will take you past some of them.

Activities

Mountaineering Señor Enrique Veloz (tel 960916) is the president of the Asociación de Andinismo de Chimborazo. He has climbed Chimborazo and the other peaks many times and can guide you himself or arrange a good guide. This is fairly priced but not cheap, and it is not for the beginner mountaineer. For more information see my *Climbing & Hiking in Ecuador*. For a close look at the mountain you can hire a pickup truck near the railway station. This would take you as far as the parking lot below the climbers' hut for about US$10-15 depending on the vehicle and your bargaining abilities.

Places to Stay – bottom end

Most hotels are in the town centre a couple of km away from the main bus terminal. If you want to stay near the terminal, you'll find the clean *Residencial Puruha* across the street behind it. They charge US$1.70 per person and have hot water.

The best selection of cheap hotels is near the train station. The *autoferro* leaves at 5 am, so avoid rooms facing the tracks. The cheapest is probably the *Residencial Colonial* which charges about US$1 and has hot water. Other hotels for a dollar are less attractive. They include the residencials *Villa Ester, Guayas, Chimborazo* and *Guayaquil*. I prefer the *Residencial Camba Huasi* for US$1.40 per person. It is a block from the station and hence quieter, has friendly staff, spacious rooms and hot showers. Other places with hot water but facing the station are the hotels *Americano, Atahualpa* and *Ecuador,* and the *Residencial Venecia*. They are all about US$1.40 each.

Places to Stay – middle

Hotel Imperio is quite good value for US$2.80 per person with private bath. The rather old-fashioned *Hotel Metro* is recommended for friendly staff and clean rooms. They charge US$3.50 and US$3 per person for rooms with and without private baths. There's hot water and a restaurant. New, clean and good is the *Hotel Whymper* at US$3.50 per person. Rooms are arranged in blocks of four and there is a bathroom with hot water for each block. There is also a breakfast cafeteria.

The older *Hotel Segovia* charges US$3.50 each for rooms with private bath, but the restaurant *El Cafetal* below is rather expensive for what you get. Two good hotels are the *Humboldt* and the newer *Hostal Los Shyris*, which have comfortable rooms with private baths for US$4.50 each. Cafeterias are attached.

In front of the main bus terminal is the comfortable and new *Hotel Las Retamas*, which has a restaurant and charges US$5.50 per person in rooms with private baths, hot water and TV.

Places to Stay – top end

For long-term stays, the *Apart Hotel Liribamba* is spacious, clean and comfortable. Some rooms are arranged as apartments with kitchen facilities. Prices are US$9, 13, 17 and 20 for singles, doubles, triples and quads, all with private baths. For private kitchen add about US$3 per apartment.

The best hotel in town is on Avenida Argentinos and a long way from the centre. It's the *Hotel El Galpón* and is highly recommended for the rich and/or luxury loving. About US$20 and US$28 single and double.

Places to Eat

Most restaurants in Riobamba are fairly basic and cheap and there are many of them. Budget travellers are recommended to try the four-course lunch for 70c at the simple and homely *Restaurant Kikirimian*. There are several cheap restaurants near the railway station, some of which are rather grimy but others are quite good; try *Restaurant Oriente* and *Monaco*. Not quite as cheap but excellent value is *Restaurant La Biblia* – they have good meals and you might try their fresh pineapple juice for 20c.

For breakfast, *Restaurant Cafeteria El Pailón* is reasonable, as is the *Fuente* underneath the post office. As usual, there are several inexpensive *chifas*, of which the *Chung Wah* and *Internacional* are especially recommended. For dining with a little style try the restaurants *Candilejas, Monarca* or *La Cabaña Montecarlo*. They are less expensive than they look and even the most impoverished budget traveller can afford a night out at a place with a clean tablecloth once in a while.

One of the fanciest places in town, and fairly expensive by Ecuadorean standards, is the good German-run *Restaurant León Rojo*, located just off the west end of the map at Avenida D L Borges 37-47.

Entertainment

Nightlife is extremely limited. I could find nothing except the three movie theatres on the map. They advertise in *El Libertador*, the local daily paper.

Getting There

Air There is a secondary airport which is used for military and emergency services only.

Rail The service to Guayaquil and Cuenca was disrupted by the 1982/83 El Niño floods which washed out over 80 km of the track beyond Riobamba. It is unlikely that services will resume before the end of 1986 – quite possibly much later. At this time there is only one daily *autoferro* to Quito which leaves at 5 am, costs 70c and takes about five hours. It is usually full and advance booking is recommended. Enquire at the train station in the town centre.

Bus The main bus terminal is almost two km north-west of the town centre. Unfortunately, not all buses leave from there. Northbound buses for Quito (US$1.40, four hours) and intermediate points are frequent. Also frequent are buses for Guayaquil (US$1.75, five hours). There are two buses at 7 and 9 pm for Machala

(US$2.75, 10 hours) and Huaquillas (US$3.25, 12 hours) if you're heading for Peru.

If you're headed south you'll only find three buses a day for Cuenca with Patria bus company. They leave at 5.30 and 7.30 am and 7.30 pm and cost about US$2.50 for the ride which can take from nine to 12 hours. The Pan American highway south of Alausí is in terrible condition and there are frequent landslides – buses for Cuenca may well go via the western lowlands (El Triunfo) and then back up into the Sierra. Buses for Alausí leave about every hour with CTA and cost 70c for the 1½-hour ride, but trying to continue from there to Cuenca can be problematical.

Three blocks south of the main bus terminal (turn left out of the front entrance) is a smaller terminal with frequent local buses for Cajabamba and Balbanera; fare is 15c.

For buses to Baños and the Oriente you have to go to the Oriente bus terminal on Avenidas Espejo and Luz Elisa Borja almost four km away. There is no direct bus linking the two terminals – a taxi should be about 50c. Once in a while there are buses leaving the main terminal for Baños – it's a matter of luck. If you're arriving in Riobamba from the Oriente, you may find that your bus makes a swing through the centre before ending up at the Oriente terminal.

Getting Around

Bus North of the main bus terminal, behind a church with a blue dome, is a local bus stop for the city centre nearly two km away. These buses run along Avenida León Borges, which turns into 10 de Agosto near the railway station. Here there is a good selection of hotels. To return to the main terminal, take any bus marked 'Terminal' on Avenida Primera Constituente. The fare is 5c.

To visit the villages of Guano and Santa Teresita, take a 10c bus ride from the stop at Avenidas Pichincha and New York.

GUANO & SANTA TERESITA

These small villages are a few km north of Riobamba and make an ideal day trip. Guano is an important carpetmaking centre and although it's unlikely that many travellers will have room in their luggage for a couple of souvenir carpets, it is nevertheless interesting to see this cottage industry. In Guano you should get off the bus at the central plaza, where several carpet stores are to be found, and then continue down Avenida García Moreno, which will take you past several more. There are no hotels or restaurants.

From the main plaza you can continue with a 5c bus ride to Santa Teresita a few km away. The bus terminates at the end of the road and you turn right and head down the hill for about 20 minutes to the Balneario. Here there are swimming pools fed by natural springs. The water is quite cool (22°C or 71°F) but the views of Tungurahua and El Altar are marvellous. There is a basic cafeteria, and camping is permitted.

The round trip from Riobamba will take about six hours if you take it leisurely and have a swim in the pool. There are frequent buses during daylight hours and it's a good chance to see some of the local countryside.

CAJABAMBA

The southbound Pan American highway actually heads west out of Riobamba until it reaches a cement factory 10 km away. Here the road forks, with the west fork continuing to Guaranda and the main highway heading south-west to Cajabamba about seven km further. Cajabamba was founded in 1534 and was historically important until it was devastated by the 1797 earthquake which killed several thousands of its inhabitants. Most of the survivors founded nearby Riobamba, but a few remained and their descendants still live here. As you arrive, look up to your right and you'll see a huge scar on the hillside – the only sign of the landslide which caused much of the damage in

1797. Most of the buses from Riobamba continue down the Pan American highway beyond Cajabamba; if you want to see some of the old town you should get off at the entrance which is at the junction of the main highway and Avenida 2 de Agosto on the right. Most bus drivers stop here. There's little to see; if you head down 2 de Agosto you'll soon come to the History Museum on your right, which contains about a dozen fragments of carved rock dating from before the earthquake. It's not worth seeing, but maybe in the future the museum will have a proper exhibit. Continuing down the road, you come to the earthquake-damaged town church on your left. There are no hotels.

Returning to the Pan American, you'll see a few food stalls and very basic restaurants. Heading south on the main highway, you soon pass open fields which are the site of the interesting weekly market. There are no permanent buildings; the Indians just lay out their wares in neat rows. Every Sunday morning the bare fields are transformed by a bustling but surprisingly orderly throng who buy, sell and barter produce. Quechua rather than Spanish is spoken and there are no tourist items; this is one of the more traditional markets in the Ecuadorean highlands. Amazingly, it takes place right by the side of the Pan American highway – a measure of just how rural this part of Ecuador is.

Most buses from Riobamba continue about four km beyond Cajabamba to Lake Colta – an interesting place. The road climbs gently to a notch in the hill to the south and here is found the little chapel of La Balbanera. It is built on the site of the earliest church in Ecuador, which dates from 15 August 1534, though only a few stones at the front survived the devastating earthquake of 1797. The church has been almost completely rebuilt and the curious traveller can enter to inspect its simple interior and look at the usual disaster paintings. In La Balbanera one painting carries the explanation: 'On the 17th of May, 1959, the train derailed, setting the whole convoy on fire. Sr Juan Peñafiel, the brakeman, prayed to the Divine Lady of La Balbanera and her miracle saved the train near Alausí.'

Looking almost due north of the chapel, you can see Chimborazo looming up from 30 km away. Next to the chapel are a few basic restaurants and the more elaborate *La Balbanera* tourist restaurant where you can sample local dishes. A little to the south of the chapel there is a road fork. This is where the decision must be made whether to continue south on the Pan American or take the 100-km detour to the right via the junction of El Triunfo and then return to the Pan American at Cañar. Frequent road closures caused by landslides sometimes make the detour impossible to avoid.

Opposite the road fork is Lake Colta. Its blue expanse is often choked up by reeds, which form an important crop for the local Colta Indians. Sometimes you can see the Coltas' rafts on the lake; the Indians cut the reeds for use as cattle fodder or for the reed mats and baskets for which they are famous. Some of the more traditional Colta Indian women can be readily identified by their habit of dyeing the front fringes of their hair a startling golden colour. If you have the time or inclination you could walk around the lake in a couple of hours.

GUAMOTE

From the Cajabamba region the southbound Pan American highway roughly follows the railway and crosses the tracks quite often. Some 30 km beyond Cajabamba you reach the village of Guamote, which has a Thursday market. Until 1982 it had some importance because of its railway station, but the trains haven't run for some years and it's rather a forgotten little place now. There is one basic pensión near the train tracks.

ALAUSÍ

Almost 50 km south of Guamote you reach Alausí, which is near the head of the

Chanchán River valley down which the railway runs to the coast. Just below Alausí begins the famous Nariz del Diablo, where a hair-raising series of railway switchbacks negotiate the steep descent towards the lowlands. Unfortunately, this is the area where the most damage was done by the landslides caused by the torrential rains of the 1982-1983 El Niño. Alausí used to be a popular highland resort for Guayaquileños wishing to get away from the unpleasant heat and humidity of the coast while experiencing one of the world's great feats of railway engineering. Although the railway doesn't run, the hotels remain, often empty. Everyone hopes that the railway will reopen – but I'd be very much surprised to see it running before 1987. Forgotten by the tourists, Alausí nevertheless retains some importance as an agricultural centre.

There is a movie theatre that shows badly scratched and distorted kung fu movies and an IETEL office if you need to call your mother.

Places to Stay & Eat

The hotels are all on Avenida 5 de Junio. There are no first-class hotels and the best seems to be the *Hotel Gampala*, which has hot water and charges about US$2 per person. For US$1.60 you can stay at the clean *Hotel Panamericano*, which has hot water in the mornings only and a basic restaurant below. *Hotel Ecuador* also has a basic restaurant and can provide hot showers around the back for a fee of 20c if you ask in advance. The rooms are a dollar per person. The *Residencial Tequendama* looks pretty basic but has hot water and charges US$1.20 per person.

Apart from the hotel restaurants, there are a couple of other basic places to eat.

Getting There

Bus Buses from Riobamba (80c, 1½ hours) arrive every hour or so, but to go further south is sometimes impossible and you might get stuck in Alausí. Buses turn off the Pan American highway and drop down into town, arriving on the main street, Avenida 5 de Junio, where they normally stop near the Hotel Panamericano. Pickup trucks act as buses for nearby destinations and leave from this street. Some of the rides can be quite spectacular, especially the one to Achupallas about 23 km to the south-east. Make sure that any sightseeing ride you take is coming back to Alausí, as there are few, if any, places to stay in these villages. Buses for Cuenca, when they're running, also leave from the main street.

Cuenca & The Southern Highlands

The three southern Sierra provinces, Cañar, Azuay and Loja, are noticeably different from the seven highland provinces to the north. Geographically they are much lower, with very few peaks reaching 4000 metres. The topography is rugged nevertheless, and communications with the rest of Ecuador have only been developed relatively recently. Cuenca, the major city of the region and Ecuador's third largest, didn't have paved highway connections with Guayaquil and Quito until the 1960s, and even today these highways are often in bad shape. The area is rich in history, and until recently its isolation has left the region with a strong flavour of the colonial past.

The southern highlands had a colourful history even before the Spanish conquest. These were the lands of the Cañari Indians, an independent culture with exceptional skill in producing gold jewellery and other metalwork, fine weavings and ceramics. In the late 15th century the Cañaris were conquered by the Incas, who built several major centres. These included the city of Tomebamba near present-day Cuenca, and the fortress of Ingapirca – the best-preserved pre-colonial ruin found in Ecuador today. The Inca influence was short lived, however, and the Spaniards under Pizarro were in control by the 1530s. Cuenca was (re)founded relatively late in 1557. Several other important towns of the region were founded earlier, such as Loja in 1548.

Remnants of the colonial era are more likely to be seen here than anywhere else in the country, except Quito. Although progress is slowly catching up with the southern Sierra, this area is still a long way behind the coast and northern highlands. Today's traveller is struck by the paucity of large cities in the southern highlands. Apart from Cuenca and Loja, there are no towns with a population of over 20,000 inhabitants. There are many villages with old balconied houses and cobbled streets, and there is a strong tradition of handicrafts ranging from jewellery-making to weaving. A journey through the provinces of Cañar, Azuay and Loja is a journey into the past.

CUENCA

Barely half a century before the arrival of the Spaniards, the powerful Inca Tupac (or Topa) Yupanqui was undertaking the difficult conquest of the Cañari Indians, who struggled bravely to stem the expansion of the Inca empire. After several years of bitter fighting, Tupac Yupanqui's forces prevailed. The Inca began the construction of a major city whose splendour and importance was to rival that of the imperial capital of Cuzco. The Indians told of sun temples covered with gold sheets and palaces built with the finest skill of Cuzqueño stonemasons, but what happened to Tomebamba, as the city was called, is shrouded in mystery. By the time the Spanish chronicler Cieza de León passed through in 1547, Tomebamba lay largely in ruins, although well-stocked storehouses indicated how great it recently had been. Today it is difficult to imagine Tomebamba's splendour, for all that remains are a few recently excavated Inca walls by the river.

This river bears the name of the Inca city and divides Cuenca in half. South of the river lie fairly recent suburbs and the modern university. To the north is the heart of the colonial city. Although Cuenca has expanded to become Ecuador's third largest town with 151,000 inhabitants, it still retains a pleasantly provincial air and the old centre has churches dating from the 16th and 17th centuries. The earliest building is the original cathedral whose construction began in 1557, the year Cuenca was founded by the Spanish

Cuenca

conquerors. There are cobbled streets and red-tiled roofs, art galleries and flower markets, shady plazas and museums. The majority of the hotels, too, are located near the centre and thus the traveller can conveniently enjoy a relaxing few days in this colonial city.

Information

The IETEL and post office are located next door to one another on the corner of Gran Colombia and Presidente Borrero.

The DITURIS information office is on

Benigno Malo, half a block from the main plaza. They are friendly and they do try to help. As usual, though, they seem to be geared mostly to tourists staying in the best hotel in town for one night and wishing to 'see' Cuenca in three hours. Still, they're better than most other tourist offices and should be able to help with up-to-date museum information, etc. It's a good place to go if you want to help someone practice their English.

Almost opposite the DITURIS office is the Municipalidad, where you can buy the

1	Residencial La Alborada	37	Old Cathedral
2	Hostal Londres	38	Cambio Sur Money Changer
3	Hotel España	39	Internacional Hotel Paris
4	Residencial Tito	40	Hotel Atahualpa
5	Hostel El Galeon	41	Ristorante Pizzeria Italiane
6	Pensión Taiwan	42	Teatro Sucre
7	Residencial Florida	43	Cafeteria Roma
8	Pensióna Andaluz	44	Teatro Casa de Cultura
9	Residencial Norte & Colombia	45	Intituto de Folklore
10	Residencial La Ramada	46	MAG Office
11	Restaurant Bulcón Quiteño	47	Monsalve English magazines
12	Residencial Atenas	48	Chifa Pack How
13	Hotel Majestic	49	Restaurant La Carreta
14	Cine 9 de Octubre	50	Restaurant El Jardin
15	Residencial Niza	51	Restaurant Casa China
16	Cine España	52	Cambistral Money Changer
17	El Paraiso Vegetarian Restaurant	53	Municipal Hall
18	Residencial Siberia	54	Casa de Cultura
19	Hotel El Conquistador	55	DITURIS office
20	Post Office	56	Flower market
21	IETEL	57	Hotel Catedral
22	Hotel El Dorado	58	Pensión Azuay
23	Hotel Internacional	59	Residencial Granada
24	Residencial Amazonas	60	San Sebastian Church
25	Teatro Cuenca	61	Museum of Modern Art
26	Residencial Sto. Domingo	62	Hotel Alli Tiana
27	Sto. Domingo Church	63	Hotel Milan
28	Hotel Residencial Emperador	64	Restaurant El Inca
29	St. Cenaculo Church	65	San Francisco Church
30	Residencial Paris	66	Hotel Cantabri
31	Hotel Pichincha	67	Hotel Crespo
32	Residencial El Inca	68	Hotel Crespo Annex
33	Gran Hotel	69	Municipal Museum
34	New Cathedral	70	Inca ruins
35	Pio Pio Chicken Restaurant	71	Banco Central Museum
36	TAME		

best available map of the city. It's a very good, up-to-date map and costs about US$1.50, but don't be surprised if it's sold out.

There are several bookshops but English-language books are almost unavailable. The Monsalve bookstore has a very mediocre selection of English-language magazines and occasionally one of the magazine stalls around the main plaza has a month-old copy of *Newsweek*.

Money When I was last in Cuenca it was impossible to exchange foreign currency in the banks. You had to go to the exchange houses, which paid within 1% of the best Quito rate. They were open from 9 am to 6 pm Monday through Friday and from 9 am to noon on Saturday. There wasn't a great difference between places. Two are shown on the map. Dollars were easy to change but other currencies were difficult or impossible. It is quite possible that banking regulations will change, enabling banks to cash foreign currency in the future.

Things to See

The River Tomebamba is attractively lined with old colonial buildings, and washerwomen still lay out their clothes to dry on its grassy banks. A pleasant walk is along Avenida 3 de Noviembre, which follows the north bank of the river. The following selection of places of interest to the visitor begins near the south-eastern end of the river, moves north-west into the town centre, and finally moves out to the west. All the sites are marked on the city map and the complete walk out along the river and back via the places mentioned is about six km.

Padre Crespi Museum If you happen to like museums, the good news is that you'll find quite a selection in Cuenca, although they aren't as good as the museums in Quito or Guayaquil. The bad news is that the most famous Cuenca museum, the wonderful rambling collection of Padre Crespi, has

been closed indefinitely since the Padre's death in 1982. The collection has been taken over by the Banco Central but it was not available for viewing when I was last in Cuenca.

Museo del Banco Central This museum has recently moved away from its old location in the downtown bank. It is now found at the south-east part of town near the River Tomebamba and is not very obvious (no sign). The entrance gate is on Calle Larga (see map) and the building is across open grounds. The guard at the gate will indicate the way but you should have your passport. It is free and open from 9 am to 4 pm Tuesday through Friday and from 9 am to noon on Saturday. There is a permanent collection of old black-and-white photographs of Cuenca and a changing exhibit which is often very good. When I was last there this was about the evolution of man and it was most interesting to see this admittedly familiar subject explained from an Ecuadorean point of view using local examples.

Inca Ruins Walking back along Calle Larga and along the river, you come to the ruins on Avenida Todos los Santos. There are some fine niches and walls but most of the stonework was destroyed to build colonial buildings. There are a few explanatory signs in Spanish. If you're coming from Peru the ruins will seem rather lacklustre.

Municipal Museum Further along Calle Larga you come to the Municipal Museum, which is open from 8 am to 1 pm and 3 to 5 pm Monday through Friday. Religious sculptures, colonial furniture and paintings are on display. They have a fine collection of Indian artefacts but only a few were on show recently. The 1984 canonization of St Miguel, who came from the Cuenca area, meant that a display of the life of the saint took up several rooms. Exhibits change frequently.

Instituto Azuaya de Folklore From a block west of the Municipal Museum, head north to Luis Cordero 722 and the institution is on the 3rd floor, up a rather grimy staircase. They are open from 10 am to noon and 3 to 5 pm Monday through Friday. It's free and there is a small but worthwhile exhibit of pottery, traditional musical instruments, native and regional costumes, and various handicrafts. Explanations are in Spanish and a guide is sometimes available. A tip is appreciated.

Parque Calderón The main plaza is half a block away. The dominant building is the **new Cathedral** with its huge blue domes. It is particularly attractive when illuminated, although the lighting hours are unpredictable. The interior is rather stark. Almost unnoticed on the other side of the park is the squat **old Cathedral**, which was closed for renovation for the visit of Pope John Paul to Ecuador in 1985.

Casa de Cultura At the south-west corner of Parque Calderón is the Casa de Cultura. There is a good art gallery here with frequently changing exhibits. Most paintings are by local artists and are for sale but there is absolutely no pressure to buy. In fact it's hard to find a salesperson if you should happen to see a work that you're seriously interested in. There's also a bookshop of art-oriented Spanish-language books.

Other Attractions At the corner of Sucre and Aguirre is the small **Plaza de Carmen** where there is a colourful daily flower market in front of the church. (Turning left here brings you to the **San Francisco market**.) Continuing down Sucre, you come to the **Parque Miguel León**, which is also known as the Plaza San Sebastián. This is a quiet and pleasant park with the interesting old Church of San Sebastián at the north end. The park seems to be developing into an 'artists' quarter,' with a mural of infant art on one wall, a couple of art galleries, and the **Modern Art Museum**

at the south end. This is free and open from 9 am to 1 pm and 3 to 6 pm Monday through Friday and on Saturday morning. They plan on opening on Sundays too; it's worth checking if that is your only free day.

You can return back into the centre along Bolívar and look into the colonial **Church of San Cenáculo** as you go. This also was closed for cleaning recently but will probably be open by the time you read this. After San Cenáculo, continue into the centre along Gran Colombia, the main handicraft shop street in Cuenca. Soon you pass the **Church of Santo Domingo** on your left, which has some fine carved wooden doors and colonial paintings inside. A couple of blocks further is **Productos Andinos** at Gran Colombia 6-24. This Indian-run store sells most kinds of handicrafts at reasonable prices. Crafts experts claim that this is the best store of its kind in Cuenca but there are many more to choose from in the area. The main plaza is only a block to the south.

Market day is Thursday, with a smaller market on Saturday. There are two main **market areas**: one around the Church of San Francisco and the other at the plaza by Avenidas Mariscal Lamar and Hermano Miguel. The market is mainly for locals rather than tourists, and crafts shoppers will do better to look along Gran Colombia. The markets are nevertheless lively and interesting but watch your belongings – pickpockets have been reported. The market continues on a smaller scale on other days of the week.

Las Cajas National Recreation Area
This recreation area lies about 30 km west of Cuenca and is famous for its many beautiful lakes. It is rugged hiking and camping country. Buses from Cuenca leave at 6.30 am from the Church of San Sebastián for the two-hour ride and there is a return bus in the afternoon. There is a refuge where you can sleep for a fee, and camping is allowed. A permit used to cost US$1 but I've heard recent reports that

it's now an exorbitant US$10. The park is administered by the Ministerio de Agricultura y Ganadería. The MAG offices in downtown Cuenca will give you further information, maps and permits.

Fiestas

3 November is Cuenca Day and combines with 1 and 2 November (All Saints' Day and All Souls' Day) to form an important holiday period for the city. The markets are in full swing and there is music and dancing. Hotel rooms may be rather difficult to find at this time.

Carnaval, as in other parts of Ecuador, is celebrated with boisterous water fights. No one is spared – I saw a whole bucket of water poured over an old nun's head from a balcony! Cuenca seems to be more enamoured of these soggy celebrations than the rest of the country; Easter and New Year's are also popular with water-throwers. Protect your camera gear. There is a colourful city parade on Christmas Eve.

Places to Stay

Hotels are often full for the celebrations 1-3 November and your choice will be limited – though there are so many places listed below that you're bound to find somewhere. Prices tend to rise during the fiestas. For some reason, almost all hotels (except a few of the most desperately cheap) seem to have hot or at least tepid water. So you can assume that hot water is available unless I mention otherwise. I also noticed that several hotels have inexpensive rooms with private baths which cost little more than rooms with shared bathrooms. You might want to consider treating yourself to this luxury, even if travelling on a budget. There are half a dozen hotels within a few hundred metres of the bus terminal, but most are a km or more away in the downtown area.

Places to Stay – bus terminal area

Directly opposite the front of the terminal is the *Residencial Los Alamos*, which has a simple restaurant attached. They charge US$2 and US$4 per person for clean rooms with shared and private baths. Turning right out of the terminal and heading down Avenida España for about five minutes, you reach the *Residencial La Alborada*, which charges US$2 each.

A little further, by the traffic circle, is the friendly *Hotel España*, which is US$1.50 each or US$2.30 with a private bath. Both are clean and good. Within a block of the traffic circle are the *Hostal Londres* and *Residencial Tito*, both of which charge US$1.80 each; the *Tito* also has rooms with a private bath for US$3 each and a restaurant below – it has been recommended by several travellers. Also recommended is the modern and clean *Hostal El Galeon*, a block beyond the *Tito*. It has spacious rooms with private bathrooms for US$3.50/US$6, single/double. *El Galeon* is about 700 metres from the bus terminal; all the hotels listed below are a km or more from the terminal.

Places to Stay – bottom end

If you're really low on money head for the market area by Cueva and Sangurima. Here you'll find the basic but adequate *Residencial Norte*, which charges just 70c per person for inside rooms and 90c for a room with a window. There are some other similarly priced cheapies nearby but I wouldn't recommend them unless you're desperate. These include the pensiones *Andaluz* and *Taiwan* and the *Residencial Florida*. Next door to the *Norte* is the *Residencial Colombia*, which is rather better but charges US$1.50 each. Around the corner is the *La Ramada*, which charges from US$1.20-1.50 each depending on the room. The best hotel in this market area is the *Residencial Niza*, which is clean and friendly. The staff always chatted to me when I went in and out and tried to answer my questions when they could. They charge US$2 each in rooms with shared baths or US$2.50 single and US$4.60 double for a room with a private bath.

There are several good, cheap hotels further into the town centre. For US$1.20 each try the *Residencial Siberia*, which is old but friendly and pleasant – they have lots of flowers at the entrance. One of the best cheap hotels is the friendly *Residencial Inca*, which has long been used by budget travellers and is still only US$1 per person. A simple restaurant is attached. Two clean residencials for US$1.50 each are the *Amazonas* and *Granada*, the latter with a great view from the roof. Also clean and quiet is the *Residencial Santo Domingo* at US$1.70 each. For US$2 and US$2.20 each there are the clean but unremarkable *Hotel Emperador* and *Pichincha*. The extremely cheap and basic *Pensión Azuay* and *Hotel Cantabri* have nothing to recommend them except their cheapness.

If you are trying to economize but would like a simple and clean room with a private bath, try the following selection. The *Residencial Atenas* charges US$2.30 and US$4 for comfortable singles and doubles but their left-luggage facilities have been criticized. The old and somewhat run-down *Hotel Majestic* has friendly staff and their spacious rooms go for US$2.50 per person. Similarly priced is the recommended and friendly *Hotel Milan*; try to get a room with a balcony – some superb views. The *Gran Hotel* at US$2.80 each has also been recommended – both these last two have good luggage storage facilities. Some of these hotels have cheaper rooms with shared baths.

Places to Stay – middle

For about US$3.50 each you can stay at the oldish and rather stately *Hotel Internacional* or the recently remodelled *Residencial Paris* (not to be confused with the *Internacional Hotel Paris*). Both have private baths and even telephones in the rooms. *Hotel Alli Tiana* charges US$5.50 each and has some rooms with good views.

Places to Stay – top end

Brand new and modern-looking in a quiet part of town is the *Hotel Atahualpa*, which charges US$7.50 single and US$12 double. The highly recommended *Hotel Crespo* has a great variety of rooms with an equally great range of prices, from moderate to relatively expensive. They have rooms in their main building and in the annex across the street. Some rooms have inside windows, others have street windows or river views. Prices are US$6-14 single and US$7.50-18 double. There is a good restaurant.

The good *Hotel Catedral* charges about US$9 single and US$14 double, but the friendly management gives discounts to Peace Corps workers and similar organizations – use your imagination. They have a good restaurant. The *Internacional Hotel Paris* and *Hotel El Conquistador* are both good, modern, recommended and have restaurants. They charge about US$11 single and US$16 double.

The fanciest hotel downtown is the *El Dorado*, which has been criticized for snotty staff (maybe they've changed). Expect to pay US$22 for a single and US$26 double. Finally, if you want luxury and prefer staying out of town, try the expensive, Swiss-run *Hotel La Laguna* on Avenida Ordoñez Lazo, at the northwestern edge of Cuenca.

Places to Eat

Paradoxically, the finest restaurant in town is opposite one of the cheapest good ones. *Restaurant El Jardín* has been described as the best restaurant in Ecuador; this is a matter of opinion but it's certainly very good value. You can eat well here for US$5. Almost opposite it is *La Carreta*, which serves good meals for under a dollar.

The areas around the two markets have plenty of cheap restaurants. One of the best near the San Francisco market is *Restaurant El Inca*, where a decent set meal can run as low as 70c. On Avenida Sangurima you can find several cheap places, of which the *Balcón Quiteño* is recommended. Local people eat here –

always a good sign. On the first block of Avenida Sangurima there are good *chifas* next to and opposite the *Hotel España*. Other *chifas* are shown on the map – the *Chifa Hong Kong* isn't because they made the classic errors of cooking a fly in my food and then overcharging me.

On the main square is the *Pio Pio* chicken restaurant, which has good coffee. Also on the main plaza is the *Raymypampa* restaurant under the new cathedral. It looks quite nice but has the slowest service I've ever encountered anywhere. Turn this too your advantage – order a coffee and write letters home. Just off the plaza is the rather undistinguished entrance of the *Cafeteria Roma*. Inside it is quite spacious and has a slightly tarnished but nevertheless charming old world décor. Although their prices aren't dirt cheap, they do serve good Italian food and I recommend it. Another Italian place is the *Ristorante Pizzeria Italiana* out on the Plaza San Blas. It's also good but I like the Roma better. If you're looking for vegetarian food try the very simple *El Paraiso*.

The best hotels in town have good restaurants open to the general public; you can relax inexpensively with coffee and croissants in pleasant surroundings. The *Internacional Hotel Paris* has a good and very moderately priced restaurant, *El Conquistador* has some of the best coffee in town and *El Dorado* can give you breakfast from 6.30 am, though it's not so good for other meals.

If you're leaving town – or arriving, for that matter – you can eat at the main bus terminal. They have a 24-hour snack bar and a decent restaurant open during the day.

Entertainment

Though Cuenca is Ecuador's third largest city, entertainment is minimal. *El Mercurio* is the Cuenca newspaper for listings of movies at the half dozen cinemas. The *Teatro Casa de Cultura* is not the same place as the *Casa de Cultura*, which occasionally also has movies or lectures – both are shown on the map. The expensive *El Dorado Hotel* has a nightclub and there's a discotheque weekends at the *Hotel Alli Tiana*. There are a couple of other disco or show possibilities on the same block – irregular dates. I suggest you bring a good long novel if you need entertainment.

Getting There & Around

Air The Aeropuerto Mariscal Lamar passenger terminal is conveniently located on Avenida España only two km from the heart of town. Taxis are about 50c and city buses pass the terminal frequently, although they tend to be rather full just after a plane arrives. Downtown, buses depart from the stop by the flower market on Padre Aguirre – not all are marked so ask the drivers.

Flight schedules to and from Cuenca change several times a year so you should make local enquiries about these. There are usually daily flights to and from Guayaquil for about US$10 and two or three flights a day to Quito costing US$16. For flights to cities south of Cuenca you have to fly to Guayaquil and then take another flight back to your final destination. This is expensive and inconvenient but it is possible that there will be direct flights to Loja in future. For flights to cities to the north you must change in Guayaquil or Quito.

Most flights are with TAME, which has its downtown office by the central plaza. Business hours are 9.30 am to 12.30 pm and 2 to 5 pm on weekdays, subject to change. Their airport desk is open for incoming and outgoing flights. SAN-Saeta also has begun services to Quito. They were in the process of opening a new office downtown recently – ask at a travel agency, the tourist office, or try the airport.

Rail The railway station is on the south-eastern outskirts of town. There used to be a daily service north to Sibambe with connections to Guayaquil and Quito, but these have been halted because of damage to the track during the 1982/83 El Niño floods. It is unlikely that service will resume before 1987 and maybe much later.

Bus A new and well-organized Terminal Terrestre was opened in November 1983 and most long-distance buses now arrive and leave from here. It is located on Avenida España on the way to the airport and about 1½ km from the town centre. City buses leave from in front of the terminal for the centre (5c) and buses for the terminal leave from the bus stop on Padre Aguirre by the flower market. Most (but not all) buses are marked 'Terminal' so ask the driver to be sure.

There are literally dozens of different bus companies with offices in the terminal. Some run two or three buses every hour, others run two or three every week. Some run fast, small and cramped minibuses (or *busetas*) with guaranteed seating, others use huge but slow old coaches with more leg room but standing passengers as well. You should check out the various possibilities and find the one most convenient for you.

Buses leave for Guayaquil (US$2.50, five hours) every few minutes. Buses for Azogues (25c, 45 minutes) leave at least every hour, many continuing to Cañar (45c, 1½ hours) and Alausí if the road is open. For Quito (US$3-4, nine to 14 hours depending on route and road conditions) there are buses about every hour. For destinations between Alausí and Quito there are several departures every day but times and costs vary depending on road conditions and routes taken. Buses leave for Machala (US$2.20, five hours) about every hour; a few continue to Huaquillas but it's usually quicker to change buses in Machala. There are six or seven buses a day to Saraguro (US$1.90, 4½ hours) continuing to Loja (US$2.40, seven hours). For destinations south of Loja it is best to change in Loja. There are three or

four buses a day to Macas (US$2.40, 10 hours) and a couple of buses to Gualaquiza (US$2, seven hours) if you want to go into the southern Oriente. There is a passenger information desk at the terminal where you can ask about other unusual destinations.

Buses to Gualacéo for the Sunday market depart from the corner of Avenidas Espan'a and Benalcázar about 100 metres south-west of the main terminal. They leave every few minutes on market day and less frequently on weekdays for the 40-minute, 25c ride. Ask in the main terminal for buses continuing to Sígsig; they leave almost hourly with CITES (40c, 1½ hours).

Local buses (5c) for Baños leave from Avenida Gen Torres by the San Francisco market. At Baños you'll find hot springs with public pools and restaurants.

AZOGUES

About 35 km north of Cuenca on the Pan American highway lies Azogues. It is a quiet, small town of only 15,000 inhabitants, yet it is the capital of the province of Cañar. 'Azogues' literally means 'quicksilver' and derives from the mercury-rich ores supposedly found in the area; I could find no evidence of mercury extraction. The town is more important for its panama hat industry and Saturday market, and is worth visiting for its church. It is a possible alternative to Cuenca as a base for visiting Biblián, Cañar and Ingapirca to the north.

Information

The IETEL office is on the main plaza. Filanbanco will reluctantly exchange dollars at a bad rate – it's better to go to Cuenca.

Things to See

The most interesting place to visit is the **Church of San Francisco**, which dominates the town from a hill to the south-east. You can't see it when you arrive at the bus terminal but if you head generally south-

Azoguez

Not to Scale

east and then climb up the Avenida de la Virgen, you'll reach it in about half an hour. From the church there are sweeping views of the town, the surrounding countryside, and several other churches perched on the top of nearby hills. Hilltops seem to be the place to build churches in this region. Inside San Francisco there is a beautiful gilt altar. The building is sometimes illuminated at night and, sitting on the dark hill, it looks almost as if it were floating in mid-air.

Another church worth visiting is that of Biblian. This village is some nine km north of Azogues on the Pan American; there are plenty of buses from the terminal. The **Santuario de la Virgen del Rocío** (or Sanctuary of the Virgin of the Dew), as the church is called, is highly visible to the right of the main highway on a steep hill dominating Biblian. It is one of the most attractive churches I've seen and looks more like a fairy-tale princess's palace than it does a church. Keep your eyes open for it even if you're just driving straight through Biblian. There is an annual pilgrimage here on 8 September. There's also a weekly market on Sunday.

Both these churches were renovated in late 1984 for the pope's visit in 1985, so they should be looking clean and bright. In fact, buildings on all the main streets in Azogues were whitewashed, and walking the streets of the town and admiring the colonial architecture is very pleasant. As you stroll, keep your eyes open for signs of the panama hat industry. Avenida 3 de Noviembre is a good street to see hats being blocked and sold. The main market is on this street and is where the bustling Saturday morning market is held. There is also a smaller market on the Plaza San Francisco in front of the church – it's worth going to for the view.

If you spend the night and want something to do, try the movie theatre. There's only one.

Places to Stay & Eat

Despite its provincial capital status, Azogues does not yet have any particularly good hotels. The best place in town is across the highway from the bus terminal and down a small hill. This is the small, clean and family-run *Residencial y Restaurant Azogues*. All the rooms have communal showers and there is hot water. They charge US$2.50 per person and are often full.

At the bus station there is the basic *Hotel Cordillera* for US$2.30 each. Closer to the town centre is the more basic still *Pensión Tropical* at US$1.50 each. They're OK but have no hot showers. Public baths charge 20c for a hot shower and there are two marked on the map.

The best place to eat is at the *Residencial y Restaurant Azogues* but their menu is often limited. Three inexpensive but quite acceptable restaurants are shown on the map: the *Gypsy*, *Copacabana* and *El Padrino*.

Getting There

There is a train station but, as you've gathered by now, services were indefinitely suspended in 1983.

The bus terminal is right on the Pan American highway, which is renamed 24 de Mayo as it goes through Azogues. For buses to Cuenca or Cañar it is often best to stand on the highway and wait for one to come by – often Cuenca-Cañar buses don't pull into the terminal. The fare to either Cuenca or Cañar shouldn't be more than about 30c although one driver tried to charge me twice that. There are direct buses from Azogues to Cuenca with Empresa Auto Via but their buses are very old, very slow, and pick up everybody and their chickens – interesting and worthwhile if you're not in any hurry. From the terminal there are several departures a day for Quito, Guayaquil and Machala. For other destinations it is best to go to Cuenca and change buses.

CAÑAR & INGAPIRCA

Although Ingapirca is the major Inca site in Ecuador it is difficult to get to and nobody seems to know much about the ruins. They have never been 'lost,' as was Machu Picchu – indeed, the Frenchman Charles-Marie de La Condamine drew accurate plans of them as far back as 1739. The ruins are referred to as a fortress, but its garrison – if there was one – must have been quite small. Archaeologists think that the main structure, an *usnu* elliptical platform known as the Temple of the Sun, had religious and ceremonial purposes. This building boasts some of the Inca's finest mortarless stonework and has several of the typical trapezoidal niches and doorways which are a hallmark of Inca construction. The less-well-preserved buildings were probably storehouses and the complex may have been used as a *tambo* or stopping place for runners carrying imperial messages from Quito to Tomebamba.

At Ingapirca there is a small village with an occasionally open craft shop/museum by the church on the plaza. There are no restaurants or accommodation and the few stores sell only the most basic of food items. There is a weekly market on Fridays.

The ruins are about a km away from the village. There is as yet no entrance fee and no proper amenities, although an on-site museum was under construction in 1985 and it is hoped that it will be open soon. There is a shelter by the construction work with basic toilet facilities and benches but you can't sleep there.

Places to Stay & Eat

Cañar has some simple places to stay. The basic *Pensión Guayaquil* on the street of the same name charges US$1.20 per person and 30c extra for hot water. The *Residencial Patricia* is found over the store at 3 de Noviembre and Bolívar. Their sign had fallen down; maybe it's up again now. They have hot water and charge US$1.50 per person. If these are all full you can find accommodation in unsigned private houses if you ask around. Places to eat are not particularly note-worthy and most close by about 7 pm. Market day is Sunday.

Getting There

Although Ingapirca is Ecuador's most important Inca ruin, visiting it cheaply is not straightforward as there are no direct bus services. A few tourist agencies in Cuenca organize day trips but charge US$15 per person and need a five-person minimum. It would be better to rent a taxi for the day, which should cost under US$20 – bargain for the best rate.

To make an economical visit, you must first take a bus to Cañar (45c, 1½ hours from Cuenca). About two km before Cañar there is a signed turnoff to Ingapirca on your right. You can wait here for a passing vehicle to take you the 15 km to the ruins; expect to pay about 30c for the ride. You can walk/hitch but still are expected to pay if you get a ride. Vehicles pass by about once an hour. This is probably the easiest way to get to Ingapirca by public transport, but leave early or you may get stuck without a ride back. There are no facilities at Ingapirca.

The bus from Cuenca continues through Cañar to El Tambo. From here there is a shorter (eight km) road to Ingapirca but it was closed for repair recently. It is passable on foot and is the shortest walk from the Pan American. I'm told that there is a very basic place to stay in El Tambo but I've never tried it.

There is a train station about three or four km from Ingapirca – if they ever reopen it.

Pickup trucks leave Cañar for Ingapirca when they have a load. There are no set departure times or places. Ask around. You could probably hire a truck to take you there for about US$3.

GUALACÉO, CHORDELEG & SÍGSIG

These three villages are all famous for their Sunday markets. If you started from Cuenca early in the morning you could easily visit all three markets and be back in Cuenca in the afternoon. The best-

1 Residencial Español
2 IETEL
3 Gran Hostal Gualaceo
4 Residencial Gualaceo
5 Teatro Mariscal

Gualaceo

(Not to Scale)

known markets are at Gualacéo and Chordeleg, which are within three or four km of one another. Gualacéo has the biggest market and sells mainly produce, animals and household goods. Chordeleg's market is smaller but important for textiles and jewellery – it is one of Ecuador's most famous jewellery centres. Sígsig market is further away from Cuenca and less visited by tourists. All three villages are good examples of old-fashioned colonial towns.

Gualacéo

In addition to being an important market town, Gualacéo has some importance as a tourist resort and is prettily located by a river. There are several restaurants by the river and the stroll is pleasant. The town is quite progressive and has a large and spacious modern church with good stained-glass windows. There are several restaurants and places to stay as well as an IETEL office and a cinema.

Places to Stay & Eat The best place to stay in town is the *Gran Hostal Gualacéo*, which charged me an incredibly cheap US$1.30 for a room with a private bath and hot water. I can't believe that these prices will last but it must be the best hotel deal in Ecuador. The other two hotels are the residencials *Gualacéo* and *Español*. They charge US$1 and have hot water, sometimes. About 20 minutes out of town is the new *Hostería La Ribera* (see map), which is by the river and has a restaurant and small swimming pool. They charge US$8 and US$12 single and double with private bath but are open to bargaining, especially for stays of more than one night.

Gualacéo has several barely adequate restaurants on the east side of the market. You'll find more restaurants by the river – one of the best is *Los Sauces*. It is designed for weekend relaxation with skittles, volleyball and tennis, as well as food and beer. The tennis courts are a far cry from

Wimbledon! Most of the riverside places are closed midweek.

Chordeleg

Chordeleg has many stores selling a great variety of crafts – some people complain that it is too 'touristy.' Maybe it is; it's especially popular with Guayaquileños looking for highland bargains. On the other hand, if you're shopping for souvenirs or gifts you can choose from gold and silver filigree jewellery, woodcarvings, pottery, textiles, panama hats and embroidered clothing.

There is a pleasant central plaza with a small modern church containing simple but attractive stained-glass windows. Also on the plaza is an excellent museum. It's just a small village museum, yet it manages to pack more into it than many bigger city museums. It's open from 8 am to 5 pm daily except Monday and is free. There are very informative displays about the history and techniques of many of the local handicrafts such as filigreed metalwork, panama hatmaking and *ikat* weaving. Guides are available. It helps if you understand Spanish.

Places to Eat There is nowhere to stay in Chordeleg but you can find a couple of simple restaurants.

Sígsig

Sígsig is a pleasant old colonial village but nothing happens here except the Sunday market. There are a couple of restaurants on the main market plaza. A few blocks from the plaza is the CITES bus office. Opposite it is a store that will rent you a room. The ride out here from Cuenca is nice.

Getting to Gualacéo, Chordeleg & Sígsig

Buses from Cuenca take about 40 minutes to reach Gualacéo and leave every few minutes on market day and about every hour on weekdays. You can continue the three or four km to Chordeleg on foot or take a local bus (see map for locations).

Buses pass the Chordeleg plaza for Sígsig at least once an hour and charge 20c for the 40-minute ride. Sit on the right-hand side of the bus for good views of the river canyon on the way to Sígsig. CITES buses return from Sígsig to Cuenca about every hour for 40c. Three buses a week (Monday, Wednesday and Saturday at 6 am) leave Sígsig for Gualaquiza if the road is passable.

PAUTE

A few km before you reach Gualacéo, the road forks. The left-hand fork takes you up the Paute River valley to the village of the same name. Nearby is the Distilería Uzhupud, which makes several of the local liquors.

Places to Stay

Also near the village is the *Hostería Uzhupud*, an excellent hotel in pleasant countryside. They have a very good restaurant, a swimming pool, tennis courts and an amazing garden which contains hundreds (I've heard thousands) of varieties of flowers, including dozens of species of orchids. They charge about US$15.

ONA

The Pan American Highway heads south from Cuenca to Loja via the towns of Oña and Saraguro. The road climbs steadily from Cuenca and there are good views of *páramo* moorlands and the southern Ecuadorean Andes. Oña is reached after about 2½ hours and the bus sometimes stops here to refuel. The interesting and ancient petrol pump is generator-driven. The attendant has to switch on the generator before he can deliver the fuel, and then he switches it off – a good measure of how frequently vehicles stop in Oña. It's a one-street town with a couple of simple restaurants and a basic pensión – there's not much reason to stop here.

SARAGURO

Just beyond Oña, the road crosses the

provincial line into Loja and continues rising and falling through the eerie *páramo* scenery until it reaches Saraguro, 4½ hours, 165 km and US$1.80 south of Cuenca.

The town is named after the Saraguro Indians, who originally came from the Lake Titicaca region in Peru but became colonists in this region under the Incas. They are readily identifiable by their traditional dress. Both men and women wear flat white felt hats with wide brims. The men sport a single pigtail and wear a black poncho but perhaps the most unusual part of their attire is their knee-length black or navy-blue shorts which are sometimes covered with an odd little white apron. They carry double shoulder bags with one pouch in front and one behind for a balanced load. The women wear heavy pleated black skirts and shawls fastened with ornate silver pins. The pins are known as *topos* and are highly prized.

The Saraguros were well known for their jewellery but this craft seems to be dying out. Cattle-raising is their main occupation and they are to be seen on foot driving their herds to tropical pastures in the 28 de Mayo area. Wherever they go, they normally wear their traditional clothing and are the most successful Indian group of the southern Ecuadorean highlands. Their market day is Sunday.

Places to Stay & Eat

There are no real hotels, but if you ask around you'll be shown houses where lodgers are taken. There's one next to the *Helados* sign on Calle Loja, just off the main plaza. There are two or three basic restaurants, of which the best is the *Salón Cristal* behind the church.

Getting There

Loja, the provincial capital, is 60 km to the south and CTS buses leave Saraguro six or eight times a day for the two-hour ride, which costs 60c. The CTS bus office is a block from the main plaza. They also have buses leaving for various small villages in the area. For Cuenca, it is best to wait in the plaza for a northbound bus from Loja to pass by.

LOJA

From Saraguro the road drops steadily to Loja at 2225 metres. It was founded by the Spanish captain, Alonso de Mercadillo, on 8 December 1548, and so is one of the oldest towns in Ecuador. None of the earliest buildings survive, although houses from the 18th century can be found. With over 71,000 inhabitants, Loja is both an important provincial capital and a college town, with two universities, a music conservatory and a law school.

Loja is situated very close to the Oriente and the surrounding countryside is green and pleasant. The people are proud of the great variety of plant species found in the region. They tell the story of the beautiful Countess of Chinchón, wife of an early 17th-century Peruvian viceroy, who was dying of malaria. A Franciscan monk cured her with quinine extracted from the bark of a tree found in the Loja area. After her recovery, fame of the 'miraculous' properties of the tree spread throughout the Spanish empire and the world. Today the tree is called the cinchona after the countess. Alexander von Humboldt, the German scientist and explorer, visited the area in 1802 and called it 'the garden of Ecuador.' The British botanist Richard Spruce also mounted an expedition here in the mid-19th century.

Although the town itself is not exceptionally interesting, travellers on their way to Peru via the border town of Macará find this a convenient place to stop. The highland route to Peru through Loja and Macará is slower and rougher but much more scenic than the more frequented route through the coastal towns of Machala and Huaquillas.

Information

The post office is in the municipal

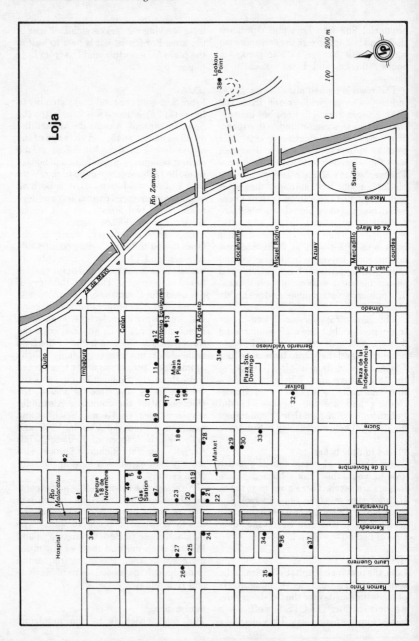

building on the north side of the main plaza. It is not very obvious, so ask. The IETEL office is a block away. There are no exchange houses and the only bank which will change dollars is the Banco Central, whose rate was almost 20% lower than exchange houses in Cuenca. They won't change sucres into dollars. Peruvian soles are also difficult to negotiate and a bad rate is given. It is better to change money in Macará.

Two local newspapers, *El Mundo* and *El Siglo*, carry only local news. Guayaquil newspapers are available by about 8 am and Quito papers arrive by late morning.

Things to See

A short but pleasant walk is east from the centre and across the River Zamora (where washerwomen can sometimes be seen at work). Then climb up the small hill to the statue of the Virgin of Loja, who is protected by a caged (stone) lion. Here there is a rather damaged lookout with good city views.

The cathedral is on the main plaza, and from August to November it contains the miraculous Virgen del Cisne (Virgin of the

Swan), carved in the late 1500s by Diego de Robles. During other months of the year the statue is kept at the village of El Cisne, some 70 km away. Both the cathedral and the church of Santo Domingo have interesting painted interiors and elaborate statues.

The weekly market is on Sunday, but Saturdays and Mondays also seem to be busy. The day of the Virgen del Cisne is celebrated on 8 September, and an annual international produce fair is held for about four or five days on either side of the 8th. (It's called 'international' because Peruvians attend it.)

Places to Stay

Loja appears to have an excess of accommodation. I counted over two dozen hotels and many of them were nearly empty. Maybe they fill up for the annual fiestas. Some of the hotels were closed and others were open but I couldn't find anyone to show me a room. The lack of guests may well mean that the owners will be willing to bargain. The hotels are close together so wander around until you find one that appeals to you.

1	Continela del Sur (buses)	20	Hotel Miraflores
2	Viajeros (buses)	21	Hotel American
3	Transportes Saraguro (buses)	22	Hotels Quinara, Riviera, Inca
4	Turismo Oriental (buses)	23	Hotel Saraguressss Internacional
5	Hostal Don Juan & Residencial Sta. Marianita	24	Hotel Río Amazonas
		25	Transportes Loja Terminal & Pensión
6	Hotel Metropolitan	26	Pensión Guayaquil de mis Amores
7	Restaurant Rey Neptuno	27	Restaurant Suizo-Lojano
8	Hotel Mexico	28	Hotels Austral & Internacional
9	Banco Central	29	Hostal Crystal & Hotel Loja
10	Restaurant Andaluz	30	Residencial Caribe
11	Post Office	31	Cine El Dorado
12	TAME	32	Teatro Popular
13	IETEL	33	Hotel Imperial
14	Cathedral	34	Restaurant Americano
15	Pizzeria Geminis & Chifa Asia	35	Residencial San Andres
16	Cine Velez	36	Transportes Cajanuma
17	Cafeteria Glacier	37	Transportes Sur-Oriente
18	Hotels Acapulco, Lourdes, Cueubamba	38	Virgin of Loja
19	Hotel Paris		

Places to Stay – bottom end

One of the cheapest places is the *Residencial Santa Marianita*, which is clean and secure but has only cold water. They charge US$1.20 per person. Similar prices are charged at the *Hotel American*, *Hotel Mexico* and *Residencial Caribe*.

For US$1.50 each try hotels *Londres*, *Acapulco* and *Cuxubamba*. These are all located next to one another and are clean, pleasant and have hot water. The last-named also has some rooms with private baths for US$2.50 each. The *Hostal Don Juan* also charges US$1.50.

For better rooms with hot water and private bathrooms try the *Hotel Metropolitan* for US$2.50 per person, or the friendly *Hotel Miraflores* for US$3 with a private bath and US$2 without.

There are several hotels near the *Transportes Loja Terminal*. The place right above the terminal is cheap but very noisy. Across the street is the unfriendly *Pensión Guayaquil de Mis Amores*, which charges US$2 per person in rooms with private baths but only cold water. I don't like either of them. There are other good hotels near this terminal but they are more expensive.

Places to Stay – middle

There are several very comfortable and reasonably priced hotels. *Hotel Paris* charges US$3 per person for rooms with private bathrooms and hot water. It's been recommended by several travellers but I've heard mixed reports. Good value is the *Hotel Inca*, which charges US$3.50 each for clean rooms with private bath, carpeting and TV (though Loja programming can best be described as lacklustre!). Even better is the *Hotel Rio Amazonas* which offers all the above plus a room phone and a restaurant for US$4.50 single and US$6.50 double. It is conveniently located a block away from the Loja bus terminal. Other clean hotels with private bathrooms in this price range are the *Saraguros Internacional*, *Riviera* and *Quinara*.

The best place in town is the new *Hotel Imperial*, located a few blocks away from everybody else. They charge about US$8 single and US$12 double.

Places to Eat

On the west side of the main plaza you have the choice of Chinese or Italian at the *Chifa Asia* and the *Pizzeria Geminis*. Both are good. Just up from the plaza is the more elegant *Restaurant Andaluz*, and around the corner the *Cafeteria Glacier* is OK for breakfasts and snacks. *Restaurant Suizo-Lojano* by the Loja bus terminal is reasonable and has a variety of food. Also good is the *Restaurant Americano* a few blocks to the south. I couldn't find any outstanding restaurants.

Entertainment

There are three movie theatres, of which the *Cine Velez* on the main plaza usually shows the best films. Above the *Cine El Dorado* there is the *La Rosa* discotheque, open at weekends, but it seems teenage rather than adult oriented.

Getting There

Air Loja is served by La Tola airport, which is in Catamayo some 30 km to the west. At this time, TAME has daily flights (except Sundays) to Guayaquil. You have to leave Loja at 5 am to be at the airport by 6 am for the 6.45 am flight, which costs about US$9.50. There are no buses at that time, but TAME will help organize shared taxis for about US$1.50 per passenger. Alternatively, spend the night in Catamayo. TAME has announced that it will begin a thrice-weekly direct service to Quito (via Cuenca?). Check with their office at the corner of the main plaza in Loja for up-to-date information.

Bus There are many different bus terminals in Loja but the most important is the Transportes Loja Terminal on Avenida 10 de Agosto and Guerrero. Their buses are often booked up several hours or a day in advance, so you should book early. The booking office is crowded, noisy and intimidating, so be prepared. There are two desks: one for same-day bookings and the other for departures on future dates. Once you've sorted out which is which, you can ask the clerk at what times buses are available and buy your ticket. There are four daily buses to Quito (US$4.50, 18 hours); four buses to Macará (US$1.80, seven hours); eight buses to Zamora (80c, three hours); four buses to Machala (US$2.10, eight hours); five buses to Guayaquil (US$3.20, 11 hours); one night bus at 10.30 pm to Huaquillas (US$2.90, 10 hours); and various other departures to intermediate points. It's a very busy terminal.

There are several terminals around the Parque 18 de Noviembre. Centinela del Sur has five daily departures for Machala. Co-op Viajeros has seven daily buses to Cuenca (US$2.40, seven hours) and Turismo Oriental has a single night bus to Cuenca. Transportes Saraguro has six or seven buses a day to – you guessed it – Saraguro (60c, two hours). Some of these continue on to remote communities beyond Saraguro, such as Selva Alegre and Manú.

For buses to Vilcabamba you have to go to Transportes Cajanuma or Transportes Sur-Oriente, both of which have four buses a day that take one hour and cost 45c. A few of their buses continue south as far as Valladolid.

There are a few other infrequent buses going to remote and rarely visited villages in the surrounding mountains. Ask around. These are most likely to run at weekends for the Loja market.

VILCABAMBA

A minor road heads due south from Loja and drops steadily through green mountainous scenery to Vilcabamba, some 30 km away. En route you pass through the village of Malacatos, distinguished by a large church with three blue domes visible from a great distance. Malacatos has a Sunday market and there is a basic restaurant, *Salón Estrellita* behind the main plaza.

Vilcabamba has for many years been famous as 'the valley of longevity.' Inhabitants supposedly lived to be a 100 or more, and some claimed to be 120 years old. This was attributed to their simple, hard-working lifestyle and the excellent local climate. Scientific investigation has been unable to substantiate these beliefs but the legend persists and gives rise to some minor local tourism. The climate certainly is very pleasant and the surrounding countryside offers lovely walks.

Most of the town surrounds the main square, where there is a church, an IETEL office, a few simple stores and town's total choice of eating and accommodation possibilities. On Calle Vega just down from the church is an *Artesanías* sign where they sell a few local handicrafts.

Places to Stay & Eat

There are two basic restaurants and the clean and friendly *Hotel Valle Sagrado*, which charges US$1 per person, on the main square.

About a km from the main plaza, on the very outskirts of town, is the modern *Parador Turistico Vilcabamba*, which has a restaurant, bar and rooms with private baths for about US$6 per person.

Getting There

There is a Transportes Sur-Oriente bus office on the main plaza and buses return to Loja every hour or so.

CATAMAYO

Loja was founded twice. The first time was in 1546, on what is now Catamayo; the second time on its present site two years later. Despite its long history, Catamayo is a totally unremarkable town except for its airport, La Tola, which serves Loja 30 km away.

Places to Stay

It is possible to stay here although accommodation is basic. There are three hotels. *Hotel Lacita* is a few blocks from the central plaza, the *San Marcos* is on the plaza itself, and the *Turis* is on the corner of the plaza. The last is the cleanest-looking at US$1.50 per person. There are several basic restaurants on and near the plaza, and a market as well.

Getting There

There are frequent buses from the plaza to Loja with Transportes Catamayo. There are also slow buses to Quito and Guayaquil. Local buses can take you to explore the small villages to the north and south of Catamayo. A taxi to the airport is about 50c.

About 25 km after Catamayo the road forks. The north fork goes to Machala via the colonial gold-mining towns of Portovelo and Zaruma in the province of El Oro. The south-west fork goes through Catacocha to the border town of Macará.

CATACOCHA

It's a scenic but bumpy seven-hour ride from Loja to Macará. Catacocha is the halfway point and the only place you could break the journey. It's a very rural village and on market day (Sunday) it seems as if horses outnumber vehicles.

Places to Stay & Eat

There are two basic hotels, both a couple of blocks from the main plaza but in different directions. They are the *Hotel Guayaquil* and *Turismo*. Both charge about US$1.20 each per night. There are a few basic restaurants.

MACARÁ

From Loja at 2225 metres, through Catacocha at about 1700 metres, the road continues to drop steadily to Macará at a hot and dusty 500 metres above sea level. Macará is a small and unimportant town on the Peruvian border. The faster and more convenient coastal route carries almost 100% of the international traffic. The main advantage to the Macará route is the scenic descent from Loja.

Information

Although there is a bank in Macará, it does not have foreign exchange facilities. Because of the low volume of border traffic, there are few people who will change money. If you ask around, however, you will always find someone. Rates for exchanging soles into sucres and vice versa are inferior to using US cash dollars, so try to arrive at the border with as little local cash as possible. Exchange rates for cash dollars were better with Macará street changers than with the bank at Loja but worse than with the exchange houses in Cuenca. If possible, try to ascertain exchange rates before arrival at the border by talking with travellers going the other way.

There is an IETEL office and a ratty movie theatre.

Places to Stay & Eat

There are four hotels. The best, and the most expensive, is the DITURIS-run *Parador Turistico* on the outskirts of Macará on the way to the border. It has simple, clean rooms with private baths and is excellent value for US$3.50 single, US$6 double and US$8.50 triple. There is a restaurant, which is the best place to eat if you're staying here.

There are three cheap and basic hotels in the town centre. They only have cold water but the weather is warm enough that it isn't a great hardship. *Hotel Internacional* is conveniently located over the *Transportes Loja* bus terminal; hence it is often full and can get very noisy. *Hotel Amazonas* is on the same street and quieter. *Hotel Guayaquil* is located over a store and you should ask the store owners for rooms. It is occasionally closed. All three hotels charge about US$1 per night.

There are a couple of basic restaurants opposite the bus terminal but they are only open at meal times and have limited menus. For mid-afternoon snacks try the *Fuente de Soda*, which isn't very good but at least it's open.

1	Transportes Loja & Hotel Internacianel
2	Fuente de Soda
3	Movie Theatre
4	IETEL
5	Peruvian Consulate

Not to Scale

Getting There

Air There are two flights a week to Guayaquil with TAME, using small aircraft such as Twin Otters or Avros. Flights are at 1 pm Monday and Friday and cost US$9.50. There is no airline office; enquire at the airstrip a few minutes' walk from the town centre.

Bus Transportes Loja is the main bus company. The following schedule was in effect in late 1984. Buses are available to:

Loja – 3 am, 1 pm and 4 pm, US$1.80, seven hours
Machala – 6 am, US$2.60, 12 hours
Guayaquil – 6 pm, US$4, 15 hours
Quito – 10 am, US$5.20, 22 hours
Santo Domingo – 1.30 pm, US$4.50, 18 hours

These times are rough estimates. The journeys are tiring and uncomfortable, and you are recommended to go to Loja and break up the journey. If you really must get to the other destinations fast, you should go via the coast.

Crossing the Peruvian Border

Macará is about an hour's walk away from the border at the Río Macará. Pickup trucks leave the market once or twice an hour and charge about 15c. You can take a taxi (usually a pickup truck) for 60c. Vehicles wait at the border to pick up passengers from Peru. Peruvian soles are usually accepted.

At the border there is one fly-blown restaurant where you can get a cold drink. Border crossings are from 8 am to 6 pm daily with irregular lunch hours. Formalities are fairly relaxed as long as your documents are in order.

Travellers entering Ecuador are rarely asked to show exit tickets or money. A valid passport and tourist card are needed for Ecuador. If arriving, you will be given a tourist card at the border; if leaving, you will be expected to surrender the card you received on arrival to the border authorities.

Travellers entering Peru are occasionally asked for a ticket out of the country, especially those who require a visa. If you don't require a visa you probably won't be asked. If you are, and you don't have an airline ticket out of Lima, you can usually satisfy this requirement by buying a return bus ticket to Sullana, the nearest large town and over 200 km away. The unused portion of the ticket is non-refundable. Most nationalities, however, need only a valid passport and tourist card which is obtainable from the border authorities. 'Gringo' exceptions are Australians, New Zealanders and French citizens who do require visas. There is a Peruvian consul in Macará – if in any doubt, check. The consulate is open from 9 am to 1 pm Monday through Friday.

Facilities for accommodation, transport and food are inferior on the Peruvian side and it is best to stay in Macará if possible. It is difficult to get transport into Peru in the afternoon and evening; therefore crossing the border in the morning is advisable.

The Southern Oriente

Oriente literally means the orient, or east, and is the term used by Ecuadoreans for all of their Amazon basin lowlands east of the Andes. The words *selva* or *jungla* are not used for the area as a whole, although *selva* can refer to a particular part of the forest of the Oriente. Even though the Amazon river itself does not flow through Ecuador, every one of Ecuador's rivers east of the Andean divide eventually empties into the Amazon and hence all of the Oriente can properly be referred to as being part of the upper Amazon basin. The correct term for most of the basin's vegetation is 'rain forest'; popular usage, however, refers to this lush tropical growth as jungle.

A glance at any Ecuadorean map will show its claim to a large section of jungle extending beyond Iquitos. The basis of this claim has a long history. After independence in 1822, the new republic claimed lands as far as the River Marañon in the south, and far eastwards into what is now Brazil. This remote and difficult-to-control area was slowly settled by increasing numbers of Peruvians (as well as a few Colombians and Brazilians). Ecuador gradually lost lands to these countries. In 1941 matters came to a head and war with Peru broke out. Each country accused the other of beginning the aggression. The following year a treaty at Rio de Janeiro ended the war and Peru was allotted a huge section of what had been Ecuador. The Ecuadoreans have never officially accepted the full terms of this treaty, claiming that it was bulldozed through when most of the world was occupied with WW II; that Peru invaded them; that the limits of the treaty were geographically invalid because a small section in the Cordillera del Cóndor in the south-east was ambiguously defined; and that the land was theirs anyway. Internationally, however, the border as drawn up by the

1942 treaty is accepted. If you should ever fly from Miami to Iquitos on a regularly scheduled jet service, rest assured that you will be landing in Peru!

This dispute affects the traveller in several ways. The south-eastern border region is still very sensitive and there are skirmishes every few years. The last major battles were in early 1981, when several soldiers were killed and aircraft shot down in an area only 20 km from the main road through the southern Oriente. Sabre-rattling continues intermittently. While journeying through the Oriente, even on the well-travelled tourist routes, you should always have documentation on hand, as passport checks at military checkpoints are not uncommon. These are usually quick and hassle-free, assuming your papers are in order. The dispute also means that crossing the border into the Peruvian jungle is no longer possible for foreign travellers (though various Indian groups do so all the time). So if you were hoping to descend from Ecuador to the Amazon in river boats or canoes, forget it. Finally, try not to wave non-Ecuadorean maps of the region under peoples' noses. One friend had maps of Peru confiscated by customs officers at Quito airport, because the Peruvian maps naturally didn't show the Ecuadorean claim. It should be emphasized that the area is safe to travel in at this time.

The Oriente can be conveniently divided into north and south by the Río Pastaza. The main southern Oriente road begins at Loja and goes through Zamora north to Macas. Beyond Macas the road is unfinished and you have to continue either on foot or by air to Puyo on the north side of the Pastaza.

Most travellers to the Oriente visit the northern region, which admittedly has much more to offer the tourist. Indeed, the southern Oriente is the least-visited part of Ecuador and has a real sense of remoteness. Perhaps that is why I particularly enjoyed travelling through it.

There are two surface routes into the southern Oriente. The most frequently used is from Cuenca through Limón (officially named on most maps as General L Plaza Gutiérrez) to Macas. The other route runs from Loja through Zamora and continues north to Limón, where it joins the first route.

ZAMORA

Although Zamora is only 40 km by road from Loja, the journey takes almost three hours. The road climbs dustily from Loja over a 2500-metre-high pass and then drops tortuously along the Zamora River valley to the town at 970 metres above sea level. The scenery soon becomes tropical, the vegetation thicker, and you begin seeing strange plants such as the giant tree fern. There are good views in either direction, but the right-hand side of the bus is the best.

Zamora was first founded by the Spanish in 1549, but the colony soon died out because of Indian attacks. It was refounded in 1800 but remained very small. A local old-timer recalls that when he arrived in Zamora in the 1930s, there were only half a dozen buildings. In 1953 it became the provincial capital when the province of Zamora-Chinchipe was created, although it was still extremely small and isolated. The first vehicle did not arrive in town until 1962. Zamora is now experiencing a boom since the recent discovery of gold in Nambija, a few km to the north. The sudden influx of miners has strained the resources of the area somewhat, and food costs here are relatively high. The present population of Zamora is something around 6000.

Zamora

1	Hotel Maguna
2	Post Office & IETEL
3	Comedor de Don Pepe
4	Residencial Venecia
5	Hotel Amazonas
6	Hotel Zamora
7	Bus Office
8	Restaurant Caribe (bus stop)
9	Sheraton Restaurant

Saraguro Indians with their typical black shorts are sometimes seen in the Zamora area. They frequently arrive on foot, driving their cattle on the trail from Saraguro, through 28 de Mayo, to the Zamora-Yanzatza road. North of Zamora, Shuar Indians may also be seen, as well as colonists and miners. The whole area definitely has a frontier feel to it.

Military Checkpoint

The recent conflict with Peru took place close to Zamora. This, combined with the present gold boom, means that there is a high-profile military presence in Zamora. There are military checkpoints on both sides of town. You have to check in and register your passport at the main checkpoint three km from the north-east side of town, on the road to Gualaquiza.

When I arrived from Loja, I had to show my passport at the minor checkpoint west of Zamora. Then I was accompanied into the town itself by an armed soldier who insisted that I go with him to the main checkpoint to register my passport. I couldn't do this at the first checkpoint, nor could I persuade him that I would do it on my way out of town, and I couldn't book myself into a hotel room and get rid of my luggage first. My only (minor) victory was insisting that he paid my bus fare to the main checkpoint three km out of town. This is without a doubt the most intimidating passport check I've had in two years of travelling all over Ecuador. Nevertheless, the armed soldier was polite and friendly (if insistent!), and there were no real hassles. At the main checkpoint I had to explain my presence – they just aren't used to seeing tourists here. Whatever your feelings are, keep your cool and insist that you are a *turista* visiting the Oriente and taking buses from Loja to Gualaquiza and Cuenca or wherever. This is absolutely not the time to express your interest in the Peruvian border or your fervent hopes to make a fortune in the goldfields. Foreigners are not allowed there anyway. After all this, they didn't even stamp my passport.

Once you've checked in, you're on your own. They don't provide a staff car to take you back into town, so it's a three-km walk, or you can wait for a passing bus (one or two an hour).

Maybe, by the time you read this, it will be possible to register on the Loja side of town, thus avoiding the lengthy hassle described above. If you arrive in Zamora from the north on your way out to Loja, it will probably be easier as you will pass by the main checkpoint on your way to town. If you're lucky, you won't get stopped at all. Maybe I just came across a particularly officious official, or some brigadier was passing through and they wanted to impress him. If you're entering the Oriente through Zamora, cheer yourself with the thought that this is the most difficult of all the checkpoints.

Information

There's not much to do. The main plaza is a concrete affair with few trees and little shade. The IETEL and post office are on it. There is a bank but they don't do foreign exchange. There's a movie theatre on the northern outskirts of town by the river. The town is planning a tree-lined riverside avenue two km long. You could try the Saturday-night discotheque over the *Sheraton Restaurant*. Most restaurants are closed by 8 pm, so eat early. The weather is not too hot, with daytime temperatures averaging about 20°C and pleasant evenings with few insects.

Places to Stay & Eat

The three cheap hotels are all clustered together a block away from the plaza. The best and cleanest of these is the *Hotel Zamora*, which charges US$1.50 per person. They have some good balcony rooms which you should ask for. *Hotel Amazonas* and *Residencia Venecia* are not as good and charge US$1.40. None of them have private bathrooms or hot water, but you have to start getting used to that in the Oriente. Anyway, cold showers are refreshing in the hot weather.

A brand-new hotel opened in 1984 and provides quite luxurious services. *Hotel Maguna* has rooms with private baths, carpeting, TV and telephone for about US$4 per person. These are 'promotional' prices to advertise the new hotel and may well go up in future. Some of the rooms have excellent balcony views of the Río Zamora.

There are several restaurants on the main street, Avenida Diego de Vaca. *Comedor de Don Pepe* on the main plaza is quite good. *Restaurant Caribe* is full of flies but convenient if waiting for a bus. Menus are sometimes limited and the meal of the day is often the best choice.

Getting There

Bus A new bus terminal is under construction on the east side of the market. Meanwhile, buses arrive and depart from the market; the corner in front of the Restaurant Caribe is the place to wait. There is a bus office but its hours are irregular.

Transportes Loja run about eight buses a day to Loja (80c, three hours). Zamora-Chinchipe buses are open-sided trucks with uncomfortable bench seats designed for midgets. They provide frequent services to nearby villages as far north as Yanzatza. There is no scheduled service at this time from Zamora north to Gualaquiza and beyond. You have to wait outside the Restaurant Caribe for a northbound bus from Loja to pass. Enough passengers normally get off at Zamora that it's not very difficult to get a seat to continue north. Some of these buses go only as far as Yanzatza (50c, 1½ hours); only two or three a day continue as far as Gualaquiza (US$1.20, 4½ hours).

YANZATZA

The northbound road to Yanzatza follows the left bank of the Río Zamora, so the best views are to be had on the right of the bus. There are beautiful vistas of open stretches of the river with heavily forested hills on either side, often with tropical trees flowering in bright reds, yellows and purples. The bus goes through many little Indian hamlets and *fincas* growing a variety of tropical produce such as coffee, sugar cane and citrus fruit. The road also goes near the Nambija mining area, so the journey is enlivened by the various

interesting characters getting on and off the bus.

The first village of any size north of Zamora is Yanzatza, 1½ hours away. In 1970 it consisted of only a couple of shacks, but since the Nambija gold boom it has become one of the fastest-growing towns in the province. Its population is now in excess of three thousand and there are several restaurants and a couple of basic hotels. These are likely to be full of miners, so it's probably best to continue to Gualaquiza. The hotels *Amazonas* and *Central* are both just off the main square.

GUALAQUIZA

North of Yanzatza the population thins and houses are seen infrequently. The road continues to follow the left bank of the gently dropping Río Zamora and there are fine tropical views. Sit on the right of the bus. The road crosses the provincial line into Morona Santiago province near the tiny village of Los Encuentros and continues to El Pangui, where there is the basic *Hotel El Cóndor* on the one street. Just north of this village the road drops suddenly and a lovely jungle panorama stretches out below.

A few km before reaching Gualaquiza, the Río Cuchipamba is crossed. A new steel bridge is planned, but meanwhile all traffic must cross the river by a decrepit wooden raft capable of transporting only one vehicle at a time. Most passengers get off the bus – you can cross on a footbridge.

Gualaquiza is a pretty little village of about three thousand inhabitants. The church on the main plaza looks like a toy building, and there are cobbled streets and houses with attractive balconies. The town has a Spanish colonial air. There are also pleasant walks in the surrounding countryside. Gualaquiza closes down early and is definitely *tranquilo*.

Places to Stay & Eat

Accommodation is limited – this is a little-visited town. On the main plaza is the simple *Residencial Amazonas*, which charges US$1.50 each. It is probably better than the *Pensión Oriental* on the main street. Also on the main street is the *Bar Restaurant Gualaquiza*, as good as any of the few restaurants. There is a small market just off the main street.

Getting There

There are several bus companies on the main street, Calle Gonzalo Pezantes Lefebre. Transportes Sucúa, El Cóndor and Oriental each have two or three departures a day for various destinations. Ask around. You can go south (Zamora and Loja), north (Limón, Sucúa and Macas) or west (Cuenca). The next town to the north is Limón (US$1.30, four hours). To Macas it's US$2.60, 8½ hours.

LIMÓN (General L Plaza Gutiérrez)

Limón (population 2300) is a totally unprepossessing town whose main importance is that it lies at the junction of the roads to Cuenca, Macas and Zamora. From Gualaquiza the road passes through pretty but sparsely populated countryside until it reaches the missions of San Juan Bosco and Plan de Milagro (also known as Indanza), about an hour before Limón.

Places to Stay & Eat

Limón is a typical small Ecuadorean jungle town with one main street lined with two hotels and several simple restaurants and bus offices. Both the *Residencial Paraiso* and *Amazonas* are basic but clean and charge US$1 each. Avoid getting rooms on the street, as bus drivers park their buses with engines running while they have a midnight snack or early-morning breakfast. Exhaust fumes fill your room and the noise keeps you awake.

Getting There

Buses from Limón are available to the north, south and west several times a day with various companies who have their offices along the main street. Few buses originate in Limón, however, so departure times are at best approximate. If you have arrived from the south, this is where you join the road from Cuenca. If you are going to Macas, sit on the right-hand side of the bus, as there are good views of the Río Upano.

MÉNDEZ

This quiet little village of 1250 inhabitants is passed through on the way to Sucúa. It is 60c and less than two hours from Limón. On the corner of its shady plaza are the very simple pensiones *Miranda* and *Ruiz*, both charging the usual dollar. There are one or two restaurants and the houses have red-tiled roofs and flowery gardens.

SUCÚA

Sucúa, population 4000, is one of the more interesting villages in the southern Oriente. It is the major centre of the Shuar Indians, who were formerly called the Jivaro and were infamous for shrinking the heads of their defeated enemies. This practice still occurred as recently as only two generations ago and the *tsantsas*, as the shrunken heads are called, can still be seen in various museums, notably the Municipal Museum in Guayaquil. Most of today's Shuar look very Ecuadorean in jeans and T-shirts, but you still see older Indians with elaborate facial or body tattoos.

There is a pleasant main plaza with shady trees, tropical flowers, cicadas and birds. From the plaza, walk down the main street (Avenida Francisco Orellana) and you'll come to the Shuar Centre on your left, about a km away. Here you can buy booklets and obtain further information about the Shuar. They have become missionized, as have most of the surviving Oriente Indian groups, so you won't be shown *tsantsas*; other crafts are, however, on display. There is also a mission hospital and a movie theatre.

Places to Stay & Eat

A good hotel is the clean *Hotel Cumanda*, which charges US$2 per night and is on the plaza. Similar is the *Hotel Oriente*, down the main street close to the Shuar Centre. They have a restaurant. The cheapest place in town is the basic *Hotel Colón*, just off the plaza on the main street. There are several restaurants by this corner, including the *Bar Restaurant Rincón Oriental*, probably the best restaurant in the southern Oriente. The waiters wear bow ties and charge about 15c more than the basic places. Definitely worth it.

Getting There

Air For several years, the airstrip at Sucúa provided regular service to Puyo with TAO. In mid-1984, however, the new airport at Macas was opened with a runway capable of taking large planes; that airport has now largely superseded the strip at Sucúa. Ask at the office by the airstrip if any regular flights are still operating. Aircraft can be chartered for flights into the interior of the Oriente; ask at the Shuar centre or the mission. Villages in the interior are for Indians and missionaries – there are no facilities for tourists.

Bus Pickup trucks for Macas (35c, one hour) leave at frequent intervals from 6 am to 5.30 pm every day. Departures are from the corner of the main plaza near the Hotel Cumanda.

Southbound buses pass by the restaurants on the main street at the corner of the plaza. Services are better from Macas.

MACAS

This small (population 6000) but important town is the capital of the province of Morona-Santiago and is the end of the road for most travellers. It has four centuries of history as a Spanish trading and missionary outpost, and an old mule trail still joins Macas with the highlands near Riobamba. A road is planned which will follow this trail, but it is unlikely to be completed in the near future. A road north to Puyo is also projected but it stops about two hours north of Macas, so the only existing road link with Quito is via Cuenca.

Despite its history, Macas is essentially a modern and developing town. There is a new bus terminal and airport, and the main plaza was completed only in 1983. A new cathedral is being built on a small hill above the main plaza. It's a large, scaffolded, concrete monstrosity at present, but maybe one day . . . . Almost hidden behind the cathedral is the quaint and simple old wooden church containing some well-carved stations of the cross. From the cathedral hill there's a view of the town and, on a clear day, the often smoking volcano Sangay some 40 km to the north-west. At 5230 metres, it is the seventh highest mountain in Ecuador and one of the most active volcanoes in the world.

Information

There are both IETEL and post offices. The first is new and the second is old. It is likely that a new post office will be built by the main plaza. There is no movie theatre or other entertainment.

Places to Stay & Eat

There are eight hotels in Macas. They all seem to charge a uniform US$1.50 each except the *Pensión Turismo*, which is a few cents cheaper but also the most run down. The *Residencial Upano* is pretty run down too. The best (or at least the most popular) place is the simple *Hotel Encalada*, which also has one of the best restaurants in town. If that's full, the *Hotel Amazonas* is also quite good. There are others marked on the map; none of them are particularly noteworthy. None of these hotels has hot water or private bathrooms.

Macas is a fast-developing town and new hotels are under construction. One, near the bus terminal, is marked on the map. It is expected to be the most

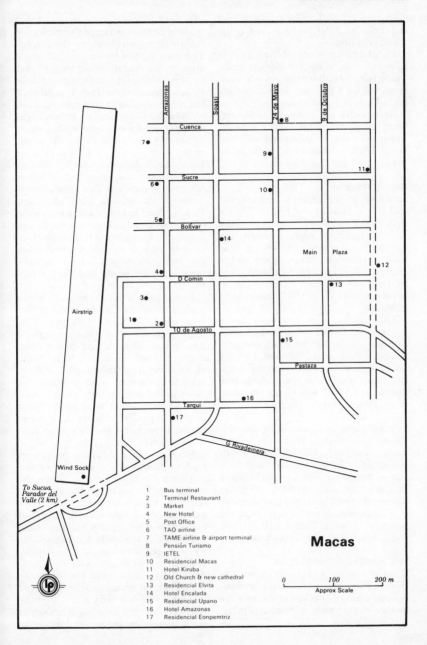

Macas

1 Bus terminal
2 Terminal Restaurant
3 Market
4 New Hotel
5 Post Office
6 TAO airline
7 TAME airline & airport terminal
8 Pensión Turismo
9 IETEL
10 Residencial Macas
11 Hotel Kiruba
12 Old Church & new cathedral
13 Residencial Elvita
14 Hotel Encalada
15 Residencial Upano
16 Hotel Amazonas
17 Residencial Eonpemtriz

0   100   200 m
Approx Scale

To Sucua,
Parador del
Valle (2 km)

Wind Sock

Airstrip

Amazonas
Soasti
24 de Mayo
9 de Octubre

Cuenca
Sucre
Bolívar
D Comin
10 de Agosto
Pastaza
Tarqui
G Rivadeinera

Main   Plaza

comfortable hotel in town – indeed, in the whole province.

About two km south of town, on the road to Sucúa, is the *Parador del Valle*, which has clean, bungalow-style accommodation for US$7 double with private bath. There is a restaurant.

Restaurants are generally lacklustre. Most people eat at the *Hotel Encalada*, which has good set meals and a limited menu. There is a reasonable restaurant by the bus terminal and a few others.

Getting There

Air TAME has two flights a week to Quito at 2 pm on Monday and Friday. Tickets cost US$12 and are obtainable from the TAME office in the airport building. Half the town's population and even people from surrounding villages come to the airport to see the large, four-prop plane land and take off. There's a festive feeling in the air – after all, there's little else to do in Macas.

TAO has flights on most weekdays to Pastaza near Puyo. Pastaza is also known as Shell – it used to be an oil company airstrip. Flights cost US$9 and, because small, light aircraft are normally used, they give a good aerial look at the jungle. Seating is limited and flights are often booked up several days in advance.

Bus All departures are from the new Terminal Terrestre. There are several departures a day for Cuenca (US$2.40, 10 hours) and Gualaquiza (US$2.60, 8½ hours). Buses and pickup trucks to Sucúa (35c, one hour) are frequent. Transportes Macas runs small buses and pickup trucks to various remote northern parts of the province, including Chiguaza (US$1, two hours) hourly during daylight hours.

THE JUNGLE FROM MACAS

There are various ways to see more of the Oriente from Macas. It should be mentioned, however, that the best centre for tourism in the jungle is Misahuallí in the northern Oriente.

Many Ecuadorean maps show tracks or trails leading from Macas into the interior. These are usually overgrown; transportation to the Shuar Indian villages and missions further into the Oriente is mainly by light aircraft these days. It is difficult but not impossible to visit some of these villages. You can hire an *expreso* light aircraft to take you to some of the better-known centres such as Taisha. With luck or the right contacts, flights have been arranged with the mission aircraft. Visiting nearby Shuar centres on foot or bus is fairly straightforward. There are frequent buses to the mission of Sevilla (Don Bosco), about an hour's walk away on the other side of the Río Upano. A new bridge is being built; at present there is a rickety wooden suspension bridge which takes only one vehicle at a time. All the passengers disembark and walk across the bridge, and the bus follows.

From Sevilla you can head south on foot along a broad track to the village of San Luis, about four hours' walk away. This makes a good day trip and en route you'll pass cultivated areas and Indian huts, where you may be invited to try some yucca *chicha*. This traditional Shuar drink is made by the women, who grind up the yucca by chewing it and then spit it into a bowl where it is left to ferment. If this doesn't appeal to you, bring a water bottle. There are no facilities of any kind beyond Sevilla.

Buses go north along a fairly good gravel road to various destinations up to and including the Río Chiguaza, where the road stops. The bus passes through Shuar territory and you can see a few of their oval-shaped, bamboo-caned, thatched huts on the sides of the road. Most of the Indians riding the bus look unremarkably western, but occasionally a beautifully beaded bracelet or tattooed face is seen. At the Río Chiguaza the bus returns to Macas but you can continue on foot if you wish. A canoe will ferry you across the river and then you have to ask the way to the villages of 24 de Mayo and Arapicos, where another canoe will ferry you across the Río Palora. There are no facilities at these villages although, if you're lucky, you may find a pickup truck going from Arapicos to Palora where there is a very basic pensión. You may have to walk as far as Palora, as the road is often impassable. From Palora there are three buses a day to Puyo, in the northern Oriente. Locals say that if you take the first morning bus from Macas to Chiguaza, you can walk to Palora in one long day. I've never tried it.

The Northern Oriente

North of the Río Pastaza are the provinces of Pastaza and Napo, which together form the northern Oriente.

Unlike the southern Oriente, the northern Oriente is well connected with two roads to Quito and hence is the most visited part of Ecuador's jungle. In one long day of bus riding, you can go from Quito to the oil boom town of Lago Agrio in the far north-eastern jungle, or to the tourist centre of Misahuallí in the central Oriente. Various round trips can be made by bus, boat and air. If your time is limited, the quickest of these is the bus journey from Quito through Ambato, Baños, Puyo, Tena, Baeza and back to Quito. This can be done in two long days and gives a good look at the jungle where it meets the eastern slopes of the Andes.

A longer and highly recommended trip can be made by omitting the Tena-Baeza section and going instead via Misahuallí and down the Río Napo to Coca, and then continuing by bus to Lago Agrio and back to Quito through Baeza. Such a trip will give a very good look at many facets of the Ecuadorean Oriente and is not beyond anyone's resources. It is feasible in four days, but at least a week or more is recommended. The journey could be broken at either Coca or Lago Agrio, both of which have regular air services to Quito. The trip can be done in reverse but this isn't recommended, as the river portion is against the current and takes over twice as long.

THE ROAD TO PUYO

If I were to choose just one stretch of road in Ecuador for the best views of the upper Amazon basin, I would have difficulty in improving upon the drive from Baños to Puyo.

The road follows the Pastaza River canyon as it drops steadily from Baños at 1800 metres to Puyo at 950 metres. This

road has recently been rebuilt, and buses now regularly make the through journey. Just beyond the famous Agoyan waterfall, now site of a new hydro-electric project, the road passes through a tunnel. A few km further, a waterfall splashes from the overhanging cliff onto the road – quite a surprise if you're hitch-hiking in the back of a pickup truck.

Waterfalls frequently cascade into the canyon, and one of the most impressive is by the village of Río Verde, 20 km beyond Baños. You have to walk down a short trail to a suspension bridge to appreciate it properly; ask at the village. As the road drops further, the vegetation rapidly becomes more tropical and the walls of the Pastaza canyon are covered with bromeliads, giant tree ferns, orchids and flowering trees. Near the small community of Mera the canyon walls spread apart, and you see a breathtaking view of the River Pastaza meandering away to the south-east through the vast, rolling plains of the Amazon basin. The right side of the bus is best for views. There is no higher land between here and the Atlantic, almost 4000 km to the east.

SHELL

Shell is a few km beyond Mera and the two communities together are often called Shell-Mera. At Shell is the Pastaza airstrip, serving Puyo which is about 10 km away. This is the most important airstrip in the province of Pastaza. There is also a military checkpoint here.

Military Checkpoint

All foreign travellers arriving in the Oriente through Shell must register with the army. The procedure is efficient and straightforward. Buses on the way to Puyo stop by the checkpoint and wait while foreigners disembark and register. You have to fill out a form with the usual details (age, nationality, etc) and present your passport and the tourist card which you received on entry into Ecuador. You'll be asked your destination and the purpose of your visit. *'Turismo'* is the safest and most obvious answer. Your passport will be stamped by the Brigada de Selva No 20 and you'll be free to go. The whole procedure takes only a minute and the bus drivers are so used to it that they'll wait as a matter of course. The only possible problem is if you only have a few days left on your visa – they like you to have at least 10 days before going into the Oriente. The stamp is important; it will be inspected by the port captain at Misahuallí before you can take the boat downriver. It may also be inspected at other places in the Oriente. If you arrive at Puyo by air you should also register. The checkpoint is five minutes' walk east of the airport on the one main street of town. If you are leaving the Oriente through Puyo, you may or may not have to register.

Places to Stay & Eat

There are three basic hotels, of which the *Cordillera* is probably the best. It charges about US$1.20 a night. There are a few simple restaurants. You won't get lost – it's a one-street town with the airport at the west end on the way to Baños, and the checkpoint near the east end on the way to Puyo. Everything else lies in between.

Getting There

Air There are no regular flights from Shell to Quito. Flights with TAO leave most mornings for Macas aboard light aircraft and cost US$9.50. Seating is limited and tends to be booked up ahead. The TAO office is in the airport. There are various other companies (Condor, ATESA) in Shell which can provide light aircraft for chartered flights to other jungle strips. Shell is also a major US missionary centre and there are schools, churches and hospitals. The missions often have flights into the Oriente and can provide emergency services.

Bus Most people going through Shell will already be on a bus through to Puyo. Should you need a bus to Puyo, wait by the military checkpoint, where pickup trucks leave for Puyo every half hour and charge about 15c. If you want to go to Baños or Ambato, also wait by the checkpoint for buses from Puyo, which will pick you up if they have room.

PUYO

Puyo, with a population of about 11,000, is the provincial capital of Pastaza. Until the early '70s it had a real 'frontier' atmosphere, and was the most important town in the Oriente. Since the discovery of oil, however, the frontier has been pushed deep into the jungle and now Lago Agrio vies for the claim of being Ecuador's most important Oriente town.

Information

There are IETEL and post offices marked on the map. Two banks are also marked. The Banco de Fomento doesn't change money but one of the managers will buy cash dollars as a 'favour' at unfavourable rates. The new Banco Internacional was still under construction when I was last in Puyo, but it should be open by now and I've heard rumours that it may exchange money. An auto spares dealer near the Banco de Fomento also buys cash dollars at unfavourable rates when he's in the mood. 'Unfavourable' means about 10 or 15% less than in Quito.

Things to See

If you can get up at dawn you'll often see a spectacular view of jagged snow peaks rising up over a jungle covered with rolling morning mists. Later in the morning, the mountains usually disappear into the clouds. The jagged peaks belong to El Altar (5319 metres), the fifth highest mountain in Ecuador and about 50 km to the south-east. Sangay (5230 metres) is also occasionally seen. A good view can be had from the main plaza.

El Tucan gift shop on the plaza has a

Puyo

Río Puyo

1   Hospital Turingia
2   IETEL
3   Auto spares store (change money)
4   Residencial Gioconda
5   Hotel Tucan
6   Banco de Fomento
7   Transportes San Francisco
8   Rincon Ambateño Restaurant
9   Teatro Amazonas
10 Residencial El Alamo
11 Pensión Paris
12 Pensión Guayaquil
13 Restaurant Mistral
14 Hotels Europa & California
15 El Tucan gift shop
16 Post Office
17 New Banco Internacional
18 Buses Centinela del Oriente

To Tena

Footbridge
Steps
Main Plaza
Church
Sucre
Bolivar

To Baños

Marin

19 Peña Bar
20 Pensión Susanita
21 Hotel Europa Internacional
22 Residencial Santa & Pensión Georginita
23 Hotel Granada & Pensión Victoria
24 Pensión Tungurahua
25 Residencial Ecuador

Market

Atahualpa
Francisco de Orellana
Amazonas

Old bus terminal

24 de Mayo

0   100   200 m

good variety of handicrafts and functions almost as a museum. It's worth a look and if this is as far into the Oriente as you plan on going, you can buy balsa models, bead and feather necklaces, blowguns and other jungle crafts. During the day you can go swimming in the river. If you're a birdwatcher you'll see a good variety of jungle species near the river.

For nightlife, there is the Amazonas movie theatre which shows kung-fu movies to the accompaniment of encouraging yells from the local kids. You could see how the newly opened Peña Bar is doing; they plan on having live music at weekends.

Places to Stay

There's no shortage of accommodation in

Puyo but there are frequent water shortages. When I was last here in late 1984, none of the cheaper hotels had any water at all and you had to swim in the river. The water system is currently being repaired. If you need a shower, ensure that there is running water before renting a room.

Places to Stay – bottom end

Hotel Granada at US$1.20 per person, and behind it the very simple *Pensión Victoria* for US$1, have been recommended by budget travellers. They are both by the old bus terminal. There are several other places near here in this price range. These include the very basic *Pensión Georginita* and the somewhat better *Residencial Santa* and *Pensión Tungurahua*. The *Residencial Ecuador* is old but well looked after and has pretty flowers in the balconies. Closer to the centre of town are some cheap and run-down hotels such as the *Pensión Guayaquil* and *Paris* and the *Residencial El Alamo* and *Susanita*. I must confess to a no more than cursory examination of these – they don't look up to much.

The *Residencial Gioconda*, near the Transportes San Francisco bus office, looks quite good for US$1.50 per person; some rooms are with private baths. It was full when I tried it – often the sign of good value. *Hotel Tucan* nearby charges US$2 per person for rooms with communal baths. They seem unfriendly. If you want to be fairly sure of a constant water supply and reasonable comfort, I recommend either the hotels *California* or *Europa*, which are next door to one another on 9 de Octubre. They both charge US$2.50 per person with a communal bath and US$3 each for rooms with a private bath. The *Europa* has hot water and a good view from the roof.

Places to Stay – top end *Hotel Europa Internacional* (as opposed to the Hotel Europa) is a new and modern hotel in the town centre which charges about US$6.50 single and US$11 double for rooms with a bath. It will have to be seen how it withstands the ravages of time. A similarly priced hotel, which has been a Puyo institution for years and has aged charmingly, is the highly recommended *Hostal Turingia* on the outskirts of town towards Baños. They have accommodation in bungalows with private bath and hot water. The bungalows are set in a tropical garden with a good collection of orchids. There is a good restaurant.

Places to Eat
Puyo cannot be recommended to gourmands. One of its better restaurants, and it's by no means fancy, is the *Rincón Ambateño*, which has been here for a long time and has various car-rallying trophies on the walls. The *Mistral* is good for breakfast and OK during the rest of the day. It is decorated with a rather bizarre collection of prints ranging from posters of the Beatles to photographs of local Indian tribes. There are several other places. The better hotels have adequate restaurants, of which the *Turingia* is the best.

Getting There
Air Pickup trucks providing service to Shell for the Pastaza airstrip leave from the intersection known as the 'Y' – it's marked with a 'Y' on the map.

Bus The old bus terminal is marked on the map, but few buses depart or arrive there any more. A new terminal to the south-west of town is projected but is nowhere near completion. Meanwhile, most buses leave from the Transportes San Francisco office. This company has frequent buses to Ambato (US$1, three hours), a few of which continue to Quito (US$1.80, six hours) and Riobamba. The only buses to Tena (US$1, three hours) leave at 6.30 and 8.45 am so if you want to catch one later in the day you have to wait for a bus passing (*el paso*) from Ambato. These may well have standing space only and during weekends can be completely full. The early morning buses are usually booked the day before.

Centinela del Oriente runs ancient buses to various small villages in the surrounding jungle. The most important of these is Palora, where there is a basic pensión and from where you can continue south by pickup truck (if you are lucky), foot and canoe ferry to Chiguaza near Macas in the southern Oriente. (For more information about this journey, see the section on Macas.) Buses for Palora leave three times a day for the three-hour ride, which involves two river crossings.

PUERTO NAPO
The narrow, gravelled road from Puyo into the Oriente heads almost due north, passing small homesteads and occasional

banana plantations until the road crosses the provincial line into Napo. About seven km from Tena, Puerto Napo is reached. There is only one place to stay, *Hotel Palandacocha*. A road fork to the right leads to Misahuallí, 17 km away, or you can continue north to Tena.

You can wait here for a vehicle to take you to Misahuallí. Many buses/trucks to Misahuallí come from Tena and there is often a scramble for seats. It is probably easier though not necessarily faster to go into Tena and take a bus back to Misahuallí from there.

TENA

Tena, at about 500 metres above sea level, is the capital of the province of Napo. This province, with an area of over 52,000 square km – almost a fifth of the country – is the largest in Ecuador. Its capital, however, has a population of only 6000. Tena was founded in 1560, and was the most easterly of Ecuador's early colonial missionary and trading outposts. There were several Indian uprisings in the early days, notably in 1578 when Jumandy, chief of the Quijos, led an unsuccessful revolt against the Spaniards. Tena survived, though many early Oriente towns were completely wiped out by other Indian attacks. Today, the area is largely agricultural, with cattle ranches and coffee or banana plantations. It is pleasantly located at the junction of the Tena and Pano rivers and is a minor centre for Ecuadorean tourism. The average year-round temperature is 24°C, with the rivers having a moderating effect on the climate.

15 November is the anniversary of Tena's foundation and is the time for colourful processions and other festivities. While visiting the town during one of their fiestas, I had one of those unusual experiences which make travelling all the more fun. I was sitting quietly in my hotel room, making notes for the Tena city map, when there was a knock on the door. I opened up, and two officious-looking gentlemen in plain clothes walked in.

Perhaps it's the sign of a guilty conscience, but my first thought was, 'Oh, no, what am I in for now?' The gentlemen introduced themselves as the organizers of the Tena beauty pageant which was being held that evening to elect 'Señorita Tena, 1984.' They had heard that a Spanish-speaking foreigner was in town and would I be kind enough to help judge the contest, as they wanted some non-biased judges for a fair vote!

I don't normally hold beauty contests in very high esteem, but I couldn't refuse. The evening turned out to be riotous fun, with each señorita having her wildly cheering following of relatives, friends and neighbours, and a sound system which screeched maniacally at inopportune moments. Perhaps the most memorable segment of the evening's events was when the MC asked the contestants a question, taken out of a sealed envelope. One of the young ladies, flustered by the rapt attention of several thousand listeners, nervously began to pick her nose before she realized what she was doing. The crowd roared with a mixture of rage and delight. Although I enjoyed myself, I haven't noticed any recent change in my opinion of beauty contests.

Information

There are the usual IETEL and post offices, the latter difficult to find as there is no sign. It is inside the provincial government offices at the west end of the main plaza. Money-changing facilities are limited; the bank will sometimes change cash dollars but not travellers' cheques. The mission may be able to help. Although there is an airstrip at the north end of town, there are no regularly scheduled flights. A DITURIS information office is under construction on the main road south of town – maybe it'll be open by the time this is published.

Things to See

There's not much to do in town. Most people visit the nearby village of Archidona

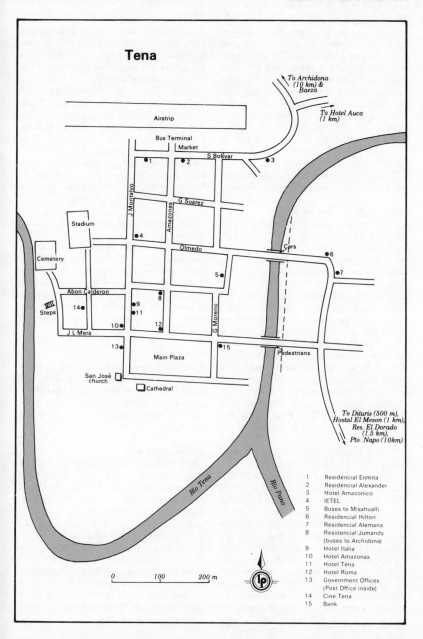

Tena

To Archidona (10 km) & Baeza

To Hotel Auca (1 km)

Airstrip

Bus Terminal

Market

S Bolívar

J Montalvo

G Suárez

Amazonas

Stadium

Olmedo

Cars

Cemetery

Abon Calderón

Steps

J L Mera

G Moreno

Main Plaza

Pedestrians

San José church

Cathedral

To Dituris (500 m),
Hostal El Meson (1 km),
Res. El Dorado
(1.5 km),
Pto. Napo (10km)

Río Tena

Río Pano

0   100   200 m

1	Residencial Enmita
2	Residencial Alexander
3	Hotel Amazonico
4	IETEL
5	Buses to Misahualli
6	Residencial Hilton
7	Residencial Alemana
8	Residencial Jumandy (buses to Archidona)
9	Hotel Italia
10	Hotel Amazonas
11	Hotel Tena
12	Hotel Roma
13	Government Offices (Post Office inside)
14	Cine Tena
15	Bank

and the caves of Jumandy. If you're interested in looking for tropical birds, the steps leading down to the Río Tena near the cemetery are a good place for bird-watching. The volcano occasionally seen looming up out of the jungle, roughly 50 km north of Tena, is the 3900-metre Sumaco. Although popularly considered extinct, recent vulcanological studies indicate that it is merely dormant so travellers to the region may have a surprise one of these years.

There is one movie theatre. Occasionally the San José mission also shows movies.

Places to Stay – bottom end

The cheapest hotels are in the town centre but they all suffer from water shortages. Make sure there is running water if you don't want to bathe in the river. The most expensive of the 'downtown' hotels is the *Hotel Italia*, which charges US$2 per person in rooms with private bath – not much use if there's no water! It doesn't appear well looked after and the restaurant below was ankle-deep in greasy napkins when I went in for a drink; I didn't look at the rooms. Cheaper and better is the *Hotel Amazonas* across the street, which is much cleaner and charges US$1.50 each but has only communal showers. The cheapest place in town (and it looks it) is the *Hotel Tena* for about US$1.20. Inexplicably, the *Hotel Roma* and *Residencial Jumandy* were temporarily closed last time I visited Tena; they look as if they're in the US$1.50 price range.

Accommodation away from the centre costs a little more but is usually worth it. The residencials *Alexander* and *Enmita* and the *Hotel Amazonico* are all close to the main bus terminal. The newest is the clean Alexander, which has pleasant rooms with communal showers for US$2 per person and with private bathroom for US$3 each. The Enmita and Amazonico both charge US$3 per person in rooms with a private bath – both have their own private water supply which normally carries them through any water shortage

and they are therefore recommended. The Amazonico has bungalow-style accommodation and the Enmita is run by a friendly lady who also manages one of the best restaurants in town.

Across the bridge in Bellavista is the somewhat unfriendly *Residencial Hilton*, which charges US$4 for a double room and won't give a lower price to singles. They have communal showers. Nearby, the friendly *Residencial Alemán* charges US$3 per person in rooms with a private bath. Similarly priced are the *Hostal El Mesón* and *Residencial El Dorado* but they are a long walk south of town.

Places to Stay – top end

The best place in town is the DITURIS-run *Hotel Auca* (tel Tena 161), about two km north-east of the town centre. They have spacious grounds by the river, a restaurant and bar, a discotheque (which they'll open up, they told me, for a couple of paying guests) and a casino . . . ?! They charge US$6.50 and US$11.50 single and double with private bathroom.

Places to Eat

There are a number of small and inexpensive restaurants but I always seem to end up eating at the *Residencial Enmita* – some Peace Corps volunteers told me it was the best place in town. It's not expensive.

Getting There & Around

There are three places to catch buses. The main terminal at the end of Avenida Amazonas has several companies with buses to various long-distance destinations. There are several departures a day for Quito (US$2.60, nine hours); both the southern (via Puyo) and northern (via Baeza) routes are used. The latter route is shorter and a little less frequented but you shouldn't have much difficulty in getting a bus out the day after you arrive if you want to make the short Oriente circuit from Quito via Puyo, Tena and Baeza. Flota Jumandy run about four buses a day to

Lago Agrio (US$3, nine hours). These times are approximate; bad roads, old buses and inclement weather make all journey times in the Oriente notoriously unreliable.

Local buses leave from other places. For Archidona (10c, 15 minutes), buses leave about every half hour during daylight hours from in front of the Residencial Jumandy. Equally frequent services for Misahuallí (30c, 45 minutes) leave from the west of the river between the two bridges.

ARCHIDONA

Archidona is a small mission village founded in 1560, the same year as Tena, 10 km to the south. Although the village boasts a movie theatre and a couple of basic restaurants, there are no hotels. The main reason for visiting Archidona is to see the main plaza, which is a small but very well laid out forest of tropical palms, vines, ferns, flowers and trees. The plaza is crossed with paths from which you can admire the varied flora – it came as a real surprise to see such a beautiful plaza in so small a village. It is probably the mission's work. Their carefully but strangely painted concrete block church is also very colourful. A good day to visit Archidona is on Sunday, when the local Quijos Indians come to their weekly market and to hear mass.

From the plaza you can take a bus to Cotundo and ask to be dropped at the entrance to the Cuevas de Jumandy, about five km north of Archidona. There are three main branches in the cave system, which apparently has not yet been fully explored. There is a cafeteria by the caves but there are no other facilities. You must bring your own lights to see the stalagmites and other formations within. Entry costs 50c.

The next town of any importance to the north is Baeza, about 100 km away. This is at the junction with the Lago Agrio-Quito road and will be described later in this chapter.

MISAHUALLÍ

This small village is marked on many maps as Puerto Misahuallí, and is at the end of the road running from Puerto Napo along the north bank of the Río Napo. It is the best place in Ecuador – indeed, one of the best places on the continent – to see some of the jungle conveniently and cheaply. You can easily get here by bus from Quito in a day, so it is suitable for the traveller with a limited amount of time as well as money. However, before you grab your hammock and pith helmet and jump on the next bus, you should realize that this isn't virgin jungle. The area has been long colonized and most mammals (monkey, wild pig, jaguar, capybara) have been either hunted down or had their habitats encroached upon to the point where they cannot survive. What you will see, if you keep your eyes open or, better still, with a local guide, is a variety of jungle birds, tropical flowers, army ants and other insects, and hundreds of dazzling butterflies. In addition there is a colourful Sunday river market when brightly painted dugout canoes arrive in town with cargoes of jungle produce, and all the nearby inhabitants, from local Indians to hardy gold prospectors, come to buy, sell and trade.

Buses can usually reach Misahuallí in any weather, but extremely high or low water levels can disrupt river services. The 'dry' season – though it can still rain – is November and December. The wettest months are June through August.

If you do want an excursion deep into the jungle, that too can be arranged in Misahuallí. This will require time, patience, flexibility and money – but still it is less expensive than jungle expeditions in other countries. Finally, if you want a reasonable amount of comfort – or even luxury – that is available further downriver, but not at Misahuallí.

Information

Money For shorter trips, sucres are the preferred method of payment. For the 10-

day trips, cash dollars are usually acceptable. There are no proper exchange facilities in Misahualli', although the Hostal Jaguar will often change small amounts of cash dollars at about 5% below the Quito rate. It is best to bring a good supply of sucres from the highlands.

Post There is no post office as such in Misahualli, and mail takes months to arrive. From Europe to Quito usually takes about two weeks, and from Quito to Misahualli about two months. If you have the time, you can make postal enquiries and reservations with the guide of your choice by writing to him at Misahualli, Provincia de Napo, Ecuador. For a long tour, it's best to go to Misahualli' at the beginning of your stay in Ecuador and make arrangements in advance.

Things to See

The various restaurants in Misahualli are good places to meet potential travelling companions for excursions, or to pick the brains of travellers returning from a trip. Good places are Douglas Clarke's Restaurant Dayuma, Carlos Lastra's bar just off the corner of the main square by the military post, and the El Paisano restaurant just beyond it. It's a small village; you'll be able to 'cruise' the likely places in a few minutes.

There is an 'outdoor movie theatre' near the Residencial El Balcón de Napo which shows movies on dry nights. The picture is projected, or distorted, on a screen consisting of an off-white bed sheet flapping gently in the tropical evening breeze. The generated power supply fluctuates, causing the characters to alternately speak their parts in fast Mickey Mouse fashion or a slow draaawl. Seating is on the ground (bring something to sit on). Babies scream, kids yell, teenagers fight, adults gossip, the occasional bat swoops through the projector beam, and everyone has a great time. Don't go for the movie!

If you want to see some of the river without taking a tour, you can take a regularly scheduled boat trip as far as Coca on any day of the week.

Jungle Tours

Even if you don't normally enjoy organized tours, you should consider joining one in Misahualli if you want to see some of the jungle, particularly if this is your first visit. There are many guides available in Misahualli, and they offer a variety of tours ranging from one to 10 days in duration. Usually you have to get a group together to make it economical. Travellers pass through Misahualli every day and it's a small place; if you're alone you'll meet others very soon.

One of the best guides is Douglas Clarke, who has been offering guide services for many years. He used to be a butterfly collector but now works exclusively as a jungle guide. His son Wilfrid and his sister Billy often work with him. He does a simple one-day walk which is a good introduction to the jungle – various plant and insect species are pointed out, and a swim under a hidden waterfall can be included. He also does two-to four-day trips, which include camping in the jungle at his camp where all necessary equipment is provided. Some canoeing in dugouts as well as hiking is involved. Finally, he will organize a 10-day trip which takes you far down the Río Napo and back up the Aguarico with a good chance of seeing wildlife such as macaws, parrots, toucans and rarer bird species; and animals such as caymans, various monkey species and perhaps wild pigs, anteaters, or – with a great deal of luck – a jungle cat. This is a rugged expedition and there is little comfort. It is not for the faint-hearted.

You can find Douglas Clarke at the Dayuma Lodge half a block from the plaza in Misahualli. He speaks only a few words of English (none of the guides in Misahualli are fluent English speakers), but he has a photo album which will give you a good idea of what to expect on his trips. Everything, including cooked meals, is included in the cost. He charges US$5 per person for the one-day walk, and about US$12 per person per day on his two– to four-day trips. You normally need a minimum of four people at these prices. For the 10-day trip he charges US$1500 for 10 participants (ie US$15 per person per day). If your party is smaller, the per-person costs go up proportionately, and with a bigger party you have to negotiate.

Douglas Clarke is but one example of the type of guide services available in Misahuallí. There are many others and you have to shop around to get exactly what you want. Douglas' prices are amongst the highest in Misahuallí and you can find similar tours offered for up to 25% lower. On the other hand, by saving yourself US$3 a day you may find that the standard of guide service, environmental concern, care for the 'client,' or quality of the food is other than what you would have liked.

Another outfitter who has been around for a long time is Héctor Fiallos. He runs Fluvial River Tours, which has a little office on the plaza and is headquartered at the Residencial Sacha by the river. He is Douglas' main competitor and runs similar but cheaper tours. I've heard very mixed reviews of his operation. In addition to running the standard one– to 10-day tours, he also does trips to visit the villages of 'primitive' Auca Indians two or three days' walk into the jungle.

I feel strongly that these kind of tours are not to be encouraged. The guides are rarely sensitive to the needs of the Indians who are undergoing the painful process of integration into 20th-century life. Many guides are just inexperienced local young-sters trying to make a living, and through simple ignorance or sheer bravado the Indians are treated in a degrading or abusive manner. As often as twice a week, groups of tourists are taken to gawk at 'real' Indians in the 'real' jungle. The Indians stare miserably and with little interest at the frequent hordes of tourists and the parade of goods that to us seems

basic: backpacks, not one but two pairs of shoes and a change of clothing, sleeping bag, rain gear, sunglasses, cameras, penknives, cigarette lighters, plastic water bottles, canned food and so on. The tourists expect and demand the basic necessities of water and a place to sleep, but the Indians' thoughts about the matter are ignored and little is given in return.

If you want to see the Indians it is best to wait until they come to you. A few of the more adventurous and acculturated Aucas usually come to the Sunday market in Misahuallí, where you can see them and they can see you in an unstrained and uncompromising atmosphere.

There are many other guides other than Douglas Clarke and Héctor Fiallos. Most of them started working with either Douglas or Héctor and decided to branch off on their own. Carlos Lastra is one such; he is very friendly and does a good job. I enjoyed being with him. Two other outfitters whom I haven't met but who have been recommended are Walter Vasco and Julio Angeles. These, and others, usually have signs or booths up in the corner of the main square.

Make sure that whoever you choose gives you a good deal. Work the details out carefully beforehand to avoid confusion or disappointment. Common sense dictates making sure that costs, food, equipment, itinerary and group numbers are all discussed thoroughly before the tour. The most important matter to settle is the guide; a good guide will be able to show you much you would have missed on your own, particularly if you convey your enthusiasm and interest by asking ques-tions. An inadequate guide will spoil the trip. A common problem is that a group makes arrangements with an outfitter and then an inferior guide is supplied at the last moment. All the outfitters are guilty of this to a greater or lesser extent and Fluvial River Tours in particular has built up quite a reputation for this. Douglas Clarke obviously can't join every group himself, but at least he tells you so from the beginning and tries to find a suitable guide for you. If you want a specific guide, you may have to wait until he is available.

Make sure you meet with your guide before you leave. Can you communicate adequately? Has he done this before? Can he show you the *achiote* plant (whose red berries are crushed to make decorative body paints)? Can he find the vine which, when cut, provides water fit to drink? Will he take you for a swim by a waterfall or fishing in a dugout canoe or bird-watching or whatever it is you want? What will he cook for dinner and breakfast? Will he hunt for game? – the area is overhunted and a no-hunting policy is encouraged. A few questions like these will soon tell you if you and the guide are going to have a good trip together. Most people have a great time, especially if they plan their excursion carefully.

Places to Stay & Eat

None of the accommodation in Misahuallí is expensive or luxurious. Water and electricity failures are the rule rather than the exception in all these places. On the plaza you'll find the *Residencial El Balcón de Napo* which has small concrete block rooms, some of them like jail cells. The rooms with a window are OK. The residencial is fairly clean by jungle standards, though the showers are a bit grungy. They charge US$1, as does the rambling old *Residencial La Posada*, which has a hodgepodge arrangement of creaky wooden rooms and somewhat dubious bathroom facilities.

On the corner of the plaza is the nice-looking (from the outside) *Hostal Jaguar*. They charge US$1.20 per person and some of the rooms are airless cells, but they do have a couple of better rooms with a private bathroom, inexplicably at the same price. They'll probably begin charging more now that the word is out! Across the street from the Jaguar and a half block from the plaza is Douglas Clarke's new *Dayuma Lodge*, behind the restaurant.

The lodge is a small, wooden, jungle-style building with four rooms. Two rooms have four bunks each and the other two have six bunks each, dormitory-style. One of each of these has a private bathroom and there is also a communal bathroom. If there's two or more of you, you can normally have a room to yourselves, but if you're alone you may have to share. Prices vary from 50c if you use your own sleeping bag in a room without a private shower, to US$1.50 each if you want bedding and a private shower.

The *Residencial Sacha* is pleasantly located down by the river. It has basic, jungle-cabin-style accommodation for US$1.20 each. Finally, the folks at *El Paisano* restaurant have rooms to let and are building a small hotel.

All the hotels have some kind of restaurant. The *Dayuma* and *El Paisano* are both good. El Paisano is 100 metres from the plaza on the road past the military post. They serve good vegetarian fare, as well as meat dishes. The *Sacha* has riverside dining but erratic service. *La Posada* serves ice cream.

There are two expensive tourist lodges down the Río Napo. The nearest is *Hotel Anaconda* on Anaconda Island, about an hour from Misahuallí. This is a fairly comfortable jungle-style lodge (bamboo walls and thatched roofs), but there is no electricity. Rooms come with private bathrooms and mosquito screens, and the meals (included in the price) are good. They charge about US$25 per person, per day. Canoe trips and jungle excursions from the island are available at extra cost, more expensive than from Misahuallí. You'll see pet animals such as monkeys and peccaries.

Further downriver is the much more expensive *Hotel Jaguar*, about 1½ hours from Misahuallí. This is a comfortable modern hotel on the banks of the Río Napo. You can make reservations for it in Quito (agency at Ramírez Dávalos 653, tel 239400), but usually this involves an all-inclusive jungle tour package from Quito lasting three or more days. It is possible to enquire in Misahualli' about shorter or cheaper stays.

Getting There

Boat Motorized dugout canoes leave from the port for various destinations downriver. The port is a block away from the plaza. The major destination is Francisco de Orellana, but everybody calls it by its popular name of Coca. There are daily boats at 11.30 am which hold about 20 passengers, so it is best to try and buy your ticket in advance to ensure a seat. There are two companies, which have departures on alternate days. One has its office under the Residencial La Posada, and the other is across the street, half a block closer to the river. Tickets cost US$5 for foreigners and US$3.50 for Ecuadoreans, so if you have any kind of residency visa, use it.

Arrive early for the departure. First you must register your passport with the Port Captain, a simple formality but you can't leave without it. Ask for the Capitanía; it's on the waterfront. Then find your boat and choose a seat, which are taken on a first-come, first-served basis. The front seats give better forward views but are narrower, the middle seats are wider and more comfortable, the back seats are close to the noise and fumes of the engine. Read the section on dugout canoes in the Getting Around chapter for more information.

The journey to Coca takes about six hours in normal conditions, but abnormally high or low river levels can disrupt services for days or even weeks. En route to Coca, several points of interest are passed. These are, in geographical order, the village of Ahuano, Hotel Anaconda on Anaconda Island, Hotel Jaguar, the village of Santa Rosa and the village of Bellavista, which is the approximate halfway point to Coca. Usually two motorized canoes per day leave for these destinations, so it is possible to do a short trip downriver and return on another boat later in the day. There are no facilities at

the villages. Enquire at the boat offices about times of departure and return.

Even on the trip down to Coca you won't see much wildlife, as the area is heavily colonized. Little houses on stilts huddle on the bank, prospectors wash sand or pan for gold by the river's edge, colonists wave and whistle for a ride, and impossibly tiny dugout canoes, loaded to the gunwales with an Indian family perched on a pile of bananas, are steadily and gracefully poled upriver. A sudden rain shower can enhance the beauty of the river. The jungle glows verdantly in the late afternoon sun, and a few pure white clouds suspended in a perfectly blue sky contrast dramatically with the muddy flowing river. It's worth the discomfort.

If you want to hire your own dugout (with boatman) you can do so from the port of Misahuallí, but it's expensive. To hire a canoe to take you to Coca will cost about US$90, for example.

Bus Buses leave from in front of the Residencial La Posada on the plaza, about every 30 minutes during daylight hours. The only destination is Tena, where you can make connections elsewhere. The ride costs 30c and takes –3/4 of an hour.

COCA

All Ecuadorean maps show the official name of Puerto Francisco de Orellana, but I've never heard this town referred to by any name other than Coca. It is located at the junction of the Río Coca and the Río Napo (hence its popular name). Its official name derives from the fact that Francisco de Orellana came through here on his way to 'discover' the Amazon in 1542. The Río Napo is Ecuador's major tributary into the Amazon. Indeed, it is at the point where Ecuador's Río Napo and Peru's Río Marañon meet that the Amazon continues as a single river.

The Coca of today is a sprawling oil town with little to recommend it other than its convenience as an overnight spot after you arrive from Misahuallí. There

are no street signs, and every road is unpaved and hence covered with dust, puddles or mud depending on the season. Most of the buildings are just shacks and the place has a real shanty-town appearance – they don't even have a town plaza.

Information

The IETEL office, unlike most of Ecuador, is open only from 9 am to noon and 2 to 5 pm, and 7 to 9 pm Monday through Saturday. On Sunday it is open during the morning and evening hours only. There is a post office but service is very slow. There are no proper money exchange facilities. All travellers arriving and departing by river must register with the Port Captain at the Capitanía by the landing dock. I was treated extremely courteously here. There's not much to do apart from drink beer, go to the movie theatre, or go to bed.

Places to Stay & Eat

The hotel nearest the port is also one of the cheapest and is reasonably clean but often crowded – the *Pensión Rossita* at US$1.20 per night. In the 'town centre' is the best *Hotel El Auca*, which is set in a garden and isn't bad. They charge US$2.20 each or US$3 in rooms with a private bath, and they are often full by nightfall. There are also three basic residencials across the street: the *Tungurahua, Ecuador* and *Lojanita*, in descending order of appearance. They charge about US$1-1.50 each. If all else fails, try the very basic *Residencial Turingo*.

Hotel Auca has a halfway decent restaurant although the menu is limited. The next best is *Restaurant El Rey*. It's in a neighbourhood of rather sleazy and questionable bars – but maybe that's what you were looking for anyway. The area is not dangerous. *Restaurant El Costenito* is new, clean and simple. There are several others.

The *Hacienda Primavera*, two hours downriver, offers simple but clean rooms or camping space. Good, home-cooked meals are available. There are pleasant walks and lakes in the nearby jungle. The hotel has been recommended, though I've never been there. They have a representative in Quito for further information – Señor Rodríguez, PO Box 1085, Quito, Ecuador, tel 510387. The street address is Venezuela 1716, Quito. Prices are moderate.

Getting There & Around

Air The runway has been improved and a regular service to Quito has recently been restarted by TAME. Flights leave fairly early in the morning on Monday, Wednesday and Friday. Tickets cost about US$11 and are available from the TAME office by the river, a short way east of the bridge. Flights are not always full and you can sometimes buy tickets at the airport before the flight if the TAME office is closed when you arrive. Hotel El Auca has timetables in the lobby.

It is occasionally possible to fly with an oil company plane, which might be cheaper, or free. You need the usual combination of luck, contacts, and being at the right place at the right time.

Boat The trip to Misahuallí takes about 14 hours, so you are advised to take the trip in the opposite direction, from Misahuallí to Coca, which takes only six hours. Departures are at 8 am daily and tickets and information are available from the Capitanía. The trip is sometimes broken and passengers camp out by the river – be prepared.

The Capitanía can also inform you about getting a boat further downriver. The next destination of interest is the Hacienda Primavera, about two hours downriver. An hour or two further is the ex-American mission of Limoncocha. Nearby is a school and Oriente museum at Pompeya but there is no tourist accommodation. Boat services here are irregular, infrequent and comparatively expensive.

There are very few services to Nuevo

Rocafuerte on the Peruvian border. Since the 1981 Peruvian/Ecuadorean war, you need a permit from the military camp in Coca to continue downriver. This is normally refused unless you are travelling with an organized tour group from Misahuallí or on the *Flotel Orellana*. Entering Peru at this point is prohibited.

Flotel Orellana This large, flat-bottomed river boat has three decks and about two dozen double cabins. It is operated by Metropolitan Touring, Ecuador's biggest travel agency, and the prices are commensurate with this. The tours are fairly good and an English-speaking naturalist guide accompanies the boat to explain the wildlife and surroundings. Day trips to shore are taken in dugout canoes and nights are spent in relative luxury aboard the *Flotel*, which provides good food, a bar and lectures about the jungle. The boat is based in Coca and normally steams downriver, where there is less colonization and a better chance of seeing wildlife. This is certainly the most comfortable way of seeing Ecuador's Oriente.

Voyages on the *Flotel* last anywhere from three days to a week. These tours are all-inclusive from Quito (normally you arrive and leave by air, included in the price) and cost in the region of US$50 per person per day. It may be possible to alter the itinerary to allow you to bus down to Coca and meet the *Flotel* there. Full information can be had from Metropolitan Touring, PO Box 2542, Quito, Ecuador, tel 524400, telex 2482 METOUR ED. The street address is Avenida Amazonas 239, Quito.

Bus Transportes Baños and Transportes Jumandy are the two main bus companies, each with their own office – see map. Baños have five buses a day and Jumandy have two morning buses to Lago Agrio. Most of these continue to Quito and one or two to Tena. To Lago Agrio costs US$1 and takes from two to four hours depending on the wait at the ferries (there are two

river crossings). To Quito is US$3 and about 12 to 14 gruelling hours.

LAGO AGRIO

The bus ride from Coca to Lago Agrio gives an interesting look at how the discovery of oil has changed the Oriente. Fifteen years ago, this was all virgin jungle and communications were limited to mission airstrips and river travel. Today there are roads and buses, and there are always signs of the oil industry – the pipeline, oil wells or trucks.

A short way north of Coca you have to wait for an ancient car ferry to take the bus across the Río Coca. There are soft drink stands to help you wait. The bus heads east and passes the belching wells of the Sacha oil works. It continues through the small oil town of La Joya de las Sachas, where there are a few restaurants and two basic residencials – the *Carmita* and *Zaruma*. The road is narrow but in good condition and paved in places. It follows the oil pipeline most of the way, and there are several stretches with fine scenery and vistas of the jungle. You'll frequently see tropical birds; one of the most common is the all-black ani with a long, drooping tail and extremely thick bill. The bus passes occasional small communities and reaches the Río Aguarico. Here another ferry takes the bus across the river. The town of Lago Agrio is a few km beyond.

Lago Agrio is one of the fastest-growing towns in Ecuador. Since the discovery of oil, it has changed from literally virgin jungle to the most important of Ecuador's oil towns. It now has a growing population of over 8000. A road has been built from Quito and there are daily flights. There are new road links with Colombia and a modern hotel has been opened. Lago Agrio became the capital of its *cantón* in 1979; the streets are beginning to be paved and a new town plaza has been laid out on the north-western edge of town. Avenida Quito is the main route from Quito to Coca and is still the main street and town centre, but the town is planning

Top: Colonial Cuenca, Tomebamba River (RR)
Left: Quito at dusk and Mt Cayambe (RR)
Right: Quevedo river market (RR)

Top: Cofan Indian children (RR)
Left: Oriente boy (RR)
Right: Group of Cofan Indians passing under a breadfruit tree (RR)

to spread around the plaza. Lago Agrio is lobbying to have the province of Napo divided into two, with the southern half keeping the present capital of Tena and the northern half having Lago Agrio as its new capital. It will be interesting to watch Lago Agrio's progress over the next decade.

Although it's the oldest, biggest and 'best' of Ecuador's oil towns, Lago Agrio is still just an oil town, and an oil town is an oil town. Most travellers spend as little time here as possible; it's simply a convenient overnight stop. The drive from the jungle up into the Andes is very beautiful and it's a good idea to rest in Lago Agrio and leave refreshed on a morning bus if you're headed to Quito, so that you can appreciate the scenery. Also, you can use Lago Agrio as a base for further excursions into the jungle on the road which is being pushed ever deeper into the Oriente.

Note that Lago Agrio is often called simply 'Lago' by the locals.

Information

The IETEL office, unlike the rest of Ecuador, is open from 8 am to 10 pm on weekdays, and from 8 am to noon and 8 to 10 pm on Sunday. The post office (closed weekends) is up some rickety stairs near the *casa de cambio* and looks like it's in the front room of a private home. Nevertheless, a letter I mailed from there to the USA arrived safely.

The two cinemas sometimes show fairly good English-language films.

Money Lago Agrio is only 20 km south of the Colombian border and exchange facilities exist mainly to deal with Colombian pesos, though dollars can also be negotiated. The *casa de cambio* is open irregularly (ie when they have some sucres) and they'll change cash dollars, but travellers' cheques may be refused. Usually you have to wait a few hours for 'authorization' to change money. The Banco de Fomento normally deals only with pesos. The Banco Internacional, projected to open sometime in 1985, often accepts dollars in other towns so it might do the same here. Expect to pay a commission of at least 5% if you do change money. As usual, it's best to change it in the highlands.

Things to See

There's a Sunday-morning market which can be quite interesting when the local Cofan Indians come into town to buy staples and sell their handicrafts, such as necklaces made of seeds and iridescent beetle wings. The men often wear a typical one-piece, knee-length smock called a *kushma*, along with a headband around their short hair. This latter may be made of porcupine quills. The women look very handsome in brightly patterned flounced skirts, short blouses which expose an inch of midriff (a great way to keep cool), bright red lips (they love lipstick), and some of the most beautiful long dark hair I've seen anywhere. They are related to the Sequoia people and there used to be tens of thousands of them before early contacts with whites decimated them, mainly by disease. This, unfortunately, is the history of most Amazonian Indian groups. Before the discovery of oil, most Cofans' exposure to non-Indian people was limited to the occasional missionary and they still remain quite shy, as opposed to the Otavaleño Indians, for example. They live in several river villages near Lago Agrio but there are no restaurant or accommodation facilities there.

Places to Stay

Lago Agrio is a fast-growing town and new hotels open every year. Some hotels (eg the *Hotel La Mexicana*) are expanding upwards. The top floor has the advantage of being newer and hence cleaner, but then there's the disadvantage of being closer to the roof, the sun and the heat. It's worth looking at different rooms in the same hotel to see what's best for you. Most hotels provide a mosquito net with

Lago Agrio

1	TAME Office	13	Transportes Centinela del Norte
2	Hostal El Cofan		& Pensión Marsella
3	Banco Internacional	14	Residencial La Mexicana
	(under construction)		& Hotel Utopia
4	Banco de Fomento	15	Hotel Oro Negro
5	IETEL	16	Vaquero Bar
6	Cine Amazonas	17	Transportes Zaracay
7	Hotel Cabaña	18	Casa de Cambio
8	Residencial Chimborazo	19	Post Office
9	Transportes Baños	20	Hotel Machala & Residencial Casino
10	Residencial El Dorado	21	Restaurant Chifa Rey Coreano
11	Residencial Baños	22	Hotel Oriental & Transportes Jumandy
12	Transportes Baños	23	Hotel Ambato
	& Residencial Hilton	24	Cine Oriente

the bed. Although spraying keeps the mosquito population in Lago Agrio down to a minimum, you should look for beds with these nets, especially if you're not taking malarial pills.

Places to Stay – bottom end

There are plenty of budget hotels which are cheap, basic and usually look horrible

because the rate of deterioration of cheap architecture in the humid jungle is very fast. Some of the oldest and cheapest places are getting a bit rank, so the sensitive might consider it worthwhile staying somewhere more expensive. The standard budget travellers' hotel seems to be the *Hotel Oro Negro*, which looks like a run-down jail though the rooms are kept clean. They charge US$1.50 each. Similarly priced are the *Residencial Hilton* and the *Hotel Machala*, which both look OK. The following hotels are all about US$1.50 or less and don't look as good: the hotels *Ambato* and *Oriental*; the residencials *Baños*, *Casino*, *El Dorado*, *Chimborazo*; and the *Pensión Marsella*.

Residencial La Mexicana has some rooms for US$1.50 and others for US$3 per person. These are new, have private baths and are fair value. If you stay here, have a good look around, as some of the rooms are definitely better than others. *Hotel Utopia* is basic but cleaner than most and charges US$2 each. *Hotel Cabaña* is similarly priced.

Places to Stay – top end

The best in town is the new and modern *Hostal El Cofan*, which charges about US$8/13 single/double with private bathrooms. It's often full, so get there early.

Places to Eat

Best value meals are in the restaurant of the *Hotel Utopia*, which charges US$1 for a hearty set meal and also has a varied menu. The *Hotel Machala* restaurant is also good, although a little more expensive. The *Hostal El Cofan* restaurant is supposedly the best in town. It is good, and not too expensive, but I found it a bit antiseptic. The *Rey Coreano* is a good *chifa*. There are plenty of other cheap places to choose from if you don't like this selection.

After supper, you might want to mosey over to the *Vaquero Bar* with its swing doors and wild west atmosphere. It makes a change from the beer-swilling ambience of most Oriente bars.

Getting There & Around

Air Lago Agrio boasts the best air schedule from the Oriente to Quito. TAME has a flight daily (except Sunday) at 11 am which costs US$10. They have an office downtown which is usually open on weekdays but their hours are quite erratic.

Often everyone packs up and goes to the airport when the plane from Quito arrives about 10.30 am. You can sometimes buy tickets at the airport if the flight isn't full (about half the time). The airport is about five km east of town and there is a TAME pickup truck which takes people from the office to the airport for 20c about an hour before the flight. Taxis (which are usually yellow pickup trucks) cost up to US$2 but you can go as cheaply as US$1 if you bargain hard.

If you are arriving in Lago Agrio by air, you'll see several buses waiting at the airstrip. Unfortunately, most of these are oil company vehicles picking up workers on the flight and they can't or won't give you a ride. If you ask around, however, you'll eventually find something. One of the buses is usually a public bus, and the TAME people often take passengers back in their truck. There are usually taxis hanging around – see if you can share with someone. The tropically hot or wet five-km walk is not recommended.

The airport is also used by the local oil companies, of which Texaco seems to be the biggest. They can occasionally be persuaded to give travellers a ride, but with TAME's daily flight to Quito, this is often more trouble than it's worth.

I had an amusing experience once, flying from Quito to Lago Agrio. At the Quito airport I ran into an anthropologist I knew. He was accompanying a Cofan couple who had been in hospital in Quito and who were now returning home. He explained that it was the first flight for both of them and they spoke a lot of Cofan and very little Spanish – could I keep an eye on them? Of course; I was delighted to do so, though I couldn't imagine that there would be any problems. And so off I set with my new Cofan friends.

Our first little problem was with the X-ray machine. I convinced them that no harm would come to their little bundles, so they put them onto the conveyor belt and then walked to the waiting plane. They didn't realize that the X-ray machine didn't automatically deliver all hand luggage to the plane – and after all, with all the automated devices to be seen in Quito, why not? So I called the Cofans back for their bundles and they looked at me with some disgust; obviously this fancy machine was no good at all.

We clambered aboard the aircraft and the next thing to deal with were the seat belts. They couldn't quite understand why the stewardess was buckling them in and seemed rather worried when they couldn't unbuckle their belts. A quick demonstration of the fast release device on the seat belts seemed in order. Once we were airborne, they started to complain of an earache. I tried to show them how to equalize the pressure in their ears and there followed a hilarious episode as we held our noses and swallowed and blew and snorted and sprayed. Finally, through the giggles and general uproar, I managed to convey, in sign language, how to get rid of the pain in their ears.

It was a short flight, and soon we were preparing to land at Lago Agrio. I had made sure that the Cofans had gotten window seats, thinking that they would enjoy the views. Instead, as we came in to land, one of the Cofans firmly covered the window with a blanket and then took a couple of very quick, tentative peeks before closing her eyes tightly shut. We landed safely.

Bus There is no main bus terminal and most bus companies have their offices on or near the main street, Avenida Quito. Buses to Quito cost about US$2.60 and take eight to 11 hours. The following companies have buses to Quito: Transportes Baños, Transportes Jumandy, Transportes Centinela del Norte, Transportes Zaracay. Each company has a variety of buses ranging from slow, noisy old monsters to smaller and faster buses; they all seem to break down periodically so I can't recommend one in particular because you'll only blame me if your bus breaks down! Most of these companies also have services to either Coca (US$1, two to four hours) or Tena (US$2.50, seven to 10 hours). For some strange reason, Transportes Zaracay has buses to Santo Domingo.

You can continue further into the Oriente with Transportes Jumandy, which have a daily 1 pm bus to Tarapoa (US$1, 2½ hours). Transportes Putumayo also has buses to Tarapoa. Their buses are known as *rancheros* and are open-sided trucks with uncomfortable narrow bench seats. They also run three rancheros every morning to the Río San Miguel, at the Colombian border (40c, one hour). Buses to Shushufindi are also available. The roads into the Oriente from Lago Agrio are constantly being improved and expanded; ask at Transportes Putumayo for the most recent information.

Crossing the Colombian Border

It's certainly possible to enter Colombia from Lago Agrio; the border is less than 20 km to the north and there's always a few Colombians in town. However, I've never met any gringos who have either entered or left Colombia via this border crossing. The area is notorious for smugglers, and the Colombian side has been called 'dangerous' by Ecuadorean locals. I wonder if the same is said of Ecuador by the Colombians. At any rate, if you decide that this little adventure is for you, take care, guard your belongings, and I'd enjoy hearing about your experiences – if you survive!

To get to the border, take a Transportes Putumayo bus to the Río San Miguel. Then take a dugout canoe to the Colombian side – I'm told this takes about an hour. When you arrive in Colombia, you'll find occasional buses to take you to Puerto Asis from where you can get road, air and river transportation to other parts of Colombia. For more information on getting into Colombia, see under Tulcán.

TARAPOA

This is Ecuador's newest boom town. It's an oil town about 60 km east of Lago Agrio and the road (and a few buses) go there. At this time there's nothing except a few shacks and the oil works, but already they have two flights a week to Quito, on Tuesday and Thursday mornings. Ask at TAME for more information about this service. Apparently there's also a basic place to stay. Some maps mark a road continuing from Tarapoa to Puerto El Carmen de Putumayo, which is at the junction of the San Miguel and Putumayo rivers and another entry point into Colombia. This road doesn't exist yet, but if Tarapoa continues booming, it may be built one year.

BAEZA

The road west of Lago Agrio roughly follows the Río Aguarico for some 50 km before turning south-west and beginning the long climb up into the Andes by following the valley of the Río Quijos. There are two major landmarks on this ascent. To the right of the road is the 3485-metre volcano Reventador, which means 'the exploder' and which had a period of major activity in the late 1970s. Unfortunately, it's obscured by cloud more often than not. On the left of the road, about 95 km from Lago Agrio, are the San Rafael Falls, about 145 metres high and the biggest in Ecuador. To see them properly you can get off the bus just beyond the tiny community of Río Reventador, at a concrete block hut with an INECEL sign on the left of the road. From here it's about 2½ km down a steep track to the falls. You can camp here or go back to Río Reventador, where you can sleep on the floor of the store/bar. Flag a bus down when you want to go on, and be prepared to wait, as the buses are sometimes full.

Beyond Río Reventador the road continues climbing, following both the trans-Ecuadorean oil pipeline and the Río Quijos all the way. There are enchanting views of beautiful cloud forest full of strange species of birds and plants. Several small communities with little to recommend them are passed, and Baeza is reached about 170 km and six hours from Lago Agrio.

Baeza is on the junction with the road to Tena and is the most important village between Lago Agrio and the Quito valley. It was an old, established Spanish missionary and trading outpost, having been first founded in 1548 and re-founded three

more times since. The pass from Baeza via Papallacta to the Quito valley was known well before the conquest, but the road from Baeza to Lago Agrio has been opened only by the oil boom, so Baeza is both a historical and geographical junction. It is also a good, quiet spot to stay for walks in the surrounding hills. The low Andean plants and bird life are outstanding.

Places to Stay & Eat

Facilities are very limited, however. There is only the basic but clean *Hotel Samay*, which charges US$1 a night. There are a couple of simple restaurants. If the Samay is full (very unusual; Baeza is a small town) you can go down to the village of Borja, about four km before Baeza, which also has a basic pensión.

Getting There

There are no bus stations in these villages. You must flag down passing buses and hope that they have room.

PAPALLACTA

The westbound road from Baeza continues climbing steadily until the village of Papallacta is reached, some 40 km beyond. About a km beyond the village, on the left, are the Aguas Termales or natural hot springs of Papallacta. They're not overly developed and their setting is grand; on a clear day you can see the snow-capped Antisana (5704 metres) about 15 km to the south. The hottest spring is very hot, and there's a refreshing cold plunge pool. It costs about 20c to get in, and changing rooms and toilet facilities are provided, but nothing else. It's possible to camp by the springs. In Papallacta there is a small, basic, unsigned pensión and a simple restaurant.

Quito is only 60 km away, but the drive is difficult and spectacular. The road climbs over the Eastern Cordillera of the Andes via a pass which is sometimes snow covered; it is nearly 4100 metres in height. If you're driving up from the Oriente, be prepared for the cold. Beyond the pass is the valley of Quito.

To get to Papallacta from Quito isn't straightforward. Most bus companies which go to Tena or Lago Agrio won't sell you a ticket unless you are going all the way to the Oriente. You have to wait until departure time and then hop onto the bus and buy a pro-rated ticket from the driver. The problem is that the buses are often full (that's why they didn't want to sell you a ticket for such a short distance in the first place) and even if they're not, some drivers will try and charge you the full price to Lago Agrio, because 'That's what this company does.' The best company to use is the little-known Centinela del Norte which, instead of having its office at the main terminal, has an office at Calle López and Avenida Chile near the old town in Quito. They can usually be persuaded to sell you tickets to Papallacta.

The Western Lowlands

A physical map of Ecuador shows the country divided neatly into two by the massive range of the Andes. To the east lie the jungles of the upper Amazon basin, and to the west you find the coastal lowlands. The western drop of the Andes is dramatic and steeper than the eastern side. Lowlands of below 300 metres are soon reached; from Ecuador's highest peak, Chimborazo at 6310 metres, it is only 50 km due west to the 300-metre contour, a gradient of about 12%. It does not stay low all the way to the coast, however. After dropping to almost sea level, the land rises again in a barren, scrubby and almost uninhabited range of 700-metre-high hills before dropping to the coast. Thus the coastal lowlands are subdivided into the coast itself, west of the coastal hills, and the flat lowlands lying east of the hills and west of the Andes. It is the latter which are described in this chapter.

Some people's impression of Ecuador is that it is a 'banana republic' – one of those tropical countries that produce bananas and little else. Indeed, until the export of oil began in 1972, bananas were Ecuador's most important product and they remain the country's major agricultural export. The western lowlands were once forested, but much of this has now been cleared to develop agriculture. Fortunately, the land is fertile and huge banana and palm tree plantations are seen by travellers through this area. It has not been much developed touristically and many people rush through it on their way to the coast or highlands. If you're interested in seeing some of the tropical 'banana republic' Ecuador – the kind of countryside that was typically Ecuadorean before the recent oil boom – then it is worth taking a couple of days to travel slowly through this area instead of rushing through.

One of the most frequently used routes from the highlands to the western lowlands is from Quito to Santo Domingo. From here you can head south, through Quevedo and Babahoyo in the lowland province of Los Rios, to Guayaquil on the coast. This is the travellers' route I follow in this chapter.

THE ROAD TO SANTO DOMINGO

From Quito, the bus heads south through the 'Avenue of the Volcanoes' to Aloag, where the Pan American highway is joined by the road into the lowlands. The bus often refuels here and is surrounded by hordes of snack sellers lustily hawking their delicacies. *Aziuuuzias!* seems to be a frequently heard cry; the dry biscuits are usually sold here.

The descent into the lowlands is a spectacular and sometimes terrifying one. You are strongly advised to try and make the journey in the morning, as in the afternoon both the passengers' and the driver's views are often obscured by fog. Despite almost non-existent visibility, the drivers hurtle down the western slopes of the Andes at breakneck speeds. Amazingly, accidents are very rare but near misses somewhat more common.

The road begins in high *páramo*, with views of the extinct volcanoes Atacazo and Corazón to the north and south. The tortuous descent follows the left bank of the Río Pilatón and occasionally waterfalls cascade into the narrow gorge. The road passes the village of Cornejo Astorga (also known as Tandapi) and follows the Toachi River valley. The vegetation starts becoming increasingly tropical and if you're lucky you may see orchids growing on the side of the road. The higher temperatures are noticeable by the time you pull into the village of Alluriquín. Both these villages have basic hotels and restaurants; the best of these is the *Hotel*

Florida in Alluriquín, but few travellers stay in these villages. They seem to be overnight stops for truck drivers doing the long slow haul from the lowlands up to Quito.

About 17 km before Santo Domingo is a famous hotel run by the aristocratic and very charming Señora Tina Garzón, who emigrated to Ecuador from Russia many years ago. The hotel is called, appropriately enough, *Tinalandia* and is the haunt of bird-watchers and naturalists. There is a nine-hole golf course next to the hotel, but otherwise the extensive grounds have been left largely undisturbed except for a few nature trails. The bird-watching is excellent and Tinalandia boasts a list of over 150 sub-tropical species. It is definitely worthwhile if you enjoy birding. The accommodation is very comfortable and the food is excellent but you'll have to pay about US$30 per person per day (including all meals). However, I met an Australian/New Zealander naturalist couple who were staying in budget hotels but decided to splurge for a couple of days at Tinalandia. They weren't disappointed. The hotel is sometimes booked by bird-watching groups so you have to take your chances. There is no telephone and if you want to make a reservation you have to write to Tinalandia, Santo Domingo.

Shortly before reaching Santo Domingo you pass an oil pressure station. The road has been following the Trans-Andean pipeline for the last third of its distance. If your bus is continuing beyond Santo Domingo it may avoid the town altogether because there are a couple of by-passes; normally, however, even long-distance buses pull into the town for a break.

SANTO DOMINGO
Santo Domingo de los Colorados, as it is officially known, has a population of 67,000 and is important as a road hub with major roads heading north, south, east and west. Located at only 500 metres and just 130 km from Quito, this is the nearest lowland tropical town easily accessible

from the capital and hence it is a popular weekend destination for Quiteños.

The town used to be famous for the Colorado Indians who painted their faces with black stripes and dyed their bowl-shaped haircuts a brilliant red using achiote. You can buy postcards of them all over Ecuador, but the Indians are now fairly westernized and you are unlikely to see them in their traditional finery except by going to one of their nearby villages and paying them to dress up. The villages are on the road to Quevedo. Some of the older Indians, notably the headman Abraham Salazacon and his brother Gabriel, have built up reputations as medicine men and people come from the capital to be cured.

Information
Because Sunday is the main market day, the town closes down on Mondays. There are the usual IETEL and post offices, and the Banco Internacional (open Tuesday through Saturday) will exchange US dollars at rates surprisingly close to Quito's.

Things to See
Santo Domingo is a convenient city in which to make bus connections or break a long journey. There are lively street markets (see map) and a busy Sunday market, but otherwise it's not a particularly interesting town. There is one cinema.

The Río Toachi is nearby and city buses go there. Just across the river is a not very well developed and unexciting resort village with a few restaurants, a swimming pool (or go in the river), and some games courts.

Places to Stay – bottom end
There are many extremely basic hotels near the main square and bus terminal areas. There are four on or within half a block of the main plaza: the *Dormicentro, Astoria, Pichinchas* and *Europa*, all of which look very cheap and pretty bad – I

Sto. Domingo de los Colorados

4 Residencial La Fuente
5 IETEL
6 Residencial Noroña
7 Residencial Ontaneda
8 Residencial Ambato
9 Hostal Brisas
10 Banco Internacional
11 Chifa Nueva Hong Kong
12 Teatro Amazonas
13 Chifa Happy
14 Post Office
15 Residencial San Martin
16 Transportes Andina
17 Transportes Aloag
18 Transportes Sucre
19 Transportes Zaracat
20 Transportes Esmeraldas
21 Transportes Ambato & Ecuador
22 Transportes Occidentales
23 Hotel Caleta
24 Pensións Turista & San Jose
25 **Pollos Gus (Chicken Restaurant)**
26 Hotel Amambay
27 Residencial Ramada
28 Residencial Madrid
29 Hotel El Colorado

1 Lions Traffic Circle to
Hotel Toachi (500 m)
Hotel Zaracay (850 m)
Río Toachi (4 km) & Quito (130 km)
2 Hostal Lucy
3 Hostal Roma

0   100   200 m

didn't even go in. Better are the simple but clean *Pensión San José* and *Turistica*, the latter with hot showers. Almost all the cheap hotels have only cold water, which isn't much hardship in the warm weather. These two places are both US$1 each, as is the *Residencial Madrid*, which is acceptably clean but check the rooms beforehand; many are windowless and apt to be stuffy.

For US$1.20 (US$4 for rooms with private bath) the *Residencial Noroña* is recommended for good-sized, clean rooms close to the buses. The similarly priced *Residencial Ambato* around the corner is OK but the *Residencial Ontaneda* is overpriced at US$2-3 depending on the room (though a few of the rooms aren't bad). Right across from the bus offices is the clean and helpful *Residencial San Martín*, but make sure your room doesn't face the buses. They charge US$1.50, as does the good, clean *Residencial Ramada* near the market.

A little upmarket is the *Hostal Brisas* at US$2, or US$3 with private bath. *Hotel Amambay* also has clean rooms with private bath for US$3 per person but you're still looking at cold water and there are a lot of stairs to climb. *Hotel Caleta* is clean and pleasant but make sure the cold showers work. They charge US$3.50 each in rooms with private baths and have a reasonable restaurant. The new *Hotel El Colorado* is huge and has spacious rooms with private baths for about US$4 each; worth checking if you want reasonably priced comfort.

If you want to stay away from the town centre, head out on Avenida Quito, where you'll pass a good variety of hotels. Closest to town is the basic *Residencial La Fuente*, soon followed by the *Hostal Roma*, which is good if you want to stay out of town cheaply. They charge US$1.20, or US$2 for rooms with a private bath, and there is a restaurant. Spartan but clean rooms with comfortable beds and private bathrooms cost US$2.20 per person at the *Hotel Lucy*; a good restaurant too.

Places to Stay – top end

Continuing out along Avenida Quito, you'll come to the two best hotels in town. First is the *Hotel Toachi*, US$6 per person in rooms with private shower and hot water, a swimming pool and a restaurant. Further out is the well-known *Hotel Zaracay*, which charges US$20 for a double room with bath. The food is excellent and the rooms are in jungle-style cabins with thatched roofs. There are pleasant gardens and a swimming pool which was under repair recently – look to see if there's water before diving in!

Places to Eat

The better hotels have reasonable restaurants but otherwise there aren't any particularly noteworthy ones. There are plenty of inexpensive *chifas*; two good ones are on the main square (see map). A plastic, clean, US-style fried chicken restaurant has recently opened under the name of *Pollos Gus*. There are cheap and basic restaurants next to the bus offices but they don't have much except for the set meal – OK if you're in a hurry.

Getting There & Around

Bus There is no central bus terminal but most companies have offices around 29 de Mayo and Tulcán, with the exception of Transportes Occidentales, which has its office at 29 de Mayo and Cuenca, about five blocks away. If you go to the main bus office area you'll find the drivers' assistants yelling out destinations and it's easy to find the bus you want. Quito (US$1, 2½ hours) and Guayaquil (US$1.80, five hours) are the most frequent destinations with buses leaving at least once an hour with various companies. Make sure you take a small *buseta* if you're in a hurry to get to Guayaquil, as the larger buses can take two hours longer. It's easy enough to get buses to intermediate points such as Quevedo or Daule, but if you want to go to Babahoyo you'll find fewer buses, as most southbound buses take the Daule road beyond Quevedo.

If you're heading south to Peru and don't want to change at Guayaquil, then go with Transportes Occidentales, who have several departures a day to Machala (US$2.50, eight hours). Their buses are fairly slow but are large and reasonably comfortable.

There are buses about every hour to Esmeraldas on the north coast (US$1.40, 3½ hours) with Transportes Esmeraldas and less frequently with Transportes Ambato. This journey could be broken at either La Concordia or Quinindé (officially Rosa Zárate), both of which have simple hotels but otherwise are of little interest.

Buses also go to the central coast but not as frequently as to Esmeraldas. Bahía de Caráquez (US$2, six hours) and Manta (US$2.20, seven hours) are both served by Reina del Camino, who don't seem to have an office in Santo Domingo. Unless they've opened one recently, you'll have to wait for one of these buses to swing through town. They won't stop if they are full. The companies with offices in Santo Domingo don't have many departures to the central coast; your best bet is Transportes Esmeraldas.

These are general guidelines and you'll find that most of the companies go in most directions to a greater or lesser extent. Just check out the different offices.

There is a local bus plaza at the west end of Avenida 3 de Julio where you can find beat-up old bone-shakers to take you to nearby villages. It can be interesting to take one of these buses just to see the countryside, but make sure that there is a return bus, as these villages often don't have restaurants, let alone a place to stay. You can also find buses here returning to Quito via La Concordia and (San Miguel de) los Bancos, an uncomfortable eight-hour ride but with beautiful scenery.

Finally, the most useful city bus runs east along Avenida Quito and takes you past the *Hotel Toachi* and *Zaracay* on the way to the Río Toachi swimming area. Take any bus marked 'Río Toachi.'

QUEVEDO

It's a little over 100 km from Santo Domingo to Quevedo on a gently dropping paved road. During the first 15 km you see frequent signs on the sides of the road advertising the homes of Colorado Indian *curanderos* or medicine men. This is where you go if you want to see them, but expect to pay for cures and for photography.

There are little villages about every 20 km along this road. The most important is Buena Fé, about 20 km before Quevedo. Buena Fé has a couple of basic hotels on the main street. The land is agricultural with many banana plantations and, as you get closer to Quevedo, African palm and papaya groves. The palm is important for vegetable oil.

One of the first things I noticed in Quevedo was a strange smell, rather like stale beer. I thought there was a brewery in town but I was told that it was *tamarindo*, a brown, bean-like fruit popular in fruit juices. Quevedo, with about 70,000 inhabitants, is an important road hub and market town, and *tamarindo* and many other products pass through here. At only 145 metres above sea level, the town is hot but the mountains are not far away. There are many hotels and it is a good place to break the journey from Latacunga to the coast, if you're going that way. For some reason, the Ecuadorean Chinese community has settled in this bustling and progressive town, so there are many good *chifas* and other Chinese-run businesses.

Information

There are the usual IETEL and post offices, the latter poorly marked and you can't tell it's there when it's closed. The Banco Internacional will change US dollars but at a rate of some 3% less than Quito.

Things to See

As you might expect in a growing market town, there are markets. The daily early

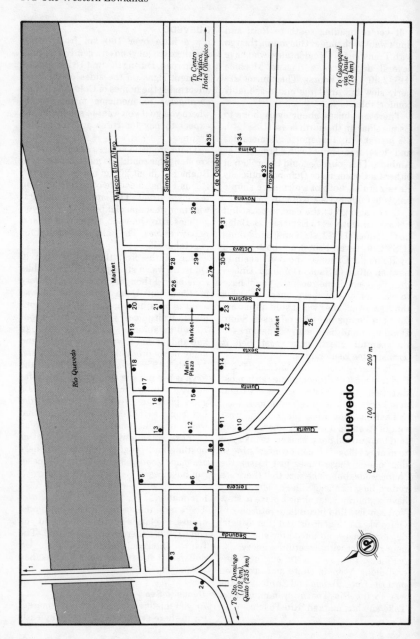

morning produce market on the Malecón by the river is quite colourful and it's pleasant to walk along the river before it gets hot. The market at Septima and Progreso has plenty of plastic junk but also hammocks if you need one.

The coastal influence begins to be felt here and there are some nightclubs. The *Zodiac* is open at weekends and has a 'couples only' rule. The less respectable *El Sotano* looks more like a pick-up joint and is open most nights. There are two cinemas.

Places to Stay – bottom end

There are many cheap hotels in Quevedo but the half dozen or so I visited looked depressingly similar – peeling walls, a lumpy bed, a broken window or no window at all. Some of the rooms were marginally better than others, so it is worth asking to see another room if you don't like the first you see. For US$1 each you can stay at the reasonably clean *Hotel Santa*, but they charge an extra 20c for rooms with windows which tend to look out on the noisy main street. For US$1.20 you can stay at the basic *Residencial Mirador, Quito* and *Hotel Guayaquil*, the last with some slightly more expensive rooms with private bath. For US$1.50 there is the *Pensión Vilmita* which is clean but nonetheless just your basic cell. Others in the US$1-1.50 price range are the *Las Brisas* (broken windows and shabby but some rooms with river views) and the pensiones *Ideal, Patricia, Nueva Esperanza, Charito, Azuay, Marianela, Guayas* and *Rocxi*, none of which look particularly enticing.

Even if you're on a budget it's worth checking out the *Hotel Imperial* by the river, US$2 each but new and clean. The rooms all have private bathrooms (cold water) with soap and towel provided, and there are fans. Many of the rooms have river views (excellent view from the roof). It's very secure and you have to ring the bell to get in.

Places to Stay – top end

There are several slightly more expensive hotels. The *Hotel Orellana* charges US$3

1	To Latacunga (177 km) & Guayaquil via Babahoyo Also Av. Guayaquil restaurants	17	Pensión Patricia
2	Buse 'de paso' to Quito	18	Hotel El Condado
3	Hotel Orellana	19	Post Office
4	Flota Bolívar (to Portoviejo)	20	Hotel Imperial
5	Residencial Las Brisas	21	El Sotano Disco
6	Buses CIA to Guayaquil	22	Cine Chan
7	Residencial Vilmita	23	Hotel Santa & Express Sucre (to Cuenca)
8	Hotel Ejecutivo Continental & Buses TIA to Guayaquil	24	IETEL
9	Banco Internacional	25	Transportes Cotopaxi (to Latacunga)
10	Pensión Ideal	26	Pensión Nueva Esperanza
11	Transportes Sucre (to Guayaquil & Sto. Domingo)	27	Hotel Continental
12	Hotel Guayaquil	28	Residencial Charito
13	Trans Ecador	29	Residencial Quito
14	Church	30	Pensión Azuay
15	Cine Quevedo	31	Chifa Rama Dorada
16	Flota Babahoyo Internacional	32	Pensións Mariannela & Guayas
		33	Pensión Rocxi
		34	Zodiac Disco & Barra Bar
		35	Residencial Mirador

each but doesn't seem much better than the *Imperial*. *Hotel Condado* boasts air conditioning and private bathrooms for US$3.50 each or a dollar less without the air conditioning. Perhaps the newest and best is *Hotel Ejecutivo Internacional* – all you international executive travellers can get an air-conditioned room for a very reasonable US$4 (with a private bathroom). *Hotel Continental* charges US$4.50 each but not all its rooms are air conditioned.

Finally, on the eastern edge of town is the comparatively expensive *Hotel Olímpico* tourist complex, complete with swimming pool, restaurant, bar etc.

Many of the cheaper hotels suffer from water shortages so check that it's running if you want to shower immediately. People often swim in the river.

Places to Eat

With its large Chinese community, Quevedo has plenty of *chifas*. *Chifa Rama Dorada* is one of the fanciest, but still not too expensive, and there are many others along the same street, Avenida 7 de Octubre (Quevedo Day).

Another good place to go is across the river. If you just keep going straight after the bridge, you'll be walking along Avenida Guayaquil which, after half a dozen blocks, makes a large Y. One arm goes to Latacunga and the other to Babahoyo. Between the bridge and the Y are dozens of restaurants, ranging from little street stands to bigger *comedors* and fish restaurants. There's a good choice of places, it's colourful, and it's worth a look.

Getting There

Boat Although the Río Quevedo is wide and deep enough for boats and eventually runs into the Pacific at Guayaquil, there is little river traffic. It is generally cheaper to use the good road connections to the coast. A few dugouts chug up and down and there's usually a raft of bamboo logs floating through, but figure on using the bus to get anywhere.

Bus There is no central bus terminal so you have to roam the streets looking for the various terminals; the main ones are on the map. Quevedo is 180 km from Guayaquil by flat road and 235 km from Quito by mountainous road so it's not surprising that the bus situation heavily favours Guayaquil. In fact, there aren't any direct buses to Quito. Transportes Ecuador has buses from Guayaquil to Quito several times a day but they are often full by the time they pass through Quevedo. It's better to stand at the town exit at the end of Avenida 7 de Octubre and wait for a bus *de paso* heading for Quito, or to take one of the frequent Transportes Sucre buses to Santo Domingo where you can change to equally frequent buses to Quito. Don't confuse Transportes Sucre with Express Sucre, which has only three daily buses to Cuenca.

Buses to Guayaquil (US$1.20) are very frequent and take from 2½ to four hours depending on the bus. All companies seem to have both large, slow buses and small, fast ones. Ask at Transportes Sucre, TIA and CIA companies. These normally go via Daule. If you want to go via Babahoyo, you should go with FBI – which translates, inoffensively, into Flota Babahoyo Internacional.

Other bus companies you should know about are Transportes Cotopaxi and Flota Bolívar. The first runs seven buses a day to Latacunga, about seven hours by dirt road. The second has an 8 am and a 1 pm bus to Portoviejo, about five hours by dirt road. This route, from Latacunga via Quevedo to Portoviejo, is one of the least frequently travelled and also one of the prettiest highland-to-coast routes. The buses are old, crowded and uncomfortable but the journey more interesting than the standard routes.

SOUTH OF QUEVEDO

If your southbound bus crosses the Río Quevedo bridge, then you are going to Babahoyo; if it doesn't, then you are heading to Daule.

About 20 km away from Quevedo you reach Empalmé – or Velasco Ibarra, as it's officially called. Here the road forks, westbound on a dirt road to Portoviejo and southbound on paved road to Guayaquil. Empalmé is a busy little junction town with several basic restaurants and pensiones. You're in the heart of banana country here and it continues that way to Balzar, another small market town with a basic hotel.

Near Palestina the good road surface turns to gravel and the going gets slower – evidence of the disastrous floods of 1982/83. Also around Palestina the banana plantations give way to rice paddies, and *piladoras* are frequently seen along the road. These are husking and drying factories with tons of rice spread out on huge concrete slabs to dry in the sun (assuming you're travelling in the dry season). Not everyone can afford the commercial *piladoras* and often you see a poor *campesino* spreading out his few bushels of rice to dry on the tarmac on the side of the road. In other areas, similar *piladoras* are used to dry various crops such as coffee.

About –3/4 of the way to Guayaquil, you'll reach Daule. This is another small commercial and agricultural centre with basic hotels. You cross the Río Daule and though you can see a few outboard-powered dugouts, few people travel to Guayaquil that way, as it is prohibitively expensive compared to the bus. Three hours after leaving Quevedo, the bus gets to Guayaquil, Ecuador's major port and largest city.

BABAHOYO

With about 45,000 inhabitants, Babahoyo is the capital of the flat agricultural province of Los Rios. North of it lie banana and palm plantations, south of it are rice paddies and some cattle raising. The ride from Babahoyo to Guayaquil is often made very pretty by the sight of huge flocks of white cattle egrets.

Babahoyo, only seven metres above sea level and located on the banks of the Río Babahoyo, was badly flooded during the 1982/83 El Niño. To get some idea of what the flood was like, go to the library at the edge of the river. The flood-retaining walls, some six metres high in the dry season, have been completely washed away in places. The water level reached the library entrance, which is on a small patio about half a metre higher than the surrounding streets – all of which were flooded for several weeks. The inhabitants waded knee deep from house to house or used canoes. An interesting feature of the river is the floating houses which were there before the floods; they just rose and fell with the waters. A few drifted loose but most remained undamaged. You can cross the river for a few cents; there are frequent departures from the dock.

The church on the central plaza has a large modern mural of the Virgin and Child decorating the entire front. The otherwise pleasing effect is marred somewhat by the massive rusty iron doors, which look more like the doors of a maximum security prison than the entrance to a place of worship.

Although it's not exactly exciting, Babahoyo is a bustling and energetic town with much commercial activity. The downtown streets are very busy and, for some strange reason, I found myself liking the place.

Information

The post office is in the government buildings on the central plaza. There is an IETEL office but no money-changing facilities.

Places to Stay

There's plenty to choose from. The *Mesón Popular* rents very basic boxes for US$1.20 per person, but at least it's locked up and looks secure. Similarly priced is the basic *Hotel Zaida*, which has a few rooms with river views. Even cheaper is the *Residencial Babahoyo*, livable for US$1.

Babahoyo

1	Library	12	Church
2	Hotel Zaida	13	Flota Bolívar
3	Teatro Babahoyo	14	Transportes El Dorado
4	Hotels Cachari & Los Rios	15	Residencial Ensueño & Bus Companies
5	Hotel Riberas del Babahoyo		(Flota Babahoyo, Interprovincial etc.)
6	Hotel San Marcos	16	Hotel Capitol
7	Pensión Sanchez	17	Residencial Azucena
8	Residencial Babahoyo	18	Mesón Popular
9	Hotel Reina Maria	19	Restaurant Munich
10	Hotel Dorado Gigante	20	Jimmy's Club
11	IETEL		

Other cheap places are the *Pensión Sanchez* (really basic little concrete boxes) and *Hotel Los Rios*, which is next to the fanciest place in town, *Hotel Cachari*. The latter charge from US$4.50-7 per person depending on whether you want air conditioning, river views, etc. It looks pretty good if you want some comfort.

There's also the *Hotel San Marcos*, with rooms starting around US$1.20 each, though you'll pay twice that for rooms with a private bath. The *Residencial Ensueño* is about US$1.50 each but is next to the FBI bus station and apt to be noisy. *Hotel Dorado Gigante* has fairly clean, spacious rooms with private bath for US$2 each, but when I was there I was asked if I wanted the room for a while or for the night.... Although a little more expensive, *Hotel Riberas* is good value with clean rooms costing from US$2-4.50 each depending on whether you have fan, air conditioning, private bathroom, river view. Finally, the *Hotel Capitol* is being remodelled but looks as if it's going to be a good – though not very cheap – hotel.

Places to Eat
There are many *chifas* in the town centre, especially on General Barona east of the central plaza. A good one is below the *Hotel Cachari*. Near *El Rosado* is a nice corner café with outdoor tables from which to watch the activity of the plaza. A good cheap place for an outdoor (or indoor) lunch is the *Restaurant Munich*.

Entertainment
There is one cinema. If you're there at the weekend you can poke your head into *Jimmy's Club* – I have no idea what it's like.

Getting There
Bus There is no proper central terminal but most companies have departures from or near the block bounded by 5 de Junio and Bolívar. Most companies have frequent service to Guayaquil (40c, 1½ hours). You can also get buses to most towns in the province.

North Coast

Unlike the coast of Peru to the south, Ecuador has warm water bathing its coast and swimming is pleasant year round. There are beautiful palm-fringed sandy beaches which, unfortunately, suffered greatly during the 1982/83 El Niño floods. Many of the beaches were destroyed (palm trees uprooted, the sand washed away, and oceanfront buildings and streets damaged) but are recovering slowly. There are still many scars of the disaster, but hotels are, for the most part, open and functioning normally and it is expected that the beaches will return to their former beauty in the next few years.

There are two definite seasons on the coast. The rainy season runs from December to June and the dry season during the rest of the year. The rainy season is hot and humid as well as wet and the climate in the lowlands is uncomfortable. At this time, strangely enough, people flock to the beaches. I suppose the rationale is that if it is hot, humid, wet and stickily uncomfortable, you may as well go to the beach and cool off in the sea. January to March seem to be popular months. The biggest problem at this time is that the rain can make roads slow or impassable but generally the main roads remain open year round. During the dry season there are often fewer tourists than during the wet!

Travelling along the coast is varied and exciting. If you were to begin in the north and work your way southwards, you would travel by motorized dugout, normal bus, *ranchero* bus, poled dugout and on foot.

SAN LORENZO

There are no roads to San Lorenzo and most travellers arrive by train or boat. The train ride down from Ibarra in the highlands is beautiful and takes all day. San Lorenzo itself is not very attractive. There are no beaches and most people use it just as an overnight stop before continuing to Esmeraldas. It is a small village with a couple of main streets centered around the railway tracks. *Marimba* music can sometimes be heard in town but there are no special bars or nightclubs; ask around.

Information

There are no proper money-changing facilities. If you ask around you'll find people will change small amounts of Colombian currency or US dollars. It is possible to arrive in San Lorenzo by boat from Tumaco in Colombia but there is no immigration office and you have to go to Ibarra or Esmeraldas and ask at the DITURIS or police stations there about getting your passport stamped. You may have to go to Quito. There is an IETEL office.

Places to Stay & Eat

None of the few hotels in San Lorenzo are very good so if you like some comforts you will be uncomfortable here. None of the rooms have private bathrooms, air conditioning or other amenities. They should have a bed and a mosquito net; the mosquitoes can be bad, especially in the wet months. Bring insect repellant or mosquito coils. None of the hotels charge more than US$1.50 per person. One of the best to stay in is the *Hotel Imperial* by the railway tracks. They are helpful with information. Also helpful is *Residencias Ibarra* over the restaurant of the same name. There are a couple of other basic places if these are full – it's a small town so you won't have difficulty in finding them. If arriving by train, it is a good idea to try and find a place to stay quickly because everyone else will be looking.

Apart from the *Ibarra*, you can eat seafood at *La Red* or in the market. There are a few other basic restaurants. None of them are great and it's best to stick to seafood, which will be fresh.

Getting There

Rail The *autoferro* leaves daily from San Lorenzo at 6.30 am for Ibarra. Try to book your seat the day before or get to the station early, as the train is usually full. More information on this service is found in the Ibarra section.

Boat General enquiries about boat services are best directed at the Capitanía on the waterfront. They have lists of departing and arriving boats.

There are boats most days to Tumaco in Colombia, but make sure you have all the necessary visas (see Facts for the Visitor). Few people take this route; the journey is done in motorized dugouts, costs about US$7 and takes most of the day. It can get both very wet and sunny so protect yourself and your gear.

Other motorized dugouts go to San Pedro (where there is a beach but no accommodation), to Limones (officially called Valdéz), and to La Tola. Limones (US$1, 1¼ hours) and La Tola (US$1.50, two hours) are served by several boats a day and are the usual destinations of most travellers. If you take a morning boat to La Tola, you can connect with a bus on to Esmeraldas. Tickets are sold in San Lorenzo for the complete journey. The bus portion takes about four or five hours from La Tola to Esmeraldas, so the whole trip from San Lorenzo to Esmeraldas can be done in one day and costs about US$3. Accommodation in Limones and La Tola is worse than in San Lorenzo, so many travellers make the straight through trip.

It is also possible to take a steamer all the way from San Lorenzo to Esmeraldas, but this isn't highly recommended. You don't see much of the countryside and the boats are cargo vessels that are dirty, hot and uncomfortable. Service is irregular – about twice a week.

The motorized dugout journey to Limones and La Tola (boats to La Tola normally stop in Limones) is much more pleasant. The dugouts are small enough to travel through the coastal mangrove swamps and you'll see much more scenery than you will from the larger steamer. Keep your eyes open for the black scissor-tailed frigate birds circling overhead, squadrons of pelicans gliding by, and schools of jellyfish floating past the boat.

LIMONES

This town at the mouth of the Río Cayapa is more important than San Lorenzo, despite the latter's railway connections. The only way into Limones is by boat and you can also take boats up the Cayapa to visit the Cayapa Indian village of Borbón. The Cayapas are famous for their basket-work and there are stores in Esmeraldas and Limones selling their work. Make sure there is a return boat, as there are no places in Borbón at which to stay or eat. The road from Esmeraldas along the coast has a branch to Borbón and a bus service is planned. Timber is logged in this area and floated down the river to Limones, where there is a sawmill. There are few amenities in town and the two hotels are pretty rough.

You can get from Limones to Esmeraldas on a twice-weekly boat; ask at the Capitanía. It is easier to go on to La Tola and take the bus.

LA TOLA

This village is the beginning or end of the road, depending on which direction you're headed. The bus journey to Esmeraldas is bumpy and uncomfortable. It is very dusty in the dry season and muddy in the wet. There are good views of the coastal scenery and I persuaded the driver to let me ride on the roof of the bus, which was better than being squashed inside. I don't recommend this during the rainy season. Watch out for sunburn during the dry. The bird life along the coast is varied and spectacular; I enjoyed looking at trees filled with hundreds of roosting white cattle egrets.

Places to Stay & Eat
There are no hotels, though stranded travellers will be given somewhere to sleep. There are a few stores where you can buy snacks.

Getting There
Buses with the La Costeñita company take five hours to Esmeraldas and cost US$2. If you take a morning bus from Esmeraldas you will connect with a boat to San Lorenzo and vice versa, so there is no reason to stay in La Tola.

ESMERALDAS
This important city of about 91,000 inhabitants is capital of the province of Esmeraldas. It was near here that the Spanish conquistadors made their first landfall in Ecuador. Esmeraldas has been a major port throughout Ecuador's history. Although fishing and shipping are important, the recent construction of an oil refinery near the terminal of the trans-Andean oil pipeline has provided Esmeraldas with a new source of income and employment.

This is of little interest to most tourists who spend the night and continue south-west to the towns of Atacames, Súa and Muisne, where the best beaches are to be found. Esmeraldas itself also has beaches in the suburb of Las Palmas, but they are not as good.

Information
The unsigned post office is up the stairs from the IETEL office on the waterfront. The IETEL office was extraordinarily efficient when I was last there – they connected me with Quito in two minutes. The market across from the IETEL office is open daily and sells Cayapa basketry among other things.

There is a DITURIS tourist information office half a block from the main plaza. There is no sign or street number so you find it by going up the stairs of the nondescript office building marked on the map.

1	IETEL & Post Office	22	Transportes Esmeraldas
2	Hotel Turismo	23	Nuevo Hotel
3	Hotel Chaberrin Internacional	24	Residencial Liz
4	Hotel Rita	25	Residencial Dominguez
5	Banco Central	26	Pensión 9 de Octubre
6	Hotel Barracón	27	Transportes Occidentales &
7	Gruta Disoteca, Hotel Valparaiso		Pensión Elsita
8	Aero Taxi Arrivals	28	Portón 26 Disco
9	Cita buses	29	Hotel Galeon
10	Aero Taxi Departures	30	Hotel Roma 1
11	Hotel Royal	31	Residencial Sulema
12	Cinema	32	Hotel Roma 2
13	Transportes La Costeñita	33	Hotel Americano
14	Transportes La Costeñita main terminal	34	Hotel Diana
15	Residencial Bolívar	35	Filanbanco
16	Hostal Isabelita	36	Hotel Korea
17	Reina del Camino (buses) &	37	Banco de Pichincha
	Residencial Paquita	38	Fish and vegetable market
18	TAME	39	Hotel Suiza
19	Tourist Office (2nd floor)	40	Two blocks to Apartment
20	Cine Bolívar		Hotel Esmeraldas
21	Cine Variedades		

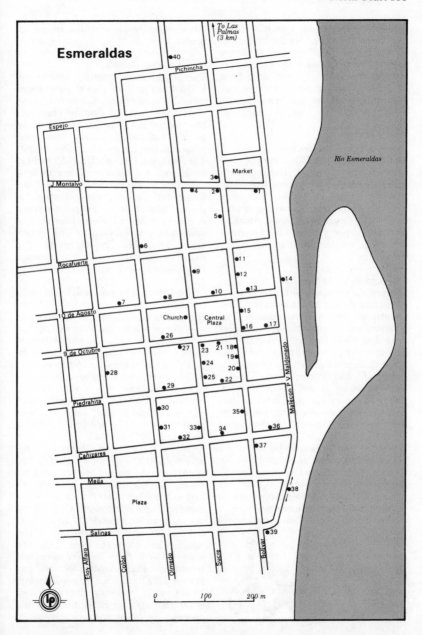

Esmeraldas

To Las Palmas (3 km)

Pichincha

Espejo

Río Esmeraldas

Market

J Montalvo

Rocafuerte

1O de Agosto

Church

Central Plaza

9 de Octubre

Malecón P. V. Maldonado

Piedrahita

Cañizares

Mejía

Plaza

Salinas

Eloy Alfaro

Colón

Olmedo

Sucre

Bolívar

0   100   200 m

Money changers don't exist and last time I was in Esmeraldas the banks told me that it was 'illegal' for them to change money. This was, apparently, a temporary economic measure and has since been lifted. It is best to arrive with enough sucres, however, as the banks remain erratic with their foreign exchange policies.

Places to Stay – Esmeraldas

There are many hotels but the cheapest ones are not too good. Esmeraldas is definitely not the place to come looking for quaint or memorable hotels. There seem to be quite a few travellers in Esmeraldas (especially Ecuadorean holiday-makers and businesspeople) and hotels are sometimes full. You may want to stay in Las Palmas.

Places to Stay – bottom end

Many of the cheapest hotels are close to bus terminals and apt to be noisy. They are also not very well looked after. The following are among the very cheapest (less than US$1.50 each) but otherwise have little to recommend them: pensiones *Elsita, Quito* and *9 de Octubre*; residencials *Paquita, Liz* and *Bolívar*; hostals *Isabelita* and *Valparaiso 1*; and *Hotel Suiza*. Of these, the ones not right next to bus terminals are generally a little better; the *Residencial Liz* is one of the better cheapies.

Slightly more expensive but not much better is the *Nuevo Hotel* at US$1.70. Cleaner, but criticized as noisy, is the *Residencial Dominguez* at US$2 per person. The last three mentioned are all on the same block of Avenida Sucre south of the central plaza. There are several

other cheap hotels within a couple of blocks.

Places to Stay – middle

There is a better selection if you can afford US$3-4 each, but check your room carefully, as the higher-priced hotels are sometimes no better than the cheapest. Most of the rooms in this section boast private bathrooms, mostly with cold water, but check to see if they are working. The *Residencial Sulena* (US$3.50 each) is clean, well-lit and secure. There are fans in the rooms but its most commendable feature is the many plants decorating the place. The front yard is a popular evening venue for volleyball. *Hotel Americano* is new, clean and good value for US$3 single and US$5 double. They charge an extra dollar per person for air conditioning. *Hotel Galeon* is well kept for US$3.80 per person.

Hotel Korea is expensive at US$3 each. *Hotel Diana* has rooms for US$3.50 per person. The rooms have TV and telephone and the nice little old lady behind the reception desk told me to phone down if the water wasn't running. The place looks as if it has some character. *Hotel Roma 2* is US$3.50 each, but many of its rooms are without windows and it shouldn't be confused with the better and more expensive *Hotel Roma 1*, which has some good rooms with TV and phone at US$5 single and US$9 double.

Hotels *Turismo* and *Chaberrin Internacional* both charge US$4 each. The first is dirty and the second has beds with no sheets. Not all the rooms have private bathrooms. These hotels are not recommended. *Hotel Rita* charges US$10 for a double room and looks sleazy. *Hotel Royal* is US$3.50 each but unfriendly – they wouldn't let me look at a room. 'Take it or leave it.' I left it. *Hotel Barracón* has a good restaurant and clean rooms for US$4 per person; US$1 more for air conditioning. Unfortunately, they suffer from occasional water shortages so check to see if it's running.

Places to Stay – top end

Apart Hotel Esmeraldas charges US$13 single and US$19 double and is the best in town.

Places to Stay – Las Palmas

There are half a dozen hotels in this beach suburb and most of them are fairly expensive. The two exceptions are the clean, family-run *Residencial Mechita* and the *Hostal Familiar*, both of which charge US$1.50 each for basic rooms. The remaining hotels all charge about US$10 single and US$16 double and are very comfortable. The *Atahualpa Hotel* is in a large house with a flower garden and the *Hotel Cayapas* also has a pleasant garden. *Hotel del Mar* is new and closest to the beach. Some rooms have ocean views and US dollars are accepted. *Hotel Hipocampo* has a pleasant patio to sit out on and is also new.

Places to Eat

The most expensive hotels have decent restaurants. The two restaurants on opposite corners of Avenidas Rocafuerte and Sucre are quite good and reasonably priced. Although there are no outstanding restaurants in downtown Esmeraldas, the food in the many small *comedors* is often very good. There are many dishes typical of the coast and sometimes found only in this province. Fish and other seafood are more common than meat and are usually served with a mountain of plain white rice, boiled beans and plantains. The plantains are sometimes boiled whole (very stodgy to my taste) or are sliced and fried to make *patacones* – very tasty. Raw seafood is often marinated to make *ceviche*, which is very good. Seafood *cocado* is cooked with coconut to impart a delicate flavour. *Cocadas*, on the other hand, are sweet bars of grated coconut cooked in sugar and sold on bus journeys throughout the province.

In Las Palmas you can find cheap, no-name beach-hut restaurants which have limited menus because they only serve whatever was caught that day. The food is often delicious. There are a few more expensive restaurants near the hotels; some of them quite elegant, such as the *Restaurant Atenas*. *Bayardo's Restaurant* has also been recommended.

Entertainment

The coast is known for its lively African-influenced music. There are no particular places where you can go to listen to shows; you have to catch as catch can. Impromptu gatherings are the norm. The best way is to make friends with the locals and ask them. There are discos, but they are usually open only at weekends. Two are marked on the map and the *Porton 26 Disco* has been recommended though I've never danced there. There are three cinemas, of which the *Ciné Bolívar* is the most comfortable.

Getting There

Air There is a flight to Quito every day except Sunday. It leaves about 8.30 am and costs about US$10. The TAME office just off the corner of the main plaza will sell you a ticket. The major problem is that the airport is about 25 km away from town across the Río Esmeraldas. TAME will help by providing a bus (50c per passenger) or taxi service to the airport. Incoming passengers are met by the bus.

Boat The Capitanía is on the right side of the road linking downtown with Las Palmas, just before you get to Las Palmas. They can give information about which boats are going where, and then you have to talk to the captain of the boat directly. Boats occasionally go to Guayaquil and other coastal ports but the most frequent sailings are for Limones. It is much more convenient to travel by land and you see more.

There is an immigration office near the Capitanía should you be arriving from Colombia.

Bus There is no central bus terminal. There is a direct road to Quito via Santo Domingo. The fastest service is with Aerotaxi (US$2.20, five hours) but they drive suicidally fast. Slower and a few cents cheaper are Transportes Occidentales and Transportes Esmeraldas. Buses are frequent.

Transportes Occidentales also has frequent buses to Guayaquil (US$2.70, nine hours) and an early evening bus to Machala (US$3.50, 12 hours) if you want to go to Peru the next day. Guayaquil is also served by Transportes Esmeraldas. CITA has four buses a day to Ambato. Reina del Camino has five buses a day to Portoviejo (US$3, nine hours) and a couple to Bahía de Caráquez (US$2.90, eight hours).

For provincial buses go to the Transportes La Costen'ita offices (there are two, a block apart from one another). Most of the buses leave from the waterfront office. Buses to Atacames and Súa (25c, less than an hour) leave every 45 minutes from 6.30 am to 8 pm. There are eight buses a day to Muisne (US$1, three hours). Buses to La Tola leave six times a day and the US$3 ticket includes the boat to San Lorenzo. Take a morning bus to ensure that you don't have to overnight in La Tola. Many buses also go to other small provincial villages.

Getting Around

Take a 5c Las Palmas bus along Avenida Bolívar to get to the port and beaches.

ATACAMES

This small resort town, about 30 km west of Esmeraldas, has built up a reputation among travellers as one of the best places to go for a relaxed and inexpensive beach vacation. It certainly is cheaper and less developed than the beaches in the Guayaquil area, and despite the recent flood damage remains particularly popular with budget travellers. Accommodation can be found inexpensively right on the oceanfront – it's great to be able to walk out of

your room straight onto the beach. There's not much reason for going into the town centre unless you need to make a phone call at the IETEL office.

Nightlife is variable. I've been here when nothing was happening and other times when every bar was hopping. I can't recommend anywhere in particular; if there's anything going on you'll hear it!

Warning

There is a powerful undertow and no lifeguards. People get drowned every year so keep within your limits.

Thieves thrive wherever there is a conglomeration of travellers. This is certainly true of beach areas, and Atacames is no exception. Camping is not recommended because thieves cut through the tent material and rob you even if you're asleep inside the tent. It is best to stay in a beach cabin or hotel room and make sure that it has secure locks on the doors and shutters on the windows.

Assaults have been reported by people walking the beaches late at night. If you want a midnight beach stroll, go in a group.

Bring insect repellant or mosquito coils, especially in the wet months. The cheapest hotels often have rats, so stay in a medium-priced hotel to minimize the chances of seeing them if it worries you.

Although the chance of being bitten by a sea snake is remote, every once in a while they get washed up on the beaches. Don't pick them up, as they are venomous.

Places to Stay

Atacames can get rather full at weekends, especially holiday weekends, so you are advised to try and arrive midweek. January through March is the high season, when prices tend to rise. At other times you can try bargaining, especially if you arrive midweek and plan on staying a few days. The low season tends to be June through August.

There are a couple of places closer to the town centre near the place where the bus lets you off but most hotels are on or close to the beach. To get to the beach, you have to cross the footbridge, as vehicles don't go there. New hotels, or old hotels reopened under new management and name, open frequently and you'll probably find a few others. Always check your room or cabin for security before you rent it.

Most showers have brackish water (which is quite salty) and only the more expensive hotels have fresh-water showers.

Places to Stay – bottom end

For the cheapest accommodation the best selection is to your right after you cross the footbridge. The first cheap place you come to is the *Residencial Bachita*, which was recently repainted but looks rather like a barracks building. They charge US$2 each. It is set back a block from the beach, as are the *Residencial Primavera* and *Hotel Balboa*, both of which charge US$1.50 each and are run down. Further down the beach is the *San Baye*, one of the cheapest places. They charge US$2 for a room with two beds. Some rooms have a private bathroom for US$1 extra. At the far end of the beach are the quiet and laid-back *Cabinas Chavalito* – tiny A-frame beach cabins with two beds for US$3 a cabin. They are basic but quite acceptable and they have a little restaurant so you don't have to go back to the main tourist area.

If you turn left at the footbridge you'll see the *Hotel Paco Foco*, which was temporarily closed recently but doesn't look very expensive. At the other far end of the beach is the *Hotel Eden*, also inexpensive. If all the beachfront cheapies are full, you can try the basic and run-down *Hotel Bellavista* near the bus stop.

Places to Stay – middle

The first mid-range place you come to if you turn right at the footbridge is the *Hostería Los Bohíos*, which has pleasant and clean bungalows with private bath for US$7.50 a double. Next door is the *Hotel Atalaya*, which has clean rooms with private bath for US$6 double. Both places are good and secure but they aren't right next to the beach. Closer to the beach is the *Hotel Tahiti*, which has a restaurant, simple but clean cabins and rooms with and without baths. Prices range from about US$4-7 double, depending on which rooms you get. The staff are friendly and lock up your valuables for you. The private baths have brackish water but there is a communal fresh-water shower too.

Heading left from the beach, you'll eventually come to *Cabañas Roger*. They charge a minimum US$5 per person and have a bewildering system of taxes and extra charges for rooms with a sea view or with a private kitchen (refrigerator and stove). All the rooms have private showers and some of them are new and look good. Some of the bungalows are suitable for up to six people and you could probably bargain for a better rate. They'll happily explain their prices to you so you won't get slapped with a 'sea view tax' as you're about to leave.

Places to Stay – top end

To the left across the footbridge you'll find the comfortable bungalows of *Cabañas Costa del Sol*, about US$13 double. They have a good restaurant. Heading in the opposite direction, you'll find the new, clean and modern bungalows of the *Hotel Juan Sebastian* set in a flower garden. They charge from US$5-10 per person depending on the room and the season. They also have a restaurant and bar. Similarly priced, but on the main road, is the good *Hotel Las Vegas*.

Places to Eat

There are many simple *comedors* close to the beach near the footbridge. They all tend to serve the same thing, ie whatever was caught that morning. Make sure you ask the price before you get served or you may be overcharged. All the *comedors* reem to be much of a likeness, so wander around till you find one that you fancy. The *Pelican* is one of the nicer-looking ones and has a good choice of food.

Getting There

Bus All buses stop at the corner of the main road by the Disco La Barca; there is no bus terminal. You pay for your ticket when you board the bus. Buses for Esmeraldas (25c, 45 minutes) normally begin from Súa and there are plenty of seats. Most buses from Esmeraldas to Atacames continue to Súa. Buses for Muisne (80c, two hours further down the coast) are often full when they come from Esmeraldas and you may find it easier to return to Esmeraldas and then retrace your route. Alternatively, be prepared to ride on the roof.

SÚA

This is a small fishing village and is rather more bustling than Atacames. It's an interesting place to stay if you'd rather watch the boats and fishermen at work than just hang out on the beach. The fishing industry brings its attendant frigate birds, pelicans and other seabirds but also means that the small beach is dirtier than the one at Atacames. The general setting is very attractive. There is an IETEL office with one phone.

It's about a six-km walk by road from Atacames. I've also heard that you can walk along the beach at the lowest tides, but if you try this be careful not to get cut off. The 1982/83 floods washed out some of the beach and it may no longer be possible.

Places to Stay & Eat

There's much less to choose from than in Atacames. The *Residencia Quito* is a basic hotel on the road into town which charges US$1.50 each. On the waterfront are several cheap places, of which the *Hotel Súa* and *Residencial Proaño* are the cheapest but aren't up to much. The *Residencial España* has a dance floor and is liable to be noisy if it's party night –

mainly weekends. They charge US$1.50 each. Slightly better is the *Residencial Mar y Sol* for US$2 each. They also have a couple of rooms with private showers for twice that price.

If there is a group of you, try the *Cabañas Las Acacias*, which charge about US$22 for six-bed bungalows with private bath. During the off season they'll be willing to bargain, and they also have some rooms where you can stay for about US$2.50 each. It's the best cheap place in town if you can bargain them down a bit. Finally, there is the pleasant and well looked after *Hotel Chagra Ramos*, where you can get a good double room with fan and private bath for US$8 in the off season. There is a good restaurant here. Otherwise you can try the cheap *comedors* past the *Residencial España*.

Getting There

Buses to and from Esmeraldas run about every 45 minutes and arrive and leave from in front of the Residencial Mar y Sol. It takes 10 minutes to Atacames (10c) and about an hour to Esmeraldas (30c). You pay on the bus.

If you want to go further along the coast to Muisne you have to wait out of town along the main road for a bus passing from Esmeraldas (often full).

MUISNE

This is the end of the road from Esmeraldas. I have always enjoyed this little village because it is relatively remote and not many people come here. The journey is interesting. The old bus (or *ranchero*) drives along a very bumpy dirt road but the scenery is good. I rode on top of the bus and enjoyed the views of rolling green countryside with many species of tropical trees and birds. At the end of the road you have to take a motorized dugout to reach Muisne, which is on an island. Boatmen will meet the bus and take you to their boat – just follow other passengers. The fare is about 50c depending on how far the bus can get; some of the road was washed out in 1982/83.

When you disembark at Muisne you'll see the main road heading directly away from the pier into the town 'centre.' There are several cheap and basic hotels, solo women travellers should beware if the *Residencial Narcisita*. The others are all unremarkable and charge about US$1-1.50 per person. It's best to continue on the main road, past the town square, and towards the ocean. The main road deteriorates into a grassy lane and it's about a km to the beach. Turn right and you'll see a store about 100 metres down the beach. The owner rents beach cabins – basic wooden shacks that are clean, have a shower and mosquito nets. They charge US$2-3 per person depending on the season. It's definitely not fancy but is a *tranquilo* place to stay and you have a huge beach to yourself. Bring insect repellant.

There are a couple of basic restaurants (*Comedor Martha, La Moneda*) in town which serve cheap set meals at normal meal times, but don't expect anything after 7.30 pm. There's a lot of driftwood on the beach and some travellers cook their own food.

SOUTH OF MUISNE

There is no road south of Muisne, so if you want to travel further you have to try other options. If you ask around the dock in Muisne you'll sometimes hear of boats heading down the coast to Bolívar, Cojimíes or even as far as Manta. Boats are usually large motorized dugouts and stay fairly close to the coast, so it would be an interesting journey for the adventurous traveller with time to spare.

You can also head south on foot and get to Cojimíes in one day if you leave early. At low tide, pickup trucks act as buses on some sections and you can get a ride, but don't rely on them. There are several rivers to cross but you can find dugouts to ferry you for about 10 or 20c. Bring change. From Muisne, walk south along the beach for about five km; take a dugout across the river and continue seven km

along the beach past Mompiche (small store); follow a jeep track over the headland four km to Punta Suspiro; make the dugout crossing to Portete (small store); walk five km to Bolívar. Although you can sometimes catch rides, be prepared to walk the whole distance if necessary. I've done this walk twice and seen sea snakes, a beached whale, crabs galore, jellyfish, seabirds and other sea creatures along the beach.

Bolívar has a little port and if you wait and ask around you can get a boat ride to Cojimíes for about US$1.50. It may take a few hours to get a passage so leave Muisne at dawn, as there are no hotels in Bolívar. You can rent a boat for about US$15 to take you to Cojimíes if you can't get a ride.

Warning
Rain during the wet season can cause delays.

COJIMÍES
The road begins again here and there are daily buses (*rancheros*) south. They run along the coast at low tide so departure times vary. The Costa del Norte bus office is on the main street. Buses to the next village of Pedernales cost US$1 and take about 1¼ hours. Buses sometimes go further. Across the street from the bus office there is a very basic (wash in a bucket) unmarked hotel which will give you a bed for about US$1.50. There are basic restaurants. Although facilities are limited, people tend to be extra friendly in these out-of-the-way places.

PEDERNALES
There is a Costa del Norte bus office on the main street where you can buy tickets for Cojimíes or San Vicente (US$3, four hours). There are three or four departures a day. There are a couple of basic (no showers) *residencials* near the bus offices where a bed costs US$1.20-1.50.

The buses usually follow the beach and the ride is very fast on the hard-packed sand, especially between Pedernales and Cojimíes. There are some rougher stretches south of Pedernales.

JAMA

This is another one-pensión village between Pedernales and San Vicente but buses are often full on arrival.

SAN VICENTE

This resort village is a short ferry ride across the Río Chone from the more important town of Bahía de Caráquez. There are pleasant beaches and a few hotels.

Places to Stay & Eat

If you turn right from the pier you'll find two cheap and basic places for US$1 each – the *Residencial San Vicente* and *Lilita*. Behind the market there are some cheap and clean *comedors* such as the *Yessenia*.

Closer to the pier is the more expensive but good *Hotel Vacaciones*, which charges US$8 single and US$14 double. They have a pool and decent restaurant. Three km north of San Vicente on the beach is a resort hotel with family bungalows costing about US$20.

Getting There

Air There is an airstrip for light aircraft behind the market. For more information about arranging flights, contact Aerotransporte Bahía in Bahía de Caráquez.

Boat Ferries take 15 minutes to reach Bahía de Caráquez and leave several times an hour all day long. The fare is 10c. After dark it costs about US$1.25 to hire a boat to take you across (four passengers maximum). There is a car ferry. You can hire boats for trips anywhere you want for US$5 an hour.

Bus San Vicente is the main office of the Costa del Norte company and they have three buses a day to Pedernales – one to Cojimíes and two inland to Chone. The bus office is close to the boat pier.

BAHÍA DE CARÁQUEZ

This is a small (13,000 inhabitants) but nevertheless fairly important port and holiday resort. There are beaches both here and across the river in San Vicente. For some reason it is rarely visited by travellers although the beaches are as good as elsewhere and the hotels adequate. The Río Chone entrance is quite busy and you can laze around at a riverside café and watch the boats go by, or go for a ferry ride.

Information

There is a bank but they don't change foreign currency. There are both IETEL and post offices and two cinemas. To get to the best beaches go north on Avenida Montufar for about 500 metres. The strange-looking corrugated tin church on the main plaza is worth a look if you've nothing better to do.

Places to Stay

There are several cheap places, of which the cheapest and shabbiest is the *Residencial Don Antonio*. *Pensión Victoria* is also cheap and marginally better. *Pensión Miriam* is not up to much, though some rooms are a little better than others, so look around. *Hotel Palma* looks better on the outside than it is inside. Other basic hotels are the residencials *San Fernando* and *San José*. None of these is remarkable in any way; you get a bed to sleep in for US$1-1.50 per person. None of them can be recommended for being very clean or well looked after.

Hotel Americano has rooms with a private bath and air conditioning for US$7 a double, which is OK if there are two of you. A single costs US$6. The most luxurious is *La Herradura*, which has carpeted rooms with private bathroom, air conditioning and TV for US$16 a double.

Places to Eat

There are some reasonable and inexpensive cafés by the river near the dock. Down

Bahía de Caráquez

Portoviejo

by the beach at the end of Avenida Montufar there are some nice pavement restaurants such as *Los Helechos*, which is one of the more expensive but not exorbitantly so. *La Galería* on Bolívar by the main plaza has been recommended but isn't very cheap. There are a couple of cheap *chifas*.

Getting There

Air Aerotransporte Bahía have light aircraft which leave from the airstrip in San Vicente. There are no scheduled flights.

Boat There is a car ferry to San Vicente and a passenger ferry leaves from the dock several times an hour during daylight (10c, 15 minutes). San Vicente has more boats. Although Bahía de Caráquez is a coastal port, passages to other ports are not easily found.

Bus The two bus companies have offices next to one another on the south end of the waterfront. All buses out of Bahía de Caráquez climb a hill and gives good views of the Río Chone estuary; sit on the left when leaving town and look back. Coactur have buses to Portoviejo (75c, two hours) and Manta (95c, 2½ hours) every hour. Reina del Camino has several buses a day to Portoviejo, Quito (US$3, eight hours), Esmeraldas (US$2.90, eight hours), Santo Domingo and Guayaquil (US$2.50, six hours).

PORTOVIEJO

This large city of 102,000 inhabitants, founded on 12 March 1535, is one of the oldest in Ecuador. It is the capital of Manabí province, which is important for coffee and cattle. Portoviejo has a thriving agricultural processing industry and is an important commercial centre with good road connections with Quito and Guayaquil. It is a bustling town but not visited much by tourists, who prefer to head to the coast, especially for the major resort and port of Manta some 37 km away.

Information

The post office is in the government buildings on the main plaza and there is an IETEL office. The Banco Comercial and Banco de Pichincha change money. The

1	Cine Central	17	Rutas Ecuatorianas
2	Hotel Restaurant Paris	18	Cuidad de Calceta buses
3	Post Office	19	Hotel Portoviejo Plaza
4	Casa de Cultura	20	Buses Carlos A Aray
5	IETEL	21	Coactur buses
6	Hotel Cabrera Internacional	22	Pensión Guayaquil
7	Hotel Madrid	23	Pensión Cristal
8	Cine Acapulco	24	Restaurant Oasis
9	Banco Comercial de Manabi	25	TAME
10	Hotel Ejecutivo	26	CTM Aerotaxis
11	Cine Roma	27	Residencial Alfaro
12	Peña Bar Wacho	28	Hotel San Marco
13	Co-op 15 de Octubre & Co-op Jipijapa	29	Residencial Pacheco
14	Banco del Pichincha	30	Local buses
15	Cine	31	Flota Bolívar
16	Reina del Camino buses	32	Hotel Gregorio
		33	Francisco Pacheco statue

streets have both names and numbers but locals tend to use the names more frequently.

Things to See

There is a Museo de Casa de Cultura with an exhibit of traditional musical instruments, but it was closed last time I was there. You can wander down to the pleasant Parque Eloy Alfaro, where you'll find the starkest, barest modern cathedral I've ever seen. It takes the wind out of the sails of those people who complain that the Catholic church in Latin America spends all its money on gold ornaments. Next to the cathedral is a statue of Francisco Pacheco, the founder of Portoviejo.

Places to Stay – bottom end

The basic *Pensión Cristal* charges only US$1 per night but is often full by mid-afternoon so it can't be too bad. Similarly priced is the *Pensión Guayaquil*, but it looks run down and dirty. The *Residencial Alfaro* is basic but fairly clean and charges US$1.50 each. Many of its rooms are without windows. This seems to be a common problem. Many of the rooms at the *Residencial Pacheco* are also without windows but they do at least have fans. They charge US$2 per person or US$3.60 in rooms with a private bath. *Hotel Portoviejo Plaza* is conveniently situated near most of the bus offices. Unfortunately its nicest rooms look out on the street and so are noisy. The rooms are small but clean and cost US$2 per person or US$3 with a private bath. A good, clean, old and rather charming hotel is the simple *Hotel Restaurant Paris*, which has rooms with private baths for US$2.75 per person and is recommended. The good, clean *Hotel Gregorio* charges US$3 per person in rooms with private baths and US$2.50 if you use the communal bath. *Hotel Madrid* has clean and spacious rooms with fans for US$3.50 per person.

Places to Stay – middle & top end

Hotel San Marco has rooms with phone, fan and private bath but it's nothing special. They charge US$6/10 single/double. The best in town is the *Hotel Cabrera Internacional*, which has double rooms from US$9-18 depending on whether you want a room or an air-conditioned suite. *Hotel Ejecutivo* looks about the same.

Places to Eat

My favourite places are the *Peña Bar Wacho* and the *Restaurant Oasis*. The Oasis is a *chifa* on top of a shopping block with outside dining and views of the city. Inside dining is also available and it looks quite elegant but the prices are reasonable and the food good. There is an inexpensive *chifa* below the *Hotel Paris*.

Entertainment

If you're looking for some nightlife, try the *Peña Bar Wacho*, which is run by a friendly couple with the charming names of Washington Castillo P and Fatima Fernandez C. It's a small place which is open daily for typical food and has shows mainly at weekends. They feature anything from poets to folk music and it's inexpensive. Also, there are four cinemas in town.

Getting There

Air The airport is about two km west of town (taxi 60c) and there are flights to Quito at 5 pm on Monday and Friday. TAME has an office in town and will sell you a ticket for US$13.

Bus There is no central bus terminal but most of the more than 12 bus companies have offices within two blocks of the intersection of Avenida Morales and Pedro Gual.

Coactur has several buses an hour to Manta (30c, 50 minutes) which leave as soon as they are full. They also have buses for Bahía de Caráquez (75c, two hours). CTM Aerotaxi has buses for Manta.

Top: Inca Ruins of Ingapirca (RR)
Left: Guayaquil Cathedral and statue of Bolívar (TW)
Right: All Saints Church, Tomebamba River, Cuenca (RR)

Top: Fishermen at work, Atacames (RR)
Left: Balsa fishing boats, Playas (RR)
Right: Fishermen monument, Manta (RR)

Rutas Ecuatorianas has frequent service to Guayaquil (US$1.85, 3½ hours). Carlos A Aray has many buses to Santo Domingo (US$2.50, five hours) with some buses continuing to Quito (US$3.50, eight hours) or going to Guayaquil. Reina del Camino has buses to Quito, Santo Domingo, Esmeraldas (US$3, nine hours), Bahía de Caráquez and Guayaquil. Flota Bolívar has two slow old buses leaving at 8 am and 1 pm for Quevedo. Ciudad de Calceta has buses to Calceta, known for its sisal industry. Other small nearby villages, including the beaches of San Clemente and Crucita, are served by small bus companies whose buses depart near the instersection of Avenida Morales and 9 de Octubre. Co-op 15 de Octubre and Co-op Jipijapa have buses to Jipijapa about every 45 minutes.

MANTA

Manta, with 99,000 inhabitants, is the major port along the central Ecuadorean coast and an important tourist resort and commercial centre.

Manta has a long history. It was founded by Francisco Pacheco on 2 March 1535, 10 days before he founded Portoviejo. But even before its Spanish foundation, Manta was an important port named Jocay by the local Indians. These earlier inhabitants left many artefacts of the Manta culture, which thrived throughout the whole western peninsula from about 500 AD until the arrival of the conquistadors.

The pottery of the Manta culture was well made and decorated with pictures of daily life. Through these, archaeologists have learnt that the Manta people enhanced their appearance by skull deformation and tooth removal, thus increasing the backward slope of their foreheads and chins and emphasizing their large, rounded, hooked noses. This facial structure is apparent in many of the local inhabitants even today.

Also evident in their pottery as well as being recorded in detail by the early conquistadors was the Mantas' astonishing skill in seamanship. They were able to navigate as far as Panama and Peru, and claims have been made that they reached the Galápagos. Capitán Bartolome Ruiz captured a Manta balsa sailing raft in 1526 and records that of the 20 crew members, 11 threw themselves overboard in terror, and the remainder were captured for translating purposes and later freed. Similar but smaller balsa rafts can still be seen sailing the coasts today.

Not only their navigational and ceramic skills were well developed. The Mantas were also skilled stonemasons, weavers and metalworkers. People wishing to learn more about the Manta culture are directed to the museum in the town.

Information

The town is divided into two by an inlet. Manta is on the west side and Tarqui on the east. They are joined by a road bridge. Manta has the main offices and shopping areas, as well as the bus terminal. Tarqui has a bigger hotel selection and beaches.

In Manta there is a DITURIS information office in room 1J on the floor over the shopping arcade at the bottom of Calle 8. There is an impressive new IETEL building on the waterfront. The post office is difficult to find. It's up some stairs in an office building in front of the Banco Pacifico but there are no signs, so ask. The Banco Pacifico changes money, as do the exchange houses nearby. Rates vary from day to day and place to place so shop around. They are usually 2-5% lower than in Quito.

Things to See

The Municipal Museum on the third floor of the city buildings in Manta is worth a visit to understand more of the Manta culture. Although the exhibit is small, it is well laid out and labelled – but only in Spanish. Although it's officially open from 9 am to 3 pm Monday through Friday, they sometimes close for lunch.

Manta's fishing boat harbour is busy

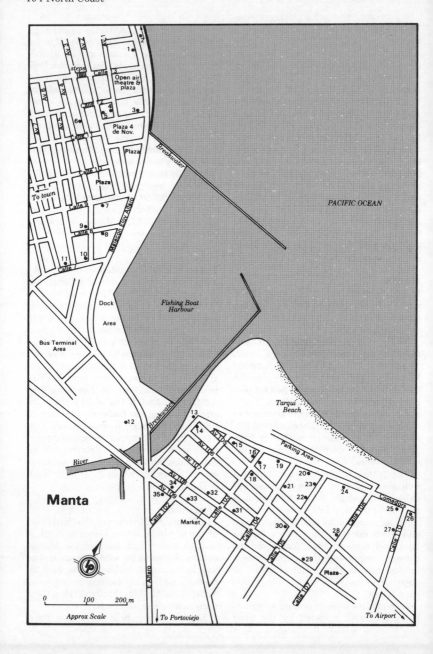

Manta

1 TAME	18 Hotel Panorama Inn
2 To Murcielago beach, Hotel Manta Imperial (1.5 km)	19 Residencial Niza
3 IETEL	20 Lligua Bar & Restaurant
4 Hotel Pacifico, Pensión Manta, Hotel Chimborazo	21 Residencial Viña del Mar
5 Exchange Houses	22 Residencial Montecarlo
6 Banco Pacifico	23 Hotel Inca
7 Municipalidad (Museum 3rd floor)	24 Hotel Las Goviotas
8 Tourist Office I J (1st floor)	25 Hotel Miami
9 Hotel Lun Fun (basic)	26 Residencial Acapulco
10 Hotel Riviera	27 Residencial Playa Brava
11 Residential Brisas del Mar	28 Residencial Astoria
12 Hotel Lun Fun (good)	29 Residencial Ideal
13 Fisherman Statue	30 Hotel Americana
14 Hotel Las Rocas	31 Pensión Tarqui
15 Hote Haddad Manabi	32 Cine Sucre
16 Boulevard Hotel	33 Hotel Rol dan Rol
17 La Cascada Bar, Restaurant & Pool	34 Residencial Chone
	35 Residencial Sante Ana

and picturesque. To get over to Tarqui, don't follow the harbour around or you'll have to swim. Cross on the bridge set back from the harbour. In Tarqui there is a huge statue of a Manabí fisherman and beyond it a protected sandy beach. At the end of the beach there are many more fishing boats. Watching them unload their cargo in the early morning is interesting. There is a bustling market in Tarqui and a cinema nearby.

The Playa Murciélago beach in Manta is less protected and has bigger waves. It is a couple of km west of the town centre along the waterfront and is less visited than the Tarqui beach.

There is an outdoor theatre in Manta which occasionally has performances, especially during the annual agriculture, fishing and tourism exposition which is held from 14-18 October. Portoviejo has a similar event at the same time. You can get more information on what's going on then from the DITURIS office in Manta.

Places to Stay – bottom end

The place to go for cheap accommodation in Manta is Avenida 1 near the Plaza 4 de Noviembre. Here there are three hotels near one another, all of which charge US$1-2 per person. They are the hotels *Pacifico* and *Chimborazo*, and *Pensión Manta*. The Hotel Pacifico looks the best

of these and has some rooms with good views. They will give cheaper rates if there is a group of you willing to share a room. Also cheap but really basic are the *Residencial Brisas del Mar* and the old *Hotel Lun Fun*.

In Tarqui, a clean and rambling old budget hotel is the *Residencial Niza*, which is near the beach and has some rooms with ocean views. They charge US$1.50 and have some rooms with up to eight beds which are cheaper per person. Similarly priced but more basic is the *Residencial Acapulco* at the other end of the beach. One of the cheapest of all is the basic *Residencial Chone*, which is reasonably clean and costs US$1 a head.

The *Residencial Playa Brava* charges US$2 for basic boxes but they do have private bathrooms. Slightly more expensive but good value is the *Residencial Viña del Mar*, which has simple but clean rooms with air conditioning and private bathroom for US$5 a double. Similarly priced is the student– and youth-group-oriented *Boulevard Hotel*, which might be a good place to meet young Ecuadorean travellers. Other cheap hotels are the residencials *Montecarlo, Astoria, Ideal* and *Santa Ana*, and the *Pensión Tarqui*.

Places to Stay – middle

Hotel Miami in Tarqui has simple but

clean rooms with private bathrooms for US$3 each. Some rooms have good ocean views. *Hotel Roldan Rol* charges US$3.50 in rooms with private bath but is near the market and likely to be noisy. *Hotel Americana* is new and clean with double rooms and private baths costing about US$7.50 with a fan. Air conditioning costs an extra US$1. Some of the upper rooms have good views. *Hotel Inca* has some pleasant rooms with air conditioning, ocean views and private bathrooms for about US$10 a double. Some rooms are not as good as others but there is a restaurant.

Hotel Panorama Inn has rooms from US$10-14 double depending on the amenities you choose. Rooms are rather worn but spacious, some with good views, and there is a restaurant. They give you pool privileges for *La Cascada* across the street. *Hotel Las Rocas* looks new and charges about the same.

In Manta there is the *Hotel Riviera*, which has rooms with private bathrooms for US$8.50 a double with fan. Air conditioning is US$1 extra.

Places to Stay – top end

The new *Hotel Lun Fun* is good and luxurious and not to be confused with the ratty old hotel of the same name. They charge about US$10 each and are conveniently located by the bus terminal. Similarly priced is the *Hotel Manta Imperial*, which is the only hotel near Manta's Murciélago beach and has a pool and all the modern amenities.

In Tarqui there are two luxurious (by Ecuadorean standards) hotels. The modern *Hotel Las Gaviotas* charges about US$23 a double. *Hotel Haddad Manabí* dates from 1931 and is Manta's oldest luxury hotel.

Places to Eat

There are plenty of cheap outdoor *comedors* on the east end of Tarqui beach which serve fresh seafood. The market is also a centre for cheap food. There are several restaurants and bars along the Tarqui waterfront, of which the *Lligua* has large servings of good and inexpensive food. For a night out you can have a rather more expensive but good meal in the more elegant *La Cascada*. The better hotels also have good restaurants.

Getting There

Air Manta is one of the few cities in Ecuador with services to both Quito and Guayaquil. The TAME office on the Manta waterfront will sell you tickets; they are open from 9 am to noon and 3 to 5 pm daily except Sunday. Flights to Quito cost US$13 and to Guayaquil US$9. The plane for Guayaquil leaves daily except Sunday at 7.45 am, and the plane for Quito leaves daily except Sunday at 9.20 am. On Sundays there is a 5 pm flight to Quito. This service is, as always, subject to change. You can buy tickets at the airport on the morning of the flight but the planes tend to be full at weekends and holidays.

The airport is about three km east of Tarqui and a taxi costs about US$1 if you bargain hard.

Bus There is a large central bus terminal in front of the fishing boat harbour in Manta and almost all buses leave from here, which makes things easy. There are several companies with buses to most major Ecuadorean cities. Journey times and prices are similar to Portoviejo's. Some of the smaller companies running buses to nearby Manabí towns and villages don't have an office in the terminal but their buses leave from there anyway and you pay aboard the bus. An example of this is Coactur to Portoviejo.

MONTECRISTI

This small village of some 8000 inhabitants is of interest to the traveller. It can be reached in 15 minutes by frequent buses from Manta's bus terminal. Buses cost 10c and stop running about 6 pm.

Montecristi is an important centre for

both the panama hat industry and wicker-work. There are many stores along the main road and along the road leading into the town centre. If you go in towards the centre and ask around, you can see various stages in the manufacture of panama hats.

The town is an old colonial one founded around 1628, when many of the inhabitants of Manta fled inland to avoid the frequent pirate plundering to which the port was subject. There are many old colonial houses left but they haven't been restored and give the village a rather tumble-down and ghostly atmosphere.

The main plaza has a beautiful church dating back to the early part of the last century. It contains a famous statue of the virgin to which miracles have been attributed and is worth a visit. In the plaza is a statue of Eloy Alfaro, who was born in Montecristi and was president of Ecuador at the beginning of the century. His tomb is in the town hall by the plaza.

There are no hotels and only a couple of basic *comedors* so it's best to stay in Manta and visit Montecristi on a day trip.

JIPIJAPA

The 'j' is pronounced as 'h' in Spanish, so this town's name is pronounced 'Hipihapa.' With a population of 27,000, it is an important centre for the panama hat industry as well as for coffee and cotton. The town market is a good place to buy panama hats.

You can get to Jipijapa by bus from Portoviejo and Manta. The 1982/83 floods cut off Jipijapa from the west coast and the road is still in bad condition but is being repaired. There are two or three buses a day with Transportes Sur de Manabí, which go to Puerto López. From there you can continue with CITM buses along the south coast to the Santa Elena peninsula.

There are a couple of basic pensiones.

South Coast

The south coast, consisting of the provinces of Guayas and El Oro, is generally much drier and more barren than the north. The weather pattern changes and the rainy season, which in the north lasts from December to May, lasts only from January to April in Guayaquil. Further west and south it becomes drier still, and by the time the Peruvian border is reached the South American coastal desert begins.

The agriculturally important lands of Los Rios province continue into Guayas and El Oro. Bananas are the most important crop and irrigation in the dry south means that plantations can continue beyond Machala. Rice, coffee, cacao and African palm are other important crops of the region. West of Guayaquil is the dry, infertile and scrubby Santa Elena peninsula with not enough rivers for irrigation. Archaeological investigation shows that the land used to be as wet and fertile as it is now in the northern coastal areas, but drought and deforestation over the last 5000 years have wrought severe changes. Pottery decorations and other remains indicate that early farmers living in the area from 3000 to 1500 BC cultivated maize (corn), manioc, beans, squash, chiles, avocados, papayas, pineapples, palms and the bottle gourd. Bananas, Ecuador's most important crop, were introduced after the Spanish conquest.

The heart of the south coast is Guayaquil, Ecuador's most important port and largest city. To the west are the popular beach resorts of Playas and Salinas and to the south another important port city, Machala, which is the normal gateway to Peru.

GUAYAQUIL

Travellers in Ecuador tend to avoid Guayaquil. It has a reputation as a hot and humid port with too many inhabitants and little of interest. It certainly does have many inhabitants, about 1,200,000 of them, and it is oppressively hot, wet and humid from January to April. I spent over two years travelling in Ecuador before I finally visited Guayaquil and I must admit to being pleasantly surprised. It does have its attractions. There is a pleasant walk along the riverfront, shady plazas, colonial buildings, friendly people and interesting museums. It's worth spending a few days.

The province of Guayas is named after the Puna Indian chief of the same name who fought bravely against first the Incas and then the Spanish. The capital of the province, Guayaquil, is named after the same chief and his wife Quill, whom he is said to have killed before drowning himself, rather than allow them to be captured by the conquistadors.

Information

The DITURIS information office is on the waterfront at the Malecón 2321 and Olmedo, up the stairs. They are officially open from 8 am to noon and 3 to 7 pm Monday through Friday, speak some English, and are helpful. The IETEL and post offices are in the same huge building comprising the block bounded by Avenidas Ballen and P Carbo.

If you want to buy English-language and other books, the best store is the Librería Científica at Luque 223. There is a public library at the Museo Municipal. Use the back entrance on Avenida 10 de Agosto for the library and the front entrance on Avenida Sucre for the museum.

If you need to get your tourist card extended, you can do so at the immigration office in the government building (Palacio de Gobierno) on the waterfront.

Consulates & Embassies The Peruvian consulate is on the sixth floor of the building at Avenida 9 de Octubre and

Chile. It is open from 8.30 am to 1 pm and 2 to 5 pm Monday through Friday. Also marked on the map are the Colombian, Argentine and US consulates.

Money Guayaquil has the best foreign exchange rate in Ecuador, usually almost 1% better than in Quito. The best places to exchange money are the *casas de cambio*, of which there are over a dozen on the first couple of blocks of Avenida 9 de Octubre by the waterfront and along the first few blocks of Avenida Pichincha. Shop around for the best rate. All *casas de cambio* are closed on Sunday and only a few are open on Saturday morning. There is a *casa de cambio* at the airport which is open at weekends to meet incoming international flights, usually in the morning.

Museums
Most of the museums concentrate on Ecuadorean archaeology and are very good.

Museo de Archaeología del Banco Pacifico
This is my favourite museum, it's small but extremely well laid out. It was almost deserted when I visited it on a Saturday afternoon, and it was a delight to wander around the exhibits and read the informative interpretations, which are in English as well as Spanish. There is also a changing art show. It is air conditioned too, so you can escape from the heat (for free) from 10 am to 5.30 pm, Tuesday through Saturday. You'll find it on the third floor of the Banco Pacifico; take the elevator.

Museo de Archaeologiáa del Banco Central
This bank also has a good archaeology museum which is open from 10 am to 6 pm Monday through Friday, and 10 am to 1 pm on weekends. It is free, well laid out, and has a varied and changing display of ceramics, textiles, metallurgy (some gold) and ceremonial masks. The descriptions are good but are only in Spanish.

Casa de Cultura The archaeology museum in the Casa de Cultura is open from 9 am to 12.30 pm and 3 to 7 pm Tuesday through Saturday. It charges 20c admission and is interesting, though not as good as the two bank museums.

Museo Municipal This museum is small but has more varied exhibits. On the ground floor there is an archaeology room, a colonial room and a changing display of modern art. The archaeology room has mainly Inca and pre-Inca ceramics with some particularly fine pieces from the Huancavilca period (circa 500 AD) and several figurines from the oldest culture in Ecuador, the Valdivia (circa 3200 BC). The colonial room has mainly religious paintings and a few household items from colonial times.

Upstairs there are modern art and ethnography rooms, inexplicably joined. Here you'll see five of the famous *tsantsas*, or shrunken heads. Other jungle artefacts include beadwork, featherwork, tools and weapons, but unfortunately very few labels. There are also regional costumes and handicrafts. Another room on this floor contains paintings of presidents and famous men, of which my favourite is a wild and eccentric-looking Theodor Wolf, the geologist after whom the highest active volcano in the Galápagos is named. All in all, a varied collection with which to pass the time. The Museo Municipal is open 9 am to noon and 3 to 7 pm Monday through Friday, 10 am to 3 pm on Saturday, and 10 am to 1 pm on Sunday. Admission is 30c.

Along the Waterfront
The majority of interesting sights are on or within a few blocks of the waterfront. It is a good idea to begin your sightseeing walk near the DITURIS office at Olmedo and the waterfront. Opposite, there is an imposing statue of José Joaquín Olmedo Maruri, an Ecuadorean poet and politician born in Guayaquil on 19 March 1789. He sits, bardlike, in a colonial armchair.

Guayaquil

Cemetery

Quisquis
1 de Mayo
9 de Octubre
Hurtado

Urdaneta

Parque

Parque del
Centenario

Olympic
Pool

Velez

Luque
Aguirre

Ballen

10 de Agosto

Sucre

Colón

Alcedo

Parque
Victoria

Market

Masote
Ejercito
G. Moreno
Antipara
Machala
Quito
P. Moncayo
P. Montufar
6 de Marzo
Caracoa

0   200 m

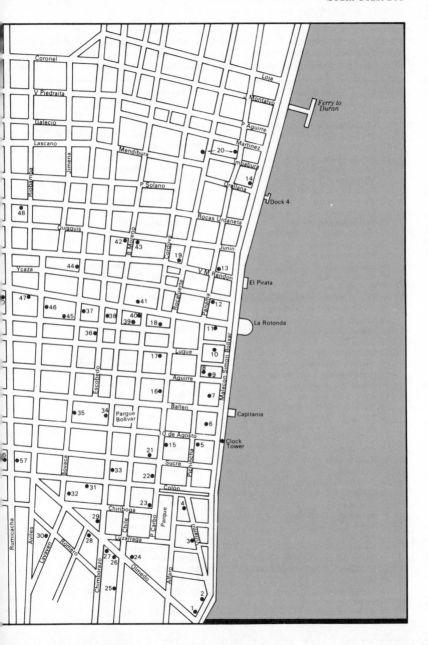

Heading north along the waterfront road called the Malecón Simon Bolívar, you pass several monuments. One is to the UN, known in Spanish as the ONU (Organización de Naciones Unidas) and another is the famous Moorish-style clock tower which dates originally from 1770 but has been replaced several times.

1 Dituris Tourist Office	46 Residencial Imperio
2 Hotel Humboldt	47 Cine 9 de Octubre
3 Hotel Orquidea Internacional	48 Hotel Imperial
4 Hotels Santa Maria, Nacional	49 Hotel Regina
& Luz de America	50 Hotel Londres
5 Hotel Italia	51 Hotel Centenario
6 Palacio Municipal	52 Buses San Luis & Transportes Oriental
7 Palacio de Gobierno	53 Transportes Esmeraldas Buses
8 Metropolitan Touring	54 Residencial Centro
9 Colombian & Argentine Conuls	55 Hotel El Inca
10 Bank of America	56 Hotel Ecuatoriano
11 Ecuatoriana	57 Residencial Medellin
12 Banco Pacifico Museo	58 Hotel Marco Polo
de Archaeologia & Hotel Moneda	59 Hotel La Buena Esperanza
13 Hotel Metropolitan	60 Cine Imperio
14 Hotel Ramada	61 Flota Imbabura Buses
15 Restaurant Napoli	62 Transportes Occidental & Cine Presidente
16 Post Office & IETEL	63 Supertaxis Cuenca, Transportes
17 Libreria Cientifica	Ecuador & Hotel Ecuador
18 Church & Plaza of San Francisco	64 Hotel Delicia
19 Church & Plaza of La Merced	65 Hotel Colón
20 Milagro Bus Companies	66 Co-op Libertad Buses
21 Museo Municipal & Library	67 Co-op Posorja Buses
22 Gran Chifa	68 Transportes Villamil Buses
23 Cifa Buses	69 Cica Buses
24 Hotel Los Angeles	70 Transportes Patria & CITA Buses
25 Hotel Residencial Espejo	71 Transportes Zaracay
26 Transportes Sucre	72 Hotel Astoria & Transportes
27 Residencial El Cisne	Gran Colombia Buses
28 Transportes Rutas Orenses	73 Transportes Andino Buses
29 Residencial Maria	74 FBI Buses
30 Ecuatoriana Pullman Buses	75 Cine Quito
31 Co-op El Oro Buses	76 Hotel Sanders
32 Flota Bolívar	77 Hotel Alexander
33 Hotel Boston	78 Cine Tauro
34 Cathedral	79 Transportes Urdaneta Buses
35 Gran Hotel Guayaquil	80 Transportes Panamerica &
36 La Palma & Cyrano Pavement Cafés	Transportes Cotopaxi
37 Cine Metro	81 Casa de Cultura (Cine &
38 Residencial Comercio	Archaeology Museum)
39 San & Saeta Airlines	82 Cine Centenario
40 Peruvian Consul	83 Transportes Santa Buses
41 Hotel Casino Boulevard,	84 Transportes Loja Buses
Teatro Guayaquil, TAME Airline	85 Reina del Camino Buses
& Galasam Tours (Edificio Pasaje)	86 Rutas Ecuatorianas Buses
42 Hotel Pauker	87 Machiavello Tours
43 Hotel Tourist	88 US Embassy & Banco Central
44 Lansa Air	Archaeology Museum
45 Hotel San Juan	89 Hotel Oro Verde

Across the street from the clock tower is the **Palacio Municipal**, an ornate grey building which is separated from the simple and solid **Palacio de Gobierno** by a small but pleasant plaza containing a statue commemorating some of the victories of the liberator, General Sucre. Both buildings were built in the 1920s, but the Palacio de Gobierno replaces the original wooden structure which was destroyed in the great fire of 1917.

Continuing along the Malecón, you soon come to the famous statue of **La Rotonda**, one of Guayaquil's more impressive monuments, particularly when it is illuminated at night. It shows the historic but enigmatic meeting between Bolívar and San Martín in 1822. Bolívar was the Venezuelan who liberated Venezuela, Colombia and Ecuador from Spanish colonial rule. San Martín was the Argentine liberator who defeated the Spanish in Chile and Peru. After their secret meeting in Guayaquil, San Martín returned to Argentina and exile to France, while Bolívar continued his triumphs in Bolivia. From La Rotonda there are good views north, along the riverfront, of the colonial district of Las Peñas at the foot of Cerro El Carmen and, far beyond, the impressive Guayaquil-Duran bridge, the biggest in the country. Two blocks away is the museum of the Banco Pacifico.

Many people like to continue along the waterfront to the picturesque colonial district of Las Peñas. Several docks are passed en route, some with restaurant boats and others which are working docks. Soon after passing the **Duran Ferry** pier you reach the end of the Malecón. This north end has a reputation for being a poor neighbourhood and tourists are advised to guard their belongings against pickpockets, especially those working the passenger exits from the Duran ferry. The ferry used to be used more by tourists because the railway station for trains to the highlands is in Duran. Now, with the disruption of the train service, almost no baggage-laden travellers come across on the ferry and the

number of thieves has dwindled. I felt that the area was quite safe.

Las Peñas

Calle Numa Pompillo Llona This street, named after the Guayaquileño (1832-1907) who wrote the national anthem, is one of my favourite sights in Las Peñas. You'll find the street at the end of the Malecón, where you'll see a short flight of stairs leading up to the small **Plaza Colón**, which has two cannon pointing out towards the river, commemorating a battle against Dutch pirates in 1624. From the corner of the plaza begins the narrow, winding Calle N P Llona. Walking up this historic street, you'll see several unobtrusive plaques set into the walls of some houses. These indicate the simple residences of past presidents. The colonial architecture has not been very much restored. Rather, it has been well looked after and is interesting to see. Several artists now live in the area and there are a few art galleries, of which the one at No 186 is currently the best known and belongs to the painter Hugo Luis Lara. Take your time – it's a short street. At the end of the street is a **brewery** which is open from 7 am to noon and 2 to 5 pm Monday through Friday. Brewery tours can be arranged.

Calle N P Llona is a dead-end street, so you retrace your footsteps to the Plaza Colón and, instead of continuing back along the Malecón, you turn right and walk past a small plaza with a brightly painted statue of a fireman (there are two fire stations near by), and past a statue of the conquistador Orellana, to the open-air theatre Bogotá. Behind the theatre is the oldest church in Guayaquil, **Santo Domingo**, which was founded in 1548, restored in 1938 and is worth a visit.

Cerro El Carmen You can continue by climbing the stairs to the right of the church and then heading left up the steep Calle Buitrón (the street of the vulture!) which will soon take you to the top of the hill, **Cerro El Carmen**. From here is a good view of the north section of the river and the impressive **Duran bridge** which is almost four km long.

Downtown Area

La Merced Return down the hill to the Malecón and walk back to the downtown area along Calle Rocafuerte. The colonial buildings blend into modern ones and after a few blocks you pass the church of La Merced. Although this building is comparatively modern (constructed in 1938), the original wooden church dated back to 1787. It's worth seeing for its richly decorated golden altar. There's a pleasant plaza in front of the church.

San Francisco Two blocks beyond the church you cross the busy Avenida 9 de Octubre, downtown Guayaquil's major thoroughfare. Here Calle Rocafuerte becomes Calle P Carbo and you find the church of San Francisco, originally built in the early 1700s, burnt in 1896, reconstructed in 1902, and now beautifully restored. The plaza in front is notable for containing Guayaquil's first public monument, unveiled on New Year's Day, 1880. It is a statue of the first Ecuadorean president, Vicente Rocafuerte, who held office from 1835-39. Ecuador's first president, Juan Flores, was a Venezuelan.

Parque Bolívar A few blocks further along P Carbo you find the Museo Municipal. A block to the right is **Parque Bolívar**, Guayaquil's most famous plaza. In its small but well laid out gardens live prehistoric-looking land iguanas of up to a metre in length, and of a species different from those found in the Galápagos. They're a surprising sight here, right in the centre of the city. Around Parque Bolívar are most of Guayaquil's first-class hotels.

Cathedral On one side of the park is the Cathedral. The original building on this site dates from 1547 but, as is common with most of Guayaquil's original wooden buildings, it burnt. The present structure was completed in 1948 and renovated in 1978. The front entrance is extremely ornately decorated but inside it is cool, simple, high vaulted and modern. High up on the white walls are some fine stained-glass windows.

Parque del Centenario From the Parque Bolívar you can head north a few blocks and walk along the modern Avenida 9 de Octubre to the huge Parque del Centenario, the city's largest plaza. A more colourful walk is along 10 de Agosto to the main market area, which is so crowded with street stalls, people and traffic that your pace slows to a crawl. Watch your belongings; pickpockets are common in market areas. In the Parque del Centenario, which covers four city blocks, there are many monuments. The most important is the great central column topped by Liberty and surrounded by the founding fathers of the country – a monument to patriotism.

Avenida 9 de Octubre continues beyond the park. At its junction with the west side of the park is the museum of the Casa de Cultura. Further along the Avenida you come to the Banco Central museum. If you continue north of the park along P Moncayo, you'll come to the **city cemetery**, which is well worth a visit. It is a dazzling white and contains hundreds of tombs, monuments and huge mausoleums.

The whole walk as described in this section can be done in two or three hours, but if you want to inspect the sights thoroughly, you could spend all day. Keep your eyes open for plaques and signs. Guayaquil is full of them and they give interesting historic information (if you understand Spanish).

Places to Stay

The Guayaquil Tourist Board controls hotel prices and each hotel is required to post their approved prices near the entrance. Perhaps surprisingly, most hotels do have the price list prominently displayed. You may be charged up to 15% tax on the listed price, though some of the cheaper hotels don't bother. During holiday periods it can be problematical finding a room, especially in the better hotels, and prices are usually higher than the listed price. Many hotels, including some of the budget ones, are registered at the DITURIS office where you can complain if you get gouged.

For some reason there are not many single rooms to be had. In the cheaper hotels I usually had two or more beds in my room when I was travelling alone. If it's not the holiday season, you can persuade many hotel owners to give you a double or triple at the price of a single. During *fiesta* time, travel with a friend or be prepared to pay for a double.

Places to Stay – bottom end

One of the best cheap hotels is the *Hotel Delicia* – secure, clean and recently painted. They charge about US$1.60 per person and have rooms with a private bath for US$2.20. Most hotels which charge less than US$2 per person are not as good. Among the cheapest are the *Hotel Residencial Espejo* and the *Residencial Maria* (US$1.20 each), and the *Residencial El Cisne* (US$1.50 each). They are very basic but marginally better than the similarly priced *Hotel Ecuatoriana*, *Residencial Medellin*, *Hotel La Buena Esperanza* and *Residencial Imperio*, which are unsavoury, dirty and generally disreputable. Some of the cheap hotels near the market double as low-class brothels, and female travellers may be improperly treated or molested.

If you can bring yourself to pay between US$2-3, you can do much better. Three basic but reasonably clean hotels are found on one block of Villamil near the waterfront. They are the *Hotel Santa Maria*, *Nacional* and *Luz de America*. Most rooms have fans and you should ask for one if they don't. Some rooms have private baths and some don't have

windows, but there's enough variety here that you should be able to find something suitable for US$2-2.50. A few blocks away is the *Hotel Boston*, which charges US$2.50 or US$3 depending on whether you have a private bathroom. The rooms are tiny, unattractive wooden boxes.

Rather isolated, but excellent value and recommended, is the *Hotel Imperial*, which has private bathrooms in all its rooms and is very clean and good. Some rooms are a little worse than others because they lack windows. Prices are US$2-2.50 per person. Six blocks away is the similarly priced *Hotel Pauker*, which is secure and friendly. The best rooms are doubles (US$4.50); the few singles are not very good. Across the street is the *Hotel Tourist*, which is not much better. It charges US$7 a double and doubles as a brothel.

Hotel El Inca has many rooms, most with bathrooms attached, and is fairly clean and secure but basic. Costs are US$3, US$5.50, US$7.50 and US$9.50 for singles, doubles, triples and quads. For US$5 a double with private bath you can stay at the *Hotel Ecuador*, which is conveniently situated for buses but is noisy. *Hotel Astoria* has very shabby rooms and their water supply is erratic. They charge US$2.20 per person or US$3 in a room with private bath. The *Hotel Marco Polo* is US$3 with bath per person, but I've heard that it's not recommended for single women. Other basic hotels in this price range are the *Residencial Centro* and *Comercio*.

Places to Stay – middle

Hotel Centenario charges US$2-5 per person and has some rooms with air conditioning, phone and private bath but nevertheless remains a basic hotel. A bit shabby but secure is the *Hotel Londres*, which charges US$3-7 per person. The rooms vary a good deal, so see several. Some have private baths, TV and windows, and all have fans. *Hotel Los Angeles* is adequate and has rooms with private bathrooms and sometimes air conditioning. They charge US$4.50 single and US$6.50 double. *Hotel Colón* has had a recent paint job and looks clean, with rooms at US$3.50 single with bath. Similarly priced is the *Hotel Sanders*, which is a bit run down but still good value. Some rooms have air conditioning. *Hotel San Juan* has rooms with air conditioning and phone at US$8 double but is very run down and many of its rooms are windowless.

A simple but clean hotel with air-conditioned rooms and private baths is the *Hotel Regina* for US$6.50 single and US$10.50 double. Very good value is the *Hotel Metropolitan*, which costs US$8.50 single and US$10.50 double. Some rooms have river views, the private bathrooms are spotless, and the management is anxious to please. Don't be put off by the fact that it's on the top floor of an office block. *Hotel Italia* is a little more expensive than this but is not as clean or comfortable. *Hotel Orquidea Internacional* is adequate for US$10 double with private bath; singles cost the same.

Places to Stay – top end

Hotel Humboldt is good value for US$12 single and US$16 double. They have a swimming pool and restaurant/bar. Also near the waterfront are the more expensive *Hotel Ramada* and the luxurious *Hotel Moneda*. The comfortable *Hotel Alexander* charges US$14 for a single. Other recommended luxurious hotels are the *Gran Hotel Guayaquil*, *Hotel Casino Boulevard* and the *Hotel Oro Verde*. The last-mentioned is the best in town and charges about US$60 for a double. The area around the *Parque Bolívar* has half a dozen comfortable first-class hotels within one block. You can take your choice and expect to pay US$25-50 a double.

Places to Eat

For breakfast I like *La Palma* and *Cyrano* pavement cafés, which are next to one another on Escobedo. They sell good coffee and croissants, and are good places at which to wake up and ease into the day. *La Palma* seems to be the most popular.

One of my favourite places for lunch is on a boat moored on the riverbank. There are several piers along the Malecón where restaurant boats are moored. A good but not too expensive one is *El Pirata*, a couple of blocks from the La Rotonda statue. They have an indoor section and an open top deck with sunshades for when the weather is good. You can eat seafood and sip a beer while you watch the busy traffic of the Malecón on one side and Guayaquil's river traffic on the other. Fragile craft paddled by banana peddlers bob close inshore and huge ocean-going vessels lumber by in mid-channel. Pleasure craft and fishing trawlers abound, and a constant stream of frigate birds, terns and seagulls fly by.

A place which I enjoy for a beer and a snack is the *Restaurant Napoli* on P Carbo, which is 'divey' but has some character. Less character is found in the modern cafeterias on Avenida 9 de Octubre, which sell such delights as hamburgers and French fries and are not very cheap. There's even an authentic *Burger King*.

A *chifa* is always a good choice for the hungry budget traveller and there are several on and around Avenida Colón. One of the very best, elegant and expensive-looking – but in fact very reasonably priced – is the *Gran Chifa* on P Carbo near Colón. A few blocks away, opposite the *Co-op El Oro* bus terminal, is the plainer and slightly cheaper *Chifa Mayflower*. There are others to choose from.

The most economical meals are to be found in and around the market area. The best and most expensive restaurants are in the first-class hotels (normally open to the public) and in the suburb of Urdesa, a few km to the north-west of downtown and best reached by taxi.

Entertainment

Read the local newspapers *El Telégrafo* and *El Universo* to find out more about what's going on. They give cinema listings of the approximately 18 cinemas in Guayaquil, of which about half are downtown and shown on the map. If you're buying the newspaper for the cinema listings, make sure that the newspaper has them. Occasionally, even the best papers omit the listing if there's been no change. English-language movies with Spanish sub-titles are often shown.

Friday newspapers advertise folk music evenings known as *peñas*, which are normally held at weekends. They are rarely cheap and always start late. A good one is *La Peña Rincón Folklorico* at Malecón 208 and Montalvo. It normally opens at 10 pm for food and drinks, and the show gets under way about midnight and continues until the early hours. Cover is US$3 and drinks aren't cheap.

If you're the athletic type, you can visit the *Olympic Pool*, which costs 30c for a two-hour period. Enquire at the entrance for times.

Guayaquil's Independence Day is 9 October (1820) and, combined with America (or Columbus) Day on 12 October (1492), it is an important local holiday period. More important still is Bolívar's birthday on 24 July (1783), followed by Guayaquil Foundation Day on 25 July (1538). The whole city parties during the last week in July, and hotel rooms may be difficult to find. Banks and other services are also disrupted.

Getting There

Air Guayaquil's Simón Bolívar airport is one of Ecuador's two international airports. If you are leaving on an international flight, there is a US$5 departure tax, payable in sucres or dollars. There is a *casa de cambio* at the airport.

There are many internal flights to all parts of the country. The most frequent are to Quito with both TAME and SAN-Saeta. If you buy your ticket with cash, the two companies will honour one another's tickets so you can arrive at the airport and leave on the next available flight if it isn't

full. There are about 10 flights a day Monday through Friday, six flights on Saturday, and four flights on Sunday. Tickets cost about US$16. Sit on the right side flying to Quito for the best views.

TAME also has flights from Guayaquil to Loja (Monday through Saturday at 5.45 am, US$9.50), Machala (Monday and Friday at 10.30 am and Tuesday, Wednesday, Thursday and Saturday at 12.30 pm, US$7.50), Macará (Monday and Friday at noon, US$9.50), Cuenca (Monday through Saturday at 10 am, Monday and Friday at 3 pm, US$9.50), and Manta (Monday through Saturday at 8.45 am, US$8.50). Fares and departure times are subject to change.

TAME operates the only scheduled flights to the Galápagos, which leave daily except Sunday at 11 am and cost US$312 for the round trip. Cheaper fares are available only to Ecuadorean residents.

Lansa used to operate light aircraft to Machala but when I enquired about this in their office in downtown Guayaquil, they told me that all their aeroplanes were out of service! They still have an office so maybe they'll buy some new planes or fix the old ones.

The airline offices are around Avenida 9 de Octubre and Chile; see the map.

Rail Train services from Guayaquil to the highlands were disrupted by the 1982/83 El Niño disaster. No trains have run since then and it is unlikely that services will resume for several years. When they do, the trains will leave from the Duran railway station, which is best reached by taking the Duran ferry from Guayaquil.

Boat The Duran ferry across the Río Guayas leaves three or four times an hour from 5 am to 9 pm daily. The crossing lasts 15 minutes and costs 3c – a great sightseeing trip! The ferry dock is on the Malecón at the foot of Avenida J Montalvo.

The *Pinzón* and *Piquero* for the Galápagos leave from Dock 4. Shipping information can be got from the Capitanía on the Malecón at the foot of Avenida Ballen.

Bus A brand-new bus terminal has almost been finished. It is located just beyond the airport and its main problem seems to be access. A newspaper article in *El Comercio* of 24 November 1984 describes how the bus terminal does not, as yet, have access roads and how the Ecuadorean Civil Airlines Authority fears that the building of access roads to the terminal will disrupt services to the airport. How the problem will be resolved remains to be seen, but at this time there are literally scores of bus companies with offices dotted all over Guayaquil. If and when the terminal is completed, bus companies will begin to move their offices to the terminal and the confusion will be greater than it is now!

The map in this book shows the present location of the most important bus offices. The following list indicates the major destinations they all serve. I begin with westbound buses and continue with buses to the south, east, north and finally back to the west again.

For the Santa Elena peninsula you can take Transportes Villamil or Co-op Posorja, which have frequent buses to Playas (65c, 1¾ hours) and Posorja (80c, two hours). Co-op Libertad and CICA have buses to Salinas (US$1, 2½ hours).

If you're headed southbound or to Peru, take CIFA, Transportes Rutas Orenses, Ecuatoriana Pullman or Co-op El Oro to Machala (US$1.50, 3½ hours) and Huaquillas (US$2, five hours). CIFA and Rutas Orenses run frequent small buses; the others run larger coaches. Transportes Loja has one bus at 6.30 pm to the border at Macará (US$4, 12 hours), and five buses to Loja (US$3.20, 10 hours).

Several companies run buses to Cuenca (US$2.20-2.60, five to seven hours). Supertaxis Cuenca and Buses San Luis run faster small buses while Transportes Oriental run larger, slower, cheaper buses. All three have buses about hourly.

Babahoyo (40c, 1½ hours) is served by Transportes Urdaneta and Flota Babahoyo Interprovincial (or FBI). Flota Bolívar has eight slow buses every day to Guaranda via Babahoyo.

For Riobamba and Ambato there are many companies taking as little as 3½ hours to Riobamba if the road is OK. All these companies are located near each other: Transportes Andino, Transportes Patria, CITA, Transportes Gran Colombia and Transportes Santa. One of the fastest is probably Transportes Andino. Transportes Cotopaxi has slow buses to Latacunga via Quevedo.

Quevedo and Santo Domingo are served by Transportes Sucre and Transportes Zaracay.

Quito (US$2.50-2.80, seven to nine hours) is served by frequent buses with Flota Imbabura, Transportes Ecuador and Transportes Panamericana. All three are close to one another so check around for what's best for you.

Transportes Esmeraldas and Transportes Occidental have about 10 buses a day to Esmeraldas (US$2.80, nine hours).

Rutas Ecuatorianas has many departures for Portoviejo (US$2, four hours), as does Reina del Camino, who also have buses to Manta and Bahía de Caráquez.

Getting Around

Airport The airport is on Avenida de las Américas, about four or five km north of downtown. A taxi from the airport to downtown will cost US$2-3. Bargain. If you cross the street in front of the airport, you can take a bus downtown. From downtown, the best bus to take to the airport is the '2 Especial,' which costs 5c and takes about a half hour. It runs along the Malecón but is sometimes full, so you should leave yourself plenty of time or take a taxi – often only US$1 from downtown.

Bus City buses are cheap (5c) but are always crowded and the system is complicated. They are mainly designed to get workers and commuters from the housing districts to downtown and back again, and are not much use for riding around downtown. They never seem to go exactly where you want to go, and what with waiting for them and battling the traffic, you'd be better off walking, which is what I always did. The downtown area is less than two km square so it's easy to walk anywhere.

The DITURIS information office can help you with bus information if you want to go out into the suburbs, though there isn't much to see there.

Taxi If you really must get somewhere in a hurry, you won't get there much quicker on a city bus. Take a taxi but make sure you ask the fare first because Guayaquil taxi drivers have the worst reputation in the country for overcharging. They're fine once the fare has been settled, though. You should be able to get between any two points downtown for well under US$1.

Car Rental If you're feeling affluent, you can rent a car; if you're not, then forget it because it's not cheap. There are several car rental agencies at the airport. Expect to pay at least US$30 per day for a small car. Make sure that insurance, tax and mileage are included. If you find a cheaper deal, ensure that the car you get isn't about to break down.

PROGRESO

Progreso is officially known as Gómez Rendón and is a village about 70 km south-east of Guayaquil. Here the road forks and you head west to Salinas and the Santa Elena peninsula or south to the resort of Playas. The road fork is Progeso's claim to fame; there's no reason to stop here.

From Guayaquil to Progreso the paved road passes through very dry scrubland. It is amazing how quickly the land changes from the wet rice-growing areas in the north and east of Guayaquil to the dry lands of the west. Despite the dryness, the scenery is quite attractive and interesting, with strange bottle-shaped kapok trees and bright flowers dotting the hilly landscape.

PLAYAS

From Progreso the road deteriorates into gravel (though it is in the process of being paved) and heads due south for 30 km to Playas, the beach resort nearest Guayaquil. It is also an important fishing village. A generation ago, many of the fishing craft were small balsa rafts with one sail – similar in design to the boats used up and down the coast for many centuries before the Spanish conquest. Now, motor-driven dugouts and other more modern craft are frequently used, but you can still see a few of the old balsa rafts in action. This is one of the most interesting things to look for in Playas. They were coming in at the west end of the beach when I was last there but, of course, this depends on winds and tides.

Because of its proximity to Guayaquil, there are many holiday homes in Playas. It is quite a bustling little resort during the busy seasons (Christmas to Easter and July to September) but feels almost like a ghost town at other times of year. In the high season all the hotels are open and prices may rise a little; in other months many of the hotels, especially the cheaper ones, close down. Those which are open have few guests and will sometimes lower their prices to have you stay there. Try bargaining.

The Teatro Playas cinema is often closed in the low season too.

Places to Stay – bottom end

The cheapest hotels often don't have running water and are extremely basic – many close during the low season. The best of the cheapies seem to be the *Hotel California* and *Hostería Costa Verde*. They charge about US$1.50 each and have water. Cheaper still are the *Casa de Piedra* (over the Peluquería Oriente hairdresser), the *Hotel Turismo* and the *Residencial*

Playas

Turismo (also known as the *Tropical*). Ask if they have water.

For US$2 each you can stay at the *Hotel Miraglia*. It's a sprawling old wooden building but the rooms are adequate – some have private bathrooms. *Residencial Costa Azul* has tiny box-like singles for US$2 and better doubles with private bath for US$6. *Hotel Marianela* is quite good for US$2.50 per person in rooms with private baths. They will probably bargain if there is a group of you in the low season.

El Galeon has been recently repainted and looks good. They are friendly, have an inexpensive but good restaurant, and are recommended. Rooms with private bathrooms and mosquito netting are US$3 per person.

Places to Stay – middle

Hotel Playas has simple but clean rooms with private bathrooms for US$7 single and US$11 double. They have a restaurant. *Residencial Cattan* provides a bed and three good meals a day for US$11 per person. The rooms have private baths and are clean but the showers only have brackish water. They seem unwilling to provide accommodation without meals but their restaurant is recommended.

If you want to stay out of town you can head roughly east on Avenida J R Aguilera to the *Hostería Delfín* about a km away. Also near here is the *Hostería Gaviota*. These are the best two hotels in the Playas area and have decent restaurants and pleasant rooms which cost a little more than in town.

Places to Eat

Inexpensive beach restaurants serve fresh seafood and are all fairly similar to one another. The better hotels have good restaurants; the one below the *Hotel Galeon* is recommended as being good, cheap and open to the public.

Getting There

Transportes Villamil and Posorja are the bus companies with services to Guayaquil (65c, 1¾ hours). Bus schedules tend to be flexible and buses often leave from the store/bar at the corner of Avenida Paquisha and Avenida Guayaquil.

Both these companies usually pick up passengers for Posorja if the bus from Guayaquil is continuing there. Transportes 9 de Marzo has frequent pickup trucks to Posorja (20c, 30 minutes).

Services are normally to Guayaquil, though occasionally a bus will go to the Santa Elena peninsula. You could go to Progreso and change, but buses from Guayaquil to Santa Elena are often full during holidays.

POSORJA

Although the road from Playas to Posorja follows the coast, it is just far enough inland so you get no views of the sea until you arrive in Posorja. The road is good but the scenery not particularly attractive. A few km out of Playas you go through the old village of El Morro, which is less important than it used to be. There is a huge old wooden church with dilapidated bamboo walls and three white wooden towers; the place is falling into disrepair.

Posorja is an attractive little fishing village with many working boats and hundreds of seabirds wheeling overhead. The beach is dirty and not good for swimming. Posorja is best visited on a day trip. There are two very basic pensiones. One is literally on the point of disintegrating and the other looks like a particularly sleazy whorehouse – neither are recommended.

SANTA ELENA PENINSULA

As you continue westward from Progreso the land becomes increasingly dry and scrubby, the kapok trees giving way to interminable forests of five-metre-high cactus. Few people and little animal life is seen, though herds of tough, half-wild goats seem to thrive. Some of the few inhabitants scratch a living from burning the scrub to make charcoal and occasionally you see someone on the side of the road with bags of charcoal.

As you arrive in Santa Elena the landscape changes. Not that it becomes any less dry, but it becomes built up. There are three towns on the peninsula and they all seem to run into one another. Thus the peninsula is almost completely a dusty urban zone with few open spaces. Santa Elena itself is the least important of the towns from the traveller's point of view, though it does have a nearby oilworks and is the home of the peninsula's radio station. *Residencial El Cisne* is a clean, basic hotel on the main square. The other towns on the peninsula are La Libertad and Salinas, the main resort.

LA LIBERTAD

La Libertad is the largest town on the peninsula, with some 42,000 inhabitants. It is a fishing village and port of some importance and is more interesting to visit (especially in the low season) than Salinas. The floods of the 1982/83 El Nin'o caused severe damage to the waterfront and low-lying streets, and many streets are blocked by repair work. A new plaza has been built at the east end of the Malecón and the modern IETEL office is here. There is a bustling market and a cinema.

Places to Stay – bottom end

One of the cheapest hotels on the whole peninsula is the basic but friendly *Residencial Libertad*, which is US$1.50 each. Also cheap is the *Residencial Reina del Pacifico*, US$1.50 per person in rather horrible little boxes (though they have a few better rooms with private bath for US$5). Next door is the *Turis Palm* with unfriendly service and basic rooms at US$2 per person or US$3 with private bathroom. Friendly, and on the seafront, is the *Hotel Villa Maria*, rather the worse for wear since the 1982/83 floods. Rooms with a view are US$2 each. Other US$1.50-2 possibilities include the *Centenario Hotel, Hotel Lido* and the *Residencial Zambano* – none of them too special.

Places to Stay – middle

Hotel Palatino is reasonable value though nothing special. Rooms are US$3.50 (US$5 with private bathroom) per person and are cleaner than the rooms with private bathrooms at the grubby *Hotel Estrella del Mar*. The Estrella charges US$3.50 per person and has the potential of improving with better management. The hotel is quite new but suffers from water shortages and general indifference. In this price bracket is the *Hotel Collins Carrera* – it's worse.

The best place in town is the DITURIS-run *Hotel Samarina* on the waterfront about a km north-west of the town. They have a restaurant, a swimming pool and clean rooms for about US$6 single and US$10 double.

Places to Eat

Most restaurants are on Avenida 9 de Octubre or Guayaquil. There are several cheap *chifas* and *comedors* near the *Residencial Reina del Pacifico* and on the way up to the market.

Getting There

La Libertad is the centre of bus services on the peninsula. For Guayaquil (US$1, 2½ to three hours) there are several choices. Transportes Reina Turismo has large but slow buses which leave only in the early hours (4.30 to 8.30 am). Transportes Libertad Peninsula has buses about every hour all day long. CICA has no office at this time but has the fastest and most frequent service. Their buses leave across the street from the Residencials Reina del Pacifico and Turis Palm on Avenida 9 de Octubre. The CICA buses from Guayaquil continue to Salinas and then return to Guayaquil from Salinas via La Libertad.

To get to Santa Elena you take a pickup truck. They depart frequently from Avenida Robles Bordero near Guayaquil. Frequent buses to Salinas run all day from Calle 8 and either Avenida 2 or 4. To visit the wild and undeveloped beach of Carnero (with

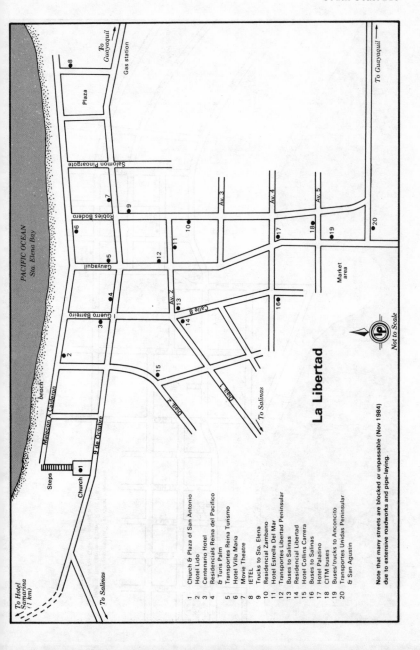

La Libertad

Not to Scale

1 Church & Plaza of San Antonio
2 Hotel Lido
3 Centenario Hotel
4 Residencials Reina del Pacifico
5 Transportes Reina Turismo
6 Hotel Villa Maria
7 Movie Theatre
8 IETEL
9 Trucks to Sta. Elena
10 Residencial Zambano
11 Hotel Estrella Del Mar
12 Transportes Libertad Peninsular
13 Buses to Salinas
14 Residencial Liberdad
15 Hotel Collins Carrera
16 Buses to Salinas
17 Hotel Palatino
18 CITM buses
19 Buses/trucks to Anconcito
20 Transportes Unidas Peninsular
     & San Agustin

Note that many streets are blocked or unpassable (Nov 1984)
due to extensive roadworks and pipe-laying.

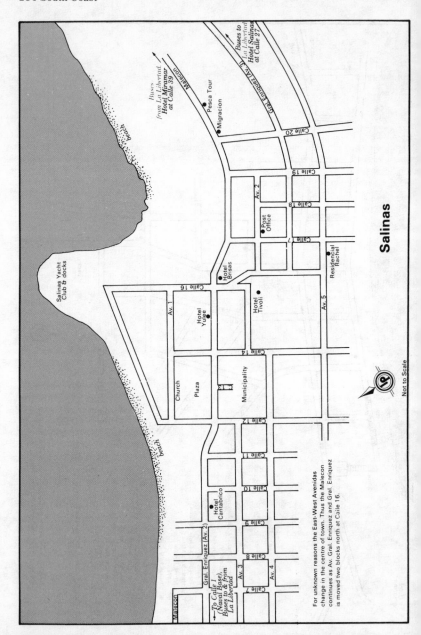

Salinas

Not to Scale

For unknown reasons the East-West Avenidas change in the centre of town. Thus the Malecon continues as Av. Gral. Enriquez and Gral. Enriquez is moved two blocks north at Calle 16.

Buses to
Hotel Salinas
at Calle 27

Buses to
Hotel Miramar
at Calle 39

Buses
from La Libertad.

La Libertad

Gral. Enriquez

Calle 20

Pesca Tour

Migracion

Malecon

Av. 2

Calle 19

Calle 18

Post
Office

Calle 7

Av. 5

Residencial
Rachel

Salinas Yacht
Club & docks

beach

Hotel
Brisas

Calle 16

Av. 1

Hotel
Yulee

Calle 14

Hotel
Tivoli

Church

Plaza

Municipality

Calle 12

Calle 11

Calle 10

Calle 9

Calle 8

Hotel
Cantabrico

Gral. Enriquez (Av. 2)

Av. 3

Av. 4

Malecon

← To Calle 1
(Naval Base)
Buses to & from
La Libertad.

beach

the fishing village of Anconcito and the oil town of Ancón), take one of the frequent buses or pickup trucks leaving from near the market on Avenida Guayaquil and Avenida 5. Near here is Transportes San Agustín, which has *rancheros* running further east along the coast to the fishing village of Chanduy. There is no accommodation in these places.

For going north along the coast to the fishing villages of Palmar, Ayangue, Manglaralto (60c, 1½ hours) and Puerto López (US$1, 2½ hours) you take *rancheros*, buses and trucks with Transportes Peninsulares Unidas or CITM. The first one has departures about every half hour but few of the vehicles make it as far as Manglaralto. Most go as far as Palmar and some go to Ayangue. CITM has two buses a day that go as far as Puerto López and sometimes two more going as far as Manglaralto.

SALINAS

This important resort town is on the tip of the Santa Elena peninsula. About 150 km west of Guayaquil, it is the most westerly town on the Ecuadorean mainland. Unfortunately, you cannot go to the very furthest point as there is a naval base there.

Salinas is called the 'best' resort in Ecuador and its casinos, expensive hotels and high-rise condos make it the haunt of affluent Ecuadoreans. It's expensive and quite busy during the season (Christmas to Easter and July to September) and expensive and dead in the off season. The beaches are pleasant but not spectacular and the general effect rather spoilt by the high-rise backdrop. I prefer the less-developed beaches of Playas or the north coast.

There is a yacht club and, should you arrive in your own boat, you'll find *Migración* on the waterfront. Also on the waterfront is Pesca Tour, who do expensive deep-sea fishing trips and provide all the equipment.

Places to Stay

There are some very good hotels but they are not cheap. I visited Salinas in November and found half the hotels closed. The cheapest open place I found was the old and tumble-down *Hotel Tivoli*, which had rooms with private bathrooms at US$3.50 per person. Other hotels in the US$3-5 per person range are the *Hotel Yulee*, which is recommended but was closed; the *Hotel Brisas* with an open door but no receptionist; and the *Residencial Rachel*, the cheapest-looking of all. November is a rather dead month.

Hotel Cantabrico is good value if you eat all your meals there. They charge US$9 per person in basic but clean rooms with private bathrooms, and all three meals are included. If you don't want to eat here you pay US$7 for the room. They have a rather dusty garden with hammocks to lie around in.

The modern *Hotel Salinas* charges US$10 for good and comfortable double rooms with private bathrooms but I would expect to pay a little more in the high season. The most expensive place in town is the *Hotel Miramar*, which boasts air-conditioned rooms, a casino, swimming pool, bar and restaurant. They charge about US$20 for a double in the low season.

Places to Eat

There are various restaurants, bars and discos along the waterfront between Calles 19 and 25 but they're mostly closed in the low season. *Restaurant Caracol* on Calle 6 at the waterfront is good and medium priced.

Getting There

Buses enter town along the Malecón and continue to the naval base. Here they turn around and head back to La Libertad along Gral Enriquez. Most buses go only as far as La Libertad. Those that continue to Guayaquil usually stop at La Libertad for up to an hour to pick up more passengers.

NORTH ALONG THE COAST

From La Libertad many buses run north along the coast. Most go only a short way but a few make it as far as Puerto López. The beaches are often very good but there is no accommodation until Manglaralto. There are several fishing villages where Guayaquileños have holiday homes. Palmar and Ayangue are the most popular. The views are good, so sit on the left or ocean side of the bus.

The most interesting sight is the literally hundreds of local fishermen surf-fishing. They catch shrimp with hand nets stretched between a framework of two crossed poles, at the end of which a couple of floats are attached. Wading knee deep in the surf, they push these hand nets up and down the beach. It looks ridiculously like a lawn-mowing convention gone crazy.

The road is quite good until Valdivia. This is the site of Ecuador's oldest culture. There is a small museum but the best pieces are in Guayaquil museums. North of Valdivia the road deteriorates and the dry landscape begins to get a little wetter. The cactus and scrub give way to stunted trees and the occasional banana plantation.

At Manglaralto there are no hotels, but for US$1.50 I found a bed with a friendly family by asking around. You can do this in the other villages too. There are a couple of basic *comedors* and an IETEL office on the main square. You can easily do the round trip from La Libertad in a day if you just want to sightsee and swim from some beaches.

Puerto López is the most northerly village reached by bus from La Libertad. It's a busy fishing village and has a clean, basic *residencial* on the waterfront. It was temporarily cut off by washed-out roads after the 1982/83 floods but is getting back to normal. Transportes Sur de Manabi has a few buses every day which take you to Jipijapa (see North Coast chapter).

1 Hotel/Bus Ecuatoriana
2 Cuidad de Piñas Buses
3 CIFA buses to Guayaquil
4 Encalada Hotel
5 Rutas Orenses
6 Chifa Central Restaurant
7 Residencial Mercy
8 Hotel Perla del Pacifico
9 Money Exchange
10 Gran Hotel Machala
11 Residencial Paula
12 Teatro Tauro
13 Residencial Almacha
14 Hotel Oro
15 Residencial Pichincha
16 Cinema
17 Residencial Machala
18 Residencial La Internacional
19 IETEL
20 Panamericana Buses
21 Transportes Occidentales
22 Residencia de Oro
23 Tourist Office (2nd floor)
24 CIFA buses to Huaquillas
25 Rizzo Hotel
26 Peruvian Consul

MACHALA

South of Guayaquil is the important city of Machala, the capital of the province of El Oro. With about 106,000 inhabitants, it is Ecuador's fourth largest city. It lies in an important banana-growing area and during the 200-km drive from Guayaquil you pass many plantations of bananas, coffee, pineapple and citrus fruits. About halfway to Machala you pass through Naranjal, an important agricultural centre but otherwise of little interest.

Despite its economic importance, Machala is not of great tourist interest. Most travellers on their way to and from Peru pass through here but few people stay more than a night. It is not totally devoid of interest, however. The local international port is Puerto Bolívar, only seven km away and worth a look. Machala has a highly touted International Banana and Agricultural Festival during the third week in September which the Ecuadorean tourist authorities assure me is of great

interest to tourists. I'm afraid I missed it.

Information

Most streets in Machala are both named and numbered. (I use names.) The DITURIS information office is on the second floor of the office block on Avenida Bolívar at Guayas. They are open somewhat erratically on weekdays. The IETEL office is several blocks away from the centre on 9 de Octubre. There is a *casa de cambio* at Paez 17-23 which changes both US dollars cash and travellers' cheques at rates about 4% lower than Guayaquil and Quito. The French, Australians and New Zealanders need visas to enter Peru and there is a Peruvian consulate open from 8 am to 1 pm Monday through Friday.

Things to See

The international port, Puerto Bolívar, is reached by the No 1 local bus from Machala's main plaza. I've heard claims that it has some coastal nightlife but I couldn't discover any. There are some seafood restaurants by the waterfront and you can hire motorized dugouts to go for a cruise among the mangroves and watch the birdlife. For about US$1 you can go as far as the island of Jambelí, where there is a beach but no facilities. There is plenty of coastal boat traffic to watch as you sip a beer in a waterfront restaurant.

There are a couple of cinemas, of which the Teatro Tauro is the best.

Places to Stay

Machala has a better variety of hotels than does the border town of Huaquillas, so travellers are better off staying there. The border is not open until 8 am, so by taking a 6 am bus you can still be in Huaquillas by the time the border opens.

Places to Stay – bottom end

Most of the cheap hotels have only cold water but the weather is hot enough that it's not a great hardship. The cheapest place in town is the extremely basic *Residencial de Oro*, which charges only 80c per person. Other basic places are the *Residencial Almacha* which looks very dirty, the *Residencial Pichincha* which looks a little better, and the *Residencial Mercy*. All charge US$1.20 each.

Somewhat cleaner and better looking is the *Residencial La Internacional* for US$1.50 per person and the *Residencial Machala* for US$2. Also US$2 each is the *Residencial Paula*, which has some rooms with private baths for another dollar. The best value in this price range is the clean and well-run *Gran Hotel Machala*, which has simple rooms for US$2 each or US$3 per person with private bathroom. *Hotel Ecuatoriana Pullman* is conveniently located above the bus terminal and some rooms are surprisingly quiet. It's a bit run down and has rather grubby private bathrooms in the rooms which cost US$2.50 per person. These last two have some rooms with air-conditioning.

Places to Stay – middle & top end

Comfortable rooms with private bathrooms, air conditioning and sometimes TV are available for about US$9 single and US$14 double at the hotels *Encalada*, *Perla de Pacifico* and *Oro*. They all have restaurants and the *Encalada* has a discotheque.

The best hotel in town, complete with swimming pool and casino, is the *Rizzo Hotel*, which charges about US$13 single and US$20 double.

Places to Eat

There are many *chifas*, of which the *Restaurant Chifa Central* is recommended as having a wide variety of good and reasonably priced meals. There are also several places on or within a block of the main square. The best hotels have more expensive restaurants but the food is good.

Getting There

Air Flights from Machala to Guayaquil leave about noon with TAME every day except Sunday. The fare is US$7.50. You can connect with a Guayaquil-Quito flight to be in the capital the same evening for about US$23.00.

There isn't a downtown TAME office at this time, so you should go to the airport to purchase your ticket. It is about 1-1/2 km from the town centre and a taxi will cost about 60c.

Lansa also has an office at the airport and they have light aircraft for flights to Guayaquil. Their services were temporarily suspended in 1984 but you could check to see if they've resumed flights yet.

Bus There is no central bus terminal. To get to the Peruvian border at Huaquillas (60c, two hours) it's best to go with CIFA, who leave at very frequent intervals from the corner of Bolívar and Guayas. Make sure your documents are in order and not packed deep in your luggage as there are two or three passport checks en route. You will be asked to leave the bus to register but the driver is used to this and will wait for you.

CIFA buses also go to Guayaquil (US$1.50, 3½ hours) from their depot on Avenida 9 de Octubre near Colón. There are several other companies in the area. Rutas Orenses has efficient and frequent service to Guayaquil in small buses and Ecuatoriana-Pullman in larger coaches.

Transportes Occidentales and Panamericana have several large coaches a day to Quito (US$3.40, 10 to 12 hours). Transportes Occidentales also has a few buses to Esmeraldas. Ciudad de Piñas has nine buses a day to Piñas, a few of which continue to Loja. They also have one or two buses to Cuenca (US$2, five hours).

HUAQUILLAS

This dusty one-street town is of importance only because it is at Ecuador's border with Peru. It has a population of about 20,000 (though it doesn't look it) and is 80 km from Machala.

The bus from Machala passes through banana and palm plantations and the dusty market towns of Santa Rosa and Arenillas. There are two or three passport checks en route but these take only a minute (assuming your passport is in order).

There is a busy street market by the border and the place is full of Peruvians shopping on day passes. It's a run-down and dirty town and not a particularly attractive introduction to Ecuador if you're arriving from Peru. Almost everything happens on the one long street.

Money

There are no banks in Huaquillas or Aguas Verdes, so you have to rely on street moneychangers. They will try to give you a very bad rate but will soon become more reasonable if you can show that you know what the real rate is. Check with other travellers going the opposite way for up-to-date exchange rates.

If you are leaving Ecuador for Peru, it is best to try and get rid of as many sucres as you can in Ecuador and arrive in Peru with dollars. Peruvian moneychangers will give you a better rate for dollars than in Ecuador and, if you bargain hard and change US$100 or more, you can get 1 or 2% better rates than in Lima. There is no black market.

If arriving in Ecuador you can get within 2% of the Quito rate from street changers if you bargain hard. Again, it is best to use dollars. You can always change sucres to soles and soles to sucres, but the dollar remains king. Other major foreign currencies can be exchanged, but less favourably, and fewer changers want to deal with them.

Places to Stay

There are several cheap hotels on the main street near the immigration office. None of them are particularly good. One of the cheapest is the basic *Residencial Loja* behind the immigration office. They charge US$1.20 each. Next door is the slightly better *Residencial Bucanero* for

US$2 each. There are several more in this price range down the street but I can't work up much enthusiasm for these either. Hotels tend to be full by early afternoon and you may have to take whatever is available or go to Machala.

There is one good hotel run by DITURIS. The *Parador Turistico Huaquillas* is about 1½ km away from the border on the right side of the main road out of town. You can take a taxi for about 40c or walk. They charge US$5 single and US$8 double and have simple but clean rooms with fans and private bathrooms. There is a restaurant.

Places to Eat
There aren't any particularly good restaurants. There is a café behind the immigration office where travellers and moneychangers often hang out. Other places are along the main street.

Getting There
CIFA buses run frequently to Machala (60c, two hours). There is no main bus office but you'll see buses on the main street a block or two beyond the immigration office. A few buses go to Quito (US$3.80, 13 hours) or Guayaquil (US$2, 5½ hours), but it's usually easier to go to Machala and change unless you're in a great hurry.

Crossing the Peruvian Border
The border is the Río Zarumilla, which is crossed by an international bridge. From the bridge, the main road, thronged with market stalls, stretches out through Huaquillas. The Ecuadorean Immigration Office is on the left side about 200 metres from the bridge and is identified by the yellow/blue/red-striped Ecuadorean flag. All entrance and exit formalities are carried out here. Dozens of small boys will offer their services as luggage carriers and guides. The many moneychangers (identified by the ubiquitous black attaché case) will show you the immigration office. You won't have any difficulty in finding it.

The Ecuadorean Immigration Office is open daily from 8 am to noon and 2 to 5 pm. The Peruvian office is open one hour later.

If you are leaving Ecuador, the procedure is as follows. Go to the immigration office and present your passport and T3 tourist card (the duplicate copy of the small document you filled out on arrival). You will receive an exit stamp in your passport and the immigration authorities will keep your T3 card. There are no costs involved. If you have lost your T3 card, you should be able to get a free replacement at the border, assuming that the stamp in your passport has not expired. If you have overstayed your permitted time by a few days you can usually persuade the immigration official to charge you a fine right there and then – expect to pay no more than US$10. If you get sent back to Guayaquil you will still have to pay a fine, so it's best to get it over with. You can usually get away with a few days over the limit by telling the official how much you loved Ecuador and that you didn't realize how much time had passed.

As you cross the international bridge you will be asked to show the exit stamp in your passport to the Ecuadorean bridge guard. On the Peruvian side (now called Aguas Verdes instead of Huaquillas) you normally have to show your passport to the bridge guard, but full entrance formalities are carried out in the new immigration building about three km from the border. About 300 metres from the bridge there are *colectivo* taxis to take you there. Most European nationalities (except the French) don't need a visa for Peru. Neither do North Americans. Australians and New Zealanders do. Visas are not obtainable in either Aguas Verdes or Huaquillas and you have to go back to the Peruvian consul in Machala if you haven't got one. Other nationalities normally just need a tourist card, available at the Peruvian immigration office. Although an exit ticket out of Peru is officially required, gringo travellers are rarely asked for this unless they look thoroughly disreputable.

Other Latin American travellers are often asked for an exit ticket, however, so if you're a non-Peruvian Latin American (or travelling with one) be prepared for this eventuality. There is a bus office in Aguas Verdes which sells (nonrefundable) bus tickets out of Peru. The immigration official will tell you where it is. A bribe may help here.

If you are arriving in Ecuador you first need an exit stamp in your passport from the Peruvian authorities. After walking across the international bridge, continue 200 metres to the Ecuadorean Immigration Office. Entrance formalities are usually straightforward. No tourists need a visa but everyone needs a tourist card, available free at the office. If you're not entering as a tourist, you need a student, resident, worker or business visa which must be

obtained from an Ecuadorean embassy, usually the one that serves your home country. Exit tickets from Ecuador and sufficient funds (US$20 per day) are legally required but are very rarely asked for. You will receive your T3 card (keep it for when you leave) and an identical stamp in your passport allowing you up to 90 days' stay. Usually, only 30 days are given but it is easy to obtain a renewal in Quito or Guayaquil.

Note that you are allowed only 90 days per year in Ecuador. If you've already been in the country for 90 days and try and return, you will be refused entry. If you have an exit ticket from Quito or Guayaquil international airport, you can usually get a 72-hour transit visa just to get you to the airport and out of the country.

Galápagos Islands

The Galápagos are a group of volcanic islands which lie about 1000 km west of Ecuador in the Pacific Ocean. They consist of 13 major islands, six small islands and scores of islets of which only some are named. Five of the islands are inhabited with a total population of about 6000 people who make a living from tourism, fishing and farming.

Most of the islands have two – and sometimes three – names. The earliest charts gave the islands both Spanish and English names, and the Ecuadorean government assigned official names in 1892. Thus an island can have a Spanish, English and official name. The official names are used here, with popular names in brackets.

The main reason for visiting the islands is to observe the incredibly tame and unique wildlife for which the Galápagos are world famous. Here, you can swim with sea lions, float eye-to-eye with a penguin, watch a blue-footed booby feed its young right next to you, and try to avoid stepping on iguanas scurrying over the lava. The wildlife is truly phenomenal. The scenery is barren and volcanic and has its own haunting beauty – though some people find it bare and ugly. A visit to the Galápagos is for the wilderness and wildlife enthusiast, not for the average sun-seeker.

Compared to the rest of your travels in Ecuador, the Galápagos are very expensive to visit. Flying from the mainland and spending a week cruising the islands will cost US$500 for even the most economic of budget travellers. Therefore the trip is not recommended unless you are really interested in wildlife. The environment is a fragile one, and the islands don't need bored visitors tramping around wondering why they are spending hundreds of dollars to sit on a rocky piece of lava under a searing equatorial sun to watch some squawking sea birds.

Every visitor must pay a US$30 park entrance fee upon arrival and will be given a full set of park rules and other informative leaflets upon arrival. The rules are for the protection of the wildlife and environment, and are mostly a matter of courtesy and common sense. Don't feed or handle the animals; don't litter; don't remove any natural object, whether living or dead; do not bring pets; do not buy objects made of sea lion teeth, tortoise, or turtle shells or other artifacts made from plants and animals; show a conservationist attitude. You are not allowed to visit the islands after dark or without a qualified guide, and a guide will accompany every boat. On all shore trips, the guide will be there to answer your questions and show you the best sites, and also to ensure that you stay on the trails and don't molest the animals.

With 20,000 tourists visiting the islands annually, it is essential to have a system of protection for the islands. The rules are sensible and necessary – they do not infringe on your enjoyment of the Galápagos. Staying on the trails is a good rule – until a sea lion goes to sleep in the middle of the trail and you are forced to go off trail to avoid the animal! The wildlife is so prolific that you'll see just as much on the trail as anywhere else, and staying on the trails protects other areas.

HISTORY

The Galápagos archipelago was discovered by accident in 1535, when the Bishop of Panama drifted off course while sailing from Panama to Peru. It is possible that the Indian inhabitants of South America were aware of the islands' existence before then, but we have no record of this.

For over three centuries after their discovery, the Galápagos were used as a base by a succession of pirates, buccaneers, sealers and whalers. The islands provided sheltered anchorage, firewood, water and an abundance of fresh food in the form of the giant Galápagos tortoises, which were caught by the thousands and stacked, alive, in ships' holds. The tortoises could survive for a year or more and thus provided fresh meat for the sailors long after they had left the islands.

The Galápagos' most famous visitor was Charles Darwin, who arrived exactly 300 years after the Bishop of Panama. He stayed for five weeks and made notes and wildlife collections which formed a central part of his theory of evolution.

For almost a century after Darwin's visit, the islands were inhabited by a few settlers and were also used as penal colonies. In 1934, the Ecuadorean government set aside some islands as wildlife sanctuaries, but the Galápagos were not declared a national park until 1959. Construction of the Charles Darwin Research Station on Santa Cruz Island began soon after, and the station started operating in 1962. Few tourists had visited the islands as yet, but by the late 1960s organized tourism began with a little over a thousand visitors per year. Now, an estimated 20,000 people visit the island every year.

WILDLIFE

The Galápagos have never been connected with the mainland, so the wildlife consists mainly of species whose ancestors were capable of crossing the 1000 km of ocean separating the islands from the mainland.

Thus the wildlife is dominated by birds (especially sea birds) and reptiles. There are a few mammals and insects but no amphibians. There are, of course, plenty of tropical fish. A good general guide to the birds, reptiles and mammals, with much background information on history and geology, is White and Epler's *Galápagos Guide*, easily and cheaply available in Quito. A brand-new guide just published by the University of Calgary Press is Michael H Jackson's *Galápagos: A Natural History Guide*. I haven't seen it yet but have heard good reports. Maps of the Galápagos are available from the IGM in Ecuador. The best map, full of useful information about wildlife, history and tourism, has just been published by Bradt Publications, 41 Nortoft Rd, Chalfont St Peter, Bucks S19 OLA, England.

Birds

There are 56 resident bird species on the Galápagos, of which 27 are endemic, found only in the Galápagos. A further dozen regular migrants are frequently seen and about 20 other migratory species are regularly but not frequently recorded. Some other species are rarely recorded. Many people are confused between a migrant, resident and endemic species. A resident lives and breeds in the island year round but the species is also found in other parts of the world. A migrant is found in the island for only part of the year. An endemic species is a resident which does not live or breed anywhere else in the world (except in captivity or by accident).

During an average week of touring the islands, most observers will see over 40 species of birds. If two weeks are spent and some of the more outlying islands are visited, over 50 species can be recorded. Of the endemic species, several will be seen by even the most casual observer. The 13 species of the famous Darwin's finches are all endemic and everyone sees some of them. All 13 species are thought to have descended from a common ancestor and their present differences in distribution, body size, beak size and shape, and feeding habits helped Darwin formulate his evolutionary theories.

The fearless mockingbirds are seen everywhere – these too are endemic. Prettier and so perhaps more interesting to the casual observer are the Galápagos doves. The endemic Galápagos hawk is frequently seen, as is the lava gull, of which only about 400 pairs are estimated to exist and which is the rarest gull in the world. Despite this, you have a very good chance of seeing one here. Also endemic is the Galápagos penguin, the world's most northerly penguin, which charms visitors with its clownlike antics.

Not endemic, but nevertheless fearless and very easy to observe, are the frigate birds and boobies, of which several species nest in the islands. The courtship displays of these birds are particularly interesting to observe, especially the football-sized bright red pouches which the mail frigate birds puff up on their throats to attract females. The aerial acrobatics of these birds are no less wonderful than their courtship displays. The beautiful red-billed tropic bird with its extremely long white tail is another species to watch for in the air.

One book particularly recommended for bird-watchers is M Harris' *A Field Guide to the Birds of the Galápagos*, published by Collins in 1974. It is sometimes available in Ecuador.

Reptiles

The prehistoric-looking reptiles found all over the islands are easily seen and approached. The most frequently seen are the iguanas, of which there are three species. The world's only marine iguanas are found on the rocky shores of most islands. They have a blackish skin which, in the males, can change to startling blues and reds during the breeding season. The row of spines along the entire length of their backs, their scaly skins, their habit of occasionally snorting little clouds of spray

into the air, and their length – which can reach almost a metre – makes them look like veritable little dragons.

The yellowish iguanas, of which there are two species, are land iguanas. They are bigger than their marine relatives. Although they are less widespread, they are still commonly seen by almost all visitors.

The most famous of the reptiles is, of course, the giant tortoise for which the islands are named. There is only one species but it has been divided into 14 subspecies. Tens of thousands were killed by whalers and sealers, particularly in the 18th and 19th centuries, and now only some 10,000 remain. A breeding project at the Charles Darwin Research Station appears to be successful and it hopes to begin re-introduction of animals into the wild. You can see both tiny yearlings and full-grown adults at the research station; this is the easiest way to see them. Although they are in enclosures, visitors are encouraged to enter the enclosures and get a good close look at these giants, some of which reach a weight of 300 kg.

Less spectacular but also endemic are the seven species of lava lizard which are frequently seen scurrying around the islands. They can reach 25 cm in length but are usually smaller and their most distinctive behavioural patterns are rapid head-bobbing and push-up stances to defend their territories and assert dominance. Less often seen are the small nocturnal lizards called geckos, of which there are nine species (eight endemic). Finally, you may see the Galápagos snake, which is a small, drab and non-poisonous species.

Mammals

The mammals are less well represented but those species which do exist are well worth seeing. The mammal you'll see the most of is the Galápagos sea lion, which is found on most islands. The territorial bulls are quite aggressive and sometimes chase swimmers out of the water, but the

Top: Boats off Plaza Island, Galapagos (TW)
Bottom: Bartolome Island, Galapagos (TW)

Top: Boat building in Puerto Ayora, Galapagos (TW)
Bottom: Brachycereus Cactus on Pahoehoe Lava, James Island, Galapagos (RR)

Top: Frigate bird with mating display pouch, Seymour Island (TW)
Bottom: Marine Iguana (RR)

females and young are extremely playful and you can often watch them swimming around you if you bring a mask and snorkel. Less common are the fur seals, which superficially look similar but on closer inspection are quite different from the sea lions. Other marine mammals you may see when cruising between the islands are whales and dolphins (especially the bottle-nosed dolphins which often surf the bow waves of the boats).

Land mammals are mainly introduced species gone wild and they create a major nuisance to the endemic species. They include feral goats, cats, dogs, rats and mice. There are two species of rice rat which are endemic to the island and are protected.

Plants

Almost 900 species of plants have been recorded in the Galápagos, of which over 200 are endemic. There are six different vegetation zones, beginning with the shore and ending with the highlands. Each zone supports different and distinctive plant species. Several books on both the flora and fauna are available; see the Books & Bookshops section in the chapter on Facts for the Visitor.

THE INHABITED ISLANDS

Although five islands are inhabited, only one is visited frequently by travellers. The

A. Blue-footed booby (TW)
B. Male magnificent frigate bird and chick (RR)
C. Male marine iguana in breeding colours (RR)
D. Galapagos hawks (RR)
E. Great blue heron (RR)
F. Immature frigate bird (RR)
G. Sea lion pups (RR)
H. Galapagos tortoise (RR)

island with the greatest population is Santa Cruz, and most travellers stay here in the small town of Puerto Ayora. Here there are a variety of hotels, restaurants and shops, and this is the place to organize any boat trip.

Baltra has a military base and the main airport, but has no facilities for tourists. Santa María (or Floreana) has a small village of a few dozen buildings on its west coast. The village is Puerto Velasco Ibarra and there is one very small but not very cheap hotel which is run, sporadically, by the Wittmers. You should make reservations in Puerto Ayora before you go, to make sure that they are expecting you. The biggest island, Isabela, has several hundred inhabitants in the small town of Puerto Villamil, where very basic accommodation can be found. The political capital of the islands is Puerto Baquerizo Moreno on San Cristóbal. Over 2000 people live here, and there are a few simple hotels charging about US$3 per person.

Information

Puerto Ayora has a post office, but no IETEL office, though one is planned. Radio messages can be sent in an emergency through INGALA. Money-changing facilities are not very good and you should change travellers' cheques on the mainland. It is easier to exchange cash than travellers' cheques. The bank usually does not exchange money. A store which changes travellers' cheques (at a poor rate) is shown on the map. Other stores will sometimes also exchange money, and some hotels will do so if you are staying there.

The Charles Darwin Research Station has an exhibition hall, an information kiosk, and tortoise-raising pens, but they do not organize tours. During the busy seasons, self-styled tour agents set up shop near the Las Ninfas Restaurant. INGALA can give you information about inter-island ferries and the Capitanía can give you information about boats to the

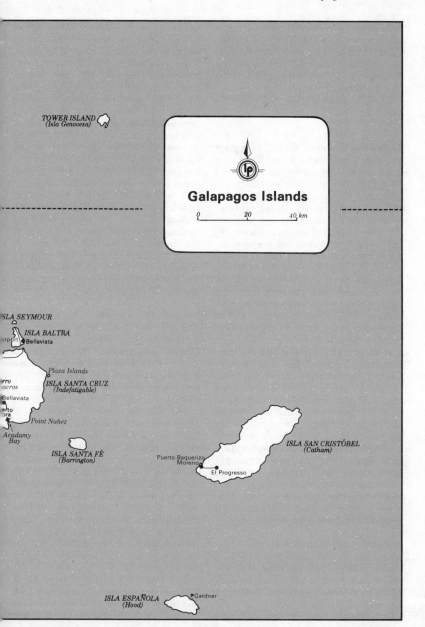

TOWER ISLAND
(Isla Genovesa)

Galapagos Islands

0   20   40 km

ISLA SEYMOUR

ISLA BALTRA
irport   Bellavista

Plaza Islands
rro   ISLA SANTA CRUZ
acros   (Indefatigable)
Bellavista
arto
ora   Point Nuñez

Acadamy
Bay

ISLA SANTA FÉ
(Barrington)

Puerto Baquerizo
Moreno

El Progresso

ISLA SAN CRISTÓBEL
(Catham)

ISLA ESPAÑOLA   Gardner
(Hood)

mainland. I have heard of plans to open a permanent tourist information office. TAME has an office open from 8 am to noon Monday through Thursday and on Saturday. It is also open from 2 to 5 pm Monday through Friday.

There is a basic hospital, a church and a movie theatre.

Activities

Snorkelling You don't have to be a great swimmer to be able to snorkel. Donning a mask and snorkel will literally open up a completely new world for you. Baby sea lions may come up and stare at you through your mask, various species of rays come slowly undulating by, and penguins dart past you in a stream of bubbles. The hundreds of species of fish are spectacularly colourful and you can watch the round, flapping shapes of sea turtles as they circle you. This won't, of course, happen immediately you enter the water, but you have a good chance of seeing most of these things if you spend, say, half an hour a day in the water during a week of cruising the islands.

A snorkel also lets you observe more sedentary forms of life. Sea urchins, starfish, sea anemones, algae and crustaceans all colourfully combine in an exotic display of underwater life. If I were to give only one piece of advice to someone visiting the Galápagos, I would say, 'Bring a snorkel and mask.' You may be able to buy them in sporting goods stores in Quito or Guayaquil, and they can sometimes be borrowed in the Galápagos, but if you definitely plan on visiting the islands, I would consider bringing a mask from home to ensure a good fit and to enable you to snorkel when you feel like it.

Places to Stay – bottom end

There are two cheap hotels in Puerto Ayora, both of which are basic, but clean and friendly, and better value than some of the more expensive places. Both are a km north of downtown on the way to the Charles Darwin Research Station. *Pensión* *Gloria* is run by Señora Gloria, whose husband is a guide. They are friendly and will help you organize a tour boat group. They have four double rooms and two triples and charge US$1 per person. Similarly priced and slightly bigger is the *Hotel Angermeyer*, run by members of the family who were among the earliest permanent residents. They are a mine of information and the hotel is in a pleasant garden. These two places are, in my opinion, the best in town for travellers who are on a tight budget and are trying to organize their own inexpensive cruise.

It is possible to camp next to the cemetery near the Charles Darwin Research Station but it still costs about a dollar and facilities are almost non-existent. Ask at the Research Station for information about this and other campsites (which are generally difficult to get to and require that you pack in your own water – for hardy and fanatic campers only).

Places to Stay – middle

The *Lobo del Mar Hotel* is popular with Ecuadorean tour groups. They charge US$2.50 per person or US$7 including all meals. They have simple rooms, some with showers, and they look clean. The hotel organizes day trips to various islands for about US$20 per passenger.

The following hotels charge about US$3-4 per person and often have private baths in the rooms: The *Palmeras* and *Salinas*, both modern and clean looking; the *Darwin* and *Santa Cruz*, fairly new and on the road out of town; and the *Elizabeth* and *Colón*, which I think are overpriced. The new *Hotel Ninfas* charges US$4.50 without and US$10.50 with meals and has private baths in all rooms. The *Hotel Castro* is usually used by tour groups booked with Señor Miguel Castro but you can always try it if you have no luck elsewhere.

The *Hotel Sol y Mar* charges about US$6 each in rooms with a private bath and serves good meals. It's very pleasantly situated right on the waterfront and marine iguanas sunbathe with the guests on the deck or walk over your feet while you're having breakfast. The owner is Señor Jimmy Perez, a colourful character who speaks English and runs Trans-Galápagos Tourism. He can find boats.

Places to Stay – top end
The best hotel in Puerto Ayora is the *Hotel Galápagos*, which charges US$29, US$52 and US$75 for comfortable single, double and triple rooms with private bath and ocean view. They serve excellent meals (about US$5, US$6 and US$7 for breakfast, lunch and supper). Across the bay from Puerto Ayora is the *Hotel Delfín* with a private beach. You need a boat to get to the hotel from Puerto Ayora.

Places to Eat
Las Ninfas Restaurant is the main meeting place during the day. They serve decent meals. The *Fragata Bar* is good for snacks and meeting people. A few other places are shown on the map.

In the evening, the rowdiest action is at *La Terraza Bar*. The *Booby Trap Disco* is quieter and serves food. *Bar La Peña* is also a good meeting place.

Shopping
You can buy the famous Galápagos T-shirts in several shops; the Fragata Bar and Boutique has the best selection. Other souvenirs available include objects made from black coral, turtle and tortoise shell. These animals are protected (coral is considered an animal) and it is illegal to use these animal products for the manufacture of novelties. The practice still continues, unfortunately, and the most effective way of stamping it out is to avoid buying these things.

Most things (T-shirts excepted) are either expensive or unavailable and you are strongly advised to stock up on suntan lotion, insect repellant, toiletries, film and medications on the mainland. Food and drink are available but the choice is limited and comparatively expensive.

A good selection of postcards is available at the post office.

Getting There
You can either go by boat or by air – I most definitely recommend air. If you go by boat you will normally waste a lot of time in Guayaquil getting one of the infrequent passages. The money you spend on hotels and food in town, plus the hassles involved, means that you really end up saving very little money, if any at all. Though the air fare is very expensive, there's nothing you can do about it.

Air Rather than spend frustrating days and weeks looking for a ship in Guayaquil, I recommend that you just get on a plane and have done with it. TAME operates morning flights daily except Sundays, from both Quito and Guayaquil. Flights from Guayaquil cost US$312 round trip and take 1½ hours to the Galápagos. From Quito, you have to check in again in Guayaquil and usually board another aircraft. The flight costs US$356 round trip. Ecuadorean nationals can fly for about US$40. Some foreign residents of Ecuador are also eligible so if you have a residence visa you should make enquiries.

It used to be that there were military logistic flights which you could wangle your way on to, but this is no longer common and I have not heard of any one who has done this for years. I heard of some travellers who tried to pull a scam by posing as Ecuadoreans and giving an Ecuadorean *cedula* number to purchase cheap tickets. They persuaded the travel agent to sell them the tickets but they were caught at the airport. Security checks in and out of the Galápagos have since been stepped up and now you have to show your identity documents three times, so forget about bluffing your way through with a cheap ticket. I have heard of some scam which gets you to the Galápagos cheaply, but apparently you have to be an Israeli citizen and the people I talked with were playing their hands very

Boat
building
area

Pelican Bay

To Sta Rosa,
Bellavista,
north of island,
ferry to Baltra
Airport

Puerto Ayora
Harbour

Park

Docks

Puerto Ayora

Not to Scale

close to their chests! I suppose that as long as the flights are expensive there will be people who will happily waste a month of their time trying to beat the system; if you're not eligible for cheap flights and you think the airfare is too expensive, then maybe you shouldn't be visiting the island anyway.

Flights to the Galápagos are often booked up well in advance but if you go to the airport you'll often find that there are many no-shows. Travel agencies book up blocks of seats for their all-inclusive Galápagos tours. First they sell them to people taking their tours but will release the seats on the day of the flight when there is no longer any hope of selling their tour. If you are tied into a definite itinerary, you should make a reservation; if you're flexible, you can buy your ticket at the airport when you want to fly. You have a better-than-even chance of getting a ticket and it's highly unlikely that you'll be turned away two days in a row.

So to get a ticket, first go to TAME. If they are sold out, try a travel agent specializing in Galápagos tours, and finally go the airport on the day of the flight if you haven't had any success at TAME or the travel agencies.

Boat If you really insist on avoiding air transport, there are four ways to get to the islands by boat: with the navy, on a cargo boat, on a cruise ship or on your own vessel.

The Navy runs the *Calicuchima*, which leaves Guayaquil about twice a month for an 11-day trip. Only about half this time is available for visiting the island, some naval bases are visited en route, and the accommodation, crew, guides and food have been criticized. The tour costs about US$330 and you can find out more from their office at Transnave on 9 de Octubre and Chile in Guayaquil. (They've moved offices several times in the last few years, so you may have to ask at the Capitanía on the waterfront.)

Cargo ships leave irregularly and charge about US$90 for a one-way trip. Three ships doing this are the *Pinzón*, *Piquero* and *Iguana*, but the first of these recently broke down and you may well have to wait

1	Entrance to Darwin Research Centre	22	Micro Mercado
	1/2 km to first buildings	23	Radio Station
2	Hotel Galapagos	24	Church
3	Cemetery	25	INGALA Office
4	Camping permitted	26	Post Office
5	Fragata Bar & Boutique	27	Capitania de Puerto
6	Bar La Peña	28	Bakery
7	Hotel Angermeyer	29	Souvenirs
8	Comercial Pelican Bay Store	30	Las Ninfas Restaurant
9	Pensión Gloria	31	Hotel Castro
10	Hotel Sol y Mar	32	Hotel Nynfas
11	Banco Nacional de Fomento	33	Hospital
12	Church	34	Store buys $ Travellers Cheques
13	Hotel Lobo de Mar	35	Café
14	Booby Trap Disco	36	Hotel Darwin
15	Town Hall (Municipalidad)	37	Pharmacy
16	Hotel Elizabeth & Store	38	TAME
17	Cinema	39	School
18	Hotel Salinas	40	Tunnel Restaurant
19	Hotel Palmeras	41	Hotel Santa Cruz
20	La Terraza Bar		
21	Hotel Colón (& Raul Jeria)		

for up to a month for a departure with one of the others. Conditions are tolerable but basic. The ships also do round trips but these are mainly for cargo purposes and not for wildlife viewing. You can go if you want to watch cargo being loaded. More information can be had from the Capitanía or at dock No 4 on Guayaquil's Malecón.

The best boats to the islands are the cruise ships which are more comfortable, have a regular schedule, offer better food and guide service, and of course are more expensive. They accommodate 90 passengers in comfortable double cabins. These seven-day tours usually cost about US$1000 inclusive and go one way by boat and return by air. Occasionally, if a tour isn't full, you can wangle a cheaper fare at the last minute. One cruise ship is the *Bucanero* operated by Gordon Tours, Baquerizo Moreno 1120 and 9 de Octubre in Guayaquil; and at Juan León Mera 566 and Carrión in Quito. Both these boats are relatively luxurious and can be booked via any good travel agent in most countries.

You can travel to the Galápagos in your own boat, but the Ecuadorean authorities give only a 72-hour transit pass to non-Galápagos boats, so you can't cruise the islands in it. You can moor the boat in Puerto Ayora and hire a Galápagos boat to visit the islands.

Tours The most economical tours are run by Galasam (Economic Galápagos Tours) and they will often sell you just an air ticket even if you don't want a tour. Galasam are at Pinto 523 and Amazonas in Quito, and at Avenida 9 de Octubre 424 (Edificio Gran Pasaje, 11th floor) in Guayaquil. Their tours are suitable for budget travellers who don't want to organize their own tour once they get to the islands. They have seven-day tours aboard small boats with six to 12 bunks in double, triple and quadruple cabins. All bedding is provided and the accommodation is clean but spartan, with little privacy. Plenty of simple but fresh food and juice is served at all meals and a

naturalist guide accompanies the boat (some guides speak English). There are no extra costs (except for bottled drinks) and the emphasis is on relaxed wildlife-watching and casual cruising rather than luxury. There are toilets, and fresh water is available for washing of faces and drinking. Bathing facilities are often buckets of seawater, though showers are available on some boats. There are pre-set itineraries which visit most of the central islands and give enough time to see the wildlife. If you want your own itinerary you have to get a group of about six together. A one-week tour costs from US$300-400 per person plus airfare, depending on the time of year. Shorter tours are available. There are weekly departures.

More luxurious tours are also available with other agencies which advertise in Quito and Guayaquil. Their boats are more comfortable, the food is better and they can cost US$100 per day or more. If you want this kind of luxury, then a good travel agent in Ecuador or at home will be able to help you with information.

Getting Around

Bus Buses from Puerto Ayora to Baltra via the ferry leave every morning that there are flights (Monday through Saturday) at 8 pm, from in front of the Hotel Colón and Raul Jería Store. The fare is about US$1.50 including the ferry. They return in the afternoon after the plane from the mainland has landed. A second and third bus will run if there is passenger demand. (The flight from Baltra to Guayaquil leaves at 1 pm.) You can use these buses to be dropped off at the villages of Bella Vista or Santa Rosa to explore some of the interior. Neither of these villages have hotels and sometimes the return bus is full with passengers from the airport. The most convenient way of seeing the interior and ensuring that you don't get stuck is to hire a bus or truck for the day with a group of other travellers. Ask at your hotel about this.

Boat INGALA can give you up-to-date details of the inter-island passenger boat services. Recently, the following services were in operation from Puerto Ayora: To San Cristóbal, US$5, Tuesdays and Thursdays. To Isabela, every other Thursday, US$5. Most inter-island transport is by private boat.

The cheapest way to get around is to charter your own boat. Most visitors arrive at Baltra Airport and have to pay US$30 national park tax. (You can't get out of the airport otherwise – the tax is levied on all visitors and it is additional to any tour prices, air fares or other arrangements you may have made.) If you arrive by boat from the mainland you will also be charged the park tax before you can land. People on yachts do not appear to be charged the park tax when arriving at Santa Cruz but if they wish to visit other islands (which they are not allowed to do on their own boat) they must also pay the park entry fee.

There are no boats or accommodation available at Baltra except by prior arrangement. You have to go to Puerto Ayora, which is the main tourist town and is located on the south end of Santa Cruz Island. You can buy a bus ticket from Baltra Airport to the ferry (50c), take a ferry across to Santa Cruz (20c) and take a bus to Puerto Ayora (US$1). The whole process takes from 2½ to four hours. Normally you can buy a through ticket, though sometimes they charge you three times for the three sections. The little desk selling bus tickets is in the corner of the departure lounge – to your left as you leave the arrival area. Buy your tickets as soon as you arrive because there is only one bus. They do a second trip if there are enough passengers.

The trip to Puerto Ayora will give you a good look at the highlands of Santa Cruz Island. Once in the town, find somewhere to sleep and then you can start looking for a boat. If you are alone or with a friend, you'll need to find some more people as even the smallest boats take four pass-

engers. There are always people in Puerto Ayora looking for boats and you should be able to get a group together quite easily in a few days. The busiest and most expensive times are June to August and December to January. You should try to avoid those months if you are economising.

Getting a group together and finding a boat is easier than it sounds. The restaurants and hotels in town will be full of travellers and boat captains will be looking for passengers. Your hotel manager can often introduce you to someone. After all, almost everyone knows everybody else so word will quickly get around. The cheapest and most basic boats are available for about US$15-20 per day per person and this should include everything. The cheaper the boat, the more rice and fish you can expect to eat, and the more crowded the accommodation.

The most important thing is to find a boat whose crew you get along with and which has a good and enthusiastic naturalist guide who will be able to point out and explain the wildlife and other items of interest. It is impossible for me to recommend any boats in particular because the owners, captains, guides, cooks, etc change frequently and, in addition, many boats make changes and improvements from year to year. You should be able to meet the naturalist guide and captain and inspect the boat before you leave, and you should have an itinerary agreed upon. It is recommended that you have the itinerary in writing to avoid disagreements between you and other passengers and the crew during the cruise. Be particularly careful to stress what you want. Some tours go out on day trips and return to a Puerto Ayora hotel at night – too much time is spent at sea. Make sure that you will sleep on the boat and tour from island to island – unless you prefer staying on dry land. Day trips are available from various hotels.

Cruise Itineraries You can go almost anywhere but it takes time to reach the more outlying islands. It is best to visit a few central islands and inspect them closely rather than trying to cram as many ports of call as possible into your cruise. Inter-island cruising will take up valuable hours of your time and you don't see very much while at sea. If you want to visit the largest island, Isabela, you'll have to allow two weeks.

Assuming you go for a cruise of four to seven days, the islands you should make an effort to visit so that you can see the most are the following: The Plazas off the east coast of Santa Cruz have sea lion,

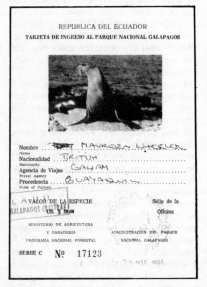

REPUBLICA DEL ECUADOR
TARJETA DE INGRESO AL PARQUE NACIONAL GALAPAGOS

Nombre ...... MAUREEN WHEELER
Name
Nacionalidad ...... BRITISH
Nationality
Agencia de Viajes ...... GALAM
Travel Agency
Procedencia ...... GUAYAQUIL
Point of Parture

VALOR DE LA ESPECIE   Sello de la
GALAPAGOS (CENTRAL) US. $ 30.00   Oficina

MINISTERIO DE AGRICULTURA
Y GANADERIA   ADMINISTRACION DEL PARQUE
PROGRAMA NACIONAL FORESTAL   NACIONAL GALAPAGOS

SERIE C   No 17123

land iguana and swallow-tailed gull colonies, a cactus forest and good snorkelling. Seymour, just north of Baltra, has both blue-footed booby and magnificent frigate bird nesting colonies. On the north shore of Santa Cruz, Caleta Tortuga Negra, or Black Turtle Cove, has marine turtles and white-tipped sharks. Isla Bartolomé on the east side of San Salvador has a small volcanic cone which you can easily climb for one of the best views of the islands. Also there are penguins, sea lions and good snorkelling. On San Salvador (often known as James) you can walk on a lava flow by Sullivan Bay on the east, and see marine iguanas, sea lions, fur seals, Galápagos hawks and many kinds of sea birds near Puerto Egas on the west. Rabida has a flamingo colony. In addition to the species mentioned, you'll see common species almost everywhere. Masked and blue-footed boobies, pelicans, mockingbirds, finches, Galápagos doves, frigate birds, lava lizards and red sally lightfoot crabs are so frequently seen that they'll become part of the normal surroundings to you.

If you have more time (say a full week) you could visit some of the other islands. The red-footed booby is found only on the more outlying islands such as Genovesa (Tower) and the small islets surrounding Santa María (Floreana). The waved albatross breeds only on Española (Hood) and the flightless Galápagos cormorant is found on the western islands of Isabela and Fernandina, which require a two-week trip.

Index

LONELY PLANET NEWSLETTER

We collect an enormous amount of information here at Lonely Planet. Apart from our research we also get a steady stream of letters from people out on he road – some of them are just one line on a postcard, others go on for pages. Plus we always have an ear to the ground for the latest on cheap airfares, new visa regulations, borders opening and closing. A lot of this information goes into our new editions or 'update supplements' in reprints. But we want to make better use of this information so, we also produce a quarterly newsletter packed full of the latest news from out on the road. It appears in January, April, July and October of each year. If you'd like an airmailed copy of the most recent newsletter just send us $7.50 for a years subscription, or $2 each for single issues. That's US$ in the US or A$ for Australia, write to:

Lonely Planet Publications
PO Box 88, South Yarra, Vic 3141, Australia
        or
Lonely Planet Publications
PO Box 2001A, Berkeley, CA 94702 USA

Lonely Planet travel guides

Africa on a Shoestring
Alaska – a travel survival kit
Australia – a travel survival kit
Bali & Lombok – a travel survival kit
Bangladesh – a travel survival kit
Burma – a travel survival kit
Bushwalking in Papua New Guinea
Canada – a travel survival kit
China – a travel survival kit
Ecuador & the Galapagos Islands
Fiji – a travel survival kit
Hong Kong, Macau & Canton – a travel survival kit
India – a travel survival kit
Indonesia – a travel survival kit
Japan – a travel survival kit
Kashmir, Ladakh & Zanskar – a travel survival kit
Kathmandu & the Kingdom of Nepal
Korea & Taiwan – a travel survival kit
Malaysia, Singapore & Brunei – a travel survival kit
Mexico – a travel survival kit
New Zealand – a travel survival kit
North-East Asia on a Shoestring
Pakistan – a travel survival kit kit
Papua New Guinea – a travel survival kit
South America on a Shoestring
South-East Asia on a Shoestring
Sri Lanka – a travel survival kit
Tahiti – a travel survival kit
Thailand – a travel survival kit
The Philippines – a travel survival kit
Tibet – a travel survival kit
Tramping in New Zealand
Travel with Children
Travellers Tales
Trekking in the Indian Himalaya
Trekking in the Nepal Himalaya
Turkey – a travel survival kit
USA West
West Asia on a Shoestring

Lonely Planet phrasebooks

Indonesia Phrasebook
China Phrasebook
Nepal Phrasebook
Thailand Phrasebook

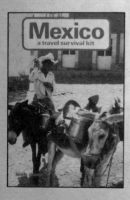

Lonely Planet travel guides are available around the world. If you can't find them, ask your bookshop to order them from one of the distributors listed below. For countries not listed or if you would like a free copy of our latest booklist write to Lonely Planet in Australia.

Australia
Lonely Planet Publications, PO Box 88, South Yarra, Victoria 3141.

Canada
Milestone Publications, PO Box 2248, Sidney, BC V8L 3S8, Canada.

Denmark
Scanvik Books aps, Store Kongensgade 59 A, DK-1264 Copenhagen K.

Hong Kong
The Book Society, GPO Box 7804.

India & Nepal
UBS Distributors, 5 Ansari Rd, New Delhi.

Israel
Geographical Tours Ltd, 8 Tverya St, Tel Aviv 63144.

Japan
Intercontinental Marketing Corp, IPO Box 5056, Tokyo 100-31.

Malaysia
MPH Distributors, 13 Jalan 13/6, Petaling Jaya, Selangor.

Netherlands
Nilsson & Lamm bv, Postbus 195, Pampuslaan 212, 1380 AD Weesp.

New Zealand
Roulston Greene Publishing Associates Ltd, Box 33850, Takapuna, Auckland 9.

Pakistan
London Book House, 281/C Tariq Rd, PECHS Karachi 29, Pakistan

Papua New Guinea see Australia

Singapore
MPH Distributors, 3rd Storey, 601 Sims Drive #03-21, Singapore 1438

Spain
Altair, Riera Alta 8, Barcelona, 08001.

Sweden
Esselte Kartcentrum AB, Vasagatan 16, S-111 20 Stockholm.

Thailand
Chalermnit, 108 Sukhumvit 53, Bangkok, 10110.

UK
Roger Lascelles, 47 York Rd, Brentford, Middlesex, TW8 0QP.

USA
Lonely Planet Publications, PO Box 2001A, Berkeley, CA 94702.

West Germany
Buchvertrieb Gerda Schettler, Postfach 64, D3415 Hattorf a H.

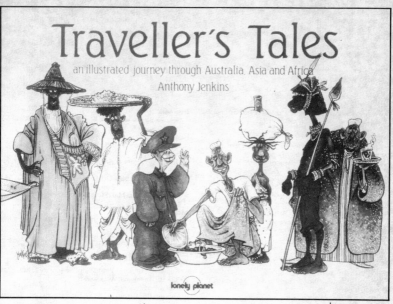

Traveller's Tales

an illustrated journey through Australia, Asia and Africa

Anthony Jenkins

lonely planet

Cartoonist Anthony Jenkins has spent several years on the road, travelling in 55 countries around the world. Along the way he has filled numerous sketchbooks with his drawings of the people he met.

This is a book of people, not places. A tattooed Iban tribesman in Sarawak, a mango seller in Cameroon, fellow travellers in Nepal . . . all are drawn with perception and (in most cases) affection.

Equally perceptive are Jenkins' written comments and descriptions of incidents during his travels. The combined result is like a series of personal illustrated letters.

This is a traveller's travel book. If you have ever endured an Indian train, watched the world go by in Kathmandu's Durbar Square or tried to post a letter in southern Africa, then opening these pages will be like meeting old friends and will probably give you itchy feet to be on the road once more.